FROM ARMAGEDDON TO THE
FALL OF ROME

From Armageddon to the Fall of Rome

*How the Myth Makers
Changed the World*

Erik Durschmied

Hodder & Stoughton

First published in Great Britain in 2002 by Hodder and Stoughton
A division of Hodder Headline

3 5 7 9 10 8 6 4 2

A CIP catalogue record for this title is available from the British Library

ISBN 0 340 82176 0

Typeset in Sabon by Palimpsest Book Production Limited,
Polmont, Stirlingshire

Printed and bound in Great Britain by
Clays Ltd, St Ives plc

Hodder and Stoughton
A division of Hodder Headline
338 Euston Road
London NW1 3BH

For Annemarie

Dedicated to those who have kept records over 3,455 years of near-uninterrupted warfare and left us their momentous accounts as sources for reflection.

Contents

Illustrations

'And when the world is overcharged with inhabitants,
Then the last remedy is Warre;
Which provideth for every man,
By Victory – or Death.'

Thomas Hobbes, *Leviathan* (II.30), 1651

Prologue

In Search of the Historic Truth

'Our ears are accustomed as of our earliest age to listen to untruths, and our minds have been saturated over the ages as the depository of suppositions. We make the truth appear as extravagant and we turn falsified tales into truth.'

These words, written four thousand years ago by Sanchoniathon, a Phoenician, still hold good today

War has been a constant factor throughout human civilisation. Accounts of the convulsions that shook the world thousands of years ago, and which have been instrumental in altering the course of history, describe mostly the victor's jubilation. Precious few are the accounts that mention the ugly backwash of merciless combat, the bloodshed and destruction that war left in its wake. We think of historic records as closely allied to the events as they really happened. That certain constants, which appear in the works of all the historians that lived during a specific period, and whose accounts have been handed down in various translations and amendments throughout the ages, are nothing but the truth. We do not ask on whose authority their story was told. A historian is always the supreme authority, since it is only through him that we penetrate into the world that he has chosen to set before us.

Over three thousand years of epic narrative, a historian's role was not to tell us how his king conducted himself, but to convince us to believe in what he wrote. Conflicts erupted to defend the 'good' against the 'evil', but when it came to doing battle, it was surprising how much the 'good' resembled the 'evil'. Both sides used precisely the same means to kill each other. In the end, the 'good' proved victorious, because every god (and recording historian) was always on the side of the 'good', the winner.

Historic truth can never be fully attained because of the falsity of records on which it is based, especially if it concerns dates, numbers and reasons for the outbreak of mortal conflict. It is not falsehood by design. For example, Herodotus, the father of historians, was a Greek who saw and recorded events as a Greek, while his country's enemies, Darius and Xerxes, were not. In Herodotus's writings, a Greek's 'convenient pretext' became a Persian's 'cunning trick'.

We know of King Alexander's every move, of his victories, but what do we know about his enemies? Greece, land of philosophers, writers and historians, left us copious records on a giant of a man – all seen from the Greek perspective. At the same time Diodorus multiplied inaccuracies when he wrote of 'the drunkard Alexander', taking notes from Hieronymus of Cardia, using Ptolemy, who tried to inflate his own importance, as his principal source.

Can we really expect a fair account of the war against the Gaul in Caesar's *De bello gallico*? After all, the author was also a general, and his account reflected his own vainglorious point of view.

The historian Flavius Josephus was a Roman citizen; but he was born Joseph ben Matthias, a Jew. Was it the Roman or was it the Jew who wrote the eye-witness account of the destruction by Roman legions of the Great Temple of Jerusalem, symbol of his own religious belief? He recorded the anxiety of the Jewish defenders before the siege, their despair, the determination to fight on, the Romans' exhilaration after victory, and the bitterness too.

But the biggest riddle of all will always be who wrote Genesis, first book of the Bible. The interpretation of this work may give a clue to our past. This has led to great controversies. The dispute continues and will probably remain history's great enigma. Was it Moses who dictated the Lord's commandments when he came down from the mountain? Or was it an amalgam of many authors, including non-monotheists? 'And God created the Heaven and the Earth . . .' The third word in the original Hebrew text is '*elohim*', for *gods*. It seems strange that such a sacred document, supposedly written by a monotheist, refers in its opening phrase to gods in the plural, whereas, in the rest of the Old Testament, God – *Yahweh* – appears in the singular. Were the ancient fathers inspired by a compilation of theological documents by Sanchoniathon,[1] a contemporary of Semiramis and believer in many gods, who wrote his analysis of the world's creation a thousand years before the coming of Moses? The Holy Scriptures were initially passed down by word of mouth in the Massorah. Around the eighth century BC, they were written down by learned men from Galilee in ancient Hebrew; in the third century BC, King Ptolemy II locked seventy wise men into individual cells and ordered them to translate the Hebrew Bible into Greek. It was in this translation, completed in just seventy days, that the term *Yahweh Sebaoth*, or god of armies, was changed into *All Powerful Lord*. This version was dissected by philosophers like Porphyrus, who engaged in a violent controversy with the saintly Eusebio, Bishop of Caesaria, who interpreted the scriptures according to the emerging faith of *Christiana alleluia!* In this manner, the original

---

[1] Sanchoniathon, *Phoenician History*, excerpts from *Fragmenta historicorum graecorum*, by C. Müller.

text of the 'Book of Books' passed many stages, translated, rectified, amended and diluted, to fit a specific period or religious need. How are we to distinguish historical fact from symbolic narration intended to convey a specific message? Our Holy Bible is not only the story of man's salvation, but is the only source of ancient historic events as they happened. There is no other work that has had a greater influence on the development of our civilisation.

The past holds two certainties: first, it never changes, and second, there's always something to discover. They still sing ballads about the great heroes of times long gone. They did not manage their affairs better in the past than modern man does now. Then, as now, battles decided the terrible business of war. The zeal with which campaigns were conducted often damaged the causes they were meant to promote. Human folly changed only in scale, but not in detail. To understand our present, nothing serves better than to study our past, with its myths, its fears, its honour, its glory, its trials and errors, and, finally, its bloody aftermath.

Perhaps Voltaire was right when he wrote: 'All our ancient history is no more than accepted fiction.' Ancient glory is mostly legends. Nobody knows what really happened then. One fact remains unshakeably anchored in narrative: antiquity did exist, and its momentous events did take place.

E.D.
Domaine de Valensole, summer 2002

Part One

Dies Iræ

(1479–1010 BC)
(Thutmosis to King David)

Introduction

A Madness of a Violent Kind

'To destroy that for which a war is undertaken seems an act of madness, and madness of a very violent kind.'

Polybius

'Because I tell you of things unknown to history, whether Greek or barbarian. It is frightful to speak of it and unbelievable to hear of it. I should gladly have passed over this disaster in silence, so that I might not get the reputation of recording something which must appear to posterity wholly degrading.'

Flavius Josephus, *War of the Jews*

Long before us, another world existed – that of antiquity. A people, in search of fertile earth, came out of the desert and marched into a land of nightmares, where nothing counted but killing, or being killed. They were confronted by a damning chain of events, a tangled web of carnage inflicted by ambitious men, interlaced with acts of treason, horror and brutality. The time we call 'the cradle of humanity' offers a sad monument to sheer ruthlessness, cruelty and horror. Nothing in our long, recorded history can compare to the sheer brutality of the distant past.

There had been conflicts before, but we do not know of them. Genocide didn't start with antiquity; it goes way back to prehistoric times. For uncountable ages mankind, alone among animal creation, has been obsessed with war. Whenever two tribes fought for territory in order to enlarge their limited food resources, it was the stronger that beat up the weaker. Man began with stones and sticks and fire-sharpened spears. The invention of the bow was an enormous advance – now he could kill his brother from a distance. With metal knives and swords came the cutting edge of war and the beginning of regimented battles. And with them slaughter.

Men began to cut through every strategic and tactical problem as Alexander cut the proverbial Gordian knot, but they also cut through every political consideration and were never paralysed by a moral dilemma in their determination to eradicate cities, tribes, entire nations. Many gave evidence of their lust for blood, an almost physical delight in slaughter for its own sake. Satisfaction never abated this terrible lust for more blood. Soldiers became hardened automata, impersonal executors of their general's whim.

There were also incredible feats of heroism, but even these personal sacrifices were sadly marred by brutality and horror in a never-ending series of conflicts and conquests. Battles were conducted, sometimes without much planning, with masses of foot-soldiers running at each other in frontal attacks, lines swaying back and forth over a growing number of dead as a result of indiscriminate slaughter. The victors shared in the spoils – the nobles were given land and the soldiers' pay was booty. Antiquity knew only winners, those who demonstrated tenacity and purpose, boldness and skill, or commanded a vastly superior force. The end result was populations beaten into a submission they could neither fathom nor control. Some stood up and fought for their rights, others submitted patiently to the caprice of their enemies. Many conquerors were reckless, barbarous, and power mad beyond description;

a few used their religious zeal in worldly matters. In the final analysis many were woefully disappointed, as anyone who commits positive evil so that doubtful good may ensue deserves to be.

History's 'foundation period' was harsh. Climatic conditions changed; from the dry interior hordes poured forth in search of grassland. What had been sufficient for primitive tribal living was no longer sufficient for a rapidly advancing civilisation. Plato, among the giants of Greek philosophy, substituting Socrates' voice for his own, predicted this worrisome aspect in his monumental work *The Republic*.[1]

SOCRATES: The country which was enough to support the original inhabitants will be too small now, and not enough.

GLAUCON: Quite true.

SOCRATES: Then a slice of our neighbour's land will be wanted by us for pasture and tillage, and they will want a slice of ours, if, like ourselves, they exceed the limit of necessity, and give themselves up to the unlimited accumulation of wealth.

GLAUCON: That, Socrates, is inevitable.

SOCRATES: And so we shall go to war, Glaucon. Shall we not?

GLAUCON: Most certainly.

SOCRATES: Then, without determining as yet whether war does good or harm, thus much we may affirm, that now we have discovered war to be derived from causes which are also the causes of almost all the evils in States, private as well as public.

[1] After a translation by B. Jowett of 1888.

Nations living in the regions blessed by nature were required to defend what needed defending. The call for more manpower with improved weapons led to greater bloodshed. Atrociously high casualties were the accepted standard for doing battle. Though the casualties of a victor were relatively modest, those suffered by the vanquished reached catastrophic numbers. At the Battle of Gaugamela, Alexander's casualties were given as 500 killed, while the Persian Darius suffered 300,000 slain. Those who managed to escape stood a chance of surviving for the next battle; the friendly wounded, who could not be treated, were 'relieved of their suffering'. All the great warriors, we are told, perished heroically by thrust of lance or flight of arrow. Nobody recorded the unheroic death of the endless thousands who expired horribly of infections or gangrene as the direct result of battle wounds.[2] The preferred medicine of the day was a talisman or some charm from a prophetess. For infectious diseases, especially those sexually transmitted, which were endemic in any fighting force, there was no cure. Potions of foxglove, sorrel, marjoram or hellebore cured anything from stomach pains to the common cold. Mushrooms provided male potency and courage. Bleeding a man white was the only remedy against snakebite. Diarrhoea, the most common of all afflictions in the field, took on epidemic proportions and often proved fatal. Battle injuries that could be healed were in general permanently incapacitating. Sword slashes were plastered over with the heated resin from the umbrella pine. Deeper cuts were sewn up with catgut. Amputated stumps were cauterised with a piece of red-hot metal sizzling on flesh. The only narcotic was a piece of hardwood clenched between the teeth, a resource reserved for those few lucky enough to receive some medical attention – the winners.

---

[2] The twentieth century's greatest improvement in the military art was not the atomic bomb but antibiotics.

The losers were left to bleed and rot. In antiquity it was certainly true that 'nothing but a battle lost can be as sad as a battle won'.

The hecatomb of death was omnipresent on every field of battle. But what brought about these horrendous casualty figures of 200,000, 300,000, 400,000? Certainly not the casualties directly caused by combat. Yet the numbers did not lie – perhaps some were artificially inflated to heighten the glory of a victorious king. But death in and after battle was certainly massive. Nobody took account of the butchery of captives that followed battle, those put to the sword or pushed over a cliff. After every victory came near-indescribable carnage. Without pity, the defeated were slaughtered, together with their wives and children – often their entire tribe. Such is the plague that, throughout the ages, has distinguished war from all other human activity.

The prospect of sudden death is always frightening. Any unaccountable event causes panic. Natural phenomena fill populations with fear – storms send them praying to their gods, thunder announces their day of judgment, and a comet portends the dissolution of all life. Credulity is always greatest in a time of calamity. It was no different then – people were smitten with fright by the prophecy that the Apocalypse was nigh and the world was coming to its end. It had a pernicious effect upon the minds of the vulgar and induced fatalism. Nations adhered to the prophesies of crazed fanatics, rabid preachers stoked the flames of terror, while ruthless conquerors manipulated their credulous populations to a pitch of ungovernable fury against 'the evil powers of their neighbours'. Seats of power were carved out, empires formed, civilisations overlapped others: Egyptian, Hebrew, Assyrian, Babylonian, Persian, Greek, Roman and Barbarian. From the fall of every one of their mighty empires emerged 'our enlightened civilisation'.

Antiquity was also an age in which the world was dominated largely by military autocracies, so that the course of history depended on the intellectual clarity and the decisions of comparatively few men. Men are only human, and react as such: all are born to greatness and all commit terrible blunders. The lessons learned were not of any great importance in the following period to any of the participants concerned. Being a king or a general does not make a man superior in any way. Only his mistakes are more costly; they lead to consequences way beyond those that follow any act of the average human. We like to think of these people as ordinary men who followed their call in a moment of need – the brave, the good and the ugly, the thinkers, the humanitarians and the butchers, every one a product of his time, believing he was fulfilling the destiny for which he had been chosen. Some clearly dominated the scene, in antiquity more than in any other historical period. And as in any other period, their vehicle was conquest by force. Some had vision and didn't plan in terms of their hordes marching to devastate neighbouring lands; they didn't dream of world domination, or founding an empire of a thousand years – because they believed that everyone was decent and would get along fine if only they could be guided along the right lines. Some men were truly larger than life – prophets, philosophers, humanitarians, and kings. They influenced history to a greater extent than ever since; they inspired their people by their example and brought their nation eternal fame.

'It being my purpose to write the lives of Alexander the king, and of Caesar, by whom Pompey was destroyed, the multitude of their great actions affords so large a field that I were to blame if I should not by way of apology forewarn my readers that I have chosen rather to epitomize the most celebrated parts of their story, than to insist at large on every particular circumstance of it. It must be borne in mind that my design is not to write histories, but lives.'[3]

3 Plutarch, *Parallel Lives* (AD 46–120).

Candidates for greatness had to have all the characteristics that made a leader in any field: the charisma to captivate and hold a loyal following; the organisational skills to run and supply an army in the field; and the determination to enforce and maintain discipline. They were conquerors, governors, administrators and judges, all wrapped in one. In the region of his conquest, the leader had to know the geographical features, the religious and racial prejudices, the taboos and superstitions of his own men as well as those of the indigenous population. He was someone who shrewdly calculated his operations and then cold-bloodedly executed them.

Some of the truly greats went on to prove that war is as much a psychological as a physical matter. In most of the immortal victories of antiquity, the actual fighting took on almost a secondary importance. 'For the profound truth of war is that the issue of battles is usually decided in the minds of the opposing commanders, not in the bodies of their men. The best history would be a register of their thoughts and emotions, with a mere background of events to throw them into relief. But the delusion to the contrary has been fostered by the typical military history, assessing the cause of a victory by statistical computations of the numbers engaged.'[4]

War is not only a science; war can become art. And these were the artists: Thutmosis, David, Themistocles, Scipio, Caesar – the ordinary great. But there were those who towered above them, the giants. Enshrined in this Olympus of the Great are Alexander the Macedonian, Hannibal the Carthaginian, and Napoleon. It was not by chance that two lived in antiquity.

If history has shown us anything, it has underlined the importance and difficulty of preparing for the unexpected. War has always come about through a fearful concentration of circumstances, and a major player in every war is the law of chance – the unforeseen and the unexpected.

[4] B.H. Liddell Hart.

Chance and good fortune, or stupidity on the part of an opponent, play a much greater role in the outcome of any battle than a victorious general is willing to admit. It is said that one should not judge a country by its generals. There are good generals just as there are bad ones. And then there are lucky generals. Each leader of men knows about the power of luck and chance; only the great admit that it exists. Most consequences of a war are predictable. History has left us with a spate of examples to teach us a lesson. But does it really?

'The only thing which history teaches us is that humanity never learns from history.'[5]

---

[5] Heinrich von Sybel, founder of the *Historische Zeitschrift* (1859), quoting Friedrich Hegel.

1

A Place Called Armageddon

Megiddo
15 May 1479 BC

'Modern history properly begins with the year 1479 BC and treats of that epoch in the story of our race which we may call territorial imperialism. For thirty-four centuries, all political ambition, whether of the individual or of the race, has aimed at geographical extension, and at the subjugation of neighbouring tribes and peoples.'
Theodore H. Robinson, *A History of Israel*, 1945

The long night of recorded slaughter began with the first chronicle of a battle, engraved in hieroglyphs on to the funeral stele of a warrior pharaoh, two centuries before the exodus of Moses.[1] It provides an account of bloodshed at har-Magiddo, the Mountain of Megiddo.[2] The Bible[3] calls the site by another name – one that has become synonymous with holocaust, a place of fire from heaven,

---

[1] Moses arrived in Canaan probably in the middle of the thirteenth century BC. 'And Abram took Sara his wife, and Lot his brother's son, and all their substance that they had gathered, and the souls that they had gotten in Haran; and they went forth to go into the land of Canaan' Genesis (12, 5).
[2] Its actual location is not well established; other sites have been named, such as Mount Carmel and Mount Zion.
[3] The Old Testament, Book of Revelations (16, 16).

where the forces of good and evil met and 'all the kings assembled to fight the ultimate battle' on the day of divine judgment – and then left behind a geography of death: a place called Armageddon!

The day began like any other since the Creation, with a golden sunrise. But then something else came to pass, overwhelming and horrible to those who lived through it and who left its record for us on the walls of Amun's temple in Thebes. They bear witness to this momentous day of the first chronicled battle in history, the day when the King of Kadesh, ruler over Syria and all the tribes of Canaan, faced up to the Pharaoh Thutmosis, third of his name.

Centuries before, Egyptian armies had invaded the lands of Canaan and had brought with them their gods as well as their oppressive yoke. Generations of Syrians had been forced to labour in abject slavery under the whip of ruthless pharaohs. That would stop now. The Kadesh was confident; with his thousands of tribesmen and hundreds of war chariots ready to strike, he would whip the young Pharaoh and send him whimpering back to Egypt. He had blocked the two possible access routes, and thus the Egyptian host would be cut off. The perfect plan. But as the Kadesh King was to find out, in war there never is such a thing as 'the perfect plan'.

'The highest gift that man can aspire to is the knowledge of the divine. All other human qualities pale before it.' Such was the grand philosophy of the ancient Egyptians. Isis, the greatest of divine powers, was creator of all, ruler over nature and the beginning of history. The Sphinx, crouching evilly before the temple, was its eternal guardian.[4] To convert the heathen tribes of the Mediterranean to the true belief of their gods was supposed to have made the pharaohs cross the Red Sea. The historic truth certainly

---

[4] Apulee, *Les Metamorphoses*, and Plutarch, *Isis and Osiris*.

lies somewhere else. The lands beyond Egypt controlled the vital trade routes east, to the Fertile Crescent and beyond. Control of the routes was tantamount to a hold over the major portion of Asia Minor. This domination was maintained with the help of a strong army. Ahmose I, founder of the XVIII Dynasty (around 1580 BC), created a professional army with precise divisional duties. Soldiers on foot were armed with a variety of shields and spears, supported by archers. The Pharaonic army's main weapon lay in its mobility; its war chariots spearheaded an attack much as a modern-day tank division strikes at the heart of the enemy's defences. Three thousand years before Rommel and Patton, an Egyptian pharaoh recognised the value of such an attack plan and developed his tactical forces around it. Three warrior kings, Ahmose, Amenhotep I and Thutmosis I, expanded their empire into Syria and from there to the Euphrates. Their campaigns were nothing more than giant raids in which a region was overrun, cities burned, prisoners slaughtered and tribes enslaved.

At the time these events took place – May 1479 BC – Egypt was ruled by the Pharaoh Thutmosis III. In his homeland he was someone special from birth. At a young age he had wisdom as well as a spiritual and military maturity that impressed the court of the ruling Pharaoh, his aunt, Queen Hatshepsut, who appointed him leader of her armies. Though she had proven herself a great administrator of her Nile empire, she had remained militarily inactive in her outlying provinces. This encouraged the outbreak of open revolt in the territories conquered by her predecessors. After the Queen's death, her nephew rose to the throne as Thutmosis III.

A movement for independence from Egypt was gaining rapid support in the land of Canaan.[5] Its driving force was

---

[5] Incorporating large parts of today's Palestine and Syria, Canaan was the strategic link between Egypt and Asia with the most important trade route in use by merchants as well as by raiding armies; it had been conquered by Pharaoh Seostris I around five hundred years earlier, in 1971 BC.

the King of Kadesh, Egypt's surrogate ruler of Syria, who strove for personal control over the biblical lands – a region as volatile 3,500 years ago as it is today. The Kadesh had called into being an army from the local city kings, 330 of them, all eager to join in his revolt. His Canaanites were a rough lot, reasonably well armed with bronze swords, metal-tipped lances and a considerable number of war chariots. Most important, they held the advantage of terrain, centred on Megiddo, the vital road junction on the northern end of the Carmel range, straddling the trade routes from Egypt to the Euphrates. The walled-in fortress controlled three roads: the Northern Road from Dor to Megiddo and Jokneam, the Southern Road from Taanach to Megiddo, and the Arah Road from Aruna up the Wadi Arah. Only this road, actually a trail, led along the confinement of a narrow river gorge, and was therefore considered too perilous for major troop movements, as any force would become too strung out and could fall prey to an ambush.

Megiddo was to become one of the most fought over places in the history of mankind. Its biblical site (Tell el-Mutesellim), rediscovered in 1903,[6] was built on a table mountain sticking out from a fertile plain that stretches into the valley of Jezreel (Joshua 17, 16). From this plain Mount Carmel rises sharply, guarding the Mediterranean shore; to its north are the hills of Galilee and the town of Nazareth, and to its right lies the massive Mount Tabor. Today the hill of Megiddo is sliced up like a wedding cake from which too many archaeological expeditions have taken a bite. The various strata show a continuous human presence lasting three thousand years. Nothing suggests that this hill was once the site of a series of decisive battles. After Thutmosis III came the army of Ramses II, and after him came the prophetess Deborah and 'a great

---

[6] By an archaeologist of the German Oriental Society.

battle was being fought by the waters of Megiddo'. Gideon surprised the Midinites there, Saul lost the battle to the Philistines, and Josiah of Judah died there. '. . . Pharaoh Necho king of Egypt went up against the king of Assyria to the river Euphrates: and king Josiah went against him, and he slew him at Megiddo, when he had seen him.' (2 Kings 23, 29). This passage from the Bible suffered in its translation. In actual fact, the Pharaoh Necho was going to the aid of the hated Assyrians, in other words 'towards' and not 'against' them, when Josiah tried to stop him.[7] A series of stables was found at Megiddo that could hold at least 450 horses and 150 chariots. 'And this is the reason of the levy which king Solomon raised; for to build . . . the wall of Jerusalem, and Hazor, and Megiddo' (1 Kings 9, 15). It was in these stables that the first Crusaders tethered their horses two thousand years later, and the Templars built the fortress of Faba on top of the biblical town. Saladin invaded the valley of Megiddo, took the fortress and killed the Crusaders in a mighty massacre. The fortress changed hands many more times. It was there, on 16 April 1799, that French General Kleber took his 1,500 French to fight the 25,000 Turks of Achmed 'the Butcher' Pasha. When Kleber was surrounded, an attack by 600 French *cuirassiers*, led by young Napoleon Bonaparte, chased the Turks across the Jordan. And on 21 September 1918, Lord Allenby, with a British Expeditionary Force, pounded two Turkish armies, the seventh (Kemal) and eighth (Jerad), into submission in the last Battle of Megiddo. That fight took place 3,397 years after the first recorded Battle of Megiddo, in 1479 BC.

Thus, over thousands of years, Megiddo became the flashpoint for religious and political upheavals. But the first battle was fought for strictly economic reasons. Pharaonic

---

[7] According to Assyrologist C.I. Gadd, translating from a parchment in the British Museum (1923).

Egypt was immensely rich, and depended on trade rather than conquest. Its traditional trade partners were the Kingdom of the Hittites, with its capital of Chattusas on the Halys, the Kingdom of the Mitanni, with Nineveh on the Tigris, and all the other people living in the Fertile Crescent around Babylon on the Euphrates. The main routes from Memphis were to Palmyra, Mari and Babylon on the Euphrates, Ashur on the Tigris, and from there downstream to Susa and Uruk. Or north via Gaza and Byblos to Ugarit and Tarsus on the Mediterranean and to Ephesus or Smyrna. He who controlled the routes controlled trade. And travel along these routes was governed by one fortress – Megiddo.

Once Pharaoh Thutmosis III, ruling from Thebes on the Nile, was informed of the growing unrest in his Canaan provinces, he reacted quickly and gathered an army of twenty thousand. It was the first time in history that a formation was called up which consisted entirely of highly trained, professional units. He divided his force into four divisions of five thousand regulars, each under a *hry ptd* (divisional commander), identifiable by their individually coloured shields. The key to the Pharaoh's strength was in his mobile strike force. His foot divisions were reinforced by the super-weapon of its day, the war chariot, drawn by two horses and driven by a handler with two to three archers as mobile artillery. These rapid deployment units were highly trained and well officered. Until the advent of the warrior genius of Thutmosis, chariots were considered simply as transportation enabling nobility to enter a battle in style; without a coherent plan of attack, they had never before been used as a solid, unified strike force to deliver a fatal impact. Furthermore, Thutmosis was the first to fully grasp the importance of support: transport, supplies and bridge-builders permitted him to cover the distance from Egypt to Gaza in only ten days. After a brief rest, he

pushed on to Yaham, located on the southern slope of
the Carmel range.

Villagers had alerted the ruler of Syria, King of Kadesh,
to a great cloud of dust coming out of the desert. This
could only signify an army on the move. The Kadesh
sent scout patrols along the two main approaches; they
reported Egyptian troop movements on both roads. Based
on these reports, he established two blocking positions on
the northern and southern approaches to Megiddo and
put all his available chariots, probably some six to seven
hundred, into position behind the hill. From there they
would be able to surge forward and attack along either of
the two roads. But he failed to cover the third approach,
the one through the Wadi Arah gorge. Thutmosis had
employed a ruse; he ordered two minor detachments to
advance along the main road and raise a great amount
of dust by dragging bundles of cut branches behind their
chariots in order to fool enemy scouts. Contrary to the
counsel of his military advisers, he then opted for the
perilous approach through the narrow Wadi Arah. With
the bulk of his army, he set out from Yaham and pushed on
unobserved to Aruna. The low, rolling plain gave way to a
series of hills, covered by a dense forest of evergreen pine.
When the army moved into the narrow defile, the canopy
of trees brought blessed relief from the heat on the open
plain. Egyptian officers scurried along the stretched-out
columns, urging their men to more speed. The pounding
of the chariot horses reverberated like thunder between the
rocky ramparts. In seven hours of forced march, Thutmosis
pushed his entire army past the dangerous passages. He
may have been surprised that his forces had encountered
no resistance, that the enemy had not put out sentries on
the cliffs lining the river gorge. His ruse had worked. The
cover of the coniferous forest ended just as the rays of a
new day peeked over the distant mountains. Thutmosis

reached the top of a ridge; in front of him the path fell away sharply into a wide plain that extended level for a great distance, a golden meadow reflecting the clear sky above, bordered by hills in the distance. A brook, fed by rushing waters from the mountainsides, divided the plain. The Pharaoh saw little of nature's beauty – all he took in was the field of hard-baked earth before him, ideal for a charge by bronze-wheeled war chariots. From the midst of the tableland, shimmering in what promised to be another hot day, a volcanic cone rose steeply. On its summit, clearly outlined against the azure sky, stood a walled fortress.

The King of Kadesh stared in surprise at the Pharaoh's army spilling from the Arah gorge and down into the Esdraelon plain (Emeq Yizreel) – right in between his two, disconnected Canaanite contingents. He dispatched messengers, ordering an immediate pull-back. This was achieved in time; now he could post his forces on the lower slope of the volcanic cone leading up to the fortress. Once more he had achieved the superior battle position. Thutmosis, facing an uphill struggle, put his foot divisions in the centre, backed up by a hundred war chariots, a minor portion of the chariots available to him. The rest he intended to use in a concerted manoeuvre on his wings. He placed these carts within easy striking range, well hidden from the enemy behind the dense foliage that rimmed the Quina brook.

The battle opened, as did every battle of antiquity, with a ceremony and a sacrifice. The King of Kadesh took a double-headed axe and went to the altar, a wooden platform erected in the centre of the field. A ram was tethered there. The King raised the axe high so that every one of his many thousand warriors could see the gleaming blade before he brought it down in a sweeping arc. He felled the sacrificial animal with a single stroke and dipped the axe into the flowing blood. Then he brandished the axe and chanted. From one end of the field to the other, his men took up the monotonous chant. They could use some cheering; many of the King's troops didn't believe they could beat a Pharaonic army on equal terms. Then all fell silent. The time for song and prayer was over; now it was time to do combat.

For a long period nothing happened; two armies faced each other without moving from their positions High above, almost invisible, eagles and vultures slowly soared and spiralled. As the sun climbed higher, and her molten rays drained the energy of the armies, patience was severely tested and nerves became frayed. The Kadesh counted on his opponent to start the offensive, attacking uphill, where the best warriors Syria and Canaan had to offer were lined up on the slopes of Mount Megiddo, while those of the Pharaoh were on the open plain, facing straight into the sun. The sun was climbing ever higher, and soon the Egyptians would begin to suffer from the heat. Still Thutmosis refused to give the order for attack; he allowed time for this to develop into a war of nerves in which he could count on the discipline of his troops and the efficiency of his water-carriers, scurrying along his lines with goatskins of water from the Quina brook. Indeed, the Egyptians were to prove themselves the more disciplined troop.

The heavily armoured men of the Kadesh were made up of nobles who considered it their obligation to prove their valour, move out in front and get slaughtered before the main clash had started. The King of Kadesh wanted to make sure that this would not happen. But he acted too late; a few of the younger Canaanite nobles, impatient over the long delay which severely tested their courage, broke ranks and moved ahead to engage in personal combat. Their personal shield-bearers, archers and sundry servants had to follow their masters without great conviction. It made them look like the mob they were. Sporadic fights broke out as more Canaanite nobles followed the first.

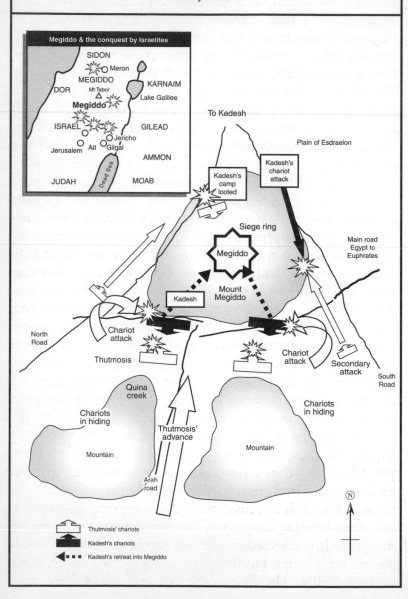

Megiddo
15 May 1479 BC

Megiddo & the conquest by Israelites

SIDON

Meron

MEGIDDO

KARNAIM

DOR

Mt Tabor

Lake Galilee

Megiddo

ISRAEL

GILEAD

Jericho

Jerusalem   Ait   Gilgal

AMMON

JUDAH   MOAB

Dead Sea

To Kadesh

Plain of Esdraelon

Kadesh's camp looted

Kadesh's chariot attack

Siege ring

Megiddo

Main road Egypt to Euphrates

Kadesh

Mount Megiddo

North Road

Chariot attack

Thutmosis

Chariot attack

Secondary attack

South Road

Quina creek

Chariots in hiding

Chariots in hiding

Mountain

Thutmosis' advance

Mountain

Arah road

N

Thutmosis' chariots

Kadesh's chariots

Kadesh's retreat into Megiddo

This led to a dangerous outward bulge in the Kadesh's fixed battle line. It left the King with no other option than to act before his entire front disintegrated. His war horns sounded the signal for a general attack. Abandoning their superior field position, they were marching into the glare of sunlight in which men and arms and mighty chariots with rearing horses shimmered in the heat. What should have been a straight line of attack began to weave like a snake. The Pharaoh Thutmosis, observing the enemy's advance from his chariot, spotted the widening fault in the Canaan formation and immediately took advantage. A sound like a huge groan swept over plain and mountain, and the ground began to shake as thousands of Egyptian warriors began to move forward. The thunder grew louder as lines of yelling men headed for each other. Like a fast-flowing river, the two huge masses swept over the field, spreading out only to come together again. The bronze tips of lances gleamed dully in the yellow light. The waves picked up speed, wrecking and tearing apart everything that came their way. And then they were at each other's throats. The entire field boiled in a weaving sea of madness, one side thundering through as the other retreated. Bodies were swept under the human flood. The Kadesh's human wave overran the Pharaoh's line, trampling across corpses. Their voices massed into an inhuman, wailing choir. A dry thorn bush burst into flames; the flames spread to a forest, adding heat and smoke to the already unbearable conditions. The dying went on unabated – men fell with gaping wounds, others staggered around gushing blood, yet others fell down from sheer exhaustion, or because their eyes smarted from the sweat, the heat and the dense smoke. Men fell because they couldn't pump enough air into their burning lungs; and those who fell were trampled or speared or crushed, to lie one upon the other like the snows on Mount Hermon when the sunset turned the summit to fire. The chaos of battle was everywhere; men were groaning and swearing and praying to whatever god they believed in. In their midst stood the King of Kadesh, with confusion all around him. He admonished his men to attack. They remained hopelessly undisciplined, and that made them vulnerable. He knew that if this continued the Pharaoh's men would come pouring around his wings; then his warriors might give in to the threat and run. And should that happen, Megiddo, and with it Canaan, was lost. For the moment, all seemed to be going well, as ever more Kadesh warriors came on hard and fast, howling like demons, ready to plunge into the mayhem. No pity was asked and none was given. Lances sliced into bellies and swords cut heads. The King of Kadesh's men weren't more than a few paces from breaking through the Pharaoh's line, and he thought the battle won.

His first indication of trouble was a flock of birds, wheeling into the sky from the copse alongside the Quina brook, before the Pharaoh's armada of sickle-whirling chariots broke their cover and raced at his men from both sides. The carts streaked straight towards the surging mass of battling warriors, raising a great cloud of dust. The Kadesh didn't know how many chariots came at them – five, six hundred, maybe more, madly careening across a no-man's-land. Within arrow distance, the chariots divided and flooded towards his flanks. The chariot-mounted archers unleashed a deadly stream of cane-shafts straight into the backs of his Canaanites. But the Egyptians also suffered greatly – carthorses were speared and sank snorting to their knees and the carts catapulted through the air, breaking the necks of the archers. Other vehicles snapped their axles and came to a sudden halt; their crews were immediately dragged from the chariots and done to death.

By virtue of their sideward turn to fend off the Egyptian chariots, the Canaanites had left their centre undefended. As the new wave of Egyptian chariots struck, a shower of arrows felled the men of Kadesh before they were crushed under bronze wheels. Their king stared across the field, to a small rise, where that cursed Pharaoh with the sun's rays bouncing off his golden helmet, this Thutmosis, sitting in his shining chariot of electrum on top of the hill, like the Angel of Death, watched his enemies die. Their blood would feed the ground so that the grass grew greener and thicker on the Plain of Esdraelon. The battle became a kaleidoscope of shifting shapes and colours. The din rose to an 'Anvil Chorus'; the centre of the plain was the belly of the beast. More and more Egyptian chariots poured from their ambush position, followed by thousands in kettle helms. A blaze of banners flew above them. Individual knots of Canaanites were trying to make their stand. The Kadesh King was raising his sword arm to rally a group of his men when a wedge of Egyptians smashed into them with spears and bronze swords. The Egyptians surged forward, throwing the Canaanites into wild flight.

The Pharaoh launched his reserves in a final chariot charge. It proved to be the most destructive. Thutmosis, at the head of three hundred chariots with their evilly spinning sickle blades, sliced through the gap between the Kadesh forces and the hill fortress. Fifty, sixty carts abreast, the Egyptian war machine raced across the field. Nothing could stop the onrush of hundreds of well-protected horses racing before the carts; their bronze wheels rolled over their defenceless enemy as a wave sweeps over the shore. The Canaanites went down all over the plateau. Great swaths opened in the Canaanite ranks. Under the impact of the crazily spinning sickles, the Kadesh line staggered, crying, bleeding, twisting and falling. Thousands of Canaanites collapsed in heaps. In these final moments, thousands paid with their lives for having dared to stand up to the might of Egypt and the military genius of a pharaoh. He left behind a field of corpses, lying like ragged dolls in terrain that had turned from the ripe gold of an autumn's morn to the red, ugly aftermath of a blooded battlefield. Armageddon!

Those who managed to escape the carnage abandoned their horses, their chariots and their arms. They scrambled uphill and clambered over the walls of Megiddo. Among the survivors was the Syrian King of Kadesh, looking down on the horrid carnage, the bloated corpses and the feeding vultures. He felt a throbbing pain behind his eyes. Previously the pain had always gone away after he had killed the men he had set out to kill. But not this time. How he cursed himself that, blinded by the heat of the battle, he had overlooked the presence of more Egyptian chariot reserves. Moments later, Pharaoh Thutmosis had put the whip to his three white stallions and – 'like God Horus armed with talons' – scattered before his carts all that was left of Syria's best warriors, who were running away as if terrified by spirits.

The Egyptians were so taken by surprise by the ease of their victory that, instead of storming an undefended fortress, they stopped their winning drive to kill the wounded and strip them of armour and jewels. It was this rush for spoils which saved some Syrians. It gave the King of Kadesh time to organise the town's defence. The wall hieroglyphs in Thebes provide no additional clue as to the length of the siege. Perhaps the defenders survived because the Pharaoh got tired of investing the fortress. The stele gives only an account of the booty recovered: 2,000 horses and 900 chariots.

Following his victory at Megiddo, Thutmosis pacified by the sword the rebellious kingdoms; their monarchs were executed and replaced by loyal nobles as surrogate kings. The Pharaoh stormed the stronghold of Kadesh, situated on the left bank of the Orontes (near Homs), then turned on the Aryans, who had invaded the fertile lands along the Great Bend of the Euphrates, and destroyed Aleppo, before he returned home to Thebes. To control the Mediterranean waters and the lands bordering it, Thutmosis ordered the construction of a war fleet. With it, he controlled Mediterranean trade and became the uncontested ruler of a vast empire. Even the far-off Babylonians and Hittites sent him ambassadors bearing precious gifts. When Thutmosis III died in 1447 BC, his reign had become the summit of Pharaonic rule.

'Thutmosis was the first to build an empire in any real sense; he was the first world-hero. He made not only a world-wide impression upon his age, but an impression of a new order . . . and today, two of this king's greatest monuments, his Heliopolitan obelisks, rise on opposite shores of the western ocean as memorials of the world's first empire builder.'[8]

In 1288 BC, another pharaoh, Ramses II, set out on the road to Megiddo, this time to teach the Hittites a lesson. The Hittite King Mutallo had gathered a force and invaded Syria. Facing him was the army of Ramses, a pale copy of his illustrious predecessor, Thutmosis III. Ramses divided his army into four divisions: Re, Amon, Naarun and Ptah. At the head of his Amon division, he crossed the Orontes river north of Shabtuna, some eight miles south of Kadesh. King Mutallo lured Ramses into a trap. He had sent 'deserters' to inform the Pharaoh about the position of the Hittite army, placing it north of the town of Kadesh. The Hittites waited in ambush across the Orontes, and as the Pharaoh's straggling Re division tried to cross it they were attacked by a great force of war chariots and driven into headless flight. Seventeen thousand of Mutallo's foot-soldiers chased the Egyptians into the Pharaoh's camp and captured it with all it contained – not only gold and jewels, but also the women, whom their warriors had basely left to their fate.

8 Obelisks in London and New York. Quote from *The Cambridge Ancient History*.

Mutallo's army became utterly distracted by plundering and the gross enjoyment of sexual pleasures. An élite unit of Ramses' mercenaries smashed into the Hittites from their rear and the Pharaoh launched his remaining chariots, at the same time as his Amon division made an about-turn and attacked the Hittites from the north. Fortune dictated that his Ptah division, which had been lagging behind, was able to join the battle. Together they put the Hittites to flight. Six thousand of them, together with their king, Mutallo, managed to escape behind the fortified walls of Kadesh. One final time the god of fortune had smiled on the Egyptians. Megiddo 2 was the last battle ever to be won by an Egyptian empire entering its decline. From a single reference in the Book of Revelation (16, 14–16) comes the concept of catastrophic holocaust and ultimate destruction, which has reigned in mankind ever since. 'For they are the spirits of devils, working miracles, which go forth unto the kings of the earth and of the whole world, to gather them to the battle of that great day of God Almighty . . . And He gathered them together into a place called in the Hebrew tongue Armageddon.'

The first Battle of Megiddo was decided by a surprise attack of mobile armour. In effect, it became history's first tank battle.

Through his victory at Megiddo, Thutmosis III ended for hundreds of years any challenge to Egypt's rule over Palestine, Syria, the Jordan valley and the Euphrates. For the following three centuries, the empire of the Pharaohs ruled supreme.

2

The Secret of the Sinnor

Jerusalem
18 August 1010 BC

'Whosoever getteth up to the sinnor and smiteth the Jebusites . . .'
2 Samuel 5, 8

. . . And thus it came to be in yonder days, when the patriarchs walked on this earth, that the Lord ordered Moses to deliver the Children of Israel from the bondage of the Pharaoh in Egypt and He promised to lead them into paradise. The Promised Land. 'Have not I brought up Israel out of the land of Egypt? and the Philistines from Caphtor?' (Amos 9, 7).

A warrior tribe from Caphtor had invaded the Promised Land and threatened Israel's very existence: the Philistines. They brought with them their gods and their culture. Whence they came, nobody knew. But where they went they left a trail of death and destruction. They rolled across countries like a human avalanche, their ox carts piled high with all their plunder. Armed with round shields and bronze swords, they had already obliterated the Hittite Empire; now it was Israel's turn. They engaged in battle, killed the Israeli leaders, and – supreme blasphemy – stole the Holy Ark. The Bible remains strangely silent on this period. Nothing much is written about the Philistines, other than the story of Samson, an Israelite who never strayed from the path of righteousness. When he refused to pay homage to their pagan gods, he was betrayed by his great love, Delilah. Captured and chained to the pagan temple, he then used his superhuman strength to crack its pillars and bring the roof crashing down on the heads of the Philistine leaders. The Hebrew prophet Samuel offered a sacrifice to the Lord, which resulted in a plague epidemic among the Philistines; frightened by their misfortune, and to appease the one the Israelis called their Lord, they returned the Holy Ark. Despite the ravages of the plague,[1] the Philistines were far from beaten and continued to inflict great harm on the Lord's children. This Philistine yoke incited the Israelites to unite and choose a king. Their prophet Samuel had promised that a *nagid* (chief) would soon come to lead them from their enslavement. The first to claim this crown was a Benjamite whose name was Saul. He took on the title of *melech* (king), but he was a despot. The King had a young shield-bearer, 'and his name was David . . .' This David was an enthusiast with the means to raise the spirits of the children of Israel and lead them to their eventual triumph. When the strength of his people had been broken and hope was gone, David set out on a mission to weld together Judah and Israel into a united front against their Philistine oppressor. In the beginning, ambition and jealousy prompted many tribal leaders to refuse him their assistance. That didn't stop him. Nothing would. He took a tribe, bowed, sullen and beaten down under a terrible yoke, and turned them into a nation of lions.

King David (1010–973 BC) is best known for killing the

---

[1] The term 'plague' encompassed every sort of epidemic, like smallpox, measles or the common cold.

Philistine champion Goliath. 'And there went out a champion named Goliath, of Gath, whose height was six cubits
and a span . . . And David put his hand in his bag, and
took thence a stone, and slang it, and smote the Philistine
in his forehead' (1 Samuel 17, 4, 49). David was not only
a giant-slayer, but also one of the great warriors of biblical
times, and the first Hebrew to unite the twelve tribes of
Judah and Israel into one great nation. Slaying the giant
Goliath (with a slingshot) brought David great popular
appeal, and this aroused the jealousy of King Saul. In
order to regain ascendancy over David, he talked his
son Jonathan and some of the Israelite tribes into doing
battle with the Philistines 'at Tanaach by the waters of
Megiddo' (Judges 5, 19). Saul and Jonathan went forth to
what was their final combat. Down from Mount Gilboa
poured the Philistines, and before Saul had time to set his
men in order an overwhelming force was upon him. They
chased Saul's small army across the plain and slaughtered
them. Having watched his son being killed, Saul threw
himself on his sword to avoid capture.[2] The corpses
of Saul and Jonathan were impaled on the walls of the
Philistine fortress of Beth-Shan. With the death of Saul,
the first kingdom of Israel had come to an end, and its
people fell into despair, without hope for atonement.

David, who lived at the time in Hebron, heard of Saul's
disaster: 'The Lord helps only him who helps himself. He
who stays put on his behind is lost.' He took matters into
his own hands and raised a small guerrilla force. Carefully
planning his operation so that he never risked a major
defeat, he and his band gradually forced the Philistines on
the defensive, while David, on the other hand, constantly
consolidated his forces, increased the size of his units from
tiny bands of men to regiments capable of attacking larger

[2] A famous painting on this subject by Pieter Brueghel hangs in Vienna's
Museum of Art.

enemy positions. In a series of ambushes in the hills and valleys of Judah, he struck where least expected and inflicted casualties on the Philistines. With every successful strike he raised the morale of the tribes, until the moment when his insurgents were able to hold a large area of Judaea against attack and he reorganised his forces into a regular army. This was when six tribes proclaimed David the King of Judah. Now he set out to unite all the twelve tribes.[3] In a smart political move, he took as wife the daughter of Saul, then quickly eliminated most of his challengers. It was to take David seven years and more battles before the tribes accepted him as their universal king. At the head of his army he moved into Syria, where he defeated the Hadarezer King of Zobah; from there he marched across the desert to the Euphrates and smashed the Aramaean King, who was poised to invade the territory of the Assyrians. In this way David saved the Assyrians from extinction, a favour which they were to repay two centuries later by wiping out Israel. David then punished the Philistines of Beth-Shan, slayers of Jonathan and Saul.

Before he turned his attention to Jebus, one more battle was fought between David's general Joab and Abner, who supported Saul's only surviving son against David's claim to the crown. Both Joab and Abner were valiant warriors and, at the appointed hour, they brought twelve of their men to the 'Pool of Gibeon' (north of Jerusalem). It was more of a western shoot-out than a battle, and it left all of them dead, except Joab.

To rule a united Judah and Israel called for a symbolic capital. There was but one place that was fit for the honour, the fortress of Jebus, built on the biblical Rock of Abraham. This sacred place would provide a uniting symbol for the

---

3 Asher, Benjamin, Dan, Ephraim, Gad, Issachar, Judah, Manasseh, Naphtali, Reuben, Simeon, Zebulun.

children of Israel. The Lord had endowed David with power and greatness of soul, and now he devoted himself to this holy cause and made a solemn engagement to place the sacred Ark in a temple he would build on the rock. But first he had to capture the town from the hostile Jebusites. This promised to be no easy task. The city was located on a cliff and surrounded by formidable walls. For weeks the men of Joab tried to overcome the solid walls, and for weeks their attempts proved futile. They stormed with ladders and were met by arrows and stones until the path up the steep slope was marked by a trail of dead and wounded. Joab advised his king that the town was so strongly defended that the only means to open its gate was by starvation. David did not want more bloodshed, but he also didn't have the time to await surrender through starvation. Some of his allied tribal forces were ready to abandon camp. He searched for a way to bring the siege to a rapid conclusion.

Lo and behold, the miracle of the Bible achieved what armed men had failed to do. The Lord, it was said, had descended one night from the heavens and opened the gate into the city. King David and his followers marched in without having to fight for it. The news of the fall of Jebus, brought about by an act of the Lord, and seen as nothing less than supernatural, spread to the remotest parts of Judah and Israel. This was a miracle, and everyone regarded it as such. Not even the King's own men knew how the miracle had been achieved.

Despite the many sieges that were to follow in the centuries to come, involving the battering down of walls and the brutality this engendered, it was three millennia before a Bible-reading British army officer discovered David's secret. The secret was concealed in ancient scriptures of which David must have had knowledge, and was contained in a brief reference to a *sinnor*. In Hebrew *sinnor* stood for gutter, but could also mean a shaft. A natural fault,

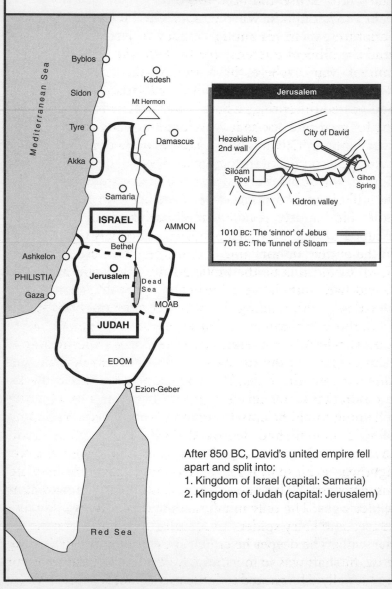

Israel United under David and Solomon
1000 BC

Mediterranean Sea

Byblos

Kadesh

Sidon

Mt Hermon

Tyre

Damascus

Akka

Samaria

ISRAEL

AMMON

Bethel

Ashkelon

PHILISTIA

Jerusalem

Dead Sea

Gaza

MOAB

JUDAH

EDOM

Ezion-Geber

Red Sea

Jerusalem

Hezekiah's 2nd wall

City of David

Siloam Pool

Gihon Spring

Kidron valley

1010 BC: The 'sinnor' of Jebus

701 BC: The Tunnel of Siloam

After 850 BC, David's united empire fell apart and split into:
1. Kingdom of Israel (capital: Samaria)
2. Kingdom of Judah (capital: Jerusalem)

widened by the ancient inhabitants of Jebus into a shaft, leading from the heart of the citadel to a source of water in the foundation rock. Over the centuries this shaft had fallen into disuse and been forgotten.

In 1867, Captain Warren, a fervent student of the Holy Scriptures, spent his annual holiday in Jerusalem. He had read the biblical reference to *Ain Sitti Maryam*, the Fountain of Mary, where the Virgin washed her clothes. A deeply religious man, he wanted to satisfy his curiosity, and visited the spring, where water bubbled from a cut in the foundation rock as it had done for many thousands of years. It hadn't always been called Fountain of Mary. Long before the coming of the Christian Messiah it was known as *Gihon*, 'the Bubbler'. As Warren cupped water in his hands, he looked up and noticed what seemed like a man-made hole. He vaguely recalled a biblical reference that had escaped armies of archaeologists: 'Whosoever getteth up to the gutter [sinnor] and smiteth the Jebusites' (2 Samuel 5, 8). Could this be the biblical sinnor, the one by which David had smitten the Jebusites? Captain Warren passed a restless night, reading the passages over and over again. *Getteth up the sinnor . . . sinnor . . . sinnor . . .*

At sunrise Warren returned to the Virgin's Fountain and, with the help of the sturdy shoulder of a German pilgrim, climbed into the hole. He was taking risks he knew he shouldn't take, but curiosity got the better of him. Holding a flaming torch, he crawled on hands and knees. Millennia of wild animals had deposited their natural refuse. Soon the torch was of no use as the shaft had narrowed and the light was so close to his face that he was afraid of burning his whiskers. All his flame did was part the dense curtain of spider webs. The only inhabitants of this underworld were striped and hairy spiders and small scorpions, scurrying up the walls. The deeper he crawled, the fouler the air got. By now the shaft was so low that it forced him to wriggle along on his belly. He wanted to leave this dreadful place, but the

prospect of doing so with the mystery as puzzling as ever
and with nothing to show repelled him. The shaft came to
a sudden end. There was precious little he could do; he was
wedged like a cork in a bottle. Given the narrowness of the
tunnel, he couldn't even reverse! The air was so stale that
breathing was difficult. He had raised a great amount of
dry dust that made him cough, to the point of choking.
He thought he was going to pass out and that nobody
would ever find him again. For a moment he no longer
cared, then his knee hit something pointed and the sharp
pain refocused his senses. He tried to relight the torch but
that proved impossible, given the enclosed space and the
limited movement of his arms. He prodded the wall with a
kind of hopeless determination, searching for cracks, when
he felt a declivity in the tunnel roof, partially blocked by
a stone. After he had managed to push the stone to one
side he felt a slight updraught of air – the hole led to an
exit somewhere above! In contortions, he worked himself
into the shaft, which led straight up. He pushed his arms
out in front, passing his hands over the smooth sides of
the vertical rock chimney, when he touched steps cut into
the rock. He knew he was close to resolving the age-old
secret. For him the only way out of the tunnel was straight
up. After a short distance, the shaft widened and turned
so that he could climb on all fours, higher and higher.
For the first time there was comfortable space around
him, and he lit his torch. He reached a cave, perhaps
a subterranean shelter, chipped from the rock. Another
disappointment awaited him – a pile of rubble blocked
the exit. He began attacking the pile, pulling at rocks
and scraping at the loose earth in between. Once again
a feeling of despondency overcame him. He prayed for a
gleam of daylight, but his prayer drew no response. His
torch had burned down, and with increasing desperation
he groped blindly at the pile; his hands fastened around
a big wedged-in stone. And then it happened: the block

tumbled down, and through the opening rushed air. Dust clouded his vision before a patch of light shone through. He forced his body through the hole, crawled on hands and knees towards the light and found himself in bright daylight inside a rubble-strewn courtyard – in the centre of Jerusalem! After three thousand years he had solved the riddle of David's conquest of Jerusalem. In his honour the tunnel was named Warren's Shaft.[4]

The rest was revealed after more investigation by archaeologists, Bible scholars and historians who followed in the footsteps of Captain Warren. Somehow King David had stumbled on the ancient scripture that mentioned the shaft – or perhaps a friendly Jebusite told him about it. The King ordered his trusted General Joab to explore this possible route. They scoured the base of the cliffs, searching for the entrance into the shaft, until one of Joab's men found it behind 'the Bubbler'. They sent a boy into the shaft, armed with a torch. Within the hour the youngster was back with the news that it did indeed lead straight up and *inside* the walls of Jebus.

Joab's dozen, specially chosen and sworn to secrecy, waited for nightfall before they ascended along the water shaft. They could not take along their cumbersome lances, not even their swords. Their only weapons were stealth and surprise. Once inside the narrow confines, they advanced with great caution; they didn't dare use light for fear of discovery, and they didn't know what strange beasts or other surprises to expect hiding in the pitch-black tunnel. They climbed higher and higher – and then stepped out into a darkened Jebus. Through the rabbit-warren of lanes, they made for the city gate. To their great relief they found

[4] Warren's discovery provided material for a heated argument among archaeologists, who argued that the exit of the shaft could not have been the sinnor of King David since it ended *outside* the city walls which protected Jebus in David's time, until another, pre-Davidian wall was dug up which showed that the exit was indeed *within* the city.

only a few guards keeping watch, and all were staring over the wall and not behind them. The sound of feet must have alerted the Jebusites posted at the gate to the danger, because some turned round. They had just enough time for a startled oath before Joab's group overpowered them, and before anyone could raise the alarm the silence of death closed their lips. The Israelites slid back the oak beam barring the heavy gate. When King David heard Joab's signal, given with a ram's horn – explained as the sound of a heavenly trumpet even to his own army – the King and his soldiers poured into the town without having to fight for it. By ruse, David took the town he renamed Yerushalaim. The secret of the sinnor died with David and Joab.[5]

With the fall of Jerusalem, and a series of astounding victories, David extended his empire from Lake Homs (Lebanon) to Ezion-Geber on the Red Sea. 'And all the elders came to the king in Hebron; and King David made a league with them in Hebron before the Lord: and they anointed David king over Israel . . . and he reigned forty years' (2 Samuel 5, 3–4). David took the titles of King of Judah and Israel, King of Jerusalem, King of Ammon, Governor of Aram (Damascus) and Edom, and King of Moab and Zobah.

'So David dwelt in the fort and called it the city of David. And David built round about.' He ordered a tabernacle to be built to shelter the Holiest of Holies, the Ark of the Covenant, but he died before construction began. To protect his united kingdom, David called into being a powerful army, an instrument with which he could dictate his will; the great changes wrought in Israel's forces were a measure of the national changes effected during this period. While David was preoccupied with administering his vast

5 In 2 Chronicles 32 there is a note about a water channel, with which King Hezekiah defended Jerusalem against the Assyrian Sennacherib – a channel that led from the Spring of Gihon into the City of David.

territories by creating a political system that united a loose federation of tribes into a coherent nation, efficiently run by a civil service, the Philistines would not be put down and gathered a new army. So King David said: 'We shall fall on them like the morning dew falls down on the dry earth and from them not a single one shall survive that day. Only once they are gone can I lead the children of Israel back to peace.' He did as he promised and fell on his enemy's vanguard in the Rephaim valley, having lain in ambush in a wood of mulberry trees. He annihilated the vanguard and caught up with the Philistines' main force at Methegamma on the coastal plain, where he routed them. After this he conquered the coastal plains around Joppa (Jaffa) and reduced the remaining Canaanite strongholds. With General Joab he moved against the Moabites, Edomites and Ammonites. 'And Joab drew nigh . . . unto the battle against the Syrians . . . And David gathered all Israel together . . . And the Syrians set themselves in array against David, and fought with him . . . and David slew the men of seven hundred chariots . . . and forty thousand horsemen' (2 Samuel 10, 13–18). While he was besieging their fortress of Madaba, a strong relief force of Aramaeans moved against David. He waylaid them in the Yarmouk gorge. With this last threat removed, David, king of a united Israel, controlled all the main roads leading from the Occident and Egypt to Asia Minor. From their depth of despair, from the yoke of the Philistines, David had delivered Israel and given it greatness. As their king, he had to protect his people, and respond to outside charges as well as challenge from within. The remainder of his reign was not an easy one. For the love of the fair Bethsabe, David had committed mortal sin: first he stole the wife of a Hittite officer, Uri, and then had him killed. He took a second wife, Achinoam, who bore him a son, Amnon. When Amnon raped his half-sister Thamar (from David's wife Bethsabe), her brother Absalom took revenge, and killed Amnon. That started a blood feud between the two royal households. Finally, Absalom revolted against his father. Chased by Joab, Absalom got his long hair entangled in the branches of a thorn tree and was killed.

The successor to David (accession to power 1006 BC) was his second son by Bethsabe, Solomon (born in 965 BC), who reorganised the army and, taking a page from the Egyptians' book, introduced the chariot as its main weapon of attack. Yet he is best known for his Solomonian judgment. Two prostitutes gave birth on the same day. In the night, one accidentally suffocated her baby while asleep. She replaced her dead infant with that of her neighbour. In the morning, its real mother, having recognised the substitution, dragged the other woman before the King. A fair decision seemed impossible. Therefore, the King ordered the infant cut in two with one half given to each of the women. One accepted the judgment, but the other fell to her knees and called out in pain: 'No, stop! I beg of you, let the child live. Hand it to this woman in one piece.' Solomon recognised the cry from the heart of the real mother and the baby was given to her.

Solomon was Israel's great builder-king. He finished the walls around Jerusalem. Most important, he concentrated on the work his father had promised – the Temple. The relic, originally a simple cedarwood casket, was sculpted by the finest artists and layered with pure gold. Two cherubim spread their wings over the Ark, a symbol of God's presence and a military rallying point for the tribes. It took the best artists from Tyre seven years before the Temple was consecrated as a sanctuary for the distinctive monotheistic Israelite religion. Its foundations of quadrangular blocks went up along the side of the mountain; a portion of these have become the Wailing Wall.

What should have been a time of respite and a long-yearned-for peace was only the calm before the storm that was to affect the destiny of the children of Israel. Solomon passed away in 926 BC and with him died the dream of a unified Israelite empire. He was followed by his son Rehoboam (accession to power 926 BC), who could not stop the renewed rivalry between the northern and southern tribes. David and Solomon's unified empire was shattered into two separate kingdoms, Judah and Israel, which then went for each other's throats over the next two hundred years, much to the delight of their neighbours. The country was attacked from three sides: by Egypt in the Sinai, the Moabites on the Golan Heights, and the Philistines along the Jordan river. In Israel and Judah, fights broke out over who should be King. Eventually Ahab, son of Omri, took command and fought the Aramaeans to a standstill on the Golan Heights. But Ahab was spotted by an Aramaean archer, who fired an arrow into his chest. Despite his mortal wound, Ahab fought on until victory was valiantly achieved.

How do we know all this? In 1868, François Klein, an Alsatian missionary, was riding on his donkey through the Sinai Desert when his attention was drawn to a slab of black basalt sticking out of the sand. Brother Klein jumped from his animal and discovered that the stone was a stele covered with ancient writing. Before he managed to decipher some of its inscription, armed Arabs surrounded him and threatened his life unless he paid them a fabulous ransom. Being but a poor monk, he was finally released – without the stone. In Jerusalem he revealed his harrowing tale to another Frenchman, Clermont-Ganneau, who had the monk draw him a map before he rushed out to inspect the site. The Frenchman could hardly believe his eyes: half buried in sand lay a portion of the original Bible. After a first glance he realised that it was written in a Moab dialect, closely related to ancient Hebrew. He dug frantically, then he, like Brother François before him, found himself surrounded by yelling Arabs. They accused him of thievery, the penalty for which was to cut off the hand of the thief. Clermont-Ganneau was not only an archaeologist, but having served in the French foreign service he was an accomplished diplomat, fluent in Arabic. With presents and much palaver he managed to calm them down. Once he gave them his solemn promise to return with a great sum of money to purchase the stone, the Arabs allowed him to make a rubbing with charcoal and paper. It was to prove a fortunate initiative.

'I am Mesha, son of Chamosh, king of Moab,' it said. '. . . I built this sanctuary to Chamosh, God of Moab, as sanctuary and refuge; for he saved me from all my oppressors and gave me dominion over all my enemies. Omri was king of Israel and oppressed Moab many days, for God Chamosh was angry with his land. And his son succeeded him and he also said: I will oppress Moab . . . but I got the upper hand of Omri and his house: and Israel perished forever . . .' It was dated 840 BC, and announced the great victory by the Moabite King Chamosh over the Israelites. 'And Israel perished forever . . .' was the vital line, since it referred to the hated King Jehoram. Here was the final proof that Jehoram did exist, thereby substantiating the story of the fall of Israel when its children forgot their covenant with the Lord, turned away from Yahweh and worshipped a pagan deity. Jehoram had offered heathen sacrifices to Baal and had not prayed to the Lord. His father, King Ahab, had brought the pagan Baal to Israel after he fell under the spell of his wife, the Phoenician temptress Jezebel (1 Kings 21, 25). And now a basalt stele – the oldest biblical document – confirmed this! It told how the mighty army of Ahab had been smitten, and only ten of his one thousand chariots got away. '. . . for the king of Syria had destroyed them and he made them like the dust by threshing . . .' Such was the fate of those who had turned away from the Lord.

Clermont-Ganneau took his stone rubbing to Paris, where the members of the Academy fêted him and offered him the sum required to purchase his sensational find.

But what he found on his return was no stone, only an ugly black smear in the sand! The Bible's oldest written document had disappeared. Avarice was the motive. The Arabs had used gunpowder to shatter it – hoping to obtain a better price by selling it off in a thousand pieces . . .[6]

Once again a water tunnel was to play a decisive role in the history of Jerusalem. 'Now in the fourteenth year of king Hezekiah did Sennacherib king of Assyria come up against all the fenced cities of Judah, and took them . . .' (2 Kings 18, 13). After taking the fortress of Lachish,[7] and impaling its entire population, the Assyrian ruler was on his way to storm Jerusalem (701 BC). 'And the king of Assyria sent Tartan and Rabsaris and Rab-shakeh from Lachish with a great host against Jerusalem . . .' (2 Kings 18, 17). With the threat of a prolonged siege, King Hezekiah knew that the only danger to his well-supplied, strongly fortified town was its lack of water. Therefore he ordered a covered aqueduct to be chipped from the rock, 500 metres long, directing the waters from the Spring of Gihon, 'the Bubbler', to the Pool of Siloam, inside the secondary defence walls of Jerusalem. 'This same Hezekiah also stopped the upper water-course of Gihon, and brought it straight down to the west side of the city of David' (2 Chronicles 32, 30).

The tunnel was discovered in 1880, when an Arab boy fell into the pool and, in his panic to keep his head above water, paddled to the other end. There, cut from the rock, he found an underground passage. It was a shaft, some 80 centimetres wide and 1.5 metres high, that wound like a snake below the Kidron Valley. This fact had archaeologists baffled: why not dig the tunnel in the shortest possible way, a straight line? Then they

[6] The Mesha stele was partly recovered. Two large pieces and eighteen smaller fragments have been assembled following the guidance of the rubbing and are on display in the Louvre.
[7] A relief of the battle for Lachish is in the British Museum in London.

discovered the ancient belief that the royal graves of David and Solomon were located somewhere down there, and Hezekiah wished to protect his great ancestors' tranquillity in death. No such graves were ever found. More likely, with the Assyrian army within weeks of reaching Jerusalem, and workmen furiously tackling the tunnel from both ends, the two teams failed to meet up, though an inscription on the tunnel wall[8] denied that. 'The boring through is finished. While they plied the pick, each toward his fellow, and yet while there were three cubits to be bored through, there was heard the voice of one calling to the other . . . then the water poured from the source to the pool twelve hundred cubits . . .'

Because of its plentiful water supply, Jerusalem held out, and the Assyrian Sennacherib had to break off his siege when he was informed that an Egyptian force was moving in on him. The Bible gives a different explanation: 'And it came to pass that night, that the angel of the Lord went out, and smote in the camp of the Assyrians an hundred fourscore and five thousand; and when they arose early in the morning, behold, they were all dead corpses. So Sennacherib king of Assyria departed . . .' (2 Kings 19, 35–6).

A shaft had once caused Jebus to fall; now another had saved Jerusalem.

The secret of how David smote the Jebusite was contained in a biblical note about a sinnor. It was conquest by stealth. David cleverly combined a 'heaven-sent miracle' with a stunning psychological victory and united Israel and Judah around one capital, Jerusalem. The city was the corner-stone with which a slayer of giants laid the foundation that turned his united kingdom into a great power.

---

[8] Cut out by the Turks at the turn of the nineteenth century and put in a museum in Istanbul.

Part Two

The Heroes

491–479 BC

(Miltiades to Themistocles)

'So perish all who do the like again . . .'
Homer, 900 BC

3

The Birth Cry of Europe

Marathon
21 September 490 BC

'Nenikikamen! – Victory is ours!'
Pheidippides, a Greek soldier, 490 BC

The ancient world was thrown into turmoil. Like a cloud of thunder a tribe of fearful warriors rode out of the east. They overran Asia Minor and liquidated its reigning houses. Their chief, who called himself Prince of Anshan-Kurush, changed his name to Cyrus, and that of his conquered dominion to Persia. Under Cyrus, Persia became a military powerhouse. He gathered an army to conquer Lydia, where their King Croesus had forged a hasty alliance with Egypt, Babylon, and a newly emerging warrior nation: Sparta. In 546 BC, the son of King Cyrus of Persia, Cambyses, invaded Lydia and defeated Croesus while Cyrus took his army against Babylon. With the death of King Belshazzar in the Battle of Ctesiphon (30 October 539 BC), Babylon fell to Cyrus. Cyrus took the title of 'King of Babylon, Sumer and Akkad and the Four Quarters of the World'. He advanced with his army along the Megiddo road towards Egypt. He met, and defeated, the Egyptians near Romani in the Sinai. In 528 BC, the King of the Four

Quarters of the World was killed during a skirmish with the Scythians.

In 521 BC, Cyrus's grandson Darius established a series of satrapies. Darius took up the grandiose scheme of Croesus when he ordered the construction of a mighty fleet with which he ruled supreme over the Mediterranean and its trade routes. Since overland travel from his western to his eastern provinces took some time, and caravans could carry only a limited amount of goods, he ordered the first Suez Canal dug.

The rule of King Darius I was the beginning of Persia's aspirations in Europe. The moment Darius launched his giant host across the Hellespont he came into conflict not only with the spears of Hellas but also the culture of the Occident which the Greeks defended. For the next two hundred years, a wave of invasions resulted in a series of battles which, in their scope and devastation, were scarcely matched in history – and never surpassed until the destruction of Europe's imperial armies by Napoleon, twenty-five centuries later.

In 520 BC Darius began planning the conquest of the known world. He began with the construction of Persepolis, a symbolic city worthy of a god-king, where merchandising was forbidden and no governing was done. Only shamans were allowed inside the sacred compound. The Persians venerated the fire of Zoroaster and the cult of Mithra; their king hailed the god Aburamazdah as the 'great one who created water and earth, its men – and me, Darius!' To his god, Darius ordered the sacrifice of horses during celebrations ending in pagan ecstasies, brought on by the consumption of potent drinks. Persepolis became an allegory for the Persian empire, and was designed to celebrate the day of the summer solstice, the triumph of the sun over the moon. Each 21 June, at precisely ten minutes past six, as the first rays from a fiery red ball rose over the desert horizon and penetrated the magnificent crown hall, His August Majesty Darius faced the sun to pronounce: 'I, Darius, great king, king of kings, king of the universe and of the tongues spoken on this near and far earth, I greet you, sun.'

King Darius, whose ambitions were matched only by his luxurious lifestyle, turned his attention to the west. It was enough to watch his troops pass on parade to know that nothing on this earth could stand up to his desire for universal hegemony. Darius decided that Persia was to be the centre of the universe, and everyone else would be reduced to satrapy. And what Darius decided was done, because his was the voice of a god. In 512 BC, with an army of 100,000, transported and supplied by 300 vessels, he crossed the Bosphorus and headed against the Scythians to avenge his grandfather's murder. Rather than stand and fight, the Scythians laid waste to the land. Darius's army got tangled up in the dense swamps of the Danube delta, and the King, tired of chasing shadows, turned north, conquering the Ukraine, moving across the Dnieper and Donets, reaching as far east as the Volga, before he ordered a turnabout and headed south towards Macedonia. The Greeks feared that he wanted to take on the project begun by his ancestor, Cyrus the Great – intermingle in one vast empire the population of Persia and that of the Occident, and subject its ethnic groups to the harsh discipline of Iran. But then Darius changed his mind and returned home. To cover his retreat, he left behind an army under General Megabazus, who successfully reduced Thrace.

Shortly after King Cyrus's death and the bloody struggle for his succession, an event took place in Athens which was to have great consequences for its future. Athens, a centre of trade, commerce and immense wealth, established the world's first democracy under Cleisthenes. This was made possible when the King of Sparta ousted the tyrant of Athens, Hippias, who fled to the court of King Darius seeking assistance against his home-town, which had kicked him out. Darius received him favourably and the danger of a Persian invasion became apparent. Athens replied by calling a citizen army into being, divided into *taxis* (regiments) under a *strategos* (general). The overall military command was handed to a *polemarch*, who remained under the political supervision of the Athens Assembly. With Sparta and other city-states, Athens formed a Peloponnesian League. When the question of who should be in command of the league was raised, Sparta outdid Athens in numbers of troops and thereby became its *de facto* leader.

The Athenian example of ousting their tyrant was closely observed by similarly oppressed cities of Asia Minor, especially the Ionian Greeks of Ephesus. A half-century before, in 546 BC, the armies of the Persian General Harpagus had defeated the Ionians and annexed their lands. When the rumour spread that Darius had been defeated by the Scythians, the Ionians of Miletus rose to throw off the yoke of their Persian overlords (499 BC) and called on the assistance of their Greek brothers across the Aegean. Sparta refused to get involved in a fight that didn't concern them, but Athens and Eretria dared to challenge Darius's role as 'King of the Four Quarters of the World' and dispatched a minor force. The Ionic Revolt failed because the cities squabbled over the question of leadership and the Persians cleverly used their internal discord to put down the rebellion (494 BC). The brutality with which it was crushed left a bitter taste and the Ionians, who were Greeks by origin, became satraps in name only which no Persian ruler could ever again fully trust.

Meanwhile, Hippias, the ousted Athenian tyrant, continued his intrigues at the Persian court. He pointed out the danger to monarchical rule when it was replaced by something the Athenians called a democracy. Athens had abetted the Ionian Revolt, and their interference in his 'private garden' so infuriated Darius that he decided to set an example. To crush the Hellenic city-state, he assembled a great number of warships plus a terrestrial force in excess of fifty thousand. Persia suffered no shortage of manpower, and its satrapies were required to supply all their able-bodied for military service. Such ethnic call-ups were spread over garrisons throughout the empire, away from their own province. It prevented the possibility of another home-based revolt, like that of the Ionians.

King Darius had become increasingly taken with *pleinoxia*, the condition described by Aristotle in his *Politics* as the situation in which a power wants more power and ends up defeated by a better-motivated power. By the autumn of 491 BC, Darius was ready to invade Greece. With this single step, he set in motion the first major struggle between the Occident and the Orient, one that was to last two hundred years and, in the end, destroy both Persia and Greece.

Persia's powerful battle fleet under the command of the Median General Datis was to land in the Bay of Marathon and lure the Athenian citizen army from its capital. A second fleet under the satrap of Lydia, Artaphernes, was to sail around Attica and strike at Athens. Darius's strategic plan was clever, but his tactical planning was inadequate and based on an over-confidence regarding numbers. When Darius reached the Bosphorus and admired the sight from the bridge of his royal yacht, he ordered two white marble steles placed alongside the seashore, 'bearing the names of all nations and tribes of whom he was the guide'.[1] Soon he would add another stele with more

[1] Herodotus, *Histories* (IV).

names – Thebes, Athens, Eretria and Corinth. That was his plan.[2]

In the first months of 490 BC, King Darius's two combined armadas sailed from Samos. A day out at sea, they were spotted by a Greek merchant vessel, which managed to escape its pursuers and rushed with the news to Athens. The city-state was in no position to confront the might of Persia on its own and called on its League partners for immediate assistance. A military dispatch roll (a rolled-up parchment, calling on all other states of the League to rush to a member's assistance) was sent with the utmost speed to the members of the Hellenic Congress. The Athenians entrusted this delicate mission to their best runner, who had won his laurels in the games of Olympia. His name was Pheidippides, and it is reported that he covered the incredible distance of 250 kilometres in less than two days. The Plataeans promised immediate help, as did the Spartans, but only after their religious Carneian festival, which happened to fall on 20 September. When Pheidippides returned with their reply to Athens, its citizens broke out in bitter oaths over Sparta's refusal to rush to their support, considering it, rightly so, as a betrayal of their pact. The situation became more critical as reports were coming in of an imminent Persian landing. Without further assistance, the only readily available defence force was sent off. Athens' hastily assembled citizen army of ten thousand, led by *polemarch* Callimachus, was given a tearful send-off by mothers and wives, kissing the warriors' hands and imploring them to stop the Persian peril. In their haste to reach Marathon before the Persians, the Athenians left behind their pack-asses and supply wagons and told the drivers to catch up as best they could. The troops lengthened their stride. Their main obstacle was the thousands of refugees flowing like an endless stream against

[2] ibid.

them, clutching their infants and bundles of possessions. But they managed somehow, and this forced march by Callimachus and his Athenians proved decisive. Their luck held; the moment they disgorged from the mountain pass into the shore flats of Marathon, where they met up with an additional one thousand Plataeans, the Persian fleet appeared around the promontory of Cape Marathon and dropped anchor in the bay. It had been a close-run thing. A few hours made all the difference. They had derailed the Persians' plan by the speed of their advance.

The Persian General Datis debarked with his army in good order, but could no longer deploy down the Athens road, as the Athenians and their allies were camped astride it, near the shrine of Heracles. This left the Persian general bottled up, with the mountain pass held by the Greeks in front and the ocean behind him. He established the camp for his fifteen thousand men behind the protection of a marsh. For a week nothing happened, except for an occasional Greek raiding party, sent out by night to intercept boats loaded with supplies. Both sides were lying opposite each other in wait; Datis awaiting the outcome of the attack on Eretria by the second Persian host under Artaphernes, and the Athenians praying for the early arrival of the promised Spartan contingent. A number of Ionian Greeks, forced as auxiliaries into the Persian army, had fled from the camp of Darius and joined up with Callimachus; some were secretly dispatched back into the enemy camp in order to incite their fellow Ionians: 'If we must fight our Greek brothers, then let us fight badly . . .', a message that was to be repeated many times over the next two centuries.

With Datis held up in the Bay of Marathon, and Artaphernes laying prolonged siege to Eretria, the Persians' strategy began to show cracks. Having failed to take possession of the passes, the Persians had to alter their plan. The obvious solution was to re-embark the troops of

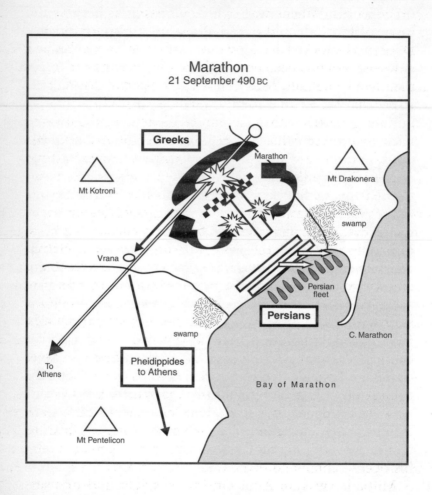

Marathon
21 September 490 BC

Datis and move on Athens by way of the sea. Therefore, it was just as vital for the Greeks to keep the Persian host tied down in Marathon as it had initially been for the Persians to draw the Athenians away from their city. In other words, Athens was safe from attack as long as the town of Eretria could hold out against Artaphernes, and Datis was blocked in a swamp. But then came the bad news: Eretria had been betrayed and the Persians had taken the town by default. Now everything hinged on Marathon. It became imperative for the *polemarch* Callimachus to initiate a battle with a favourable outcome, then hurry back to protect Athens from the danger of Artaphernes; or at least make it so costly for Datis that he needed time to resupply. Callimachus knew that he could not count on the Spartan contingent's presence until *after* their religious festivities, and that would be the evening of 21 September at the earliest. As matters were becoming urgent another piece of bad news arrived: the army of Artaphernes was getting ready to embark for Athens. He was expected to reach the city within the week. For the men at Marathon, it was now a question of days, if not hours. Callimachus held a council of war. Still without sufficient effective, he pleaded caution. His hoplite formation of élite foot troops was not strong enough to accomplish the mission. But at the same time, could the Spartans be rallied in order to play a decisive role? Time was pressing, and the Spartans nowhere near. This was a dynamic that Callimachus had to deal with. It led to a violent argument, and the *polemarch*'s plan to temporise was hotly challenged by the senior general under his overall command, Miltiades.

Miltiades was an Athenian by birthright and by usurpation the Tyrant of Chersonese. In a local revolt, he had been ousted from his capital Cardia and had fled back to Athens, where his arrival was greeted as a welcome addition to the war effort. But it also provoked a political crisis. Miltiades was violently anti-Persian and joined the party of aristocrats with that of the democrats in their drive to fight Darius. He had forcefully put across his view that Darius had to be stopped before he was given the chance to march on Athens. The design of the Persian invader was clear: conquer Athens, isolate Sparta, and the rest of Greece would fall into his hands through sheer terror; after which he would install the ousted Tyrant of Athens, Hippias, as his surrogate king. When Miltiades was shouted down in the assembly, he screamed in outrage: 'It was fated by the oracle that I should come to Athens. Horrid things are about to happen and a man like me will be needed. So do not reject me!' The Council of Elders came up with a typical politico-democratic solution: the democrat Callimachus was chosen as *polemarch* and the conservative Miltiades as his military adviser.

Miltiades, who bore a justifiable hatred ever since the day he had had to look on as a Persian raiding party killed his father, knew their ways better than anyone in the Greek camp. He now called for an immediate strike. His fear was understandable: should they let Datis and his Persians slip away into the open sea, there was no longer a way to stop them. Since he was already making preparations, this implied that the Athenians couldn't wait for the Spartans. Miltiades' argument was solid, but the council of ten generals still hesitated; Miltiades then demanded to have it put to the vote. Four were in his favour, five against. He now turned to Callimachus, who held the decisive vote. The *polemarch* gave the plan his nod. It now became a question of when. On that they couldn't agree. To precipitate a battle the following morning, Miltiades went among the troops, firing them up with patriotic slogans: 'Athens the Great, Athens the Unconquerable, each of you have drunk it in first with your mother's milk.' More cunning than fierce, he appealed to their honour and courage. He convinced them that the Persians wanted everything; they would take the land and its people as a beast rips the child from a mother's womb. The Athenians answered him with a roaring cheer and the die was cast.

This move threatened Callimachus with a revolt by his army, and he decided to advance the confrontation to the next morning. He handed the military operations to Miltiades, an old fox well versed in combat and not someone easily fazed by the prospect of having to confront a much larger force. He counted on the bravery and fighting spirit of his heavily armed hoplites. He knew their capabilities and limitations, and their major limitation was a justifiable fear of the measured advance by the enemy's line. Therefore he had to break up this advance before it could take on its final form. He would launch the initial attack with the outstanding combat formation of its time, the *phalanx*. A Greek phalanx was a compact formation with a triangular point at its head which, like a lance, pierced an enemy's line. The first rank pointed their spears at the enemy while the rear rank rested their lances on the shoulders of those in front to form a thicket of lances. With a depth ranging from eight to sixteen men, armed with thirteen-foot pikes, a phalanx was capable of well-directed manoeuvres in combat formation. The line itself allowed for narrow gaps to enable lighter-armed but faster units such as archers and slingers to pass through.

The main load of battle was carried by the *hoplites*; their heavy armour – greave, shield, helmet and pike – was expensive, and only the very rich could afford it. From an early age, it became the dream of every youngster to be chosen as a hoplite. Their training was rigorous and the best were awarded the honour of representing their respective towns at the annual Olympic competition. Their names were known and their deeds venerated. Hoplites preferred a flat field, since they advanced with a syncopated step, keeping the 'striking' foot ahead of the 'planting' foot (planted solidly on the ground for the lance thrust). Right behind a hoplite formation came the light infantry, or *psiloi*, hired from the lower classes of the cities; these were paid, but when it came to fighting for their own homes they were just as much Greeks as the nobility in front of them. *Psiloi* were poorly armoured and depended mainly on their speed, dashing forward to unleash their arrows or javelins. And finally, each city engaged a number of mercenary battalions, such as the famous slingers from Rhodes and Crete. They unleashed stones from slingshots, as David had done in biblical times when he smote Goliath. They fought, and fought well for him who paid their salary.

But there was one other difference in the opposing forces. The Persians were a drummed-together lot, made up of Medes (Persians) as well as their undependable satrap auxiliaries; the Greek hoplites were free citizens of the highest nobility. Their phalanx now faced the Persians across a flat piece of shoreline, bordered by two swamps.

At sunrise on 21 September 491 BC, after the watch fires had burnt into ash, the priests worked their great magic, calling up the spirits of the ancestors to see what the coming day would bring; they offered sacrifices to the gods on Mount Olympus to ask for their benediction. The omens were good. A double column of Athenians marched forward, hoplites in front, backed up by their spear-carriers and archers. They came to a halt between two small streams, the Charadra and the Avlona, facing the Persians of General Datis some five hundred yards away. The Persian war cries and banging of shields created a frightful noise, which drowned that of the adversary across the field. The Persians were lined up in formation with their backs against the sea, not a good position from which to start a battle. Psychologically it forced them to win. The alternative was to drown.[3]

[3] G. Rawlinson, *History of Herodotus*, London, 1880.

The outcome of the battle was most likely decided before it even began. It came about not through planning, but from necessity. Miltiades lacked the necessary manpower to ensure a decisive breakthrough in the centre, and that led to a radical shift in his tactics. Shortly before the battle commenced, and having studied the enemy's line-up, he feared that the Persians would go for his centre, split his army in two and then push the separate parts into the bordering swamps. Therefore he ordered his centre column to be weakened and reduced the ordinary eight-rank phalanx to four rows. He realised the risks involved, but this freed a substantial number of troops to boost his flanks. He ordered the wings to turn inward at an angle of 45 degrees, forming a shallow horseshoe line, and not to advance without his specific command. It is unlikely that he was aware of his winning formula.

At dawn a cloud of mist had hung over the region, but when the war horns blared and the fifes began their shrill racket, the sun, already high, blazed. The Persian troop leaders had dressed their ranks into rigid lines, deadly in their grim beauty, an array of many colours, topped by the glittering line of lances. Slowly the long line advanced, although a frontal attack into massed archers and slingers amounted to suicide. The Greek bow-men had moved ahead of their hoplites. They arrayed themselves in an appropriate manner for rapid changes of range and angle of shooting. The Persians marched, shoulder to shoulder, and when they were at a distance of 200 yards, the Greek *psiloi* peppered their line with a shower of arrows and missiles. In the next few moments, the devastation caused by every archer firing a minimum of ten shafts was great. Volleys of feather-winged shafts tore into the Persian ranks, sweeping away the Medes and their allies like leaves. Horses stumbled, men cried out, and Datis lost many good troops in his initial charge. His line became ragged as soldiers stumbled blindly ahead, straight through the hail of missiles, struggling to stay on their feet over the next twenty paces. His column became a vulnerable and sluggish line, strung out farther than he liked it to extend. Yet, instead of trying to re-form his line, he ordered the effort redoubled, thinking that with the sheer mass of flesh he could smash through the iron-tipped phalanx. For those following the downed first line it became a nightmare of stumbling over ground made mushy by corpses. Eventually they got through, and it came to a frontal impact between a thin Greek line and a howling mass of Persians. Gaps opened in the Athenians' column, a hand-breadth, then a yard, and then three men wide. Into every breach surged a hammering, gouging wave of Persians, thrust ahead by their own momentum. The Greek centre began to buckle and give under the bulk of the Persian flood, its brave defenders maintaining their shields to the fore. Holes were speedily plugged by reserves. Again and again, the Athenian centre closed ranks as they were forced into a slow retreat. Thousands of sandalled feet grabbing for a hold raised great clouds of dust; dust caked their bleeding wounds, dust covered the dead, and dust was sucked in great gulps into the lungs of the fighting. Men stormed ahead and then again retreated over the chests and faces of the fallen, trampling the living to death.

Taking advantage of the retreat of the Greek line, Datis ordered a renewed Persian attack. The Persians fed ever more troops into the fray, and soon they had punched a deep bulge into the Greek centre. But the Greek line still held. Datis, with victory in his grasp, urged his men to knock a hole through the outdrawn and steadily thinning echelon of hoplites. Some portions of the Greek chain were now down to a single rank. But they stood and they stabbed from behind linked shields. Theirs was a fury such as the Persians had never encountered in all their previous wars. The Greeks refused to give. Wherever the Greek line was about to scatter, others jumped forward, grabbing the shield and lance of their fallen comrades to plug the hole in the wall of muscle and shield; they quickly grouped together, shield to shield, lances solidly anchored in the ground. They let their enemy come up to die on the tips of their pikes. But no amount of individual heroism could halt the growing distress of the centre. Their exhausted limbs and leaden bodies could hardly hold sword or lance, their breath came ragged, their eyes were blinded by sweat. On they fought, while bodies kept piling up, Greeks and Persians. More and more the Greeks had to give. Miltiades, who showed great personal courage, had decided on a bold plan and was sticking to it. He refused the enemy his flanks. He understood what couldn't be avoided in the centre and handled the situation with astounding coolness. The climax of the battle was near.

Callimachus, who had stood most heroically in the centre, rushed to take command of the right wing, while Miltiades took over the left flank – a daring option while their centre was near collapse. This created a devilish trap. While the Athenian centreline had stretched and its measured pull-back sucked more and more of the enemy into the bulge, it brought the reinforced, angled Greek wings towards their centre. This inward wheel resulted in a double envelopment of the Persian pocket.

Men fighting for their lives in hand-to-hand combat never notice what goes on to their sides, nor to their backs; their concentration is fully directed on the enemy before them. This was the case with the Persians; they had never been nearer victory, when suddenly the reinforced Greek wings uncoiled in what became in seconds a lethal charge, fired on by their defiant roar of 'Zeus!' They burst into the open flanks of the massed Medes inside the pocket. Once the first phalanx stormed ahead of its flanking position, all others followed suit; their pent-up rage needed no command to be released. This sudden flank attack by Greek lances caught the Persians completely by surprise and stopped their advance. With insensate fury the Greek wing formations hacked and stabbed their way through the Persian ranks, granting no quarter. Persian dead littered the field in heaps between the two rapidly closing wing formations. With the lion's jaws about to snap shut, a corps of Persian cavalry rode forth in an attempt to prevent their army's encirclement. Their horses were skewered by the lance-tips of the charging phalanx. The riders broke and fled. Datis' desperate attempt to save his foot troops from annihilation had come to nothing. Within minutes his army was surrounded on three sides and buried under a hail of missiles; only one escape route was still open to them, towards the shore – and beyond that lay the treacherous deep water. Mauled and shaken, they pulled back, while more of the dreadful ironclad hoplites circled round behind and hacked them to pieces. The shore quickly became puddled with the blood of thousands. Miltiades and Callimachus were in the midst of their bravest and finest, driving before them the remainder of their enemies towards a watery death. During the final charge at the water's edge, Callimachus was struck down. He did not live to see his side's crushing victory. Nor did many Persians. They threw down their arms and ran for their ships, which had already put out to sea, abandoning their comrades to captivity, or death. Datis lost more men in the final rout than during the battle: 6,400 dead were left behind on the beach. For days afterwards, the sea washed many more bloated corpses ashore.

While the fleet of Datis retreated unmolested from Marathon Bay, a signal was flashed to his ship from somewhere on Mount Pentelicon; those who saw it assumed afterwards that it must have come from a Greek renegade, urging Datis to join an uprising planned by opponents to Athens' democratic rule. But with news that victory had been won, the rebellion never took off, especially when the conspirators learned that a powerful Spartan army was on its way to protect the city. They would have made short shrift of the rebels. It was just as well that nobody ever discovered who sent the signal. It might have started a civil war.

The same evening a strong Spartan contingent marched on to the field at Marathon, to find it strewn with corpses, with birds of prey feeding on the remains of the Persian army. There were no living about – the Persians were dead, and the Athenians had rushed off in defence of their city, after having given a decent burial to their fallen comrades in a common grave. Miltiades and his Athenians wasted no time in self-congratulation – that would come later. Generations would sing their praise of that incredible moment.[4]

Darius's army had landed to do mortal damage, and instead the Greeks had inflicted a stinging repulse. In a double envelopment, probably brought on accidentally by the dynamics of the battle but which would stand up as a tactical gem, a vast Persian host had been beaten in its own element, on land.

'Marathon was a brilliant prologue to a grand drama.'[5]

In the age of the fathers of history, Herodotus and Thucydides, Marathon presents a milestone in military history. For the first time, the legends and biblical chronicles of the past gave way to serious historical reporting. And yet it is likely that Marathon would have become just another in a series of forgotten battles had it not been for the astounding feat of one man. Still in his blood-splattered battledress, the noble Pheidippides ran

[4] It was on these accounts, given many years after the battle, that contemporary historians based their analyses.
[5] *The Cambridge Ancient History* and J.F.C. Fuller, *Battles of the Western World*.

the 42.5 kilometres from Marathon to Athens[6] to cry out:

'*Nenikikamen!*' – Victory is ours!

After which he fell over dead from loss of blood and exhaustion.

It is this sideline to history which perpetuates the immortality of the Battle of Marathon.

The Battle of Marathon presents a historical enigma. Was the double envelopment, leading to the annihilation of the Persian army, brought on by design, or did it come about accidentally? This has become a point for speculation by historians.

There can be no doubt that Miltiades exhibited the qualities of a great leader. With his moral steadfastness and flexibility, he adjusted to the given situation. His moral character stood as an example and forced his troops to maintain the physical exertion demanded. He stopped the Persians at the gates of the Occident.

Marathon was the birth cry of Europe.

---

[6] Today's marathon champions, training for years and with light equipment, do it in 2 hours and 10 minutes, but then it probably took some five or six hours.

4

The Gates of Hell

Thermopylae
9 August 480 BC

'Stranger, passing by, go tell the Spartans,
that here we lie, obedient to our laws.'
Simonides' epitaph on the stele
at Thermopylae, fifth century BC

'Again, in our Greek enterprises we present the singular spectacle of daring and deliberation, each carried to its highest point, and both united in the same person . . .'[1] If ever such a person existed, then it was Leonidas, King of Sparta. It not only required physical courage to face an overpowering enemy, but moral courage to assume responsibility for the lives – or deaths – of his own men. And once he had made his decision, he stuck to it, whatever the costs. The stand of Sparta's Threehundred at the Gates of Thermopylae remains the epic rearguard action of all time, a monument to physical courage and tenacity.

Following the death of King Darius I, his son Xshayarshan, or, as he was to be known, Xerxes (485–465 BC), took

---

[1] Thucydides in his *History of the Peloponnesian War*, translated by Richard Crawley in 1874.

power by eliminating all sibling pretenders to the Persian throne. He climbed the bloody ladder to ascendancy, then pursued his master scheme: to destroy Greece and gain undisputed control over the Aegean and Mediterranean trade routes. 'The Persian king was pushed by the gods to commit a fatal error engaging in the Second Medean War.'[2] Gods or no gods, Xerxes dispatched envoys to the Greek city-states (with the noted exception of Sparta and Athens), demanding from them an urn of earth and a jar of water as sign of their submission. When this was refused, Xerxes called on his satraps to supply him with men and arms. According to the 'father of historic writing', Herodotus, the army of Xerxes numbered in excess of two million; recent estimates put it closer to 200,000, still a formidable mass of warriors for its time. His naval forces were equally impressive; these consisted of 3,000 transport vessels and 1,207 ships of the line. Xerxes' plan for the invasion of Greece called for a crossing to the European shore by way of the Hellespont. He ordered the construction of two gigantic boat bridges, one of 314 vessels, the other of 360, held in line by six arm-thick flaxen cords and covered with planks to allow passage for his many thousand war chariots and cavalry. In the winter of 481 BC, Xerxes moved his court to Therma (Salonica). His huge war machine was ready to go into action.

The news struck without warning: a great Persian host had bridged the Hellespont, had already overrun Thrace and Macedonia and was rapidly approaching the borders of Hellas. In a typical 'everyone for himself' attitude, Thessaly switched sides and joined the ranks of the invader. The Greeks, caught in the grip of their usual internal squabble and in disunity over who should fight and who should lead, reacted timidly by dispatching a hastily collected force of ten thousand to their northern borders to stop

2 Herodotus.

the Persian host at Tempe. When part of Xerxes' forces threatened to bypass them, the Greeks turned and ran. 'A disgraceful act,' cried the older generation that had stood up valiantly to the Persian hordes at Marathon. Better to risk defeat than commit such a cowardly act, running away in the face of the enemy! Wives, who had garlanded their warrior husbands and sent them off to draw blood in order to protect their hearths and their cribs, now spat in their faces and refused them their beds. What united the Greeks was not the danger brought on by the military débâcle at Tempe, however disgraceful it may have been, but the reaction to their behaviour from their wives and mothers. They had been listening to the stories of Persian atrocities from refugees. The women told of their rape, how their teenage daughters were rounded up to be sold into soldier brothels and their sons castrated to turn them into eunuchs. The women of Greece were adamant – should their men lack the courage to defend them against such outrage, then they would form into Amazon battalions. Their delegation confronted the *polemarch*. This did it. Hellas's men were shamed into action. Their honour, and with it the honour of Greece, was at stake.

Emissaries went to the city-states with the call for a meeting of the clans, during which the women managed to extract a promise from the various representatives to raise immediately five *morai* – five thousand hoplites plus their shield-bearers. Not much of an army to face Persia's hundreds of thousands – but it had to do until more forces could be gathered and armed. The Council of Elders went to seek advice from the Oracle of Delphi: 'Stand at the end of the earth.' For any Greek, 'the end of the earth' was the land beyond the high peaks. After listening to wise men and grizzled warriors, the Elders settled on one location where a relatively minor force stood a fair chance of halting, or at least slowing up, a vastly superior army: the Three Gates of Thermopylae. Xerxes would have to take the only coastal road to Athens, and their chance of delaying his advance was in a bottleneck between mountain and sea, the Thermopylae Pass, named after a hot spring supposed to contain the secret of healing wounds. The task of stopping the Persians on land was handed to the greatest warrior of his time, the Agiad King of Sparta, Leonidas.

An overall plan of defence was devised. It called for all the forces readily available. A combined Athenian–Spartan battle fleet of 324 triremes was to block the Straits of Artemisium and Andros to prevent the Persian fleet from launching a flank attack on the troops holding Thermopylae. Compared to the Persian might, the Greek land forces were pitifully small. The Panhellenic Conference raised seven *morai*, a mixed force of Thespians, Phocians and Spartans, altogether seven to eight thousand hoplites. In what was to become an eternal saga of valour, led by Sparta's Threehundred of the *homoioi* cast (the warrior-citizens) and true to their motto 'Conquer or die!', these men were ordered to hold off the two hundred thousand foot-soldiers, cavalry and support troops of Emperor Xerxes.

The Thermopylae Pass was actually a series of three narrow passages, known as the West, the Middle and the East Gate. Hemmed in by bordering cliffs, the enemy would not be able to deploy his numerical superiority. Leonidas concentrated his allied force on a rise just after a ravine in front of the Phokian Wall of the Middle Gate; years before, the Phocians (or Phokians) had put up a stone wall, more for collecting road taxes than for any defensive objective. This crude barrier was only chest high, but defended by men willing to die for it, the Pass became virtually impregnable. But every fortress has its built-in weakness, a key that opens the gate. It was no different at Thermopylae: a mountain trail, called the Anopaea trail, bypassed it; it snaked upriver along the Asopus river gorge by skirting the citadels of Trachis and Oita, then wound across the rock-strewn northern slopes of Mount Oita and Mount Callidromos, before it cut back down to the sea, where it joined the coastal road between the Middle and the East Gate. The Spartan King did not know of its existence. Very few did; only a few local shepherds used it in springtime to put their flocks out to pasture.

To ensure the flanking protection of the Middle Gate, Leonidas deployed a blocking unit of a thousand lightly armed Phocian helots near the Citadel of Trachis. There was little chance of an attack from that quarter, and the thousand were there to screen enemy scouts and minor forays, but were not meant to prevent a major force from moving through them.

Xerxes entered the Plain of Malia (known also as the Plain of Trachis), a green pasture dotted with flocks of sheep. From there the road climbed up to the Thermopylae heights, where the Greeks were blocking his advance. He encamped his army in plain sight of the Greeks, hoping that the mere display of this immense host would panic them into flight as it had done at Tempe. This time it did not.

Seen from the Thermopylae heights, the plain was covered from end to end with tents and smoking campfires, a gigantic encampment, divided into sectors, each reserved for an ethnic group: Assyrians, Babylonians, Medes, Karians, Armenians, Cissians, Cappadocians, Arabs, Illyrians, Lydians, Bactrians, Egyptians – 'for was there one nation in Asia which Xerxes did not bring against Greece?'[3] Leonidas was impressed; not even the Titans could have equalled in scale and splendour the Persians' war train. The Persians down on the plain resembled mechanical toys, but toys that had emerged straight from Hades. Every tribe, every satrap contingent, every division was dressed in its own distinctive colour; troops marched about in slashes of red, blue, yellow and purple. Their captains stood out by virtue of their

[3] Herodotus (VII, 21).

Persian Invasion of Greece
480–479 BC

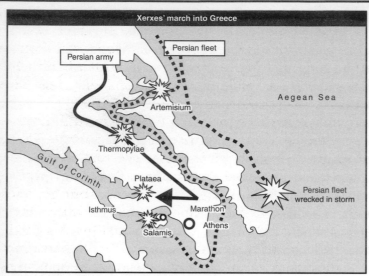

Xerxes' march into Greece

Persian fleet

Persian army

Aegean Sea

Artemisium

Thermopylae

Gulf of Corinth

Plataea

Isthmus

Marathon

Athens

Salamis

Persian fleet wrecked in storm

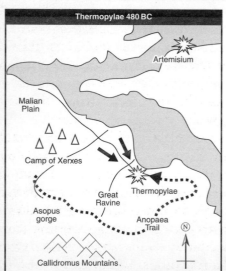

Thermopylae 480 BC

Artemisium

Malian Plain

Camp of Xerxes

Great Ravine

Thermopylae

Asopus gorge

Anopaea Trail

Callidromus Mountains

N

Sea Battle of Artemisium

Persians: over 800 ships
Athenians: 324 triremes

Battle of Thermopylae

Xerxes: 200,000 men
including 10,000 'Immortals'

Leonidas: 7,000 hoplites
including 300 Spartan bodyguards

polished breastplates; troops carried no protective armour other than leather jerkins. The exception was the Ten Thousand Immortals of the King's élite corps in shining fish-scale armour.

Above the Malian Plain a brightly illuminated path led to a magnificent tent. Placed outside the tent was an impressive throne, that of His Majesty Xerxes, son of Darius, King of Kings and Master of all the Lands. His splendour was the result of years of plundering Asia. Next it would be the turn of Greece.

Leonidas knew only too well that the main distinction between the forces was not weaponry but morale. What a difference his Greek hoplites presented – sedately garbed, but more heavily armed and protected with body armour all the way down to their leg covers of poured bronze;[4] their *aspides* (shields) were of solid oak trimmed with polished metal. Their main weapon was a thirteen-foot spear, the *sarissa*, which had already proven its value at Marathon. Every warrior-citizen was accompanied by his individual shield-bearer or *helot*; it freed the noble *homoioi* to slash or stab. A helot was required to tend the wounds of his master and, following victory, take his club and kill the wounded enemy. Behind this formidable shield wall were the archers, with dozens of bronze-headed cane shafts stuck in the ground for easy reach, and behind them the foot reserves waited to plug the holes.

The Spartan King's seven thousand versus the many hundred thousand seemed a lost cause. They weren't. The approaches to the Pass acted much like a funnel, wide at the entrance and narrow at the critical passage. There wasn't space enough to put more than ten dozen warriors into a frontal attack formation – certainly no room to throw in tens of thousands at the same time. Leonidas wished he had a few thousand more; it is certain,

---

4 Somewhat like the shin protectors of a modern football player.

had he received an additional force of only five thousand hoplites, as he had been promised, that the Persians would never have passed Thermopylae, because one on one they were no match for the Greek hoplites. Leonidas decided to use the Thespians and Arcadians to absorb the first attack, keeping his Spartans as back-up to fill gaps. Farther back he posted his reserves of Mycenaeans and Phliasians.

For three days both forces camped opposite and observed each other. There was little talk among the defenders; the eyes of the warriors were remote and insular, their minds preoccupied with the anticipation of the fight they knew must come. On the fourth day, Xerxes dispatched an envoy with the order for King Leonidas to lay down his arms. 'Come and get them,' was the Spartan's curt reply, which so infuriated His Persian Majesty that he ordered an immediate attack. Masses of Persians and their satrap armies formed up across a strip of no-man's-land, awaiting their emperor's signal. It came with the silvery wail from a horn.

The men up on the Pass heard a distant trumpet, and then a rumbling that shook the ground. Before the mass of Persians crested the rise, Leonidas performed the *spaghia*, the customary sacrifice to the goddess Artemis, by running his blade through a goat he held clamped between his knees. The blood spurted from the animal's throat and splattered the King's tunic. It was the first blood drawn in the battle for the Thermopylae Pass. Everyone was aware that there was much more blood to come.

The Persian army, a thousand wide and ten deep, marched up the long slope. As the cliffs narrowed, their front ranks were compressed, and this resulted in a great, unwieldy mass of pushing and shoving men without any chance for lateral movement. The first engagement was set off by Medean archers dashing ahead of the congested bulk to rain arrows on the Greek shield wall; with only their eye slits in horsehair-plumed helmets peeking over red-and-bronze shields, they inflicted no damage on the Greeks. The 'Greek wall of bronze' had its shields interwoven in a solid rampart; the second rank held their shields above them and slanted forward, like a roof, to ward off the cane shafts which disintegrated on impact with the bronze. The Thespians, with their long pikes planted solidly in the ground, presented a bristling iron-tipped forest to the onrush. Against this wall of shields and the armoured bodies of the Thespian hoplites, eight dozen shields wide, piled thousands of attackers, jostling and getting in each other's way in the narrow confine. 'Victory for Xerxes!' was immediately answered by the single outcry of a defiant 'Zeus Saviour!'

The initial contact came in a great crash that reverberated from the cliff walls, as the smaller, leather-covered shields of the Medes collided with the solid oak-and-bronze shields of the Thespians. Then a cloud of dust obscured everything, with only the occasional glinting of spears rising above it. The Medes, whose principal function was to deliver a lightning strike under the protection of a deluge of arrows, were armed for speed but not for impact. Coming on in a great mass and delivering their short throwing spears from fifteen to twenty yards was normally sufficient to drive any enemy to flight. This time they didn't stand a hope; they died, run through by Thespian lances. More Persians were sent into the fray; they came on, a hundred, two hundred wide and forty deep; the push from the rear ranks was so forceful that it shoved their front line onto the tips of Thespian and Arcadian pikes. Mountains of dead began to pile up in front of the wall of shields; corpses with slashed bellies and hacked-off limbs lay all around. Those who tried to retreat were cut down by the axes of their own slave-drivers, who 'did away with cowards' to stop others from running away. Whenever a charge was repulsed, no attempt was made to help the wounded or clear the field of corpses for the following wave.

The training and discipline of the Greeks were turning the situation in their favour. With courage and great sacrifice they held the wall and confronted each new attack. The helots pulled their wounded behind the shelter of the phalanx, while fresh warriors took their place to reinforce the ranks and link shields. Against this wall of bronze crashed consecutive Persian waves to be met by a thrust-and-draw with lance and sword. Every attempt was turned into a maw of slaughter. Before the Greeks' *promachoi* (first rank), a new wall had piled up – the torsos of their enemy. Subsequent waves had to clamber over hundreds of slain to get near the foe. Standing at the gate of hell, the Greeks were possessed by the divine *daimons*; their hatred of the intruder was transformed into acts of savagery and barbarism unimaginable before. In this hand-to-hand struggle, bodies themselves became the weapon; press and weight often decided the issue. Even fingers became lethal claws. The narrow confines turned into the theatrical stage of a Greek drama, where the play performed was *Death* and only confusion reigned. After each new assault, the Greek helots went out among the hundreds of wounded who cried out for help or pity. No mercy was granted, only death. Ever more Persians were broken on the bronze wall of the Greek *aspides*; decimated Medes units turned back, becoming inextricably entangled with the oncoming waves. The Greek archers were lined up in the shelter of the Phocian stone wall; their feathered missiles arced over the fighting front to smash with murderous velocity into the advancing masses. Because of the tremendous pressure from the back, wave after wave was virtually carried into the arrows and mowed down. And should one unit manage a breakthrough, then groups of Mycenaeans jumped atop the Phocian wall and hacked down on the mass of enemy heads, slicing through helmet and bone. During brief respites in the fighting, boys hurried about with goatskins of wine or water they had fetched from the Scyllian spring behind the stone wall, while the helots rushed out among the fallen to collect arrows. When the warriors manning the shield wall became too tired or suffered too many casualties, they were replaced by rested troops; then the exhausted warriors were granted a few moments of respite to rest their sword-arms. At opportune moments, a phalanx of Spartans advanced sure-footedly, keeping in perfect step to the sound of flutes, thrusting out with razor steel. More blood burst from wounds. The dry earth of Thermopylae turned into red mud.

A dozen separate attacks were delivered that day, until by nightfall a portion of Xerxes' front-line troops had been virtually wasted.

At last the Persians, finding that all their efforts to gain the pass availed to nothing, and that, whether they attacked by divisions or in any other way, it was to no purpose, withdrew to their own quarters. During these assaults, it is said that Xerxes, who was watching the battle, thrice leaped from the throne in terror for his army.

Next day he renewed the combat with no better success. The Greeks were so few that the Persians hoped to find them disabled, by reason of their wounds. But the Greeks stood solidly, drawn up in detachments according to their cities, and bore the brunt in turns. Blood splashed their arms and chests, their shields dripped with it, and the bright steel of their blades was dulled with it. When the Persians found no difference between that day and the preceding, they retired again to their quarters.[5]

Despite the overwhelming odds of thirty, forty, sometimes fifty to one, and the blind courage displayed by

---

[5] Herodotus (VII, 211–12).

some of the Medean regiments, the Persian attack stalled on the killing ground before the ancient stone wall, and many Persian leaders saw no alternative but to withdraw their platoons from the line. And so for two days Xerxes' vast host tried to break the Greek line, and for two days they were warded off, suffering great loss. The Greeks also suffered great losses. Leonidas was sacrificing Hellas's best men, but he had to buy time for the rest of Greece to rally, and he would.

At the same time as this epochal battle was conducted on land, another was fought on the sea off Cape Artemisium between Xerxes' armada and the Hellenic fleet. The Persian warships tried to force a channel for their troop transporters in order to turn Leonidas's flank, and the Greek seamen did what had to be done to stop this from happening. The Persians had too many ships to render the final outcome in doubt, and fortune smiled on the badly pressed Greeks. A severe storm disrupted the engagement. The Hellenic fleet made good its escape along the Euboean Channel and into the Bay of Eleusis, coming to anchor in the lee of the island of Salamis.

The sea battle of Artemisium was considered a Persian victory, but it taught one captain a most valuable lesson: for the Athenian Admiral Themistocles, it had shown up the vulnerable naval tactics of his adversary. The Persians had entered into battle without an overall strategy, relying entirely on a concerted push by thousands of oars driving forward many hundreds of ships of war. If such an attack could be funnelled into the narrow waist between one of the many Aegean islands, where manoeuvrability was everything and numbers accounted for little, the Greeks stood a good chance of halting the enemy, even defeating him.

On Thermopylae, the next day began equally harshly for the defenders on the Middle Gate. This day the shield wall was made up of Spartans. First they held off a charge by

Bactrian cavalry. The front rank of Spartan hoplites knelt down and planted the butts of their long *sarissas* in the ground, angled towards the eyes of the horses. The next three ranks held their lances high, points out-thrust over the heads of the kneeling first rank. They presented a wall of spiked steel, and the Bactrian horses wouldn't stand it. A few managed to close in and slaughter several in the Greek front rank, but the second file held and hacked the riders from their mounts. The Greeks shouted in triumph, and the cheer ran down their line. The Bactrians were followed by Xerxes' foot troops. Much of the fighting took place in single combat. Two Medes came rushing from Leonidas's blind side, axes high. But the Spartan archers were ready. One of the axemen died at once; the other managed to duck and the shaft ripped through his shoulder. He staggered on, till another arrow punctured his fish-scale plate as if it were made of cloth instead of metal. A dozen times, that day, the Medes charged, and were broken on the shields and spears like waves on a rocky shore.

Xerxes was furious about his generals' denigrating setbacks. Successive attacks had brought little or no results. What had started out, on the first day, as a *furioso* charge began to lack frenzy; this led to a drop in morale. A number of generals, all those His Majesty considered unworthy or having fought without sufficient courage, lost their heads to the royal executioner.

While Xerxes pondered what to do next, a raggedy-looking figure was dragged before his august presence; he gave his name as Ephialtes of Malis, the village that had given its name to the Malian Plain. Little is known about this man. Contemporary Greek historians shunned his name in shame, only to pass on the fact that this Ephialtes committed an act of treachery most vile: for a purse of gold he offered to guide a Persian division on to a secret trail, which wound around the Greek defenders. Xerxes had nothing to lose. He ordered his Immortals under their captains Orontes and Hydarnes to undertake the march across the mountains and come upon Leonidas from his undefended rear. Because of this epochal march, the Anopaea trail became the Path of the Immortals. Several thousand heavily armed men set out after darkness, with only a sliver of moon to guide them. The smallest sounds were amplified. They found their way by following the sound of the footsteps of those walking ahead; many tripped over exposed roots, curses breaking their self-imposed silence, made necessary because the Greek had told them of a Phocian blocking force farther up the gorge. They crossed the Asopus river without incident. Before sunrise they caught sight of the Phocian detachment, blocking the entrance into the narrow chasm beyond. After a brief encounter, in which only a few Phocians were killed, the rest ran off in blind panic; two had enough presence of mind to head in the direction of Leonidas.

From the Asopus gorge, the goat trail led steeply up to the rugged slopes of Mount Callidromos, through ravines and gorges, up to the watershed and down the other side. After a brief respite during the heat of the day, they crested a rise. Far below them they could see the coastal road leading from the East to the Middle Gate. The greedy Ephialtes beamed and demanded his bag of gold. Captain Orontes, carved from the same noble wood as the Greek heroes, was so incensed by this treacherous act that, with a glinting flash of steel, he cut the traitor's head from his shoulders. The disembodied head of a greedy man who had sold his king for a bag of gold rolled like a lumpy ball in the dust.

In the evening the Immortals heard the sound of thunder from the direction of the Pass, with sheets of lightning crackling across the heavens. An omen – but was it a propitious one? In fact, lightning had struck the Phocian wall the moment the first Persians had reached the last barrier and begun tearing it down. Zeus had spoken!

Since early that day, the sound of battle had never stopped. Out at sea, the Persian Navy finally pushed through the Artemisium narrows, where the Greeks had left a delaying force of two dozen triremes. The sea was covered with the flotsam of smashed timber from the ships that had gone down. On the Thermopylae heights, the carnage was more terrible than ever before. Both sides took casualties, though the Persians suffered many more than the heroic Spartans and their allies. Xerxes had thrown everyone pell-mell into the struggle to break the Spartans' resistance: Bactrian cavalry, Egyptian archers, Armenian and Cissian foot troops, Cappadocians and Arabs. The mass of attackers extended all the way down the long slope and into the Persian camp. Each consecutive wave found it more difficult to stop sliding back on the blood-soaked ground. Thousands of bloodless, dead Persians lay scattered before the wall. There was no call for quarter. The Greeks no longer cheered each other; they hacked and they speared, they fired their arrows and they died. When a Greek was mortally struck, his body was pulled back and another jumped into the breach and linked his shield to that of his neighbour. And if there were no more *homoioi* of the supreme warrior caste, then their shield-bearers took their place and fought on to the death. There were so many slain Persians that King Leonidas had another wall built of their corpses. During a break in the fighting, his battle-fatigued warriors worked furiously to pile hundreds of slain into a breast-high wall. It proved enough to stop the next three waves, but not the fourth. Five thousand heavily armed Medes came across the churned-up earth, pushing before them a herd of slaves to protect them from the missiles until they reached the wall of bodies. With their bare hands, the mass of slaves pulled at the headless, hacked corpses before Persian soldiers flooded through the holes. The Persians were fresh and the Greeks exhausted. They fell back fighting. For the first time, the Persians were about to cross the Phocian wall when the unexpected took place. Probably attracted by the superheated air and the mass of metal on the Pass heights, lightning struck the wall. For the Greeks it was a sign from heaven, and with a fierce 'Zeus Saviour!' they pushed back the attackers. Then rain that fell in sheets turned the blooded ground into ankle-deep muck.

Before the Phocian wall, the slaughter had now gone on for three days. If Leonidas could hold out a while longer, then he would force Xerxes to abandon the land route and seek a solution by sea, where the Greeks had a chance. For this to happen they needed time to prepare, and it was this time he had to buy with his delaying action. There was a limit to the suffering that could be endured. Though the Persians took frightful casualties – which owing to their numbers they could afford – the allied Lacedaemonians had just about reached the end of their endurance; their platoons had been decimated, their bodies refused to function and their brains were dulled by effort, noise and the odour of rotting flesh. Their various captains confronted Leonidas with a request to pull out, make for home and prepare for the defence of their own cities. 'Preserve our men, O lord, because they have proven their valour,' they argued. 'These are no cowards; the warriors that remain still standing up are the flower of Hellas, ready to fight another day. But not here and not now.'

No mortal is ever as lonely as the man who must make life-and-death decisions concerning his men. Leonidas had expected their demand; he knew that they couldn't hold out much longer. They had done their share of fighting. Rather than have them wasted to no purpose, he ceded to their demand. In doing so, King Leonidas of Sparta accepted the ultimate sacrifice: with his personal guard, a mere three hundred men, he would fight a rearguard action to stave off the Persian avalanche for at least one more day. This would give his allies a chance to make good their escape.

He knew, as did his men, that as surely as the sun rises every morning the Persians would assault his Spartans. All was in the hands of the gods, and into their hands Leonidas released his spirit. From them he summoned help, because only with their compassion could his thin line overcome the next test. His warriors had reached the banks of the River Styx – and on the other shore awaited death. Under the cover of darkness his allied Greeks readied themselves to pull back – Corinthians, Phliasians, Mycenaeans and Arcadians, covered by dirt and blood from the last three days. For them the fighting had ended, and they looked what they were – a tired, battle-weary lot, their helmets pushed back from their grimy faces, their eyes listless, their shoulders slouched. There was hardly one that wasn't bleeding from some wound. While they filed past the Spartans, they handed their swords to those who had broken theirs in battle and their spears to those whose shafts were stuck in some Persian. They didn't have to be ashamed; Hellas would be proud of them, they had fought with utmost valour, but now their combat was finished. There was another battle waiting for them, in front of the walls of Arcadia or Corinth. It was to the great glory of Greece that of all the city-state units only the Thebans surrendered to Xerxes.

The Spartans were on their own. After most of his allies had pulled out, Leonidas took off his helmet and wiped his hand over a grubby face. He shrugged his shoulders, lifted a steel-fisted hand, pointing at the enemy, ready to strike again, and then again. The other hand held his dented helmet. 'We must stand,' he said. The men around him gritted their teeth and decided not to make an issue of a decision of which they could foresee the consequence, even without an oracle.

During the night Leonidas received news of the disaster that had befallen his Phocian blocking force in the Asopus gorge. If the gods had chosen to aid their cause throughout the first three days they must have decided to end their support. He did the only thing left to him; he dispatched the allies who had delayed their pull-out 'to seize the exit of the path before the Persians had time to spill from it'. This force, probably as large as four thousand, including a number of hoplites, which could have blocked the Immortals, either arrived too late or were overcome by panic when they saw the size of the Persian contingent. Whatever the reason, a great number of Greek soldiers arrived exhausted down the coast in Elatea, telling of 'masses of Persians coming down from the mountain'.

King Leonidas prayed to Zeus for all the brave knights who would die on this day, and for the children and wives who would mourn them. He looked up on high and called upon the gods to protect his children in the defence of Hellas. And when the fourth dawn passed, and Xerxes sent out his men, they found the Threehundred drawn up before the wall with Leonidas's standard flying above their heads. The Threehundred locked shields, lowered their pikes and stood firm. A dozen times Xerxes sent out his archers and arrows fell like rain, but the Spartans merely lifted their shields above their heads until the squall had passed.

Meanwhile, Xerxes had been handed a message from Orontes recounting his successful circumvention of the Middle Gate. The Emperor ordered an increased frontal attack in order to divert the Spartans' attention, while his Immortals came up from the opposite direction. A Spartan rearguard was the first to die. The arrow took him in the chest and he tumbled down the slope. Before the rest of the Spartans knew what had struck them, a flight of arrows smashed into the unprotected rear of their shield wall. A hoplite dropped his spear and pirouetted slowly before he collapsed, his legs kicking convulsively. When the Spartans turned, they saw a mass of Immortals racing down from the high ground. Some Spartans, armed only with their short swords, plunged into the advancing ranks, striking and hacking. But nothing would stop the thousands of Immortals. As the Spartans had turned their full attention to the attack from their rear, the Persian auxiliaries finally hurtled in their thousands over the Phocian wall, as murderous as hunting dogs. The Spartans killed with grim efficiency. The enemy was falling all over the ridge, for numerous as they were the warriors of King Leonidas held the advantage of both weight and muscle power. The Spartans were tossing the Persians aside as though they were mushrooms. Soon the ring of dead Medes around the hill was high. Ignorant of danger, and seemingly unconcerned about losses, many more climbed over the wall and rushed up the long slope. However many the Spartans killed, there were always more hurtling over the wall, swamping the plateau like ants cutting a swath across the land they were invading.

Before the Cappadocians, Bactrians or Egyptians were given the chance to claim the victor's laurels, the Immortals launched themselves at the Spartans, for they were honourable warriors and they respected courage in others. The steel carapaces of their armours clashed, and then it was hand to hand, sword on sword, fist against fist. The flashes from polished shields, the streaks of dull bronze arrowheads in flight, blended with the rippling plumes on the helmets of warriors. Those who slipped stayed down, trampled underfoot. Heaped bodies sprawled like discarded piles of blood-soaked rags. Neither the Threehundred nor the Immortals gave an inch. They fought and they hung on to each other in death, pierced by each other's swords, uniting them on their final voyage. Lances pierced flesh and welded bronze breastplates to armour of polished fish scales. Xerxes, who observed the battle from a nearby rise, wondered for the first time about the cost of victory over Greece.

One after the other the Spartans fell. The remainder staggered on to a knoll to prepare for their last stand. Those of the Hellenes that could still stand fought on despite their horrible wounds, until they were smashed to the ground by an overwhelming number of battle-axes. 'Take prisoners only of the noble,' was their emperor's command. But the Persian auxiliaries were mad with blood and killing fever; in this final bloodbath, Persians and Hellenes annihilated each other in the most brutal manner. The slope around their hillock looked like a charnel house. A big Greek, his fist wrapped around the throat of a Bactrian, throttled the man while his own back was torn to shreds by shafts. Both men fell dead to the ground. It was the moment when each Spartan became a Hector.

The Threehundred were down to a few dozen. With no more protection than their body armour, they formed a human wall around their king, fighting off the hundreds of attackers. Orontes took charge and ordered the madly yapping satrap forces to pull back. He wanted to reserve the final combat for his Immortals. Then he noticed the figure of Leonidas, framed by the sun like a human Apollo, raising his spear with a blood-sullied arm in a final gesture of defiance. Xerxes' specific orders had been to take the King alive. He wanted to make an example of the Spartan. But here was a brave man, proud in defeat, and Orontes wouldn't allow this noble king to be seen in chains. He placed a cane shaft in his bow, took careful aim and let the winged instrument of death fly. It struck Leonidas above his protective armour. The bronze arrowhead traversed his throat and came out by the neck. Mortally struck, the noble King let go of his lance and dragged himself to a shield propped up against a heap of bodies, trying to stem the dark blood pouring from the ghastly wound. With a cry of anguish, his shield-bearer dropped to his knees to hold his king in his arms. 'Fear thy God, master of all Persians on this field of battle . . . ponder that a human avenger will step forward to vindicate our loss . . . now it is you that will become entangled in the knot of death . . .' the King whispered, before blood spilled from his mouth and his voice broke. His eyes clouded over, and then his spirit was lifted into the Olympus of all the great Hellenic heroes. A dozen Spartans, still able to stand up, fought on like cornered lions. In a final charge, they tightened their grip on their swords and then plunged into the Persians with a kind of reckless despair. It was to be their last gallant charge. Far ahead was the giant figure of a warrior, wielding a blood-dripping blade; he rammed his way into the line of Persians, lifted his sword-arm for the killing stroke, and his blade flashed down, burying itself in flesh, again and again, before an axe smashed his skull and he pitched forward. The last of the heroic Threehundred lay in eternal sleep with his face against the blood-soaked earth. It was over.

> *And where they find a mountain of the slain,*
> *Send one to climb, and looking down beneath,*
> *There they will find him at his manly length*
> *With his face up to heaven, in that red monument*
> *Which his good sword had digg'd . . .*[6]

There was one survivor. Shortly before the battle opened, a certain Aristodemus,[7] together with his friend Eurytus, was sent by King Leonidas to nearby Alpeni to receive treatment for an eye infection. No sooner had they reached the place than a helot came running after them to inform them that the Persians had struck, that the Threehundred were engaged in a fight for life and death and that every man was needed. The brave Eurytus returned and died with the rest. 'Now if only Aristodemus had been involved, if he alone had returned sick to Sparta, or if they both had gone back, I do not think the Spartans would have been angry. But one was killed and the other took advantage of the

---

[6] These words were written by Dryden in his epitaph to knightly gallantry.
[7] Aristodemus's story features prominently in Herodotus (VII, 229–32).

excuse which was open to both of them to save his skin, they could hardly help being very angry indeed.' So wrote Herodotus. 'They did not kill him but treated him just as Plato's *Laws* said a coward should be treated – pitiful clinging to life so that he could endure his infamy as long as possible.'[8] Aristodemus was shunned; the women of Sparta pointed their finger at him and called him 'The Trembler'. It was furthermore reported that the same Aristodemus tried to redeem himself during the Battle of Plataea, where he 'fought magnificently to retrieve his lost honour'.

Courage had been displayed as three hundred Spartans endured great suffering without complaint. No outcry, no prayer – all died true to their principle of 'Conquer or die!' Sparta's bravest of the brave went to their end like Homeric heroes, sacrificing their lives in a noble cause. Long before the Peloponnesian War came to an end, poets sang the praises of the Threehundred and their heroic stand at Thermopylae. Their sacrifice had bought for Greece the precious weeks necessary to prepare for the one battle that was to decide the future of the Occident.

That, and only that, was the legacy of Sparta's Three-hundred.

The final act of a Greek tragedy seemed imminent. With the fall of the Thermopylae Pass, the road to Athens was thrown open. Yet for Greece Thermopylae was more than a moral victory; it finally united its city-states behind the example of the larger-than-life-size figure of Leonidas, rest-ing in Olympus, next to Achilles and Hector. By delaying Xerxes' army, the glorious Threehundred had achieved the purpose of their heroic sacrifice. They had proven that even the mightiest of armies was vulnerable once it was robbed of its trump card – the ability to bring into action its total

8 Herodotus, *The Histories*, transl. A de Selincourt, London, 1972.

effective. This lesson was not missed by a man about to become the saviour of Greece, and the Occident.

The stand at Thermopylae proved once and for all that a given terrain limits the size of an army. The Spartans' epic stand at the Gates of Hell represents the pinnacle of temerity and sacrifice. Treason effected what courage had striven for in vain.

History records this epic last stand by recalling two names – Xerxes the aggressor and Leonidas the hero. It tends to overlook the third player in the epic drama – Ephialtes of Malis, the traitor. Five hundred years before Judas sold his messiah for thirty shekels, another scoundrel had committed such a deed most foul. The victors were about to find out: the price of freedom is not gold, but steel.

Deus ex machina.[9] As in a Greek drama, where the gods came on stage at the end of the play to decide its outcome, the gods would decide this struggle between Occident and Orient.

Thermopylae was not the end, it was only the beginning.

---

[9] Plato, *Kratylos*. Literally 'god from the machine' – i.e. appearing from the stage apparatus behind the scenes.

5

The Wooden Wall of Athens

Salamis
29 September 480 BC

'Safe shall the wooden wall continue for thee and thy children.'

The Oracle at Delphi, 480 BC

'Holy Salamis, thou shalt destroy the offspring of women, Where men scatter the seed, or where they gather the harvest . . .'

The Oracle at Delphi, quoted in Herodotus

Great men appear at moments of great need. Such was the case with the noble Athenian Themistocles. '. . . he exhibited the most indubitable signs of genius. Indeed, in this particular he has a claim in our admiration quite extraordinary and unparalleled,' wrote Thucydides of Athens. 'By his own native capacity, alike unformed and unsupplemented by study, he was the best judge in those sudden crises which admit of little or of no deliberation, and the best prophet of the future, even to its most distant possibilities . . . this extraordinary man must be allowed to have surpassed all others in the faculty of intuitively meeting an emergency.'[1]

[1] Thucydides, *The History of the Peloponnesian War*, transl. R. Crawley, London, 1874.

This emergency was happening now; they were engaged in a fight to preserve the liberty of Hellas from an invader's yoke.

Once the gates of Thermopylae were forced open, there was no further obstacle to Xerxes and his plundering hordes. They roved across Attica, razing along their way the temples of the Hellenic gods, looting Greece's treasures and burning its cities. Athens was abandoned, its citizens fled; the Acropolis was stormed and its defenders put to the sword. The Persians continued on their rampage, turning Greece into a graveyard.

While the Persian land army advanced unopposed, where was their all-powerful naval armada on which Xerxes had based his strategy? From the outset, the Persian fleet was beset by an evil omen. The Emperor had split his great fleet into two armadas; one was to enter the Gulf of Malis, engage the Greek fleet lying in wait off Artemisium, then sail south along the Euboean Channel to support his land action at Thermopylae; the second fleet was ordered to sail along the Aegean coastline and enter the same channel from the south to bottle up what was left of the Greek fleet. In his planning, the Persian Emperor did not take into account the god of weather.

The portion assigned to the Aegean skimmed along the Magnesian peninsula on a southerly course, and was about to approach the southern tip of Euboea island when the weather took a sudden change for the worse; clouds raced across the sky, bearing towards the landmass from the south-east, harbingers of a storm Greek sailors feared more than anything – the Hellespontias. It unleashed its fury; monstrous waves raced towards the Persian fleet. By order of their admiral, the noble Ariamenes, the vessels had been sailing bunched up to give mutual support in case of a Greek attack, and were too close inshore to be able to manoeuvre at will. The penteconter nearest land was caught in the backwash from the rocky shore; her deck tilted and her crew slid towards the frothing breakers that ringed the doomed ship and were flung against the cliffs by the foaming sea. Waves hit many vessels side-on, flinging them high in the air to crash down into the trough beyond. Ships were jerked broadside on to the rolling seas, lifted up and flipped end to end, spilling the helpless crew into the sea in a chaos of oars and smothering destruction. Ships that didn't capsize were carried on the crest of giant waves to be smashed against the cliffs, or broke their backs on reefs. In the ordeal, at least two hundred warships went down.[2] There were no survivors willing to bring the news to their king; those who had miraculously escaped were much too frightened to face their king's wrath. Within a few hours, half of Xerxes' armada had vanished. The Persians had dared to offend Poseidon, Lord of the Seas, and his anger was so great that he had unleashed against them his witches of the deep; his furies had pulled man and ship into their abyss.

'Safe shall the wooden wall continue for thee and thy children . . .'[3] was what the Delphic Oracle had promised the Athenians – and the 'wooden wall' was its ships, ships of war, strong and fast, with well trained and brave crews. When, five years before, the Athenian Council of Elders wanted to divide the benefit from a silver mine among themselves, it was the eloquence of Themistocles which convinced them to invest it in the construction of one hundred triremes, based on a radically new ship design.

Around 650 BC the Corinthian shipwright Aminocles developed a revolutionary new ship of war. In a narrow, sleek design everything had been sacrificed for speed. A trireme was propelled by three banks of oars (hence the name), operated by 150 oarsmen. The traditional rounded bow was replaced by a higher, squat bow (*agalma*), topped

2 Herodotus.
3 ibid.

by a high forecastle with a breast-high gunwale to protect assault troops from arrows during the initial ramming procedure. The ship's main weapon was a ten-foot bronze ram (*eperon*), jutting from the prow beneath the waterline. This *eperon*, when rammed at speed into the side of an enemy vessel, proved devastating. It snapped a ship's back, breaking her in two. Another method of rendering an enemy helpless lay in the trireme's manoeuvrability: a rapid approach, swerving at the last instant, shipping the oars while using the bronze blade on her square bow (*stolon*) to shear off the oars of the enemy, who became a sitting duck for a hoplite boarding party. Though they were relatively small in number compared to the massed fleet of Xerxes, the Persians could never match the triremes' speed, their ability to flit in and out of any situation, nor were their sailors up to the seamanship of the Greek seamen. The Corinthians couldn't see the advantage of such a ship; however the Athenians, urged on by Themistocles, did, and remodelled their fleet along the lines of Aminocles' design.[4] However, the ship had a drawback: by virtue of its slim shape a trireme was vulnerable to high winds, therefore the Greek fleet was basically an inshore fleet, designed for the protection of the homeland and not for an ocean-going attack. That fact should have been obvious to the Persian captains; their plan should have been to lure the Greek fleet out of their archipelago sea into the open, where they would be vulnerable. But the Persians were too sure of themselves. Their entire strategy was based on their numerical superiority. They considered the Aegean a Persian lake, and their emperor had given the order to keep it Persian. Not once did they take into account the tenacity of the Greeks.

'We will smite the overbearing Medes.' The Greek fleet

---

[4] The importance of his invention can be compared to the Dreadnought, based on a revolutionary new design, with its ten twelve-inch cannons mounted on five revolving turrets. It was launched by the British Navy in 1905.

commander who made this fiery boast was of stocky build, with a round head and a flowing grey beard. Captains had learned to avoid him if trouble brewed, for in an argument he always proved the more astute. Themistocles was not a warrior by nature; he thought of himself as more of a philosopher, at best a navigator, who would go to any lengths to avoid a sea battle. Yet it was his rhetoric which made his fellow Athenians overcome the fear of an alien sea; he convinced them to lift their fortified towers from mountain crags and launch them as castles on the ocean. Themistocles, more than anyone before him, realised that with its formidable insulating power the sea provided the surest line of defence.

'The news from Attica is bad.'

'You don't know how bad it really is. We must stop Xerxes. We must not allow his hordes to roam around our country.' And he repeated: 'We must stop them.'

'But, Themistocles, that is impossible.'

'Nothing is impossible.'

With an emergency at hand and the might of a Persian host marching on Athens, Themistocles based his strategy on two factors: that the Persian land forces depended entirely on their powerful navy for supplies, therefore destroying Persia's navy meant destroying its land forces; and that Greek ships were faster and could outmanoeuvre the Persians in a closed-in sea, where their mass of ships would find itself utterly congested. Themistocles' strategy involved luring the Persian armada between two of the many Greek islands. He had already chosen the site for the encounter: the Straits of Salamis, located off the southern shore of Eleusis. Into these straits led two channels, and Themistocles didn't have the means to block both. He had enough ships for only one, and he chose the narrows between the promontory of Cynosura and Piraeus, which again was split by the small island of Psyttalaeia into two narrow channels from half to three-quarters of a mile in width. Failure couldn't even be contemplated; the key to success was the isthmus with its treacherous currents and submerged rocks. When an enemy made for Piraeus or Salamis, both towns located inside the bay, he would find an approach that appeared easy, for beyond the narrow passage awaited a wide bay of calm waters. But the allure was deceptive, for the entrances were shallow, with spiky submerged reefs close to shore. Should a determined Ariamenes manage to work his way past these initial obstacles, he would still find that his numerical advantage was suddenly reduced, given the narrowness of the passage. Themistocles argued forcefully that this location would offer the Greek fleet a decided advantage. But the issue turned political; the interests of Corinth and Sparta were at stake, since his daring plan stripped the approaches to the isthmus of Corinth of their defences. As predicted, a crisis with his allies erupted several days before the decisive battle. To force the issue with his own side, and make the Persians fall for his trap, he thought of a ruse.

Speed was essential. When news arrived of the fall of Athens, it panicked many of his sea captains, lying with their ships inside the Bay of Salamis. They feared that the Persian fleet would cut off their retreat to the Corinthian isthmus; many hoisted sail, ready to take to the open sea. In this moment of crisis, the reprieve for Themistocles lay with Eurybiades, the Spartan admiral; if he could convince his Spartan ally, and pro-forma overall commander owing to his position in the Hellenic League, to stand and fight at Salamis, they stood a good chance. If not, then Greece was lost. 'With thee it rests, O Eurybiades, to save Greece,' said Themistocles. 'Hear me now and judge between the two courses. At the Isthmus of Corinth you will fight in the open sea, which is greatly to our disadvantage; there the land armies and the sea forces of the Persians will advance together. But here we shall fight in a narrow sea with a few

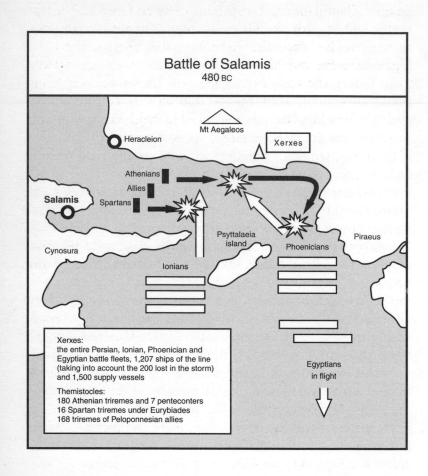

Battle of Salamis
480 BC

Mt Aegaleos

Xerxes

Heracleion

Athenians
Allies
Spartans

Salamis

Cynosura

Psyttalaeia
island

Piraeus

Phoenicians

Ionians

Xerxes:
the entire Persian, Ionian, Phoenician and
Egyptian battle fleets, 1,207 ships of the line
(taking into account the 200 lost in the storm)
and 1,500 supply vessels

Themistocles:
180 Athenian triremes and 7 penteconters
16 Spartan triremes under Eurybiades
168 triremes of Peloponnesian allies

Egyptians
in flight

ships against many, and if war follows a common course, we shall gain a great victory. Because to fight in a narrow space is favourable to us, in an open sea, to them.'

Eurybiades hesitated. The Corinthian Adeimantus voted against Themistocles. To save his beloved Greece, Themistocles had to provoke his fellow captains into battle and, to achieve his end, the Athenian was not loath to use blackmail. He did his best to discourage his allies from abandoning the fight by glaring and frowning as if being asked to sail off the edge of the world with the Devil and his brother for passengers. He held an ace up his sleeve in the form of a threat to withdraw his fleet: '. . . if thou wilt stay and behave like a brave man, all will be well, if not, we will take our families on board and go to Italy, which is ours from old and you will have lost us as allies.' He counted on the fact that without the support of the powerful Athenian trireme fleet the Spartans and Corinthians were lost. Thus Themistocles made the two allies change their minds and decide to fight it out in the Straits of Salamis.[5] There still remained the problem of the other Peloponnesian sea captains, who wanted to abandon their station. A council of war was convened, and their vote went against him. Themistocles shook his head and with a grimace of disdain left the council tent.

An incident now occurred which showed the shrewdness of the Athenian. 'I will adopt any stratagem to destroy the Medes,' Themistocles said. Returning to his ship, he gave instructions to one of his men, a certain Mylon, a sly twenty-two-year-old from Rhodes, to pass on a secret message. Mylon slipped aboard an outgoing Sicilian trader. 'Themistocles instructed him what he should say, and sent him on board of a merchant ship to the fleet of the Medes (Persian) to speak to their admiral. "The Athenian commander has sent me to you privily, without

5 Herodotus.

knowledge of the other Greeks. He is a well-wisher to your king's cause and would rather success should attend you than on his countrymen; wherefore he bids me tell you that fear has seized the Greeks and they are meditating a hasty flight. Now then it is open to you to achieve the best work that ever ye wrought, if only ye will hinder their escaping . . ."' The Persians intercepted the Sicilian trader and the Rhodian Mylon was able to deliver Themistocles' message, which was instantly relayed to Xerxes. For once, the sly Emperor did not see the trap, especially after his own spies had informed him of the open discord among the Greek sea captains. The opportunity seemed too good to be missed. He decided to make immediately for the bottled-up Greek fleet. The speed with which these events developed was staggering. From receiving Mylon's message to the eve of battle took only one day. And while Xerxes was beginning his move and the Greek captains were still arguing, the noble Aristeides, an Athenian captain, arrived out of breath in the council tent. He took Themistocles aside to tell him, 'However much the Corinthians and Spartans may wish it, they cannot now retreat; for we are all enclosed on every side by the enemy.' Themistocles' ruse had worked – the Peloponnesians were cornered and faced with no option but to prepare for battle.[6] These events took place at nightfall on 22 September 480 BC.

The Persians had sailed into the Aegean with 1,207 vessels of war of various kinds. Against this massive armada, Themistocles could put up 366 of his lightning-fast triremes and seven slower but more massive penteconters. Athens' superiority lay in its officers and ship captains, who commanded, and its men, who did battle. The bevy of Greek captains was impressive – all were professional sailors; half were traders, the other half pirates. Despite

6 ibid.

their relatively young age, they carried a great amount of seafaring experience. They had joined the defence of their country from all along the Mediterranean coast. Among them was the thirty-year-old Aristos from Piraeus, sailing in his home waters; of the same age was Kilinos from Rhodes; Euthymenos of Massalia (Marseilles) was in his mid-thirties; Karos of Heraclea was twenty-eight, but had been at sea since the age of twelve; also Kyprianos from Alalia (Corsica) and the Corinthian Adeimantus. And then there was the question of the crews' motivation and morale: while Persia counted on its vassal forces and galley slaves to fight their battles in a foreign land, the free citizens of Greece were defending their families and hearths. The night before the battle, the men boarded; some smelled of perfume, others of wine. Not one was missing. Everyone knew where he was going. The captains called out their names and assigned them to their positions.

'My men drank some of the filtered wine. I had three amphorae of sweet wine on board; fifteen *drachmas* the amphora this crook in Massalia had charged me. No good to let it go to waste,' Captain Karos said, laughing, without adding 'in case we sink', since that was not even a considered possibility. They were Greeks, and they were better! Unsinkable!

'I am pleased for your men, Karos. This way they shall row with greater strength.' Themistocles smiled. He was pleased; the spirit his crews showed was positive.

On the morning of 23 September 480 BC, the combined Persian and Phoenician fleets, with their satrap units of Ionians and Egyptians bringing up the rear, lay in three echelons before the Bay of Eleusis. Looming ahead was a rocky islet (Psyttalaeia), with its cliffs falling steeply into the sea. To their left lay the rocky shore of the island of Salamis, with its promontory of Cynosura stretching its spiky fingers into the narrow passage. Ancient legends spoke of sea dragons around these islands, monsters com-manded by the Greeks' god of the sea, Poseidon. A good number of Phoenicians, dreading the wrath of Greek gods, and who had watched a flock of black birds crossing low over their ships, wondered whether they were in the presence of a mythic manifestation of evil. Their admiral, Ariamenes, had little time to think of dragons as he listened to the dull booming of surf on both sides; still more worrisome was the vicious tide around the rocky outcrops ahead. For him this prospect was more frightening than any world of legend. The danger lay here, in these narrows. His captains would be heading in compact battle formation into a shallow and treacherous passage, which greatly constricted freedom of manoeuvre. He was still unaware that the Greek fleet was lying in wait in the lee of the promontory.

The time to do battle was near; Xerxes was installed on the high cliffs to observe his great victory. His signal was flashed to his admiral, Ariamenes, who raised his battle flag. A thousand ships hoisted their sails – and a fleet sailed into a trap. Three things combined which led to the débâcle: the congestion produced by the great number of ships jamming the treacherous passage; bad navigation and the ineptness of crews; and, lastly, the choppy seas created by currents and submerged reefs which caused unstable steering conditions. They might have been able to resolve these problems one at a time, but not in combination. Ariamenes split up his triple line of ships to enter the bay by the two channels leading around Psyttalaeia island, the half-mile-wide western channel and the mile-wide eastern approach. His left-flank attack formation consisted of the Ionian fleet, the right of the Phoenicians, with the two hundred vessels of the Egyptian fleet held in reserve to lay in ambush, should the Greeks try to make a break for the open sea.

Nothing was farther from the Greeks' mind; once forced

into battle, then battle they would do. Themistocles' plan called for the Corinthian squadron of Adeimantus to hold the western channel off Piraeus and hide under the cover of Psyttalaeia island until the signal for an all-out attack was given. The Spartan fleet of sixteen triremes under Admiral Eurybiades lay in ambush behind Cynosura peninsula, from where they could jump the Ionians as they entered through the eastern narrows. The Peloponnesians, reluctant at first but now raring to have a go at the enemy, held the centre. Themistocles, with his Athenians and Aeginetans, further augmenting the Greeks' fleet, held the left wing. As fate dictated, Themistocles was positioned along the mainland shore of Heracleion, directly below the cliffs of Mount Aegaleos, where Emperor Xerxes had taken up his grandstand seat to watch the 'sinking of the Greek fleet'. The shore around him was black with the men and horses of Xerxes' land army, stirring like excited ants as they caught sight of their proudly approaching armada.

Aboard the Greek ships final preparations had been made, cloth-wrapped and oil-dipped arrows distributed to the archers, and the braziers to ignite them lit. Helots manned the *stolôn* (bow), armed with grappling hooks, backed up by eighteen hoplites on every trireme, ready to jump across on to the enemy's decks and commit slaughter. For the tenth time, Themistocles strolled forward to the bow of his trireme, peering out to sea. Discovering that the wind was coming from land and blowing straight into the face of the enemy, he felt elated. He had succeeded in luring the Persians into the trap, and now the wind was also against them he could hardly believe his luck. The daimons stood by the Greeks.

Within minutes the Persian fleet would be entering the narrows. At the outset circumstances had served them well, but then the fickle wind turned traitor. Their captains counted on overcoming that difficulty with fifty oars per ship and crews of strong-armed men to row them.

The problem lay in their keels – some of the ships were ponderous broad-beamed sows with immense cargo holds and huge sails, which made them helpless in a strong cross-tide.

Themistocles, up by the bow's splendid bronze figurehead (*agalma*) representing the goddess Artemis, dropped to his knees; one final prayer: Zeus willing, by this evening Hellas would be delivered of the Persian menace. Or he and his valiant men would rest for ever in a watery grave. The thump of the rhythmic tambour and the swish of oars was nearer now; then an aide called out and pointed to their flank. Themistocles turned his head, blanched and cursed. The Spartans of Eurybiades, eager to settle their personal account with the Persians over the death of Leonidas and his valiant Threehundred, had jumped the gun and put their muscle to the oars. They raced ahead, cut out into the open channel – right in front of the approaching Ionians – and were immediately rammed in the side. The Spartans reeled in momentary confusion; some went straight to the bottom and some pulled back. For Themistocles, the element of surprise was apparently gone. Quite inexplicably, the Phoenician fleet, making up the bulk of Xerxes' effective, hadn't noticed this brief but furiously fought engagement; their view was screened by Psyttalaeia island, and they continued straight for the trap laid by the Corinthians.

Zeus be thanked, the precipitated Spartan move hadn't given away Themistocles' other surprise. As an experienced sailor, he knew that nothing was quite as terrible as fire at sea. He would unleash its power, and for this he had ordered specific preparations. First, all his ships brought down the big sails and foresails (*dolôn*). They would attack without their sails and do precisely what the enemy never expected him to do – proceed under oar power alone. That would make their movements easy to control. He had stripped many of his support ships of their masts and replaced them with catapults to launch basket weaves stuffed with resin and pitch. His 'gun crews' had also filled earthen jars with olive oil set to shatter on impact and ignite like napalm. And finally, scores of archers crouched behind gunwales, ready to fire broadsides of flaming arrows. Enough to create an inferno.

In Themistocles' squadron, hoplites, sailors and archers stared resolutely ahead. The water splashed restively around the piling beneath decks. Suddenly, from behind the bend of Cynosura peninsula, appeared the prows of the first line of ships of the Persian armada. And then more ships came forth. As far as the eye could see sailed hundreds of vessels of the Phoenician armada.

Themistocles aboard his command ship *Hephaïstos* ordered his *keleustes* (chief of oarsmen) to pound his drum for full speed ahead. Hundreds of straining shoulders and arms pulled on the oars (*scalmes*), their bodies moving in weird unison, the blades dipping and turning to the rhythm of a drum. The prows of the sleek triremes sliced through the crests of the waves, their lethal *eperon* hardly visible. The oarsmen gasped with effort, the perspiration drenching their eyes and pouring down their bare arms; they knew that on their effort hung the fate of Greece. The soldiers on deck held on to the gunwales, their bodies tense, waiting for the moment of impact. Themistocles and his Athenians headed for the flank of the Phoenicians, in order to drive them on to the Ionians and create confusion. Their sleek, fast triremes were infinitely better suited to respond to sudden changes in direction and therefore Themistocles had chosen the narrows as the site of the decisive encounter as here manoeuvrability would be all and mass nothing.

The Persian admiral still failed to see the trap. His view was partly obscured by Psyttalaeia, and he missed the danger of a rapidly approaching foe sweeping in on his flanks. He saw only a great fleet of Phoenicians, Ionians and Egyptians in their ordered ranks, stretching back to the watery horizon. Then their world went up in flames. A mass of flickering bright-yellow birds took flight from the Greek ships hidden behind the island, great pots of burning pitch, arcing out over the open water, trailing flame and smoke. The water absorbed some catapult balls, but a good number found the decks in their first line of battle, spreading flame when they shattered. Smoke began to rise, and then a second flight of missiles was on its way.

Around the point of the island appeared a massive object wrought in bronze. To Admiral Ariamenes' men it looked like a mace. Her sails snapped and the ship heeled over sharply as she charged around the cape. Bronze gave way to a black timber hull that cut the water in spurts with each dip of the oars. A forest of spears bristled from the ship's deck. From the top of the mast streamed a great silk banner, the sure sign of an Ionian admiral. She headed straight for the spot where more Greek fireships were lying in wait. With a thud, which sounded like a single shot but actually came from several catapults, a shower of glowing balls whipped across the open gap of water. Some fell sizzling into the sea, but the majority struck. The Persians' sails ripped open with an orange blast, burning quickly down the length of the mast. The Greeks' eyes flooded with tears as the distance between the fleets narrowed and a rancid smoke drifted across the waters. From below the deck of the big Ionian ship belched an oily black cloud, and then the vessel was gone. All that was left of her was bits of flaming sail floating on the water and a collection of flotsam.

Protected behind their high forecastle, the Greek archers waited. As more Persians jammed into the bay, they dipped their oilcloth-wrapped arrows into the braziers and let a flight of flaming missiles streak across the water; their hardened tips embedded themselves in Persian timber. Half a dozen rapid volleys struck the enemy fleet. Because of the great number of flaming missiles and the incessant volleys, the Persians were unable to remove many of the arrows before their ships caught fire.

While this long-distant engagement took place, both fleets came racing towards each other at a tremendous pace. Themistocles used his heaviest ships, the penteconters, like rams to break down a fortress's gate. His massive galleys made straight for the Phoenician and Ionian armadas, jammed in the narrows. The advantage lay with the heavier, more solidly built Greek warships. The Greek helmsmen veered their vessels and rammed their bronze spears into the side of the enemy, slicing through midship timber as a knife cuts through butter. Many were bowled over and sank rapidly without leaving a trace. Others pitched sideways, filling with water before they began to settle beneath the waves. Hundreds of Persian soldiers were thrown overboard by the initial impact; they clung to smashed timber, but were sucked under in the vortex of their sinking ships.

Over the screech of splintering wood came the persistent crump of catapult firing. Stones and great balls of fire climbed into the air. Some sent up great spouts of water as they landed, but not all fell in the sea; a great number smashed through planking and reduced men to pulp. The centre of the battle was a fiery bedlam, with Greek triremes flitting about. The Greeks used their square bows to shear off the Persians' oars and render the enemy's vessels unsteerable, then veered about to ram the helplessly drifting ships. Those still afloat had to fight fires as well as boarders. The Persian crews tried to hold the Greeks off with long poles, while Greek assault troops leapt on board, wielding swords, clubs and battle-axes. All over the Bay of Salamis the picture was one of armed men leaping from deck to deck; then they scrambled about like ants dissecting a carcass. A hundred miniature land battles took place, mostly on the decks of Persian vessels. Men fell overboard; fighters were covered in sweat and blood. The Persian mariners were no match for the heavily armed Greek hoplites whose fighting took on the appearance of a ritual, the killing of a flock of bleating sheep. On every deck was heard the sound of fighting, heavy thuds and the ring of metal on metal, intermingled with the screams of the wounded and the calls for help of the drowning.

Yet the worst destruction was caused by fire. If ever proof were needed that the greatest danger on the sea is fire, Salamis provided it. From the decks of the taller Greek ships crews continued to fling burning brands, pour glowing coals and launch Greek fire on to the hapless Persians. Vessels burst into flames; the heat of the fire stirred up a strong breeze, and the flames raced along the salty, tarred timber as more ships were set alight. From the hulks poured forth thick, oily swirls of smoke.

A Greek trireme had rowed close to a burning Persian vessel; it blew apart with a shower of sparks and crumpled into ash and burning timbers before disappearing sizzling beneath the blue water. But for every Greek ship lost a dozen Persians went down. Soon the heart of the Persian fleet was engulfed in a whirlpool of roaring flame. The stench that poured from the inferno was acrid and nauseating. Below decks, the slaves chained to their oars were roasted alive. Ships were disappearing at an alarming rate into the hideous depths. Debris and survivors clutching to flotsam covered the sea. The mighty Persian fleet was a shambles.

From his clifftop, Xerxes saw not his ultimate triumph but the end of Persia's century-old supremacy over the sea. It was accomplished by a feat of superb seamanship, as Themistocles' faster Athenians managed to turn the sluggish Phoenician armada and then drive them burning towards their Ionian comrades. It left their captains no choice but to pull away from the burning ships. So many vessels were manoeuvring and drifting about that the retreating Ionians became hopelessly entangled with the

rest of the Persian battle fleet. Coming up from behind
on the horrid spectacle, the captains of the Egyptian contingent were beset by panic. They obeyed nothing but
their frantic instinct to get away. They kept screaming
at their oarsmen to turn their vessels back to the open
sea. Eventually they reached safety, but their minds were
plagued by the certainty that their lives were forfeit to the
rage of Xerxes.

Kilinos of Rhodes was more of a pirate than anything
else; he thought like a pirate and acted like one. When
he spotted a great ship, splendidly decorated and with an
admiral's flag, its two banks of oars rhythmically lifting
and falling, he decided to make it his prize. The Persian
vessel had never taken down her sails, and it was her
undoing. As Kilinos and his men were about to board the
enemy ship, a load of flaming sulphur smashed into her
sails. The soldiers on deck suffered casualties, but not the
oarsmen, sitting a half-deck below, protected from missiles
and firepots. Up on the fighting deck the situation became
critical; fire spread quickly as more pitch pots rained down
around the ship. Smoke bellowed so thickly that Admiral
Ariamenes, whose ship it was, could no longer tell in
which direction they were steering. All around him men
were burned alive, rolling on deck and screaming in their
death throes. The smoke was thicker when he stood than
when he crawled, but crawling over blackened corpses
was hideous. With smoke and death all around him, he
managed to jump on to another vessel. He didn't even
watch his ship drifting off into the sea of fire. But he
didn't get far. Chased by the triremes of Aminias the
Decelean and Sosicles the Pedian, Ariamenes put up every
sail and fled speedily towards the open sea. Given the fresh
breeze, the admiral's new command ship might well have
escaped, had it not been for one particular incident. In the
midst of this mayhem, watching men burning and dying,
the soldiers charged with guarding the galley slaves had

abandoned their station. The oarsmen splintered the oars, ripped out the chains and poured from their lower oar deck to take advantage of this unique opportunity to regain their freedom. The Persians were caught between two lines, speared with lance and sword from the front, or slugged with broken oar and strangled by chain from behind. Those who survived the onslaught fell to their knees, bunched together around their mast, begging for mercy. All were killed, including Ariamenes.

With steady, rhythmic strokes the ships of Themistocles, Aminias, Sosicles, Kilinos, of Eurybiades, Kyprianos and Karos, and those of all the other victors, threaded their way over sunken vessels, past broken masts, burned hulls and torn sails. The Bay of Salamis had turned into the mouth of hell. An evening mist was slowly rising over the water, covering with its mantle the remnants of what hours ago had been a proud navy. Only the cries of swooping gulls and the distant thudding of waves smashing on the rocky shore could be heard. The Greeks had lost forty of their vessels, the Persians over five hundred. Their defeat was total. The splintered wreckage of the Persian imperial fleet was washed up on the shores of the country they had come to conquer. The rest was silence.

In the aftermath of victory, Themistocles suggested sailing north and destroying the two bridges across the Hellespont, but was stopped by Eurybiades, who rightly feared that such a move would prevent the Persian land army from retreating back to Asia Minor and cause them instead to lay waste to Greece. 'It is in our interest, not to destroy, but rather to build another bridge that he might make his escape with greater expedition.'

Within the year, the fate of Emperor Xerxes' Greek venture was sealed on land at Plataea (479 BC). When Xerxes crossed back into Asia, two further developments proved ill-fated omens for his army. He left behind an unco-ordinated campaign and a stockpile of mistrust. King

Pausanias of Sparta, reaping the revenge that a dying Leonidas had promised, pursued the Persian host. Xerxes worried more about his safe retreat over the Hellespont than the outcome of the battle, and left it to his general, Mardonius, to fight a rearguard action along the Asopus river. When the Spartan right wing became separated during the night from the left-wing Athenians, Mardonius launched a sudden cavalry attack. As his leading wave of riders approached the Greek phalanx, their horses shied away from the steady wall of points, edging to their right so that they gathered in front of the Greek archers and slingers. As his riders were decimated by a shower of stones and arrows, Mardonius ordered his auxiliary Ionians to come to his aid, but they abandoned him; during the night, they had received a message from their Greek blood-brothers, scratched on tablets. It was a repeat of the message of Thermopylae: 'You, that are satraps of Xerxes, if he compels you to fight us, your brothers, fight badly.' They did. General Mardonius, certainly a better military leader than King Pausanias, was killed leading his rider charge. His death decided the outcome. The Persians lost 50,000 killed, the Greeks 1,360.[7] The Greek victory was not achieved by superior leadership; the Spartan Pausanias was no Leonidas – he had not even taken part in the action. Their success was due to individual discipline and training, plus, for the first time, their clear-cut technical superiority.

Themistocles, the strategist and driving force behind the victory, never allowed his apprehension to show; nor would he ever display his relief over the fact that the enemy, which had seemed so invincible, wasn't invincible after all. He had risked everything at a moment of great danger, not merely for himself, but for all he represented.

[7] Casualty numbers as given by Plutarch.

Themistocles was a Greek legend and hero. There can be no other definition of him – his leadership qualities matched his rhetoric. Yet he stood accused by his contemporaries of taking a wild gamble at Salamis. But then he had to be something of a gambler to take on the might of Xerxes. When all was said and done, Themistocles' achievement was immense, and the gratitude owed him by Greece, as well as the Western world, no less so. The destiny of Greece had hung upon one single battle. From it blossomed a new republic and the right of men to live freely and express their thoughts freely in an open society. The entire culture of the Occident had been at stake.

Themistocles was ill rewarded. The citizens of Athens repaid him with vile accusations that left him covered in shame. He was banished for his refusal to co-operate with Pausanias of Sparta, whom he feared would usurp ultimate power. Some leading Athenians, jealous of his popularity, condemned him to death on a ridiculous charge of harbouring 'pro-Persian sympathies'. With the help of friends he managed to escape to Asia Minor, where, in one of the great reversals of history, Xerxes received him with high honours, showered him with presents and gave him a splendid palace in Magnesia. Cut off from the country he loved, Themistocles spent the last years of his life in bitterness. Never again was he allowed to return to the city he had saved from certain destruction by his wisdom, courage and genius.[8] When the King of Persia demanded that he lead an army against the Athenians, despite the shame they had heaped upon his head Themistocles stout-heartedly refused, afraid of sullying his earlier achievements. That evening, he sacrificed to the gods and, in the company of his friends, took poison. Like Socrates, who went to his death firmly believing in the immortality of the soul, Themistocles played the lead role in a Sophoclean drama.

[8] Plutarch, *Lives*.

He was vilified and accused of collaboration, when all he had tried to do was restore order after a murderous war. This was the great man's tragedy.

Two thousand five hundred years later, Napoleon Bonaparte, who liked to compare himself to Themistocles, said: 'There are only two powers in the world – the sword, and the spirit. In the long run, the sword is always defeated by the spirit.'

At Salamis, superiority in numbers was the direct cause of the disaster; other factors were the congestion of a fleet too unwieldy for the space available to it, a technical revolution in naval construction, and the use of 'massed firepower'. Yet nothing could have been accomplished without the courage of a great leader and the motivation of his crews.

Salamis destroyed the Persians' morale as a seafaring nation. It was a strategic victory that transcended the actual forces involved; it encouraged Persia's vassals to seek their independence. Tactically, Salamis was not in the same class as the sea battles of Lepanto or Trafalgar, but strategically it was more decisive in that it stopped an Asian invasion of Europe. For a thousand years, until the arrival of the Huns, Salamis safeguarded Western culture on the European continent.

With the victory of Salamis, the Golden Age of Greek philosophers was born.

Part Three

The Giants

336–202 BC

(Alexander to Scipio Africanus)

'Furor arma ministrat.'
('Fury ministers arms.')
Virgil, *Aeneid* (70 BC)

6

'I Will Not Steal Victory!'

Gaugamela
1 October 331 BC

'Quem di diligunt – adulescens moritur.'
('He whom the gods favour dies young.')
Plautus (254–184 BC), *Bacchides*

It was on a summer evening in June 336 BC that King Philip of Macedonia went to watch the performance of a drama at the Theatre of Aegea, accompanied by his son and chosen heir Alexander. The nobles of the realm and the ambassadors of allied states from the Corinthian League that he had helped to create had packed the theatre for hours. But Philip of Macedonia was not an empire-builder; such a theocratic notion was completely foreign to him.[1] He was simply his nation's caretaker, much beloved by his people. Because of his outstanding military talents the Corinthian League had chosen him as their *hegemon* (leader). Now that the region was finally at peace, he could relax and enjoy a play by one of the Greek poets.

The royal procession stopped briefly before the statue of one of the gods to allow their king, dressed in a white cloak,

---

[1] It is likely that the same held for Alexander, and that he never intended to create his Alexandrian Empire. It came as a result of his conquests.

to step alone on to the stage to salute his people. At this moment a page who had sometimes been privileged with the King's affection jumped forward and planted a dagger in the monarch's heart. King Philip stumbled a few more steps while blood spread across his white tunic, then he collapsed. The assassin tried to make his getaway, but was caught and hacked to death by the King's bodyguards. It was a tragedy in the best of Greek traditions. What heightened the drama was its epilogue. While the body of the murdered King was carried from the theatre, the name of the new King was called out: Alexander, King of Macedonia.

Vengeance for the foul deed was immediate and terrible; the corpse of the assassin was crucified, and then burned. All those suspected of conspiracy were brutally done to death. Among them was the brother of King Philip, Amyntas, who was in line for the crown; he was executed to forestall a threat to Alexander's succession.

First and foremost, Alexander, twenty, had to assert his authority in the face of a great challenge from the city-states of the League. He acted with speed. He took on Thessaly and inflicted a defeat on their army, and then acted graciously towards the prisoners to assure their assistance in his future plans. In fact this psychological move caused Thessaly to join him as an ally, and its cavalry was to prove decisive in his battles. Alexander's next move was to regain the title of *hegemon* of the Greek League forces. At first, his father's former allies didn't take him seriously; they considered him a young upstart and 'madcap'.[2] They did not reckon with the drive and will of this young monarch. At the Battle of Chaeronea, against Athens and Thebes, he led the charge of the Macedonian cavalry and pushed the enemy's infantry from the field.

[2] Demosthenes.

The human qualities of a great man were tarnished by an unfortunate affair at Thebes (335 BC). At the head of a confederation of Macedonians, Phocians, Platacans and Boeotians, Alexander marched against Thebes. Before the city's stockade, the Thebans attacked him and killed a great number of his Cretan archers, including their commander, Eurybotas. Their initial success gave them the impression of having carried the battle; they pushed forward, but then ran into an ambush set by Alexander, who reversed the situation and stormed into the city. 'In the heat of the action it was not so much the Macedonians as his allies who killed the Thebans when they ceased to defend themselves in any organized way.'[3] During the massacre of Thebes, Alexander showed for the first time an ability to apply cold-blooded methods whenever severity was called for; he continued to do so throughout his military conquests, although Thebes was perhaps the only time he used such harshness on people of his own race and country.

With the fall of Thebes, Athens submitted to him and the Corinthians elected him as their captain-general. Once the major city-states had accepted his rule, he was faced with the task of administering the country. He was greatly assisted by Parmenio and Antipater. Both were considerably older and had gathered much experience in the arts of war and diplomacy as faithful servants of his father Philip. Antipater was put in charge of Macedonia, and Parmenio looked after the possessions in Asia Minor.

Alexander's father Philip had left him a formidable military machine of professionals and patriotic citizens, an army so powerful that it could have stood up to any force until the invention of gunpowder, some eighteen centuries later. King Philip had transformed a gathering of armed

[3] Ptolemy and Arrian.

citizens and peasants into a well-armed, highly trained and motivated troop, the *pezhetairoi*, based on the Greek phalanx. The front rank of hoplites was the *pezetaeri*. For their protection they carried a round shield and for attack they were armed with the thirteen-foot *sarissa*, or pike. The *hypaspists*, the élite of the hoplites, carried a slightly shorter *sarissa* for greater manoeuvrability. Their flanks were covered by a corps of Thessalian cavalry, highly mobile and lightning fast. Between the cavalry and the slow-moving, solid phalanx, King Philip inserted battalions of *hypaspists*, more lightly armed and thereby able to move much faster. These were his 'flexible wing', able to adjust to the speed of a flanking movement by cavalry. This was to become the outstanding feature of future battles, allowing the Greek commander to change his attack formation at will and strike from the flanks without losing the overall coherence of his line. Alexander created the first mobile field artillery unit made up of light catapults, which could be carried on the backs of mules; a major improvement was a new command unit, and the speed with which his orders could be dispatched. Using excellent riders on fast horses as his personal couriers allowed him to launch simultaneous attacks or instantly exploit an enemy's blunder. The royal courier wore a distinctive uniform and had to be blindly obeyed as 'the king in person'.

Alexander's principal strike force for delivering the killing stroke was his Macedonian cavalry. He used his infantry phalanx to push into the enemy, but the cavalry was his means of achieving victory. Being an expert horseman, he knew all about rider attacks. At the age of twelve he was presented with a horse that nobody could break in, Bucephalus. He turned the horse's head into the sun so that he didn't startle it with his shadow, then quickly jumped on its back, and the horse was his.[4] The most famous of

4 Plutarch.

his cavalry units was the *agema* or 'King's Companion Squadron', so called because the King always rode into battle in their company. All were hand picked and ready to protect their sovereign with their lives. This Companion cavalry unit was the exclusive domain of Greek nobles from the equestrian class. It was to the honour of any young man and his family to be chosen as a *hetairoi* of the *agema*. A *hetairoi* stood out by virtue of his distinctive fish-scale steel armour, and the similar protection afforded his mount. These Companions were Alexander's cutting edge, the King's iron reserve for use at the appropriate moment to bring about a decisive result. All were young and noble of mind, steeped in the teachings of the great philosophers. Hephaestion was just twenty, Eutyphron, Agathocles, Klitoton, Artemidoros, Protis hardly out of their teens. From the beginning they were called upon to prove their valour. On the day of the decisive vote in the ruling council of the Corinthian League about the question of succession, his Companions stood by him at the meeting, at which he was not loath to remind his Greek allies that they had taken an oath of fidelity to *Philip and his descendants*. With that argument, backed up by his *agema* waiting outside the city walls, he was voted *hegemon*.

Alexander's ambitions were great, and for that he needed the support of all. His next problem was to find a common factor that would enable him to weld the forces of the various city-states into a single instrument of war. Their 'everyone for himself' attitude presented him with no political unity and no national Greek spirit to build on. For this to be achieved, an enemy had to be found on which all could focus their hate. Alexander managed this only too well once he promoted the idea of a crusade against Greece's perennial enemy, Persia. The Greeks were only too aware that the danger had not diminished since the days of Xerxes. A number of Persian incursions had occurred over the past 150 years – raiding parties had crossed the sea, slaughtering Greek peasants and dragging their women off into slavery. When his League partners hesitated, he black-mailed them with a threat to pull Macedonia's powerful forces from the nation's defence. With this argument he persuaded his fellow Greeks to join up. To make certain of their allegiance, he made them swear '. . . by Zeus, Earth, Sun, Poseidon, Athena and Ares, I shall abide by the peace and I shall not break my agreement with Alexander of Macedonia . . .'

Seldom has there been a man more written about than Alexander.

Alexander was of much shrewdness, most courageous, most zealous for honour and danger and most careful of religion. Most brilliant to seize on the right course of action, even where all was obscure; and where all was clear, most happy in his conjectures of likelihood; most masterly in marshalling an army and in arming and equipping it; and in uplifting the soldiers' spirits and filling them with good hopes, and brushing away anything fearful in dangers by his own want of fear – in all this most noble. And all that had to be done in uncertainty he did with the utmost daring; he was most skilled in swift anticipation and gripping of his enemy before anyone had time to fear the event.[5]

Macedonia was separated from Persia by three wide bodies of water – the Black Sea, the Sea of Marmara and the Aegean. It was obvious that the slender peace achieved by the Greek victories of Salamis (480 BC) and Plataea (479 BC) would not last for ever. For a time

---

[5] The description comes from Arrian (VII) as quoted by J. F. C Fuller. Arrian used as prime source for his *Anabasis* the records of Alexander's general, and later King of Egypt, Ptolemy.

Persia kept the peace, its court torn apart by a blood feud when Artaxerxes died without leaving issue. From the bloodshed emerged as winner the offspring of the Achaemenids, a certain Codomannus, who took on the title of his illustrious ancestor, Darius. But the third man bearing this hallowed name was nothing but a pale copy of the great Darius, who once had the firmament pass through his hands. Yet Darius III considered himself a great leader of men. His skill did not match that of his Macedonian adversary, and his army, though vastly superior in numbers, had nothing to put up against the scientific instrument fielded by Alexander. Darius III could have become a reasonably efficient king, furthering the prosperity of his vast domains, had he not committed a blatant act of war when he dispatched agents provocateurs to stir up unrest and create internecine trouble between the various Greek city-states. The provocateurs were caught and forced to talk.

In 334 BC, Alexander assembled a fleet of 182 triremes in the Strymon river, and from Pella crossed to Sestus on the Asian shore. He was accompanied by his expeditionary force of 37,000 – 32,000 infantry and 5,000 cavalry. His infantry was made up of his own Macedonian foot, the allied Greek troops, and a light Balkan mercenary unit of archers and slingers. His cavalry was a formidable arm: 1,800 Companion horsemen, 1,800 Thessalians, plus 1,500 light cavalry. The fighting men were assisted by another 60,000 auxiliaries to look after his supply train. This in itself was a considerable undertaking. Leaving aside military achievements, Alexander's organisation was perhaps the most astonishing feature of his campaign (still taught as an example in military academies). The way he managed to keep his supply train by his side without having to rely on foraging from the countryside, the manner in which he planned everything to the very last detail, was something approaching a miracle. Not even Napoleon, with more modern means of transport and better roads, could match the organisational talent of Alexander.

During the crossing, the young King halted his fleet in mid-ocean to offer sacrifices to the god Poseidon. As the ships reached the Asian coast, near the place that once had been Troy, he was the first to jump ashore, hurling his spear into the ground: 'from the gods I accept Asia, won by the spear'.[6] He was set to become King of Asia. Though Asia encompassed Persia, Alexander never did make claim to Persia's crown.

Darius III failed to stop Alexander's initial push; he accepted the advice of his generals to pull the Greeks farther inland, where he could trap and decisively beat them. Darius had commanded one of his satraps, King Memnon of Rhodes, to concentrate his forces around the Asian Gates near Dimetoka, along the Granicus river (Kocabas Cay). The leader of Memnon's army was Mithridates, a Parthian of royal blood, who arranged his 20,000 cavalry on the high embankment and his 30,000 foot-soldiers behind them, on the rise leading from the eastern riverbank.[7] In the Persian armies, many of the best foot troops were Greek mercenary units, lured to fight against their own country by the promise of gold. Alexander knew only too well that his principal danger lay with these Greek mercenaries.

Alexander, not someone to leave battles to chance, went on a personal scouting mission and discovered a dry riverbed, leading away from the Granicus. It was out of sight of Memnon's host and curved directly into their rear. Since it was the middle of June, the Granicus had become sufficiently shallow for foot troops to cross. While the two armies camped near each other across a thirty-metre-wide

6 Diodorus Siculus (XVII), drawing on the notes of Ptolemy.
7 The Persians certainly had in excess of 40,000, of which at least 20,000 holding the Persian centre were Greek mercenaries in the pay of Memnon and Darius.

stream, controversy erupted in Alexander's tent between the King and the general of his foot troops, Parmenio.[8]

'King, we cannot cross the river with our foot-soldiers in an extended line without being attacked, and most likely pushed back by the enemy's cavalry. The phalanx formation will no longer exist, as our units must climb the opposite bank in loose order.' But Alexander remained adamant, counting on the element of surprise. In the light of dawn, 13,000 Macedonian heavy foot aligned in phalanx formation along 2,000 yards. Across from them, lining the lip of the riverbank, the Persian cavalry and various light foot units waited. The combined Rhodian and Persian force enjoyed a vast numerical superiority that actually hampered their movement.

'In the morning, Alexander in bold mood took his army across the river and he was the first to draw up his army for the contest.'[9] Alexander, standing out conspicuously in his gilt armour and a white-plumed helmet, rode towards his centre. The Persians followed his every move and massed their cavalry opposite him. Thereby they failed to notice the deployment of his Thessalian cavalry assembled in the dry riverbed. The Macedonian opened his move with a feint to the centre; one unit, under the inspired leadership of his General Socrates, waded with much noise across the chest-deep river. While this action was in progress, bringing the Persian cavalry racing up to stop the attack, Alexander ordered General Parmenio to pull the bulk of the Greek army from the line. Parmenio marched with them towards the right wing, and crossed the water where the river narrowed and was fordable unmolested. Although his troops encountered a fairly swift current, they moved obliquely across the water, thereby keeping their perfect phalanx formation. This so surprised the Persians that they

[8] The account of the battle comes from Arrian, who probably drew on source material from Plutarch and Cleitarchus.
[9] ibid (XIX).

failed to react immediately. They were certainly distracted by the noise of the initial attack from down the line. It was at the moment of Parmenio's crossing that the Persians missed their unique chance for victory, preventing his men from scrambling ashore and deploying a solid line along the riverbank.[10]

A sizeable troop of Persian cavalry did attempt a disorganised attack on the Macedonian heavy infantry, but without receiving support from the mass of Persian footsoldiery, who stood by and watched the combat being played out in front of them, the Persian rider waves broke on the formidable hedge of thirteen-foot *sarissas*. Following this brief cavalry attack, both lines of infantry stood and stared fixedly at each other without making a move. Mithridates seemed confused, having witnessed the débâcle on the part of his cavalry, while the disciplined Greeks awaited the order to engage in battle. Only one man could give it: Alexander, their king and *hegemon*.

While Parmenio had stopped the Persian cavalry, the battle was still raging in the centre, turning into a heroic stand by Socrates' Macedonians in what became a suicide mission similar to that at Thermopylae. With Socrates' men still down in the water, and the mass of Persians holding the steep riverbank, the Persians soon gained the advantage. They hurled javelins and rocks on those trying to scramble up the fifteen-foot embankment and took a frightful toll. The wounded tumbled back down the steep incline to be swept off by the river and drowned. The survivors engaged in a hand-to-hand struggle to tie down as many of the enemy as possible, in order to divert their attention from another section of the battlefield.

With a critical situation on his hands, Alexander led a charge of his Companion cavalry across the flat field. They

10 Greek historians offered no explanation as to how a vastly inferior force could cross a river without being attacked, or why 100,000 soldiers never intervened in the battle. But they wrote of the heroism of Alexander and his riders.

had crossed the Granicus downstream and came thundering at the Persians on their vulnerable flank. The dust cloud from many thousand horses removed the element of surprise and the Persians had time to react. Alexander's cavalry attack was met head-on by a huge rider mass, with General Mithridates way out in front on his lightning-fast horse. Two men headed straight for each other, bent on killing, a Macedonian king and a Parthian prince, both fully aware that their clash would decide the outcome of the combat, as in most battles when an army lost its leader. In contrast to Mithridates, who wielded a wickedly sharp scimitar, Alexander was armed with the lance of the Macedonian cavalry; with the advantage of superior reach, he speared Mithridates through his fish-scale armour and knocked him from the saddle. But the speed of his stallion carried him on and he found himself surrounded by a great number of Persian riders. One of these was Rhoesaces, the Parthians' second-in-command, bent on revenge for the death of his prince. He urged his steed close to Alexander, and when the horse reared up he brought his blade down for the killing thrust. The powerful swipe from the Parthian's scimitar sheared off the plumes and a portion of the metal rim on the Greek King's helmet.

While Alexander was engaged in a fight for his life, another Persian unit commander, Spithridates, came on him from behind to run the King through but was himself mortally wounded when Cleitus, one of the King's bodyguard, sliced off the Parthian's sword-arm. While the Persians had their eyes fixed on the mêlée around the enemy king, Alexander's Thessalian cavalry managed to dash unobserved up the dry riverbed. Meanwhile, the King's Companions had cut their way through to Alexander and extracted their king from his precarious position. With their attention focused on the struggle around the Greek King, and struck by the sudden attack by his Thessalian cavalry from the rear, the Persians failed to notice Parmenio advancing with his troops in phalanx formation to cave in the Persian centre. The Greek infantry, advancing with their typical syncopated pace, pikes out front, opened large gaps through which their Macedonian cavalry could push into the Persians and their allied Greek mercenaries. The end came fast and furious. Memnon's Greek mercenaries, knowing that they couldn't expect clemency, fought on to the death. For most, this wish was granted. With the battle won, Alexander had the survivors rounded up, put in irons and sent back to Macedonia to end their days as slaves in the silver mines. All captured Persians were killed. The Greek dead were buried in their armour beside their weapons; their families were given splendid agricultural properties. The twenty-five heroes of Socrates' initial assault were buried in a common cumulus and Greece's most famous sculptor, Lysippus, was ordered to cast twenty-five bronzes.

Alexander's brilliant military career had almost come to its end on a riverbank in Asia Minor. How history would have changed, had a horse not reared, or the valiant guard Cleitus not warded off the thrust that would have cut short the life of his monarch. His miraculous escape created a myth which, from that moment on, surrounded his person; it is likely that he himself began to believe in his own immortality.

The result of Alexander's victory at the Granicus was the liberation of the predominantly Greek-populated coastal cities from the Persian yoke. But it didn't solve another problem: the Persian navy controlled the seas and, as long as this threat was present, the Greeks had to rely for their supplies on the long and difficult land route after crossing the Hellespont. Alexander had to assure control over Persia's Mediterranean ports, denying their powerful Persian fleet access. He decided to invade Cilicia (333 BC) and take possession of its coastal harbours. For this, two routes were open to him, one leading inland, via Syria, the other along the coast. He chose the one along the narrow strip of coastal plain between high mountains and sandy shore. This held advantages – it was an easier march route than the one leading parallel to it through the mountains, and it was farther removed from the Persian strongholds in Syria, where he expected Darius to assemble his main army. He sent Parmenio ahead to open the road with the Thessalian riders. They swept aside a Persian blocking force and set up camp to protect the vital passage through the Pass of Jonah.[11] From there, the road wound farther south, to Myriandros (near Iskenderun) on the Gulf of Issus; it was there that Alexander established camp to grant his army a respite. The men were tired, having marched an average of twenty miles a day, but their mood was still euphoric following their victory. Alexander used the time to receive ambassadors from the nearby towns, bearing homage and bringing gifts. He sent scouts in a southerly direction to discover the location of the Persian army, which he expected to find in front, where the mountains gave way to a wide coastal plain. On his orders, Parmenio dispatched a small unit north, in the direction of Issus, to check on the arrival of the supply train, which Alexander awaited with impatience, needing fresh troops to replenish his losses from the Granicus.

While Alexander was moving steadily southward, Darius had collected an army centred on Sochoi, a fortress straddling the road through the Amanus mountains. Reports from his satraps kept the Persian King informed of his enemy's movements. This was how he learned that Alexander had not taken the central mountain road to Sochoi but was advancing along the coastal route. It was time to spring the trap. Darius marched his force north from Sochoi, a move shielded from Alexander's scouts by the mountain

---

[11] The following accounts are taken from Alexander's court historian Callisthenes; they were subsequently rewritten by Polybius.

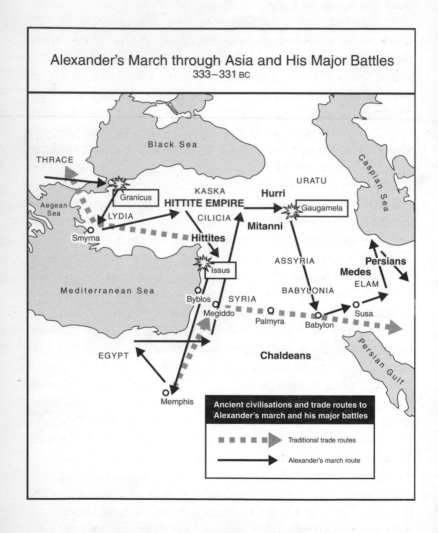

Alexander's March through Asia and His Major Battles
333–331 BC

range. Once the Persian host reached the northern end of the mountains, they headed sharp west, making for the coastal route to cut Alexander's line of communication near the town of Issus.

The scouts sent by Parmenio to locate their supply train were riding out into the open Issus plain when they noticed a big cloud of dust. 'The supplies,' they yelled, and waved frantically at the black points which came dashing towards them as a wall of cavalry emerged from the cloud. 'Persians!' They threw their horses around and rode hell-bent to warn their king. The news was a shock. The Persian army was not *in front* but *behind* him, and he was cut off from Greece and his vital supplies. He assembled his troop leaders, Sopolis, Glaucias, Aristo, Heraclides, Demetrius, and the hero of the Granicus battle, Parmenio, who broke the silence.

'*Hegemon*, what is your decision?'

'March, my friends, march! That is our only chance.'

'Farther south?'

'No! Straight at the Persian host! We shall attack and beat them, because we must!'

He had to reach the Pass of Jonah before the Persians broke through its defences, as they had done 150 years before at Thermopylae. However, Darius III was no Darius I; he was hesitant, indecisive, and mentally lazy. Rather than push resolutely towards the Greeks and catch them in an unfavourable position, he stopped his army along the Pinarus river (either the Payas or the Deli Cayi), a location unsuitable for the size of his army, too narrow for him to bring into play his full force.

Alexander and a small party rode ahead to scout the terrain. The field consisted mostly of flat ground, with long grass and no underbrush. The Pinarus river divided the plain, and on the opposite shore lay Darius with his formidable host. Alexander's party found a ford three miles to the north which would permit a crossing. Their fear, that Darius had come to the same conclusion and fortified the position, was unfounded. Instead, Darius had boxed himself into a trap, with mountains on one side and the ocean on the other. To the narrowness of this terrain, Alexander's Macedonians and Greeks were much better adapted.

Darius positioned his 30,000 Greek mercenaries to front the Pinarus river and then used another 30,000 as back-up; he also placed units in the foothills, where they would hover dangerously over Alexander's flank. The Persian had built himself a solid starting position, but then he changed his mind. He recalled his cavalry and massed them near the shore, on the only flat piece of land. This made it clear that he intended to launch his strike from there. He pulled his Greek mercenaries into the centre and replaced them with auxiliary infantry. With this move he weakened his anchoring position against the mountains. Such a major movement of troops, executed shortly before the battle, resulted in utter confusion. Units were becoming bunched together and cavalry access lanes were blocked by slower-moving units. In no time Darius had lost the numerical advantage. Rather than present a front line of sixteen men deep, Darius now had fifty to sixty men stacked up behind each other who couldn't possibly come to each other's assistance and would only step on each other's heels.

Alexander's forces, in the regulation depth of sixteen, advanced in measured pace towards the river. Parmenio was leading the Greek cavalry on the left of the phalanx, while Alexander commanded the Companions and Thessalian cavalry on the right flank. The first skirmish was between Agrianians and the Persian covering force in the hills. The phalanx entered a shallow depression which put them momentarily out of sight of Darius, a move astutely designed by Alexander to allow his phalanx to stretch in length while diminishing in depth to eight men.

His Thessalian cavalry moved in behind the advancing phalanx to be available around either flank. Two troops of his Companion cavalry moved to the extreme right flank. The cavalry commanders had received instructions to lead their riders behind the screen of the phalanx so that the enemy couldn't observe their move. When the Macedonian phalanx spilled over the top of the low ridge fronting the river, the entire line-up had been reversed. It was too late for Darius to make any further dispositions. Eighty yards from the river, the Greeks stopped briefly while Alexander rode, suspiciously noticeable by friend and foe alike, along the entire front line. 'When the two armies were already close to one another, then Alexander rode along the line, calling upon his men to be courageous and naming with appropriate honours those of the commanders, captains and mercenaries who were widely known for their reputation or for some act of prowess. And on all sides the shout came to him: "Do not delay but charge upon the enemy!"' This temporary halt of the Greek phalanx would have been Darius's great opportunity to launch his massive cavalry into a surprise attack across the river. But Darius was no Alexander; he stood frozen in his chariot like a rabbit fixed by a serpent.

To the beat of hundreds of tambours and fifes, Alexander's 31,000 men advanced steadily with their *sarissas* held high, as was their usual style in an initial attack. They were twenty yards from the shallow river when clarions blared and the right of Alexander's line burst forth at triple pace, led by the King himself, riding ahead of his élite Royal Infantry Guard. The screaming mass raced across the shallow water of the Pinarus, their long *sarissas* now dropped, their lethal steel points pointing straight ahead. Before the surprised Cardace auxiliaries were given a chance to react, the Macedonians, led by Hephaestion, captain of the Royal Guard, scrambled up the riverbank and rammed their long pikes into the bodies of the Cardace infantry. The impact was so violent and complete that Darius's left flank was thrown into chaos; the front-line units broke and tried to flee but were stopped by the lines stacked behind them. These men could hear screams, but continued to push forward, not realising the carnage that was going on in front of them. Alexander's Companion cavalry, which had been hiding behind the phalanx, splashed across the river and smashed into the rear ranks of the Cardace infantry. Their attack was so sudden and unexpected that the entire Persian left wing reeled back. Greek units were headed for Darius's position, where he was surrounded by his Royal Cavalry Guard.

While this part of the battle was going Alexander's way, his left wing had encountered a setback as the Persian cavalry put their full weight of 30,000 riders behind an attack across the river. Parmenio's 3,000 Thessalian riders were hard pressed, but then something happened to change everything. Alexander, heavily engaged on his right wing, made a sudden move for Darius's position. One or several of the Persian cavalry leaders, engaged against Parmenio, turned their horses and raced to their monarch's assistance, followed by a great number of men who thought it their duty to stay with their officers. This turnabout opened a gap in the Persian cavalry attack, one the Thessalian riders swiftly exploited. Using their greater mobility and better protection, they cut the Persians down, chased the remainder back across the river and turned the Persian right flank. All that still held was the centre. Here Darius's Greek mercenaries managed to repulse every one of the Macedonians' attempts to break through. The struggle raged most fiercely along the riverbank, where Greek fought brother Greek. No pity was given and none asked. The corpses kept piling up and the mercenaries paid a heavy price. (The loss of Darius's Greek mercenaries was to play a decisive role at Gaugamela.) Persian soldiery was fed in to fill the gaps, but nothing could stop the inevitable. With the auxiliaries on his left wing dissolved by Alexander's impetuous attack, his cavalry routed by the move of a few over-anxious officers attempting to save their king, and his Greek mercenaries getting slaughtered in the centre, Darius fled the field, followed by his cavalry, which was hotly pursued by Alexander's riders. The riverbanks and the narrow defiles leading from the river and into the mountains were choked with corpses and horses, mostly Persian. The worst carnage was where Darius's Greek mercenaries had clashed with Alexander's guardsmen. Layered pyramids of slain attested to the fierceness of the struggle. Night fell over a great victory. But Darius was still not finished – this would take one more battle. 'Issus turned out as Alexander supposed.'[12]

When Alexander, together with Hephaestion, entered the captured royal tent of King Darius, he found the King's wife, Stateira, and her children mourning the death of their husband and father. Stateira saw only the silhouette of two men in the tent's opening, both garbed in long cloaks and helmets, with spear and shield, looking portentous. The woman gathered the children around her and did her obeisance to Hephaestion, who, being the taller of the two, she thought to be the King until she was told differently. Proving his esteem for his friend, Alexander replied gallantly: 'No mistake made, noble lady, for Hephaestion too is a great leader.' Alexander then went on to reassure her that her husband Darius was alive and gave orders that the high-born family be treated not as prized prisoners but as royal guests.[13] When Darius found out about the fate of his wife, he was surprised that Alexander had not had her raped, as was common practice to seal the ultimate conquest and shame the vanquished.

*   *   *

[12] This phrase comes from Arrian. But most of the accounts of the Issus battle are from Polybius (XII), who took as his source the eye-witness account of Callisthenes.
[13] Diodorus.

Alexander's march to victory continued unabated. His next major target was the principal anchoring place of Persia's Mediterranean fleet at Tyre (Sur). The town was located on an island, virtually impregnable, fortified on all sides by fifty-metre-high walls. The only approach was by sea. As Alexander didn't command a fleet, the defenders of Tyre thought themselves invulnerable. In an example of siege warfare, Alexander outwitted the garrison when he laid a wooden causeway across the lagoon. The mole and many of the siege towers were burned by Tyrian fireships. Alexander refused to give in. He built a second jetty, then a third. From the conquered Phoenician ports, he scraped together any sort of vessel he could lay his hands on and bottled the Tyrian fleet up inside their own harbour. As for the high walls, they had been built to withstand earthquakes and siege catapults, but not heavy, lumbering pentoconters equipped with bronze rams. The walls came down and Alexander's men took the town by storm. It had taken him seven months. Tyre was completely destroyed and its inhabitants sent to work in the silver mines. His overall strategy, depriving the Persians of their seaports, proved wise. Darius was cut off from his fleet, and for Alexander the road to Egypt was open. Before he set off, an ambassador from Darius was ushered into the Greek camp. 'Great king, my emperor wishes peace. He offers you 10,000 gold talents [about $400 million] and all the lands west of the Euphrates. And' – he paused for effect – 'my emperor offers you the hand of his daughter in marriage to seal the pact.'

Alexander made his intentions clear when he replied cynically: 'Tell your emperor, I don't want his money and I don't want part of Persia, but all of it and I intend to take it. As for his daughter, tell him if I so wish I can take her and marry her without his consent.' Alexander was out to wipe Persia off the map. In November he besieged Gaza and took it by storm, and in March 331 BC he conquered

Egypt. At the Temple of Zeus Ammon in the Lybian desert west of Memphis, the priest hailed him as 'Son of Zeus'. With the fall of the southern Mediterranean seaboard, the Persians had no more harbours in which to land their ships. If Darius planned a confrontation, it had to be on land.

For a year Alexander was content to allow his troops to relax while he sketched out the construction of a new harbour, Alexandria. But his focus shifted when he received a report that Darius was assembling a huge army in Mesopotamia. Alexander acted immediately and rushed there to get ahead of his adversary. The next battle would test his capacity to adapt. For Alexander, it meant a macabre race against time, and the odds were not favourable.

Darius was beset by self-doubts as to his ability ever to beat Alexander. Every time they had met, the Greek had been a giant step ahead. The only means of stopping the Macedonian was to assemble a force so mighty that it would trample the Greek army underfoot, regardless of their king's tactical genius. In the two years since his disaster at Issus, Darius had spent his empire's fortune to rearm. He was ready to face his nemesis, having gathered half a million men, cavalry, chariots, support units, transportation. His army resembled a great city on the move.

'But the great battle of all that was fought with Darius was not, as most writers tell us, at Arbela, but at Gaugamela, which, in their language, signifies the camel's house, forasmuch as one of their ancient kings having escaped the pursuit of his enemies on a swift camel, in gratitude to his beast, settled him in this place.'[14]

What followed next was a war of nerves. Played out on the giant chessboard of northern Mesopotamia, the opening moves in the Battle of Gaugamela were almost

14 Plutarch.

as significant as the battle itself.[15] Darius had never taken
into account the problems involved in moving such an
oversized army. This great host travelled with wives, cooks
and servants, camp followers, scavengers and prostitutes.
Wherever Darius established a camp, it was too big for
stealth, too raucous to police, and totally lacking in discipline. Darius knew that it would be impossible to catch up
with Alexander in the hill country, where the Macedonian
would slip through his fingers. His army's movements were
sluggish – units got lost, while others rode off for spells of
thievery. Where Alexander and his forty thousand could
move fast and change direction at any moment, Darius
was stuck with half a million men in endlessly strung-out
columns. Therefore he was forced to stick to easy marching
country. He moved from Babylon to Arbela, the 'City of
the Four Gods'. Darius discussed this with his best general,
Mazaeus. In the general's estimation, which he was careful
to keep to himself, there was nothing right about the army;
Darius's ambitious enterprise was bound to fail through the
hubris that had mounted it. However, he advised his ruler
that their best chance was to waylay Alexander at one of
the great rivers.

Mazaeus took a vanguard of six thousand cavalry to set
the ambush. 'Hold the river,' were his confusing orders.
There were two, the Tigris and the Euphrates. Mazaeus
planned everything on intelligence received from his cavalry scouts, who had shaded Alexander's army. They were
wrong, and so was his planning. He was a good general,
but still he committed an error that was to prove decisive:
he failed to stop Alexander during the crossing of the
Euphrates at Thapsacus.

On 13 September 331 BC, Alexander's cavalry captured

---

15   For the Gaugamela campaign four important historians are available: Diodorus,
Curtius, Plutarch and Arrian. While the first three were mainly opposed to
Alexander, Arrian was pro-Greek and drew from Ptolemy and Aristobulus's
eye-witness accounts.

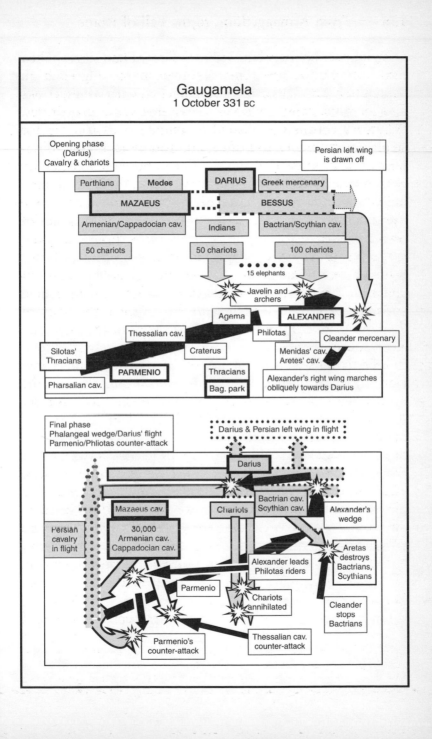

Gaugamela
1 October 331 BC

Opening phase (Darius)
Cavalry & chariots

Persian left wing is drawn off

Parthians   Medes   **DARIUS**   Greek mercenary

MAZAEUS   BESSUS

Armenian/Cappadocian cav.   Indians   Bactrian/Scythian cav.

50 chariots   50 chariots   100 chariots

• • • • • • •
15 elephants

Javelin and archers

Agema   **ALEXANDER**

Thessalian cav.   Philotas

Cleander mercenary

Silotas' Thracians   Craterus   Menidas' cav. Aretes' cav.

PARMENIO   Thracians

Pharsalian cav.   Bag. park   Alexander's right wing marches obliquely towards Darius

Final phase
Phalangeal wedge/Darius' flight
Parmenio/Phliotas counter-attack

Darius & Persian left wing in flight

Darius

Mazaeus cav.   Chariots   Bactrian cav. Scythian cav.   Alexander's wedge

Persian cavalry in flight   30,000 Armenian cav. Cappadocian cav.   Aretas destroys Bactrians, Scythians

Alexander leads Philotas riders

Parmenio   Chariots annihilated   Cleander stops Bactrians

Parmenio's counter-attack   Thessalian cav. counter-attack

a Persian scout patrol and discovered his enemy's plans. After a forced march Alexander reached the Tigris on 18 September. Mazaeus, who was lying in wait, committed a similar error here as on the Euphrates. He thought that the fast-flowing Tigris was impassable and allowed the Macedonian army to cross. Alexander's *perpetua fortuna* held,[16] and he got his entire army across before facing Mazaeus's riders, who withdrew in the face of Alexander's main army. Later accounts blamed Mazaeus's inactivity for the Persian disaster, if only to diminish Alexander's achievement.

Alexander crossed the Tigris on a day of lunar eclipse (20 September), and made sacrifices to the gods of Selene, Ge and Helios (moon, earth and sun). From there, he rushed with his entire army south with the Tigris as his western flank protection. He left his baggage train encamped on the river and proceeded with only pack animals south along the Tigris valley, with plenty of grass for his mules in the fertile plain below the Gordyenian mountains. On 25 September he encountered a troop of a thousand Persian cavalry, defeating them and taking some prisoners; they confirmed Darius's next destination, a grassy plain south of Arbela. Alexander had learned his lesson at the time of Issus, when he had been surprised by his enemy's move around his flank. Not wanting to get caught out again, this time he was keeping himself well informed of his enemy's movements. When his generals pleaded for a day's rest, he rejected their request. 'We will have to leave immediately,' he ordered. 'Darius's party is big and unwieldy. We, on the other hand, must cut down on all the unnecessary to gain in speed.' For speed he forfeited everything; he left behind all animals but his warhorses, which had to carry their own barley ration for a few days, and marched out of camp on 29 September. From the banks of the Tigris,

16 Xenophon's *Anabasis* 1.4.11.

he raced ahead with a small detachment of his Companion cavalry, leaving it to Parmenio to follow him with the bulk of his army.

Alexander was only twenty-five, but already at the peak of his powers. His greatest asset was his nerve – nothing seemed to upset him; in any crisis he kept his cool. The huge host that Darius had put into the field did not impress him. The maxim that 'only an equally great force can oppose a great force' had no meaning for the Macedonian. To his thinking, the way to oppose a mighty force was to destroy its cohesion and, once it was fragmented, deal separately with the pieces.

The Persian King lumbered with his huge force of horses, men and wagon train towards an encounter. Darius was tired, his men were tired, and he ordered a few days' rest before he moved from Arbela, the road junction between Babylon and the rest of his empire, to the River Lycus (Greater Zab), which took him another five days to cross. On 25 September, the day Alexander captured the Persian scouts, Darius finally reached a vast plain near the village of Gaugamela on the River Bumelus (Khazir).[17] This vast plain promised to provide a favourable battleground for his massive cavalry and hundreds of chariots; his generals cheered him with the assurance that here there was nothing that the cursed Macedonian could do to stop a charge by the lethal war carts.

Darius's entire plan hinged on his superior manpower. With it he would arrange a battle line so long and so thick that it would by far outreach even the thinnest of lines with which the Greek could counter it. His chariots would simply smash through the enemy's centre, and his masses of cavalry ride around the Greek flanks. The perfect plan. To make sure that absolutely nothing could stop the

[17] Gaugamela is twenty miles north-east of Mosul in Iraq. This account comes from Diodorus and Curtius.

heavy-wheeled vehicles, he ordered thousands of slaves to fill in holes and level ditches to turn the bumpy field into a billiard-table-smooth racecourse for his war chariots.

Arriving on the plain, the Greek King quickly scouted the territory and had soon figured out the likely placement of Darius's forces. While parts of his cavalry formed a screen to hide the whereabouts of his army from the enemy, he allowed his troops a few days of rest, before moving the last few miles, camping the last night only three miles from the Persians. Alexander had latterly moved so fast that it caught Darius completely unawares, and he was totally unprepared when the Greek army suddenly made its appearance on the distant heights above the plain of Gaugamela. The night before the battle, Parmenio suggested a surprise attack. This would eliminate the danger of a massed Persian rider assault, but Alexander didn't believe that he could strike a decisive blow at night. Therefore he replied curtly with his much-quoted phrase: 'I will not steal victory!' That same night, Alexander and his unit leaders rode to the top of a rise. From there they were privy to an awesome display of power. Thousands of fires lit up a military parade. An endless stream of cavalry and foot troops passed before the throne of King Darius.

'By Zeus,' mumbled Agatho of the Odrysian cavalry, 'the Persian has more horses than we have men.'

'Yes, but each of our men is worth ten of his horses,' replied Alexander, not impressed by the display. For him, what was taking place across the field was all show, and all it achieved was to tire out the army. There was something he had learned as a student of warfare. If you had to look along the shaft of an arrow from the wrong end, then the man who held it had you entirely at his mercy. He expected to see fear in your eyes because he held the power. He would gloat as he watched you squirm, and he would put off the moment of murder – until it was too late. Indeed, Darius held onto this metaphorical arrow by virtue of his overwhelming manpower, but he was not the man to fire it, or take a difficult decision.

Alexander needed a decisive victory. Darius had never lacked in manpower, nor would he ever give up war; even after the loss at Issus he had reassembled a huge army from his vast dominion. The only thing that would finish the Persian was the loss of all courage and hope following an undeniable defeat. Alexander visited the Oracle and made the customary sacrifice. He consulted his diviner Aristander for the augurs. Perhaps he believed in the Oracle, perhaps he did not – long ago he had learned that fate was no respecter of the hell of battle. Then he held a final meeting. When his generals had left and only Hephaestion remained, Alexander stepped outside the tent, then turned to his friend. 'Within hours we shall know. We must win because we are living gods.'

Gaugamela (Arbela), 1 October 331 BC.[18] As both armies established their formations, a great black bird sailed over the field. Men looked up and spoke of portents, while the bird's wings flapped across the first streaks of orange dawn like a hungry shadow, as if it had come from heaven with orders from the goddess Athena. 'The oracle is with us . . .' The Greek King and his army had slept fitfully, while Darius had kept his army under arms throughout the night. When the sun came up, they were tired. Not so the Greeks.

The day began with Alexander doing the unexpected – he turned his battle formation by several degrees. The Persian army was arrayed in a triple line of attack, spread out as far as the eye could see, far beyond the reach of the single line of Greeks confronting them in the distance. The gleam of metal was everywhere – the dawning sun flashed

---

[18] Plutarch's date: the month of Boëdromion, eleven days after a moon eclipse = 1 October 331 BC.

off polished steel and bronze shield rims. Alexander sat on his charger, slightly removed from his troops. He felt destiny awaiting him. He wouldn't become king of the known world without paying heed to his instincts rather than listening to the wise council of his friends and advisers, even if they were all heroes who had fought and won many combats. Everything was new; every battle was a new challenge, different from the last. He relied on his men; they would follow him to their own destiny.

Alexander had 7,000 cavalry and 40,000 infantry, and not a man more. He waited for the very last moment to spring his tactical plan of attack. It was pure genius. Parmenio was given the left wing and instructed to hold his position and defend against a flanking attack from the Persian riders massed in that sector. Alexander would march with his right wing at an oblique angle towards the enemy's line, hoping that such an unorthodox approach would draw out the Persians beyond the designated battle-field and throw the static enemy formation into disarray. This had never been tried before,[19] but if everyone was doing his job right it would work. He arranged his units so that they could wheel and turn and fight in all directions. He counted on Darius's known indecision and the fact that he would not be able to adapt his preset manoeuvre, even if forced to. Alexander had outwitted his enemy.

Once the battle got under way, Alexander feared that he would quickly lose the general overview. Therefore he communicated his specific orders personally to every one of his major commanders. They were to act according to his master plan, but were allowed to exploit windows of opportunity. He rode slightly ahead of his line-up. His troops presented a splendid sight, forty thousand warriors aligned in tight formation, with every archer,

---

[19] Although something similar had been described in Xenophon's *Cyropaedia* as having been used by King Cyrus.

every slinger, shield-bearer and hoplite at his appointed station. The cavalry was behind the line, out of sight of the enemy to keep Darius guessing. Menidas's cavalry was his fast-moving reserve to counter-attack flanking movements by enemy counterparts. In front of his first line were archers and javelin-throwers, the first hurdle for the dreaded war carts. They were ordered to aim only for the horses, decking them with a shower of missiles before quickly retreating behind the solid phalanx of pike-carrying hoplites. Alexander knew that the lightly armed archers would run in any case, so better to tell them to do so and keep up their courage – but only after they had unleashed at least three arrows each. If they were retreating by the King's order, they would stand, fire and then run – and not panic. In this manner he managed to control the uncontrollable. His *agema* élite and the hoplites made up his main line. They were of a different mettle and would let the initial charge run up on their planted pikes. For this principal attack with his 'mobile right wing' he aligned some of his best units: Cleander's veteran mercenaries, the Macedonian archers, a number of the Agrianians of Attalus, Aretes' light cavalry, the Paleonians under Ariosto, and the Greek mercenary cavalry of Menidas. A formidable force, but nothing compared to what faced them: forty thousand heavy Persian cavalry – as many riders as Alexander had troops – Bactrians, Dahans, Scythians, plus two hundred war chariots with archers and one million men.[20] Alexander allowed for every eventuality: 'In case of my death, Philotas will take command of my wing, and if Parmenio falls, he can be replaced by Craterus.' He checked his battle formation. First his own right wing, where next to the Companions were the Royal Squadrons of

---

[20] The figures for Persian infantry seem highly exaggerated. Other contemporary sources give them as 400,000 (Justinius). Diodorus and Plutarch both say they were all together one million. The fact is that Darius's cavalry alone equalled in strength the total effective of Alexander, cavalry and infantry.

Cleitus, Glaucius, Aristo, Sopolis, Heraclides, Demetrius, Meleager and Hegelochus. Then came the *agema* and the *hyspastis* of Nicanor. Parmenio's son Philotas commanded the right-wing cavalry. Parmenio, in charge of the left wing, had the Thessalian cavalry under Philip, the Pharsalian riders, the Odrysians under Agatho, the Thracians with Sitacles in command, Coeranus's Greek allies, and the Greek mercenaries of Andromachus. There was one more element, destined to play an important role in the battle – a portion of the Thracian infantry to guard the baggage. They were not supposed to take any part in the battle, but they would.

When he was satisfied that everything was in place, the King rode from section to section, but not on the great steed Bucephalus, who was now growing old. He wore a coat of Sicilian make, girt close about him, and over that a breastplate of thickly quilted linen, which was taken among other booty at the Battle of Issus. The helmet, which was made by Theophilus, though of iron, was so well wrought and polished that it was as bright as the most refined silver. To this was fitted a gorget of the same metal, set with precious stones. His sword, which was the weapon he most used in battle, had been given him by the King of the Citieans, and was of an admirable temper and lightness. His belt, which he also wore in all engagements, was of much richer workmanship than the rest of his armour. It was the work of the ancient Helicon, and had been presented to him by the Rhodians, as a mark of their respect for him.[21] He stopped frequently to talk with hoplite and helot, *psiloi* and Companion, encouraging all, sometimes with a laugh that shamed the cowardly into being brave. With his commanders he spoke about orders, to make certain that his instructions were understood and would be executed at his signal. Most of all, he stressed

[21] Plutarch.

that there was to be no forward move before his specific order was received, only a lateral march to draw the enemy out beyond his pre-positioned battle line.

Aristander, the King's diviner, wrapped in a white mantle with a crown of gold on his white hair, pointed at an eagle that soared high above Alexander and straight for the enemy. The Greeks gave out a loud cheer; they knew that the gods would assist him, a true son of Zeus.

Before them lay a wide stretch of grassland, sloping gently upward and topped by a low crest about half a mile distant. It would allow a good line of approach out of the line of sight of Darius. On Alexander's signal the Greek formation began to advance towards the right, closing on the enemy at an oblique angle. Once the Persians discovered this, it forced them to shift accordingly and spool out their line ever farther to their left. What was possible to achieve with an army on the march was near impossible with a force in fixed position, especially one as deep and huge as the Persian host. Units became mixed up, some moved faster than others, and some didn't move at all since their officers failed to receive or give orders to follow the general trend to their left. This unco-ordinated sideways movement left the Persian front line ragged and bulging. The general in charge of the Persian left wing, Bessus, satrap of Bactria, saw that his formations were getting more destabilised by the minute and that Alexander's advancing wing would soon proceed past the point of the 'racecourse', specially flattened for the chariot attack. There was another factor that came into play. Men and horses had been kept up all night long; they were tiring in the heat. Bessus decided that he must attack while the horses were still relatively fresh. There was nothing to be gained by waiting. His heavily armour-protected Bactrian and Scythian cavalry were ordered to attack Alexander's marching formation and halt its rightward movement.

'Sound the call for attack.' A trumpet sounded and

Bessus's heavy cavalry dashed forward, like a gigantic wall, ten thousand of them. Their attack came on fast and furious and the forward Greek units suffered heavily. Menidas, following his prearranged order, instantly brought his Companion cavalry forward to meet the onslaught and prevent the wing from being annihilated. The impact of the two rider formations, smashing into each other head-on, could be heard across the entire battlefield. Many Greek riders were thrown off their horses and continued their fight on foot, holding their shields high to protect their bodies while ramming their lances into the bellies of the Persian steeds. The Scythians and Bactrians managed to inflict heavy casualties on the Companion cavalry. But the contest between the two cavalry formations, which had turned into a mad mêlée, failed to bring about a decisive result, especially after veterans of the Greek mercenary cavalry joined in the fight and threw back the Bactrians. Alexander's battered ranks held up under the initial Persian assault. A second thrust from the Persian cavalry fared no better, although the Greek infantry swayed dangerously under its initial impact. This gave a false impression. 'The Greeks are running!' someone yelled, and a cheer passed down the entire length of the Persian line. Darius, in the belief that the Greek line had been broken, launched his sickle chariots. A mass of heavy bronze-wheeled vehicles thundered across the fairway.

Alexander's men were prepared for the chariot charge. His archers, in their advance position, nocked arrows and drew, opening their chests, pushing steeled muscles into their bows, holding the drawn arrow firm in their drawing hands, thumbs to their jaws as they took aim, before they let the shafts slide from their grasp. The arrows headed forth in a shallow arc to dispatch instant death. Within moments, the plain was strewn with fallen men and animals, but through them and over them drove another wave of chariots. Certain units in Alexander's solid phalanx swung to the side to allow the madly charging carts unhindered passage. While the chariots flew down the cleared lanes, a second curtain of arrows and javelins met them, striking deep into horseflesh. The draw horses stumbled and shrieked as arrows pierced their unprotected flanks, their wounds gaping open with the frenzied movement, catapulting their crews over their heads. Only a few crews made it, and those that did were quickly hacked to death. Without doing the slightest damage, two charges of scythe-whirling carts had been blunted. Meanwhile, the Bactrian and Scythian cavalry, many already wasted in the initial clash, were dealt with by Aretes' light cavalry. On their lighter, more mobile horses they came on like a swarm of angry hornets to deliver their blows, then quickly retreated, only to attack from a different side. This surprise assault divided the Persian horse into smaller groups. Their lances stabbed into the Persian riders, their swords cut through leather and metal, their knives buried themselves in living flesh.

A disaster was close at hand for the Bactrians and Scythians. Bessus, satrap of Bactria, dispatched an urgent call for assistance to Darius. His plea for help fell on deaf ears, because Darius's attention was by now drawn from his troubled left wing to his right wing, where his wing commander, Mazaeus, had launched his entire cavalry reserve in a massed attack against Alexander's left wing: 30,000 riders, backed by 70,000 infantry, moved forward to the sound of drums and clarions. To stop this mass from crushing his flank and exposing Alexander's army to annihilation, Parmenio deployed a mere 10,000 hoplites and 2,000 cavalry. The first stage of the Persian assault resulted in a pandemonium of screams, war horns and whinnying horses.

While Parmenio tried to stem the masses thrown against him, on Alexander's wing all was proceeding according to plan. From his vantage point the King saw the leading

Persian elements follow in parallel his own advance; this brought the men of Bessus beyond the piece of ground specially prepared for the chariot attack. It was a critical junction in the battle. Owing to the crab-like sideward movement, Alexander's flanks became dangerously exposed to a side-on attack by cavalry. Darius had it within his grasp to shift the powers of hell, and Alexander knew it. He held his breath, closely studying the huge mass of riders milling across the field, ready to strike at his flank. But Darius failed to move. And then his moment was gone.

Alexander was not only a great leader, but also a thorough student of warfare. In a battle at Leuctra in 371 BC, the Theban General Epaminondas had used a revolutionary phalangal tactic to break through a Spartan army. Following Xenophon's teaching, 'A wise general attacks there where the enemy is the weakest', Epaminondas formed his hoplites into a deeply staggered phalanx and used it as his triangular ramming block. By holding back one of his own wings and advancing on the Spartans at an oblique angle, he crushed his enemy's right wing. On an infinitely vaster scale, Gaugamela had developed like Leuctra.

This twenty-five-year-old Macedonian had a military overview never again matched until Napoleon at Austerlitz (1805). With a clearness of eye and an incredible instinct for timing, Alexander had spotted his enemy's vulnerable point. The moment to strike a decisive blow was near. Trusting in his own invulnerability, Alexander dashed along his advancing formation; he exposed himself to the hail of deadly missiles launched by the Bactrian archers, but managed to divert Bessus's attention. He gathered every available hoplite from the four most forward *speirais* (a Greek military unit sixteen men wide by sixteen men deep) and formed them into a phalanx three times its normal strength. Within minutes, a line was converted into a triangular wedge. For extra power, this wedge was strengthened with units pulled from Cleander's mercenaries, known for their ferocity. An order went out to Philotas to use his Companion cavalry to screen the wedge from a flank attack. All was set. The Greek King took a last look at Darius's centre; it was still fixed in its original location since it had failed to follow the sideward movement of its left wing. The unco-ordinated sideways shift had opened a dangerous gap in Darius's left wing, defended by a thin screen of Persian auxiliaries.

Alexander shouted orders, but it was no use screaming when the earth itself had begun to howl, horns to blare and men to yell. He had to use hand signals to make his ramming block move forward, first at a walk, then a trot. Alexander headed straight for the gap. He couldn't understand why Darius still hadn't moved his powerful cavalry to fill it. He didn't know that the Persian cavalry were fully engaged against Parmenio's wing. A ripple went along the phalanx as its long lances fell into place, and the horns sounded more furiously than ever. The trot became a run as the charge swept forward. The daring manoeuvre, together with his personal courage, was crowned with instant success. An irresistible battering ram of steel points and men shouting their fearsome '*Alalai, alalai*' smashed into the Persian line and took their frightful toll. Blow for blow and stab for stab, the triangular wedge marched in syncopated step over a carpet of corpses. They caught the Persians from the front and from the sides.

There was nothing kingly about the figure standing upright in his chariot. Darius was frozen into inactivity, as men screamed and fled before the Greek hoplites' line of advance. The terrible wedge was followed by a large number of Greek Royal Guards piling up fleeing Persian companies against his centre, creating a lamentable confusion, while an attack by the Macedonian Companion cavalry slammed at breakneck speed into his disintegrating flank. Macedonian pikes carved a path through the Persian army, slicing it into two separate sections. Suddenly, the Greek phalanx wheeled to head straight for Darius's position, clearly recognisable by his silken standard. The heroic Cleander, a giant of a man, broke into the knot of warriors from the Persian Royal Guard protecting the person of their emperor. With a swipe of his sword he split the head of a steel-clad warrior before he sat himself on the dead man's chest, breathing hard. When he raised his eyes, his stare met that of Darius. The Greek mercenary's cheek was open to the bone and his own blood mingled with that of his dead enemy. This scene of raw slaughter, played out directly in front of his chariot, was much worse for Darius than the battle itself, and suddenly made him aware of possible defeat, something he had never even contemplated. And yet he still had command of ten times as many troops as his adversary, sufficient to reverse the situation.

Because things were not going at all well for Parmenio on the Greeks' left wing. His first indication was when the ground began to shake. Then followed the drumming of hooves, and as far as the eye could see a flood of horsemen, out to gain honour, all coming straight at his thin line to win the day! The previous evening Alexander and he had taken everything into account, but had not considered that Mazaeus would concentrate his entire cavalry reserves on one single strike. Parmenio had at his disposal a few squadrons of Greek allied cavalry under Coeranus and, angled to the flank, a solid shield wall of mercenaries under Andromachus.

The Persian right-wing commander, Mazaeus, had been told to hold back until the imperial order for advance was issued. He did he know about the disaster on the left wing. He saw the opportunity to strike a crushing blow the moment Alexander detached his moving right wing from the left. This had resulted in a hole in the Greek centre, and Mazaeus decided, order or no imperial order, to launch his strike. He directed his huge rider masses to make straight for the gap. With a yell, thirty thousand Parthians, Medeans, Cappadocians and Armenians galloped for the space between the Thessalian cavalry and the Greek flank protection. The immense wave of riders looked like some cloud of dun-coloured leaves blown by a strong breeze across a field. They came on not in cleanly ordered ranks, but with their lances bobbing in any old direction. A flight of javelins and arrows met the first wave of the howling mob. For an instant it sent the front rows into stunned confusion, while the rear ranks, caught by the uncontrollable momentum of their steeds, vaulted over the fallen and rode down those who had stopped. Horses stumbled, broke their necks and those of their riders; riderless horses raced across the oncoming waves; more riders were brought down and instantly trampled to death. All this before the first thousand reached the Greek phalanx. The shock was instantaneous, the slaughter on impact unimaginable; the archers from Crete were cut down to a man and then the flank protection made up of Thracians simply dissolved.

Parmenio had lost his fighter's edge, was even accused of having been sluggish and unserviceable in this battle. Whether age impaired his courage or he secretly disliked and envied Alexander's growing greatness, he ordered a retreat to be sounded.[22] With his wing in imminent danger of collapse, Parmenio sent a dispatch rider to Alexander, asking for reinforcements. In the meantime he would hold with what he'd got. He could only pray – if Zeus allowed him time to do so. Servants and cooks were told to pick up the spears of the fallen and fill the holes in the shield wall. His troops were being mauled and trampled under the hooves of Persian cavalry. And their foot troops were eight hundred yards off and coming on fast, thousands of

[22] Callisthenes.

screaming, charging Persians; soon there would be simply too many.

While Alexander's right wing hammered at Darius's left flank, Parmenio's wing fought for its very survival. For the Greeks the situation was critical, if not hopeless. The overpowering mass of Persians could no longer be stopped. Another push and the disaster would be complete. What it needed now was for their emperor to take the lead, to provide an example and lead his reserves from the front into battle. But Darius was no Alexander. He stood in his chariot – and did nothing!

Parmenio's men would soon be confronted by a frontal attack from the onrushing waves of foot troops. They had to prevent the flood of riders from spilling out behind Alexander's wing and thereby annihilating the Greek army. Parmenio made a quick decision, which proved to be the correct one. Rather than confront an infantry attack, he rallied the Thracians of Sitacles, ordering them to execute a 180-degree turn and counter-attack the Persian cavalry. And he called upon the Thracians of the baggage guard to join in this attack. His unorthodox manoeuvre took the Persian cavalry completely by surprise; suddenly they saw themselves attacked from both sides, Thracians in front and Thracians behind. Anchoring his new line on the baggage camp, which with its piles of equipment and bales of hay prevented any passage for horses, Parmenio managed to present a solid wall of pikes, bristling like a porcupine. His Pharsalian horse joined the Thracian infantry and fought valiantly to hold off the waves of Persian charges. '. . . the commanders of the Greek troops which formed the reserve to the first phalanx, learning what had happened, smartly turned about face, according to previous orders, and so appeared in the rear of the Persian cavalry and slew large numbers of them . . .'[23] The riders' flanking

[23] Diodorus (XVII, 5).

movement had been temporarily halted, but a crisis was still at hand – the masses of rapidly approaching Persian infantry.

At the height of the battle, with his foot reserves advancing to roll up Parmenio's wing and victory in his grasp, Darius panicked. He was probably pushed into it by a minor incident that now occurred. Alexander's phalangal wedge had come dangerously close to his position, and their archers, following in their hundreds on the heels of the hoplites, sent streams of arrows into the circle of Royal Guards protecting Darius. The Emperor stared in disbelief as suddenly the belly of one of them bristled with feathered shafts, tearing the tissue and spilling his intestines. The driver of his imperial chariot, a certain Panotes, a Scythian, had put himself squarely before his emperor to protect him. Suddenly several arrows slammed into him, shearing off half of his face. Blood gushed from another wound in his neck and splattered the immaculate robe of Darius. Still suffering the shock of what he had just witnessed, and without a second thought as to consequences, the Emperor acted on impulse, and with it ended two centuries of Persian hegemony. He pushed the dying Panotes from the chariot, grabbed the reins and whipped the horses into panicky flight, but found the wheels of his chariot becoming clogged and entangled in dead bodies. He jumped on a mare and dashed off. Everyone in his army knew their king by sight and a cry rippled along the line, until it burst forth in a great roar. 'Darius is fleeing!'

Didn't he understand that, with his august person riding from the field, half of his army would try to save themselves any way they could? When the Persians on his side of the field saw how many of their comrades had been hacked, stabbed or bludgeoned to death for an emperor who was abandoning them to their fate in a cowardly fashion, it broke their will to continue the fight. They dropped their arms and dashed off after him. With this, the entire Persian left wing crumpled. 'So thick a cloud of dust was raised by the mighty mass of fugitives, that nothing could be clearly distinguished, and that thus the Macedonians lost track of Darius. The noise of the shouting and the cracking of whips served as guides to the pursuers.'[24]

Darius's left wing had become a strung-out rabble running for its life while Menidas's riders hacked down the hapless fugitives. One Persian wing was in complete disarray, but Alexander was counting on support from Parmenio to launch a pursuit. He didn't know where his general was at the moment; he had no news about his own left wing, nor what the mercenary force under Andromachus was up to.

While this battle raged, Parmenio's urgent dispatch finally reached Alexander. There was no time to lose. Should Parmenio's line collapse it would be the end. The next few moments showed Alexander's coolness in decision-taking. He wheeled his horse, and in the midst of scoring a decisive breakthrough pulled back Philotas with his Companion cavalry, plus the Thessalian cavalry, and personally led them against Mazaeus's rider mass. Alexander's cavalry was the finest, most disciplined on the field. Alexander communicated by hand signals. Thanks to the smooth fairway, ordered by Darius but never intended for a Greek cavalry charge, Alexander's élite units managed to race across the field, where they crashed into the flank of the Persians. So developed the mightiest cavalry battle of ancient history, and perhaps of all times.[25] In the first few moments, thousands of riders were unhorsed, speared and trampled. The Persians were riposting furiously in spite of their horrendous losses. Parmenio committed the remnants of his Thracians once more; they were no longer great in

---

[24] Diodorus (XII).
[25] Matched only by those of the Catalaunian Fields between Attila and Theodoric (451), the clash between the cavalry of Ney and Uxbridge at Waterloo (1815), and the Austrians versus the Prussians at Königgrätz in 1866.

numbers but nothing could diminish their fighting spirit. Alexander's wounded riders withdrew through the lanes left open for them by the advancing Grecian mercenaries of Coeranus, while a second phalanx under Simmias moved forward to close up the gaps. In a brilliantly executed charge, both movements took the Persian cavalry in the flank. The fight was over in minutes, the panic spread in every direction by bolting, riderless horses. With the Thessalian cavalry threatening his rear, Mazaeus had no choice but to call a retreat, or face annihilation. First to bolt were the Cappadocians. They didn't even wait for the order for withdrawal; they simply turned about and dashed off. The lances of Alexander's *hypaspistas* broke the rest of the Persian cavalry into scattered groups, no longer a solid wave of armoured men on horses but a disorganised horde fleeing into the great plain beyond. Nothing seemed real. Masses of Persian infantry were still advancing on Parmenio's wing when suddenly they halted in total confusion. A sound like a giant's moan came wafting across the field. Incredulously, single voices picked up the cry from their own left wing. 'Darius is fleeing!'

'The King has fled!'

Abandoned by their emperor, with his cavalry decimated, the Persian foot-soldiery were struck with hysteria. The Persian right wing collapsed like a sandcastle. Its end came with devastating swiftness; its front ranks were speared while the rear ranks broke and bolted. Big gaps appeared, immediately filled with yelling, cutting, slashing Greeks. Swords, clubs and cudgels hammered away at the groups of Persians putting up some last resistance. And then the Emperor's army was on the run, hotly pursued by the Greeks in a lust for glory. On a field churned and ploughed by thousands of wheels and sandals lay tens of thousands of shields, helmets and corpses, many face down with deep slashes in their backs, men cut down by the Greek cavalry while trying to make their getaway. Death had caught them in many ways, heroically facing the enemy or shamefully delivered upon their fleeing backs. The losses suffered by the Persians are impossible even to guess.

And then it was over. The day was won. Alexander slid from his horse; the tightness in his muscles gave way to numbness. He saw Parmenio, making his way across the field from a knot where the Grecian allied cavalry of Coeranus had grouped. They took stock of their situation. Parmenio looked in disarray, his armour askew and his helmet dented. And his face promised no cheerful news. 'We are missing Sitacles and Agatho, both went under.' Two of his best cavalry officers gone – and how many of their men?

Alexander issued two more orders: to chase the fleeing Persians to Arbela and to inflict great harm on the way, so that they would never return; and to kill the human scavengers that were moving about the field of death to strip the fallen, as they did after each battle, no matter what its outcome. Let the dead rest in peace! The Greek cavalry rode forth and did as ordered.

Alexander sat down on a knoll next to his friend Hephaestion, two figures in isolation on the field of slaughter. 'There,' Hephaestion said, pointing to a straggle of figures stumbling across the corpse-strewn ground. Shapes moved about whose unit affiliation could no longer be distinguished by their colours. There was only one colour – the red of blood.[26] Alexander stared in silence. At the blood-soaked killing-ground before him, at the bright armour of the fallen glinting in the late sun, and at the hundreds of chariots, taken with Athena's help. The immediate present was more real than any memories of his distant Greece and what his victory had achieved for his

[26] As with the numbers given for the army line-up, the casualty figures are open to doubt. Arrian gives the number of slain Persians as 300,000, Curtius 40,000 and Diodorus 90,000. In comparison, Alexander's losses are given as between 100 and 500.

country. He could not possibly imagine that a single victory could produce a result of such far-reaching consequences for the man who had accomplished it.

Alexander of Macedonia was now ruler of the known world.

Darius whipped his horses throughout the night to reach his camp at Arbela, seventy-five miles back, and when his horses gave up he forced his bodyguards to put their steeds before his chariot. Alexander and a squad of five hundred of his Companion cavalry were right behind him. They too pushed themselves and their horses until many fell over dead, the horses from exhaustion and the men from wounds they had received during the battle itself. Some just bled to death in the saddle. Alexander and his men allowed the Persian no respite; they nearly caught up with him at Ekbatana (Hamadan), where they found the ashes still glowing in his campfire. Alexander's party was down to sixty men. He took a grave risk as the chase led ever deeper into enemy territory. This hunt lasted eleven days. In the end, Alexander arrived too late. Someone else had caught up with the terrified monarch: the satrap of Bactria, Bessus. A heated argument broke out in which the Bactrian accused the cowardly monarch of having sent his Bactrians uselessly to their deaths, and then abandoned them to their fate. And so, when Alexander entered the tent of Emperor Darius III, he found the last of the Persian rulers dead on the ground, his head split from a blow by a Bactrian sword.[27]

'King Alexander, having mastered Darius in battle and having become Lord of Asia, made sacrifice to Athena of Lindus in accordance with an oracle.'[28]

*   *   *

[27] Alexander hunted down Bessus and had him executed.
[28] Engraved on a sculpture of ox heads, which Alexander himself placed in a temple in Rhodes to honour the Goddess Athena. Source: F. Jacoby, *Die Fragmente der griechischen Historiker*, Berlin, 1923.

'And it came to pass, after that Alexander the Macedonian, the son of Philip who came out of the land of Chittim [Greece], and smote Darius king of the Persians and Medes, it came to pass, after he had smitten him, that he reigned in his stead, in former time, over Greece. And he fought many battles, and won many strongholds' (1 Maccabees 1, 1).

The military genius of Alexander was twofold: his organisational talent matched his military prowess. 'The lightly-armed helots are the hands, the cavalry the legs, the hoplites are chest and armour, and the general is the head of the army,'[29] he said. As *organiser* he was without compare; as *manager* he always kept sufficient reserves to achieve victory. In battle he was incredibly inventive and utterly unpredictable. As *strategist* he achieved victory by never repeating a tactical manoeuvre. And as *conqueror* he moved with a speed that boggles the mind. (In 1991, using thousands of airplanes, it took the US-sponsored coalition eight months to set in motion Operation Desert Storm in order to effect victory over just one country.) Alexander's achievement is truly incredible; in ten short years he conquered the world – and he did it on foot.

As a man he pursued glory through conquest. He ordered cities built and settled them with traders and artists.[30] Such persons were to be transplanted from Asia to Europe, and vice versa. Thereby he intended that the people of his world should meet and peacefully intermingle. Among his great enterprises, the greatest was unquestionably the Library of Alexandria, the universal source of all wisdom. Alexander was not perfect – his close companions talked openly about his drinking bouts.[31] 'By God, he is the best man to drink with.' They even held drinking contests in which the winner sometimes died of too much alcohol. There was also the suspicion that he himself died after

29 Alexander, quoted by Iphicrates.
30 Diodorus (XVIII), after notes by Hieronymus of Cardia.
31 Plutarch in his *Moralia*, quoting Aristobulus.

drinking with his companions. 'He was earnestly invited to go to one of the friends, Medius the Thessalian, for a feast, and there, after filling himself with much wine, suddenly he uttered a loud cry, groaned and groaned, and was led off by the hands of his friends and put to bed.'[32]

It is fashionable, when examining the motives of such giants of history, to impute that they were inclined to homosexuality, and that their actions are all to be explained by the feelings that these tendencies engendered. Shortly before Alexander's death, Hephaestion, his closest friend, was found dead in Alexander's tent after an evening of festivity and much drinking (October 324 BC). The night of Hephaestion's death, Alexander had suffered from a nightmare. A sheet-wrapped apparition rose and came towards him like the lepers that had lined his army's road and begged for alms, or cursed the passers-by with threats of bad fortune. Alexander awoke in a sweat from his alcoholic stupor. When he saw how Hephaestion was lying there, his paleness shattered him. He never got over the death of his best friend. Something broke in his heart. Centuries later, evil tongues claimed that Alexander had killed his friend in a moment of insane jealousy. There is no foundation for this belief. He may well have indulged in homosexual affairs, as was the custom throughout the ages in the masculine atmosphere of men willing to fight and ready to die, but Alexander also carried with him a travelling harem of pretty girls. And then there was his wife, the Bactrian princess Roxana, married for love and not for political reasons. Whatever his sexual inclinations, these had no effect on his battles or his politics.

This King of Kings became the first true unifier of many nations of numerous races. In 324 BC he organised a momentous banquet in Susa, during which Macedonians and Persians drank from the same cup, and where ten

---

[32] Diodorus (XVII).

thousand of his men took Persian brides. Before the multitude of invited guests, gathered from every corner of his universe, the King rose to pray for world peace, 'that all the peoples of his empire might be alike partners in a Great Commonwealth and live together in harmony and the unity of heart and mind.' Without his unifying spirit, the temporary fulfilment of such a dream could never have been achieved.

He was instrumental in removing the barriers between East and West; his empire became the meeting place of the world. Greek culture spread to Rome and influenced the future of Europe to a greater extent than anything ever since. His legacy continued under four of his generals – Ptolemy, Seleucus, Antigonus and Lysimachus. Known as the *diadochi* (successors), they founded their kingdoms: the Ptolemies of Egypt, the Seleucids of Asia, the Antigonids of Macedonia and the kingdom of Asoka in India.[33] Despite his premature death and the emergence of another world power, Rome, Alexander's achievement endured. Emperor Augustus venerated him as god-king; he carried the Macedonian's effigy on his imperial seal and ordained that Alexander of Macedonia be called Alexander Magnus, the Great.

Alexander was indeed a living god.[34] Already, by 333 BC, the Ionian cities had celebrated him with shrines and sacrifices, granting him divine honours as their liberator from the Persian yoke. In the spring of 323 BC, an assembly of Greek states dispatched their ambassadors in a sacred mission to Babylon; they kneeled before the young monarch and presented him with a golden crown as King of Greece and Macedonia.

Throughout his life Alexander remembered a story his

---

[33] Asoka (293–36 BC), last ruler of the Mauryan empire, was also involved in the foundation of the kingdom of Asoka.
[34] Hyperides, *Epitaphios* 21.

great teacher Plato had told him, when he had asked the philosopher: 'Who is the happiest man?' and expected to hear: 'It is you, young prince.' To his surprise, the wise man replied: 'It was Tellos of Athens. He lived in a town that blossomed, had brave sons, watched as all had children of their own that grew up healthy. In battle he drove our enemy back before he died a hero's death. Athens buried him and still honours him greatly. So, you see, my prince, he was a happy man.' And Plato added: 'You can never tell before your death if your were happy. That everything comes together in one single man, which leads on to ultimate happiness, is impossible. The same goes for a country, a nation. In everything you undertake you must always see to the end.' The allegory of this happiest of men fitted well into Alexander's world. He could be a dreamer, never pausing, for example, in his quest to find the mystic Pillars of Heracles. He believed in miracles and signs, in wonders and omens, which, so he thought, the gods revealed to mortal man in an abundant variety of ways. When he lay dying, Alexander had the immortal phrase of Oedipus on his lips: 'In all the signs the gods themselves have given me, they never played me false.'

On 13 June 323 BC, at thirty-three years of age, Alexander of Macedonia, conqueror of the world, died. History's greatest warrior, never defeated in battle, fell victim to an invisible enemy. A mosquito bite had transmitted a blood parasite which caused the incurable fever the Romans called *mala aria* (foul air). The King was laid to rest in the city that still carries his name, Alexandria.

A mortal passed away, but his eternal belief in the one, all-encompassing Brotherhood of Man never died. It still remains the impossible dream of mankind.

'God is the common father of all, but he makes the best ones peculiarly His own.'[35]

---

[35] Plutarch.

*   *   *

Tactically, the Battle of Gaugamela was an incredible gamble that worked. Attacking a vastly superior force at an oblique angle called for both genius and audacity.

In no way does it diminish the brilliant stratagem of the Macedonian that the key to his monumental victory lay in the moment a Persian emperor panicked and fled from the field. Darius III lacked physical courage; he was a man obsessed with his personal safety who abused his leadership. At Issus he had run to fight another day. At Gaugamela he just ran.

The victory at Gaugamela made Macedonia the most powerful kingdom on earth, and Persia the weakest. With Darius dead and the Persian empire at an end, Greek soldiers hailed their beloved Alexander, who by 'right of sword' had become the King of Kings.

Gaugamela changed the map of the existing world.

7

Hannibal Ad Portas!

Cannae
2 August 216 BC

'*Hannibal at the gates!*'
Roman outcry, 216 BC

'*Flectere si nequeo superos, Acheronta movebo.*'
('If I cannot bend the gods, I will let hell loose.')
Virgil, *Aeneid* (VII, 312)

'Don't ever forget who our enemies are, my son.' Thus spoke Hamilcar Barka – *barka*, as in lightning – covered with the purple mantle of the senior field commander, his arm around his little son.

'And who are our enemies, my father?'

'*The Romans!*'

The hand of a father tightened its grip on the shoulder of a small boy. 'Swear to me upon this altar of all that is holy to us, even should I no longer be by your side to guide you, that you will continue my work – that you shall hate and fight the Romans to the death.'

They were standing before the altar of sacrifice to the great god Baal. The boy reached out and put his hand on the cold altar stone; he couldn't hide the tears of emotion in this most sacred of moments. 'Father, by all that is holy to us, I do swear this to you.'[1] Throughout his life he never forgot his oath. He was to spend the next thirty-five years away from his native land, leading its armies to greatness. His military genius was overpowering, his tactics so advanced that they are still applied in modern battles. In the face of an enemy of crushing numerical superiority, he had to be clever. He regarded the situation as the combat between a tiger (Carthage) and an elephant (Rome). If the tiger stood still, an elephant's tusks would surely gore him. But a tiger never stood still, and, after a while, the elephant fell over dead from exhaustion. He was an ardent admirer of the military genius of Alexander of Macedonia, just as his own talents were admired and copied by Julius Caesar. He was loved by his troops, feared by his enemies, and in the end betrayed by his own people.

He was Hannibal of Carthage.

With the demise of Alexander's Hellenistic empire, brought on by his untimely death, two major powers emerged, both vying for supremacy over the Mediterranean basin. One was an upstart, Rome, the other an established nation of seafaring traders of unimaginable wealth. Around 1200 BC – five hundred years before refugees from the Aegean wars (Troy) settled in a fever swamp along the Tiber river and founded a fishing village that was to go on to conquer the world – Phoenician traders established a trade centre on the northern shore of Africa. They called it the New Town, or *Kart-hadasht*, Carthage. The Carthaginians protected their trade routes with a mighty fleet. Carthage's trade flourished along the Mediterranean ports, goods and ideas were freely exchanged, and all was well – until Rome set out on its quest for world hegemony. For this, Rome put its entire effort into building up an

---

[1] The story of his oath was told to Ephesos by Hannibal in 193 BC.

army of conquest. They took the first step by defeating a combined force of Etruscans, Samnites and Gaul at Sentinum (295 BC) in a battle that decided the future of Italy for the next two millennia. Having conquered the North, the Romans next cast their eye on Sicily. This endangered the Greeks of Syracuse and Tarentum. The Greeks called for the assistance of the greatest general of his day, Pyrrhus, King of Epirus, a disciple of Alexander. Pyrrhus used elephants as his mobile shock force. These beasts so terrified the Romans that he achieved a string of victories. Yet each successive battle proved more costly to his own side, until, having thrashed the Romans at Asculum (276 BC), he exclaimed: 'Another such victory and I shall be ruined.' Once again, he had lost more men than the beaten enemy and his success became known as a Pyrrhic victory.[2] The final blow came at Beneventum (275 BC). Two Roman armies had taken the field against him and he had to prevent them from joining up. His first confrontation was against the legions of Roman consul Manius Cunius. He knew that Romans never fought at night, and he planned a forced night march to surprise the sleeping legionaries. Shortly after issuing his order, he had a premonition in which his mouth was filled with blood and his teeth were falling out, and he tried to cancel the night attack. But by this time his army was already on the march, climbing through a dense pine forest to occupy a commanding height. Unfortunately, the Epirotes had misjudged the distance and ran out of torches. While they were bumbling around in darkness, a Roman sentry heard them and raised his camp. Manius Cunius and his Roman cohorts took advantage of their commanding position on the heights, and the Battle of Beneventum ended as a Pyrrhic defeat.

---

[2] A phrase still very much in common use to describe a victory that is too costly.

* * *

The First Punic War between Rome and Carthage broke out over a minor incident. In 264 BC a conflict erupted in Sicily between Syracuse and Messana (Messina), in which both Mediterranean superpowers quickly took sides. Since Rome had never been a naval power, it could do little to prevent Carthaginian reinforcements from debarking regularly in Sicily. This pushed Rome into building a fleet, which was immediately sunk by the navigational skill of the Carthaginians in the Bay of Messana. The Romans next devised a technique of seizing an enemy's vessel by lowering a drawbridge from a higher deck; this gave a decisive edge to the superior Roman land forces, which they then embarked on their ships. With this, the Romans turned a combat on the sea into a 'land battle fought on water'. Their next encounter took place off Mylae. The Carthaginians lost fifty ships; Rome became a sea power and expelled the Carthaginians from Corsica and Sardinia. Their conquest provided them with a stepping stone on to the northern coast of Africa.

In their next battle at sea, the Romans' fleet of 330 ships met up with a much larger Carthaginian navy off Heraclea, where Rome's drawbridge army again proved victorious. For the loss of twenty-four of their own vessels, they sank ninety. But then the Roman fleet sailed rather foolishly for Africa. On the shore they were met by Carthage's cavalry under the command of a Spartan mercenary, Xanthippus, who inflicted on them a crushing defeat. They made good their escape to Sicily (255 BC), but were caught in a storm. What Carthaginian admirals had failed to achieve the weather god finished for them. The Roman disaster was complete – 284 of 364 ships went to the bottom. By a whim of nature, Carthage obtained once more control over the Mediterranean. This did not discourage the Romans, who built another fleet and were ready to attack by the time they embarked on a final exercise to perfect their tactics. They had hardly put to sea when Neptune caught them once again and their entire fleet sank (249 BC). Rome had finally run out of money and stayed off the seas. In 241 BC, after more indecisive skirmishes on land, both belligerents were so exhausted that they signed a treaty to put an end to the First Punic War. This conflict had shown up the principal weakness of both antagonists. Rome couldn't move against Carthage without a fleet, and Carthage was unable to defeat Rome's land armies. And so both put their minds to rectifying their shortcomings.

Rome's legions moved north and opened the road along the western Mediterranean. On their way they beat a Gaul force in a battle that left forty thousand of their enemy dead on the field. Carthage watched Roman expansionist ambitions with growing concern; soon it became obvious that the legions were headed for the Iberian peninsula. To forestall such a step called for a powerful land army. Carthage shipped a substantial force across the Gibraltar Straits[3] to Spain. The Carthaginian general Hamilcar Barka conquered most of the Iberian peninsula and founded a new coastal town, Alicante.[4] The last still resisting Carthage were the Orisses of the Sierra Morena.

In 229 BC, Hamilcar received a message from the King of the hostile Orisses nation inviting him to meet and discuss a territorial settlement. With a small personal escort, his son Hannibal[5] and his son-in-law Hasdrubal, Hamilcar crossed the Ebro river to meet the Oretani

---

[3] The name Gibraltar was coined a thousand years later by the Moors.
[4] According to Diodorus it was called Akra-Leuka, and only the Arabs in the seventh century called it Alicante.
[5] Hamilcar's other sons were Mago and Azarbaal, Epicide, Hasdrubal (namesake of Hamilcar's son-in-law, married to his daughter Salambo).

monarch. The King was indeed waiting for him – with a carefully laid ambush. As their small group rode through a narrow defile, rocks and boulders came tumbling down and their road was blocked by Oretani warriors. The Carthaginians managed to fight their way towards the river. All made it across – all except Hamilcar Barka, who was swept off his horse and drowned. Hannibal (247–183 BC) was still too young, therefore Hamilcar's son-in-law Hasdrubal was voted to take command. With an army of 60,000 foot troops, 8,000 cavalry and 200 war elephants, Hasdrubal took terrible revenge on the treacherous Orisses. Anyone caught was executed, and the Carthaginians made no allowances for age or sex. For this operation, Hasdrubal's army camped on a field that soon became a town they named New Carthage, or Cartagena.[6] The outcome of the Oretanian War was that Hasdrubal's army now occupied most of Spain. This presented Rome with a fait accompli. A treaty was signed which designated the Ebro river as the boundary line between the two major powers. It was Hasdrubal's wish to form a better understanding with Rome; but he proved too trusting. At an official dinner he was stabbed by a Gaul servant in Rome's pay (221 BC). There was no question who the guilty party was, nor who should lead the army of Carthage from now on: the twenty-five-year-old Hannibal.

Hannibal Barka, slight of body but with a face that showed his iron will,[7] had unbridled energy and powers of physical resistance. He was a curious compound of superstition, credulity and scepticism. He believed in the stars – for him only the stars would tell no lies. Most of all he believed in predestination. He showed superior intelligence and mental toughness, a principal

---

[6] Diodorus (XXV, 12).
[7] In 1944, a superb bronze bust of Hannibal was found during excavations in Volubilis, Morocco.

ingredient of his successes, and an extraordinary facility
for adapting instantly to the most difficult situation. He
broke with Punic army tradition, recruiting his auxiliaries
from Numidia (Algeria), Gaul (France) and the Balearic
islands, and invented an entirely new élite force, the
'commando', a unit small in numbers but mobile and
highly trained, designed to strike terror behind enemy
lines. His men paid homage to him as their living god,
and throughout his career he remained linked to them
by a spiritual bond that inspired them to heroic action.
(Napoleon based his intimate relationship with his Vieille
Garde on Hannibal's example.) This bond was created by
necessity; he emphasised the dangers of defeat and made
his soldiers fight with the courage of desperation. He was
an outstanding leader of men and a man of ideas. He
understood – two hundred years before Emperor Augustus
and 'Pax Romana' – that the world of antiquity could
only function as a unity. 'To his reckless courage in
encountering dangers, he united the greatest judgment
when in the midst of them,' wrote the Roman scribe Titus
Livius, and then added his own comment, typical of how
a Roman would describe his nation's greatest adversary:
'He held no regards for truth, and none for sanctity, no
fear of the gods, no reference for an oath, no religious
scruple.'[8] His cruelty was certainly nothing abnormal in
the age he lived in, and his perfidy no greater than that
of his enemy.

Clouds of war gathered. Rome and Carthage prepared
for the day. When the Saguntines of Spain discovered
rich silver deposits in their territory, Rome moved in and
forged an alliance with them 'to assure their protection'.
That Saguntum happened to be on the Carthaginian side
of the treaty line mattered not to the Romans, and the Ebro

[8] Titus Livius (XXI, 4).

River Treaty was doomed. Hannibal acted. In 219 BC, he attacked Saguntum and carried it by storm. Rome reacted to the 'unprovoked aggression of their ally' by dispatching a high-powered senatorial delegation to Carthage. The Romans demanded nothing less than the head of Hannibal. The leader of their delegation, Quintus Fabius Maximus, enraged over the rejection of Rome's ultimatum, stood theatrically before the Carthaginian Senate, raised a fold of his toga and slung it over his outstretched arm: '*Hic vobis bellum et pacem portamus – utrum placet sumite!* . . . In this fold I hold war or peace – choose whichever you wish.'

Carthage's Senate was insulted; its members broke into screams and curses. How dare this Roman upstart provoke them inside their sacred halls! 'Choose yourself,' they challenged the Roman proconsul. Without giving a second thought to the consequences, and in a melodramatic gesture, Fabius Maximus let his toga's fold drop.

'*Bellum!* War!' He spoke, and the Second Punic War was on its way. It lasted seventeen years and killed hundreds of thousands. Hannibal was the man to conduct it for Carthage. His cold, deliberate judgment, his experience and clear perspective, were to make him one of history's outstanding leaders. He realised that the only way to bring Rome to its knees was to challenge it on Italian soil. He sketched out a daring plan: he would travel from Cartagena, over the Pyrenees, across the wide Rhône and the snow-capped High Alps to conquer all of Italy and bring the evil empire down. For the period, and given the size of his army, this was a project full of uncertainties. A relatively small force would invade the land of a superpower that could count on near unlimited men and supplies. Hannibal defended his scheme. 'If Alexander could do it, so can I.' It was his best option for fulfilling his oath to Baal, because at the end of all the efforts and sacrifices awaited a much larger reward: world hegemony for Carthage. To achieve it, he was willing to overcome every obstacle that man and nature could put in his way. He left his brother Hasdrubal[9] with an army in Cartagena to hold down the tribes of Hispania and protect his possible retreat route. His other brother Mago, imaginative but wild, became his deputy commander and leader of the cavalry.

In the spring of 218 BC, Hannibal set off with his army on the legendary march that was to take him sixteen years. The passage across the Pyrenees went off without major difficulty. He turned north-east to avoid the coastal road, blocked by the legions of Consul Gnaeus Scipio at Massalia (Marseilles), and forded the Rhône between Avignon and Orange.[10] Once across the major water obstacle, he headed for the High Alps (in the region of Grenoble). A Numidian scout, one of the many riding around the army as flies swarm around a tired horse, pointed to 'the white wall'. 'We thought of it as a cloud, since we have entered the lands where people live up in the sky. But the clouds do not move and they are still there.' The man was frightened. 'God protect us. The white ghost will kill us all.'

Hannibal called for Magilus, the captain of his Gaul contingent. 'What is this white wall above yonder plain?'

'Mountain and ice, my lord.'

'Ice? Explain yourself.'

'When it rains in the cold months, the drops are firm and stay on the ground. Ice is very cold and very slippery, my lord.'

---

[9] Not to be confused with Hannibal's brother-in-law of the same name, who had been assassinated.
[10] Titus Livius (XXI, 58, 59).

Hannibal, who had sworn a holy oath to put the entire Roman edifice to the torch, knew that he had no choice but to cross this rock-and-ice barrier. He called on his captains: 'We must continue our great journey true to our promise. Nothing shall stop us. Have faith in me.' They did. If anybody could, he was the one to get their men across the white wall; but what about the thirty-six elephants that had survived from the original fifty? How would these creatures of a warm climate react to snow? They couldn't do without them; the beasts were a vital factor in Hannibal's strategy.[11]

The soldiers, horses and elephants climbed higher and higher. The green pine forests gave way to treeless slopes where a cold wind whistled around sharp crags and peaks and the temperature dropped rapidly. In the high regions they did not meet up with any evil mountain ghost that would block their advance, only a white mass, granular as desert sand but much colder. The alpine winds drove icy crystals into their faces; many fell victim to the ravages of frostbite and high-altitude disease. The steep, ice-covered paths made progress not only hazardous but also downright fatal. Each step was renewed pain; they slipped and then lay gasping on the crystalline ice. How pathetic, after all the battles they had come through, to fall before an enemy they could not see, only feel. The mood of the Carthaginians and their allies grew bleak as the days dragged on. Mago confronted Hannibal, wrapped in his heavy sheepskin cloak. 'We cannot go on. We will get into Italy with hardly ten thousand men.'

'And if only you and I are left, we must go on.' They

---

[11] Another defender of the mobile shock force, WWII General von Manstein, the brains behind the German blitzkrieg of 1940, wrote a student paper on Hannibal.

did. On the ninth day[12] they reached the crest of the mountain range and looked down on to the distant plains of the wide Po river basin of Cisalpine Gaul. They had little to cheer about as they found the descent even more perilous than the climb. Many slid down the icy gradients to disappear into glacier crevasses or over the cliff's edge into the black abyss. Worst off were the elephants; their flat feet couldn't prevent their huge body mass from slipping on the ice. At the bottom of some cliffs sprawled dead elephants in puddles of half-frozen blood. Eventually their suffering came to an end. Hannibal's expeditionary corps passed from the glaciers on to firm ground. But they were still not out of danger; mountain tribes unleashed stone avalanches, not to stop the army but to loot its baggage train. Altogether, the losses on the mountain in men, pack animals and precious war elephants were staggering. Hannibal had crossed the Pyrenees with 59,000, and when he reached the upper Italian plain he had 34,000 – 12,000 Africans, 8,000 Iberians and 6,000 Numidian[13] and Phoenician cavalry; not taking into account his previous battle losses, crossing the Alps had cost him 13,000 men and 30 elephants.[14]

Meanwhile, Rome's spy service operated with its customary efficiency, and Consul Publius Cornelius Scipio

[12] This is the time frame given by Titus Livius. It is unlikely that an army, with pack train and elephants, could move at such speed over 3,000-metre-high iced peaks. Polybius speaks of two months. That seems too long, unless he took into account the approach march across the foothills. A few years ago I did this route on foot. With only a backpack, it took me slightly less than one week, following Hannibal's Mt Cenis route. There is no precise historical indication as to where Hannibal crossed over the Alps; it is assumed to have been in the region of Grenoble-Briançon in the French Alps (Col de la Traversette or Col de Clapier). A local shepherd took me to a high mountain pass known in folklore as the Pass of Hannibal. From there it was a straight descent to Turin and Milan. Titus Livius indicated that the first non-hostile tribes Hannibal met were the Salassians, and they lived in this region.

[13] Ancient kingdom, today Algeria.

[14] Polybius wrote that he had seen these numbers inscribed on a bronze plaque at Cape Lacinion.

prepared a reception for the exhausted Carthaginians. For this he chose the banks of the Ticino river, but though the Romans were vastly superior in numbers and fought on territory known to them, Hannibal outwitted them. He pulled Scipio's contingent into a trap and rode him down with his Numidian cavalry. Publius Scipio the Elder was struck by an arrow and carried wounded from the field, and his army fled.

'I am not come to fight against Italians,' Hannibal said when he set free all non-Roman prisoners, 'but I shall fight on behalf of all of you against Rome.' His generosity, unusual for a time when prisoners were more likely to be butchered than released, brought many of the tribes over to his side. The next encounter took place in December 218 BC at the River Trebia, a tributary of the Po. A consular army sailed up the Adriatic to rush to the rescue of the recovered Scipio. The problem lay with the commander of the relief force, Consul Sempronius Longus, a pretentious man of no military experience who was thoroughly hated by his Gaul auxiliaries. On Scipio's advice, Sempronius built a strong blocking position fronting the river. For no apparent reason he changed his mind, crossed the river and attacked Hannibal's camp. Shortly before the battle, Hannibal's brother Mago had concealed a detachment of cavalry in a ravine, and as the combat reached its height he struck Sempronius's rear echelons and drove them against the riverbank. In the midst of the battle, Sempronius's Gaul switched sides and brought with them the head of their Roman commanders. The decision went to Hannibal – the Romans lost 30,000, Hannibal 5,000.

While Hannibal proved unbeatable in Italy, the Carthaginian Hanno went down to defeat against two legions of Publius Scipio's brother Gnaeus, who had marched from Massalia (Marseilles) to Amporia (Ampurias) in Spain. For Hannibal this was a severe shock, since it cut off his only retreat route, should things go wrong in his Italian campaign.

By the summer of 217 BC, the situation was confused, to say the least: while the Romans controlled large parts of Spain and were threatening Cartagena, Hannibal advanced down the Italian peninsula on Rome. Two new Roman armies were hastily assembled and dispatched against him, one of 40,000 men under Consul Gnaeus Geminus to block the Carthaginian's route at Arezzo in the Apennine mountains, and another of 20,000 under his co-consul, Gaius Flaminius Nepos, to Rimini on the Adriatic coast. Again Hannibal did the unexpected; he crossed the 'impassable' swamps to pop up suddenly to the rear of Flaminius Nepos on Lake Trasimene, where a battle took place on 21 June 217 BC.

Hannibal counted on his opponent's lack of tactical skill, and he was not disappointed. To block Hannibal's route, Consul Flaminius Nepos sacrificed security for speed and committed a blunder when he failed to send out scouts to locate his enemy's position. This was fatal, as the Romans' march route passed along a strip of land, in places hardly a hundred feet wide, between deep water and sheer cliff. Hannibal put a blocking force at the exit of the narrow defile. Mago, with the Numidian riders, waited in a dense forest by the road. One of Hannibal's favourite generals, Carthalo, was posted at the entry into the narrow passage. He was to put the stopper in the bottle once the Romans had passed, rendering retreat impossible. 'Until the cohorts have marched past?' he asked.

'No,' replied Hannibal, 'until you can no longer hear the sound of the last Roman. If you do it right then we will win, there can be no doubt.' In fact, his troops could use cheering. 'Do you think we can beat them?' one of his soldiers had asked him. 'Yes, there is no reason why we shouldn't. For much of my life I believed that Rome had the best soldiers in the world. Now we will beat them, because we are better.'

The morning of the battle, a blanket of fog covered the lake and its shoreline. The fog was so thick that the Romans couldn't see more than a few yards ahead. Carthalo could hear the rhythmic march of a great army passing close by; he couldn't see them, just as the Romans couldn't see his Carthaginians. He followed their passage by the loud voices of their officers and the rattle of arms as they marched past his hidden troops and jammed into the five-kilometre-long defile snaking along the shoreline. When they reached the place where the road seemed to end in water, the fog lifted momentarily. It showed the might of Rome standing around in confusion – they couldn't advance and they couldn't go back because ever more units were jamming into them from behind. Through the mist floated the wailing sound of a war horn. It was Hannibal's signal for attack, and it caught the Romans so much by surprise that many didn't even get a chance to draw their swords. The first they saw of their enemy was a mass of ghost riders appearing out of the mist – Mago's Numidians. Their horses towered above the legionaries and their hooves came down on their heads. Behind them followed the foot troops, howling like devils. Javelins tore into the Romans and arrows whistled through the air. They were unable to see from where death came, and this added to their confusion. Maniples and cohorts were quickly split up into smaller groups that lost all coherence in the milky grey mist. Along the narrow confine between road and shore, Roman units broke up and took to their heels. Those who tried to make their escape by running back along the narrow road were met by a hail of spears from Carthalo's men at the solidly blocked rear exit. The Romans fought on in desperation. Standing out by virtue of his purple coat was Consul Flaminius Nepos. He was spotted by a unit made up of Cisalpine Gaul. Years before, the same Flaminius had led a punitive expedition into their territory on the River Po; he had devastated their lands and killed their families. Now it was his turn. With his death, most of the remaining Romans put down their arms or were pushed into the lake and drowned. When the fog finally lifted, the shore was strewn with thousands of corpses – 15,000 Romans died, and another 15,000 were captured.

This was not the end. Another disaster befell the Romans when Consul Servilius, rushing to the aid of Consul Flaminius, ran into an ambush set by the Carthaginian general Maherabal. A Roman rider force of 4,000 was annihilated. A praetorian had to announce to a stunned Rome: 'We have lost a great battle.'

'Stop Hannibal!' was the citizens' outcry. During an emergency – and Hannibal's march on Rome certainly was one such – the Senate could implement the ultimate measure: replace the conventional dual consulship with a single dictator of unlimited powers. After much senatorial in-fighting, the man they picked was the same one who had declared war on Carthage: Q. Fabius Maximus. In order to pacify opposition from the Senate minority, the patricians accepted M. Minucius Rufus as his second-in-command to head the Roman cavalry; a fateful choice – the two military chieftains loathed each other. From the outset of their campaign, Minucius stirred up public opinion against the superior he mockingly referred to as *cunctator* (temporiser or coward). Hannibal counted on the fact that their rivalry would prevent the two Roman columns from combining in battle. This allowed him breathing space to forge new alliances with the Cisalpine Gaul and to provision his army, which he did by stripping the Etrurian countryside. Whatever supplies they could not carry were burned. Q. Fabius Maximus returned to Rome 'to attend an important religious festival' and handed command to Minucius, who, to his delight, stumbled into a trap and was severely mauled by Hannibal near Geronium. When Rome heard of this new disaster, the Senate sacked Minucius and ordered Q. Fabius Maximus back into the field. The extremely cautious Consul Fabius Maximus chose as his place of battle an unassailable position in a vale between two steep mountains. It was here that the historic episode of the 'night of the burning horns' took place. When Hannibal saw his route blocked, he ordered his men to tie bundles of firewood to the horns of a herd of two thousand cattle. During the night his men lit the 'horned torches' and drove the cattle along a mountain ridge. The Romans down in the valley, observing the torchlight procession of the 'Carthaginian army making good their escape over the hills', abandoned their solid position and rushed up the steep hillside to find 'a herd of cattle with burning horns'. Meanwhile, Hannibal's army passed unmolested through the undefended valley. This incident covered the Roman army and its commander with ridicule.

Now Fabius Maximus was out of favour, and Rome looked in desperation for a new tandem to lead them from adversity. Their choice fell on the patrician Lucius Aemilius Paulus and the plebeian Gaius Terentius Varro; they began their preparations for confronting the Carthaginians by raising eight legions. Never before had Rome raised an army of such size. Reinforced by contingents recalled from Corsica, Sardinia and Sicily, it totalled 85,000 legionaries plus 9,600 cavalry. In the face of such overwhelming numbers, Hannibal's force of 26,000 was meagre indeed. But the Carthaginian held two aces; the first was his Numidian cavalry, far better than anything the Romans could field, the second his audacious generals, whose superb handling of men in battle could make all the difference: Mago, Hanno, Sosylos, Carthalo, Maherabal. Furthermore he was a master of the element of surprise; time and again he had outwitted the Romans by advancing where least expected, and this time he moved so fast that he captured an undefended Roman grain-and-weapon depot on the River Aufidus (Ofanto) near the town of Cannae.

Varro and Paulus made plans that were overtaken as they spoke. 'The Carthaginians are on the march, down and out of the mountains. Their most seasoned fighters will be with Hannibal in the van. The auxiliaries will likely form a rearguard, or travel in close company. Most will be ill-armed and untrained. Such weapons as they carry are not worth our swords. Their train is burdened with women, children, herds of sheep and all their worldly goods. In short, they are vulnerable, and they do not know we will be waiting for them.' That was before both were told that the Cannae depot had fallen into the hands of their enemy. Aemilius Paulus and Terentius Varro rushed with their legions to meet Hannibal at Cannae. The Carthaginian was stuck with a scenario that involved picking the least bad of a series of bad options: with the ravaged countryside he had left behind, and a mighty host barring his front, he had to accept battle to assure the survival of his army.

How history might have changed had it not been for a curious system written into the rules of Rome's command structure. To uphold the republican principle and its dual consulship, political and military directives were divided between the two elected consuls, and called for a daily change of command from one consul to the other. Fate decided that on 1 August 216 BC the patrician Paulus should be in charge. He worried rightly about Hannibal's cavalry, and counselled restraint. They had to find a better-suited battlefield, one covered with shrubs and dissected by hillocks, which would prevent Hannibal from deploying his superior rider formations. Without adhering to Paulus's order, Varro launched an ill-conceived cavalry attack. It fizzled into a minor skirmish, but it now forced the Romans to engage in the real battle the following morning on ground ultimately favourable to Hannibal's cavalry and elephants – and on that day, legion command reverted to Varro.

When Rome established its military machine, it based its main fighting unit on 'a gathering of the clans', or a legion, with a combat strength of 10,000 men. A legion consisted of 5,000 hoplites (heavy infantry), 4,000 *velites* (light infantry), and about 800 cavalry.[15] The hoplites were divided into *hastati* (the youngest), *principes* and *triarii* (the veterans); the *velites* were kept in reserve behind the wall of hoplites. The basic unit was a maniple (company), made up of two *centuria* (platoons) under a centurion. Their protection was a square shield (*scutum*), a brass helmet and breastplate (*pectorale*); their weapons for attack were the throwing javelin (*pila*) or the heavier *hastae*, and a stabbing sword (*gladius*) – 'the result was a combination of the heavy javelin and sword like that attained in modern warfare with bayonet and muskets; the volley of javelins prepared the way for the sword encounter as volleys of musketry preceded a charge with the bayonet.'[16] Legion commanders were elected executive officials or consuls who held both military and political power. Since their promotion was based on their family's predominance in the Senate, and not on their military experience, this often resulted in bad strategy and weak leadership. Therefore, senior professional officers, called tribunes, six for every legion, were assigned to advise the consuls, and sixty centurions assisted the tribunes. At most times, Rome held eight legions under arms, of which

15 Polybius (VI, 19).
16 Mommsen, *Die Geschichte Roms*, Berlin, 1895.

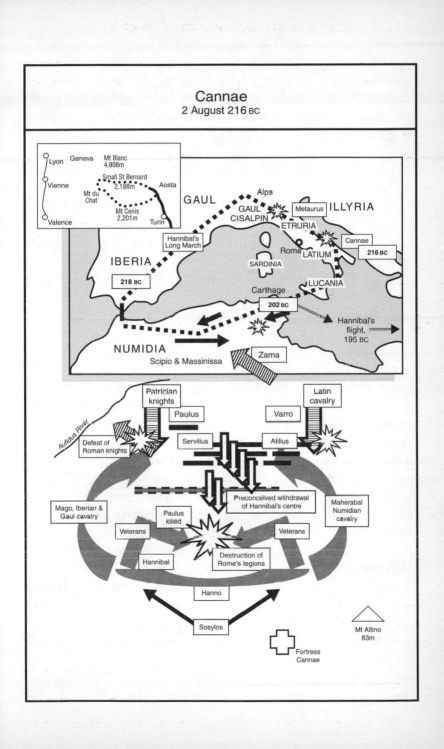

Cannae
2 August 216 BC

only four were Romans, the rest auxiliaries. A legion's principle was to achieve tactical superiority by the close interaction of maniples, attacking in staggered lines and acting individually as a miniature phalanx, which offered a great advantage since this was more flexible than a straight line of battle. Rome's war machine was formidable indeed – but they were about to meet their master.

On the morning of 2 August 216 BC, both Romans and Carthaginians took up their positions. 'Who holds the Roman command on this day?' asked the Carthaginian.

'It is Varro, my lord,' replied the leader of his heavy cavalry, the Spartan mercenary Sosylos, taller and huskier than his commander.

'The gods are lenient with us. Many of us will die, but remember, we are the sword of Carthage!' Hannibal stared across the field. When the wind blew it lifted the Roman banners. 'We'll hit hard and be away before their horsemen can form up to face us, and when they pursue we shall wheel and strike again far down their column.'

In what Napoleon was to call the 'classical masterpiece of annihilation', Hannibal came up with a genius plan. Perhaps he had taken a lesson from the Battle of Marathon, two centuries earlier. There, the strategy of flank attack had been brought about by accident; this time it was his tactical masterstroke. He saw that Varro and Paulus had stuck to the well-proven attack pattern and positioned their maniples in a three-tiered, staggered formation. They could advance in a straight line forward, but moving laterally was almost impossible. That would make it relatively easy for his elephants to punch lanes through the enemy's line-up and spread destruction and confusion. The Roman infantry numbered between 75,000 and 85,000, against

which Hannibal could put up fewer than 25,000.[17] Even
with his elephantine mobile shock force it was a gamble.
Everything depended on precise timing.

At the opposite end of the field, Paulus felt uneasy and
tried to warn Varro that Hannibal's heavy Iberian and
Gaul cavalry were nowhere in sight. His warning was
in vain. 'Worry not, Paulus,' Varro said confidently.
'Hannibal will keep them on the defensive, and we
couldn't ask for more. This is what Rome has waited
for for years, now the moment is upon us. May Jupiter
ride with us.' Varro needed much more than divine aid;
he needed a solid battle plan, and he didn't have one.
Hannibal did. He planned to pull out his heavy veteran
units and leave only his lightly armed Iberian foot and
Gaul auxiliaries to hold the centre, with his Libyans in
a second-line reserve. He was well aware that his centre
would have to cave in under Roman pressure. That was
precisely his plan.

'My warriors, before you is the might of Rome. Fight
bravely; those of you who do will be richly rewarded, but
those of you who fail will be severely punished. This I,
Hannibal Barka, promise.' Thousands cheered his words.
Hannibal looked over his array of men in the knowledge
that they were fired up. All he needed to do was guide
them in the right direction.

The Roman army was in position, ready and waiting.
For well over an hour, the legions had been lining up under
the loud-voiced commands of centurions, identifiable by
the red horsehair plumes on their helmets. The men
behind the shields were arranged in the usual phalanx,
their spear-tips tilted forward, ready to advance. Behind
the shield-bearers were the flags of the cohorts and,

[17] Polybius (III, 107). Both kept some forces back to guard their camps and
supply park.

behind them, the golden eagle of each individual legion. There were eight. On the sound of a horn, the wall of shields opened slightly to allow thousands of archers to slip through and advance to a point equal to their arrows' effective range. They formed up in a long line that spanned the entire field.

The slight figure of Hannibal was prominently displayed on a hillock He studied the enemy's line-up. His eyes watered; ever since the arduous march through the fly-infested swamps his eyesight had deteriorated by virtue of an infection that was to rob him eventually of the use of one eye. But on the morning of Cannae, what he spied through tear-clouded eyes pleased him. The Romans stood in three lines, too deep for maximum effect – a grave error. He looked at their archers, all ethnic tribesmen; there were leather-clad Etrurians, some bare-chested Gaul, helmeted and in leather kilts, much like his own Gaul; there were Cantii, Iceni and all the other auxiliaries Rome depended on to do their fighting. Hopefully they were getting tired of serving a heartless military state and wouldn't fight too hard. It was always the tribes which took the highest casualties, and it was they who left behind heaps of their dead. Their reward was the dubious honour of calling themselves Roman citizens.

The Carthaginian gathered his troop leaders and drew a diagram of his battle plan on a wax-covered tablet. 'Mago, you will take charge of the Gaul and Iberian heavy cavalry – here.' He pointed to a spot near the riverbank. 'The main rider attack is to come from our left flank; you will lead your men against the patrician cavalry. Destroy them. Maherabal, you place yourself under Mago's orders. Your Numidian cavalry is to go against the Latin cavalry on our right wing and put them out of the fight. Once you have done so, you will await my further orders. Hanno, you take command of our Libyan and Iberian foot troops in the centre. Once under attack, you will pull back slowly, but don't let the legions get through your line. Your task is to pin down the best veterans of their legions – retreat but hold the line with everything you've got until relieved. We must destroy their cavalry before we can defeat their centre. Sosylos, you command the African heavy infantry with which you will strengthen our flanks. Do not engage before you get my signal.' If his generals had questions about this unorthodox manocuvre, they kept these to themselves. All except Hanno.

'To weaken our centre may create confusion.'

'It will surprise them. What the enemy will see at the beginning of battle is our usual deployment, with our veterans against their veterans in the centre. But we will reverse the battle order, wheel out our veterans and move them obliquely to the wings. They will deliver the decisive strike against the enemy's centre once it is being pulled into our pocket.'

'You expect them to fall into the trap?'

'Yes.' Hannibal looked grim. This time it was Mago who had spoken, making his brother look as if he hadn't anticipated all eventualities. 'The enemy will not allow his veterans to break contact with our centre, keeping in step with our measured pull-back and advancing too far, thus leaving his wing auxiliaries without legion support. All depends on the destruction of the Roman cavalry.'

'It is a risk.'

'Everything in war is a risk. I will seek the omens from the augurs after the sacrifice before we engage in battle, but I am convinced of the final outcome. Obey my orders and we will meet again to celebrate a great victory.'

Hannibal's plan was not only daring, it was a radical departure from the tactical norms of warfare. His generals may have had doubts about the sanity of his manoeuvre, but their deep loyalty to their leader won out. To hide his moves from the enemy, Hannibal ordered a line of slingers ahead of the main line in order to mask the pull-out of his African veteran infantry. Sosylos divided the heavies into smaller *speiras* of 256 men each, told them to lower the tips of their lances so that their movement wouldn't be spotted from across the field, and then marched them from the centre. He placed them on both flanks, hidden behind a screen of light infantry. With this move Hannibal had stripped the centre thin – rather than the usual twelve ranks, only four would face the Roman onslaught. Everything hinged on his centre; it had to effect a slow, preconceived withdrawal and hold until Mago had taken care of the Roman cavalry. He positioned Maherabal's 4,000 Numidians, a ferocious warrior tribe from the Atlas mountains. Like the Huns of a later period, these men were born on their mounts; their initial task was to ride down the 2,000 Latin horsemen. But the principal clash would come on his left wing. That was where Hannibal positioned his heavy cavalry of 6,000 Iberians and Gaul to face Varro's 4,000 rider élite, the sons of Rome's patrician families who vied with each other not only for battle honours, but also in the aspect of outward appearance. Rome's golden youth mounted beautiful horses and their finely chiselled armour was adorned with golden symbols of war. The two dozen elephants that remained of the original fifty would be his steamroller. They were rising above the mist like miniature castles. Hannibal had formed his line of battle.

Rome's commander of the day, out to achieve glory through victory, was over-confident – a bad attitude to take into battle. His veterans outnumbered Hannibal's three to one, and with the river behind them this would ignite their fighting spirit, as retreat was impossible. Varro cut a splendid figure on his white charger; the purple coat of a Roman consul covered his chiselled breastplate. To show his utter contempt, he was sitting with his back turned on the enemy. 'Jupiter and Rome!' he shouted at the flower of Roman patrician cavalry, lined up to protect his flanks, and they answered him with a rousing cheer: 'Honour and *Patria*!' They were tough looking; individually they were good fighters. What Varro hadn't bargained for was that they were also subject to sudden fits of mass panic. 'They're on the move!' yelled one. Indeed, Hannibal had surprised them and launched his troops first. The great Battle of Cannae was under way.

Hannibal looked at his groups advancing in the centre; he saw the white tunics of the Iberians, the naked, bronzed torsos of the Gaul, all experienced slingers and archers. His light and heavy cavalry, their horses snorting and quivering, were in ambush position behind the obliquely advancing flanks. The Carthaginian wall advanced at a measured pace, its centre bulging slightly outward. The move was intended to dare the Romans – Hannibal's calculated risk that Varro would attack with his usual unrestraint, going straight for whatever was in his way. And Varro did just that, advancing hell-bent for the Carthaginian centre. Under the leadership of the tribunes Servilius and Atilius, the Roman legions came at them at a rapid pace, *hastati* in front, *principes* behind them and the *triarii* in the third line to deliver the killer stroke once the enemy's line was pierced. They had come to within two hundred yards when a mass of archers slipped past the shields of the Carthaginians' Ligurian and Gaul infantry. Their advance was so sudden that the Romans almost didn't have time to put up a protective roof of shields. A salvo of arrows tore into the Romans with devastating effect. Hundreds toppled forward; others just stood there, clutching their chests, thighs or throats, wherever an arrow had pierced them, before they sank slowly to the ground to be trampled by the next wave. They came on at a double quickstep, maniples shouting their legion's war cry until they got within javelin range. They threw their thin lances before they crashed into the Carthaginian centre at full tilt. The din was deafening, and the combat carried the lines back and forth like ships on a wild sea. Knots of fighting formed. Men prayed to their many different gods, and then went on with their business, which was killing as many of the enemy as possible. They leaned their full body weight against their shields, their left shoulder to the fore to free their right arm for their sword. Combat became an individual affair, man versus man. Struck by the full weight of the Roman principes, Hanno's centre began to waver – and did precisely what Hannibal had expected it to do. The phalanx of Iberians resisted, but they could not disengage without turning their bodies to the Romans at sword length. They fought on while retreating step by step, pulling the steel-armoured Romans with them.

For the moment, Hannibal's plan was working. With his enemy's attention focused on the centre, he sprang a full-scale rider attack on the Roman flanks. His 4,000 Numidian cavalry met up with 2,000 Latin riders. For once, the Carthaginians held a numerical superiority. Maherabal's hordes from the Atlas mountains threw themselves on to the Latin light cavalry. With their savage war cry, the Numidians virtually exploded their enemy's formation with very few losses of their own. This combat was over within minutes. The Latin horse broke and scattered; those that weren't lying dead on the ground or being trampled under the hooves tried to make it across the river. Some ended up behind the walls of Venussia or Canusium, but not many. Their success freed the Numidians for the next stage in Hannibal's tactical plan. He dispatched a rider with his order: 'To Maherabal: Do not chase after the Latinos, remain in place for my further command.'

At the same moment, Mago's mass of Iberians and Gaul made straight for the patrician cavalry of Consul Paulus and buried them beneath the weight of the much heavier Spanish horses; the Roman nobles were literally blown from their saddles. Paulus's formation was split into several groups, fighting desperately and without cohesion. They were cut down in droves. This was not a time for the kind of chivalry the noble sons had dreamed of; this was no time for heroics, just survival. When it came to sheer brutality, the nobility of Rome stood no chance against the savage professionals. Within moments, the entire Roman knighthood was driven to flight. A Roman tribune, waving his sword in a futile gesture, tried to rally the fleeing cavalrymen as they swept past him and headed for the river. With death riding on their heels, they forced their steeds into the water. Many drowned. More of Rome's noble sons died in flight than during the moment in which they had sought to gain fame through gallantry. Those who made it across staggered behind the walls of Canussium.

In the centre, Hanno's men fought like lions. How long that battle went on nobody could tell afterwards with any precision, but to the survivors it seemed like a year rather than just a few minutes. Bleeding men lay before the bristling line of lances, coughing their lives out on the blood-soaked ground. A Libyan raised his sword and brought it down on the head of a legionary at the moment the legionary speared an Iberian. Both gave out a loud groan and died simultaneously. A centurion, whose sword-arm dangled limp by his side, crushed a Gaul's head with his heavy shield. The fight for the centre of the line was conducted with berserk fury and, like a magnet, it pulled ever more Romans into the horseshoe trap.

Varro was so sure that victory was near that he ordered his available reserves of *triarii* and *velites* into the centre pocket. The Carthaginian centre was bulging so much and its line was so thinly held that it simply had to break. That was the moment Hannibal had been patiently waiting for to put his master plan into operation. Facing the Roman cavalry threat, he launched Sosylos's

African veterans: 'Order to Sosylos: Advance with all heavy infantry and strike from both flanks the Roman legions in the centre!' With a single command, Hannibal set in motion the historic double envelopment stratagem, and any subsequent general who has wanted to be called a great genius, from Caesar to Napoleon and on up to the present day, has applied 'The Cannae Stratagem' to lead his army to victory. A series of horn signals set off the second phase of the battle. The heavy African infantry, which had seen almost no action, wheeled inward and advanced rapidly towards the enemy's flanks. And from the front Hannibal launched another weapon he had held in reserve; for it to take its full, devastating effect, this situation was ideal: a tightly compressed enemy on a relatively small front.

The first the Roman commanders knew about the calamity was a sound like the trumpets of hell. The Carthaginian shield wall swung inward like a wide gate opening and exposed huge grey mountains moving towards the Roman units. African war elephants plunged into the tightly massed Romans and trampled a swath of instant death. The shrill trumpeting of the beasts heightened the terror. The Romans stood frozen in terror, while the ground about them shuddered under the impact of pile-driving feet. In several places at once big holes opened up in the Roman line, immediately to be filled by hordes of screaming Iberian and Gaul warriors, stabbing and slashing at the dazed Romans. Their only thought was to get away from the raging elephants, but a warning cry from Tribune Servilius caused them to look to their sides: from their flanks came running Sosylos's African hoplites, so fast as if they were trying to outdo each other in a contest. Only this was not an arena where a laurel wreath awaited the winner at the finish line; this was ferocious combat, where the only prize was death. Swords clashed, men shouted at the top of their voices rows of blood-and-gore-splattered warriors were fired with mortal urgency, their bodies burning up in the heat of fury. The Roman flank gave and retreated towards its own centre, compressed inside the concave bulge that was quickly tightening around them. The worn-out Romans, reeling under the shock of the elephants' charge, could not withstand the attack by thousands of battle-hardened, fresh Africans. The Roman archers unleashed their final round of arrows. One struck Sosylos in the shoulder and, in the shock of pain, he pushed his knees into his horse's flanks to support his swaying body, before the beast, which had borne him bravely through many battles, sank to its knees, the end of a javelin sticking from its pierced chest. But nothing could any longer stop the Africans.

The legions fell back. Their drums had gone silent, and their cohorts were on the verge of breaking up. Consul Varro's dream of ultimate glory ended with the savage charge of Hannibal's cavalry. It was a massacre, lances spearing bodies, swords slicing heads from bodies. Through ever more lanes opening in the centre, rode the Numidians, driving into the already broken-up Roman formations with hacking fury. The Romans put up a desperate fight, preparing themselves for the attack from the African infantry on the flanks while desperately attempting to erect a pike wall against the cavalry. Fresh from their victorious encounter with the Roman knights Mago's heavy cavalry now arrived, sweeping across the field in a knee-to-knee charge. They closed the ring around the Romans. Attacked from all sides by Maherabal's Numidians, Sosylos's Africans and Mago's Iberians and Gaul, the legions of Rome were slaughtered.

Tribune Servilius, holding on to his legion's golden eagle, yelled: 'Across the river, all back across the river!' and then he was cut down. But retreat was no longer possible; a ring of spears and lances had closed off all avenues of escape and Mago's horsemen lined up along the shore and cut down anyone attempting to make it across.

Tribune Atilius rallied his men. In a wild mêlée masses of wild Carthaginians surrounded his group fighting in desperation for their lives. Arrows and swords dealt death. The Carthaginians were upon them, and the Romans couldn't stop the tide. In the centre was Atilius, the heroic tribune. An arrow struck him in the face and another tore out his throat. He staggered a few steps and then went down. His men too were falling, sprawled among the fighting men in the blood-drenched mud, stabbed or cut open.

Consul Paulus was unsaddled by a lance that had pierced his horse. He sidestepped the thrust of another lance, grabbed his attacker by the chest and kicked him in the groin. As the Carthaginian doubled up in pain, Paulus sliced off his head. Then the Carthaginians were all around him. They came yelling, howling, brandishing spears and swords, even curved knives, ready to swamp the consul. Then his world jarred, but his eyes remained open; he staggered, sat down with a sigh and spread his hands over the blood seeping through his body armour where it had been pierced by a lance. He tried to get to his feet but his strength failed him. Then the steel tide passed over him.

When the wounded General Sosylos was helped to his feet, the Roman army was no more. It had been annihilated. Its leaders were dead or lay dying on the field. The noise of battle had abated. Soon the field would become prey to the flocks of vultures circling hungrily overhead. Amidst the butchery and the weak cries of the wounded, the Carthaginians lay down and slept, too exhausted to make camp or eat. With night came silence, the deep silence of death.

The Romans lost eight legion eagles, 2,700 patricians and officers and 50,000 legionaries[18] (70,000 according to

---

18 Titus Livius.

Polybius). Among their dead lay Consul Aemilius Paulus, former consul Servilius Geminus, and the master of cavalry Minucius Rufus, eighty Roman senators who had voluntarily joined the knightly riders, and twenty-nine military tribunes. When the count of casualties was made, Hannibal found to his dismay that he had bought his victory at a heavy price – 5,700 of his own lay dead. While the Romans would be able to replace their depleted ranks from townsfolk and peasantry across Italy, the Carthaginians could not count on such luxury. The irony of this greatly worried Hannibal; unless he could get reinforcements from Carthage, and quickly, he would soon be fighting a hopeless cause.

Carthage's altar had been reddened with the blood of its enemies. The Roman Eagle had been turned into a toothless cock. The gilded wreaths, which Rome's legions had won in its days of glory, were torn from their crimson staff.

'*Hannibal ad portas!* Hannibal before the gates!' Rome was in an uproar. An atmosphere of superstition and fear enveloped the city, its citizens willing to believe anything they were told. Scapegoats had to be found. The Senate blamed the disaster on a laxity of morals. Two vestal virgins, having falsely predicted victory, were accused of having lost their virginal oracular powers by indulging in orgies. They were buried alive. A Greek philosopher was stoned by the masses and a Gaul community was dragged to the Forum and done to death. Many of Rome's Praetorian Guard had been killed during the battle, and without their protection order broke down. Rape and pillage were rampant. Shops were looted, mansions robbed and patrician families murdered before the citizens formed a vigilante squad which re-established a semblance of order by killing the rabble on the streets.

'Hannibal began to reap the fruit of his tremendous

success. Rome and the south of Italy lay now wide open to him.'[19] Yet he would never come closer to smashing the 'evil empire' than that 2 August 216 BC. If he reckoned that Rome would now cease fighting he was sadly mistaken. In their shameful defeat, the Roman Senate sensed a powerful vehicle with which to rebuild its army along new lines, and brought young, dynamic military leaders to the fore. For this to happen, what better slogan could they possibly find than the threat of 'Hannibal ad portas'? They exhorted their citizens to defend their homeland and fight the 'cruel Carthaginian', and that iron will, engrained for centuries in its citizenry, proved to be the true strength of Rome.

Hannibal dispatched a delegation under Carthalo to negotiate a ransom in exchange for Roman prisoners. The hard-line Senate determined that it was nobler by far never to see their sons again than to admit defeat. Upon Rome's refusal to negotiate, a number of Hannibal's troop commanders – some recent allies who had suffered under the Roman yoke and switched their allegiance – wanted to kill every Roman captive. Hannibal prevented the slaughter.

'This is the moment we've waited for. Let us ride immediately on Rome,' demanded their spokesman, the Numidian Maherabal.

'No. We must not only win, but also know how to use our victory well. Yes, we have won a great battle. But Rome isn't vanquished! Not yet!'

For that to happen would take another six hundred years.

For once, the man who had never before shied from taking risks blinked. On this fateful 2 August 216 BC, with Rome's armies smashed and the road virtually open, Hannibal

---

[19] Polybius.

remained *ad portas*. *At* the gates, but never *inside* the city. He had his elephants and his siege machines; Rome had nothing but frightened citizens. Was Hannibal so shocked by the horrid spectacle on the field of Cannae and anxious to arrive at a settlement that would end further suffering? His oath to destroy all that stood for Rome hardly points to this theory. So, what was it that held him back from conquering Rome? It will remain one of history's great enigmas.

Hannibal's Cannae stratagem crowned his genius and raised him to the pinnacle of his career. With his brilliant plan he achieved that rarity in battle: the all-decisive effect of surprise. And yet historically perhaps the most stunning victory in the annals of warfare changed nothing. Rome had lost a battle but not the war.

We may well ponder how history would have changed had Hannibal passed through the *portas* and entered Rome.

8

In Death, There is No Difference

Zama
19 April 202 BC

'Qui desiderat pacem, praeparet bellum!'
('Let him who desires peace prepare for war.')
Vegetius, fourth century AD

In many wars all it took was to capture a key province, in others to destroy an army, but in most it was indispensable to take the capital city. Hannibal had brilliantly achieved the first two objectives, but so far he had failed in the third. He knew that the ultimate objective of his war was to prevent Rome's challenge for supremacy. Victory did not always demand the complete annihilation of the enemy's army, especially if he was stronger. Hannibal had always considered that the most direct way of accomplishing victory was to wear Rome out – the gradual exhaustion of his enemy's will could become the most decisive weapon in his arsenal. The Roman defeat at Cannae, while almost fatal to Rome's will to resist, was by no means militarily decisive.

Hannibal recognised where the new centre of gravity lay, and he directed his political efforts against it. Since his enemy did not have one chief leader who could be singled out, the heart of the matter was Rome itself. He had shattered its military might and now he worked hard to bring about the disintegration of its grip over the Italian confederation through political moves. He gained some initial success when the town of Capua allied with him, as did the Greeks of Syracuse and Tarentum. But while he forged alliances on land, the Punic fleet failed to gain control over the sea. Hannibal rallied Philip V of Macedonia, who controlled the best army in Greece, to his cause. In vain. Hannibal's diplomatic efforts came to nothing. King Philip's army remained in Greece to take care of local affairs, and Rome retained control over the seas, with the result that Hannibal was cut off from Carthage. All the time Rome's rebuilt army gained in size.

It was time for Rome to redeem its honour and recover its legions' eagles. It found two competent generals in the Scipio brothers, Publius and Gnaeus. They went to Spain, where they managed to rally the tribes against the Carthaginian Hasdrubal Gisco. But then they suffered a similar fate to that of Hannibal in Italy – their own Senate abandoned them, and during an attack by Numidian riders under their fierce warrior chief Massinissa, both Publius and Gnaeus Scipio were killed. Rome was once more hard pressed. It is always in times of great danger that exceptional leaders step forward. The man destined to save Rome was a student of the strategic genius of Alexander and the tactical brilliance of Hannibal. Publius Cornelius Scipio, son of Publius Scipio the Elder, was highly motivated after the death of his father and uncle at the hands of the Carthaginians. As the youngest military tribune in Rome's history, young Scipio had miraculously survived the slaughter at Cannae. During the rider débâcle he had stopped some Roman nobles from running away by putting his sword to their throats, making them swear that never again would they forsake their sacred duty to

Rome. Moments later Scipio's horse was speared, and in its death throes threw its rider headlong into the river. He drifted across to find himself, wet but unharmed, on the opposite shore. Of the many thousand dead at Cannae, fate had spared the one who was destined to become Hannibal's nemesis. Publius Cornelius Scipio was kingly in his bearing, could be charming and soft spoken, but could also curse furiously. As a Roman who had been brought up in strict military discipline, he hated inefficiency. He did not possess the overwhelming genius of a Hannibal, but he certainly took a lesson from him, contrary to all other Romans who had faced up to the Carthaginian. Hannibal became his hero figure, just as Scipio became the only Roman Hannibal ever respected.

Young Publius Cornelius Scipio provided a bright ray in Rome's days of darkness. His first chance to prove himself came in Spain. In all his actions he demonstrated an unusual mastery not only of spectacular raids on isolated targets but also long-range strategic operations. He realised that in order to defeat Carthage he had to act just as Hannibal had done when he had carried the war into Italy. Rome's war had to be carried on to African soil. Scipio provided the impetus, and despite his age of twenty-four the Senate put him in charge of their army in Hispania.

In 210 BC he began his military career with a masterstroke; he lured Hasdrubal Gisco (not to be confounded with Hannibal's brother Hasdrubal Barka) from his stronghold of Cartagena and then marched into the deserted fortress without a struggle. Hasdrubal Gisco, together with the rider masses of Numidia's King Syphax, encircled Scipio's two legions at Castra Cornelia. Faced with a hopeless situation, Scipio asked for surrender terms. While deliberately drawing out negotiations, he organised a night attack on the Carthaginian camp. It proved devastating and succeeded beyond imagination. Together with the troops of his cavalry general Laelius, Scipio's troops stole up to the Carthaginian camp and set it on fire. It wasn't planned that way, but since they were few they could ignite only the outer tent rows, unwittingly generating a terrible fire-storm. The ring of flames greedily sucked oxygen from its centre, creating temperatures near 1000°C.[1] 'It is impossible for the imagination to exaggerate the dreadful scene, so completely did it surpass in horror everything hitherto recorded.'[2] In the howling furnace that swept the camps, 40,000 Carthaginians and their auxiliaries perished.

In 207 BC Scipio confronted Hasdrubal Gisco at Ilipa (near Seville). Scipio fought a tactical set piece taken straight from the book of the great Hannibal. Against 74,000 Carthaginians and 32 elephants, he could muster only 48,000. But Publius Scipio was never daunted by superiority in numbers. He had thoroughly studied the tactics of Hasdrubal Gisco and found out that the Carthaginian always placed his veterans in the centre, and his auxiliaries on the wings. It would be no different at Ilipa. For three days he refused to give battle but always faced Hasdrubal with his veteran legions in the centre and the weaker Iberian and Gaul auxiliaries on the wings. But Scipio had no intention of wasting his valuable legionaries against Carthage's élite African veterans. Instead he planned to attack Hasdrubal's auxiliaries with his legions' maniples. Such a last-minute switch was worthy of the great Hannibal himself. And thus it came about that on the morning of the fourth day the legions moved in triple quickstep obliquely to the sides and attacked the weak flanking units. Scipio's Roman veterans drove Hasdrubal's Spanish auxiliaries into the African veterans in the centre. In the rout, one of the most thorough in history, only 6,000 of the 72,000 Carthaginians escaped the slaughter.

---

[1] A technique employed two millennia thereafter during the night bombing raids on Hamburg and Dresden. The 1945 fire-storm of Dresden surpassed the number of victims of the atomic bombs.
[2] Polybius (XIV, 1–6).

The victory provided Scipio with a stepping stone to Africa. In 206 BC he sailed to Numidia (Algeria), where he secretly met the man who was to play a decisive role in his greatest victory. The Numidian Massinissa, while fighting for Hannibal in Italy and Spain, was ousted from Numidia's throne by Syphax, the King of the Masaesyles, and that with Carthage's connivance. Massinissa seethed over this betrayal and could think only of taking revenge. After meeting Scipio, Massinissa called for his troop leaders. 'We are going to do battle.'

'Against the Romans?' they asked.

'No, we have been promised much by the Romans to fight by their side.'

'The Romans don't like us any better than the Carthaginians.' But Massinissa remained firm. Scipio's diplomatic skill and Rome's gold had persuaded this rugged leader of gigantic courage to open Rome's gateway into North Africa.

While these dealings were taking place, and ignorant of developments at home, Hannibal dispatched endless couriers to Carthage, requesting immediate assistance. The elders of Carthage ignored his pleas. They were divided into two hostile factions, the military Barkas and the commercial Hannos. The Barkas provided the generals; the Hannos were influential merchants, accusing Hannibal of draining the coffers of his country in the pursuit of a useless war. While the request for assistance was blocked, Rome used the time to rebuild its military power. The net effect of Hannibal's invasion of Italy was that it provided Rome's Senate with a rallying cause and enabled it to consolidate its position as the most powerful nation on the European continent. It accepted Scipio's strategic plan to surprise the devil on his home ground; not to fight Hannibal in Italy, but to beat Carthage in North Africa.

After years of useless wanderings nothing was decided, and Hannibal had been forced to retire with his steadily depleting forces into the toe of Italy. In the spring of 207 BC, and without taking orders from Carthage, Hannibal's brother Hasdrubal had rounded up his forces in Spain and was coming to his brother's assistance with an army numbering between 40,000 and 50,000. Suddenly, Rome was faced not with one but two Carthaginian armies and two Punic Wars on Italian soil.

Everything began with one of those minor incidents that nonetheless bear grave repercussions. To announce his imminent arrival, Hasdrubal dispatched six messengers, four Gauls and two Numidians, to convey his marching plans to Hannibal. Hannibal had already left his camp and moved to Canusium (Canossa) to await his brother. Hasdrubal's six messengers crossed the Italian peninsula undetected and were within a day's ride of Hannibal's camp when a Roman patrol intercepted them and Hasdrubal's scrolls were found. Consul Claudius Nero, possessed of great temerity, learned of Hasdrubal's battle plans and conceived a brilliant plan. He handed the command of the bulk of his army to Quintius Catius, with the order to prevent Hannibal from moving camp and joining up with his brother, while he picked a veteran élite force of 6,000 men and 1,000 riders and rushed in seven days the 250 miles to Umbria to reinforce the legions of Consul Porcius Livius Salinator, in camp on the River Metaurus (Metauro). To screen his move, he marched only by night. When Nero reached Salinator's camp, he ordered his troops to share the existing tents and hide their presence. A ceremonial procedure gave away the secret. Carthaginian scouts, riding around Consul Salinator's camp, had heard not one, but two trumpet signals reserved for the person of a consul; it signified that there were two consuls in the Roman camp. That meant two armies. Upon hearing this news, Hasdrubal decided to avoid a battle and head south on the Via Flaminia to join his brother. He ordered a withdrawal, covered by darkness, but his army got lost when their Italian guides deserted them. He found himself in an unfavourable position at sunrise. The high priestess of Baal performed the sacrificial ceremony and touched Hasdrubal's head with her fingertips. 'It's not blessing I need to pass this day, but luck,' he growled. He placed his Ligurian heavy infantry in the centre and his Gauls on a hill across from the forces of Consul Nero. Their forces were divided by a deep gully (the Ravine of San Angelo), which prevented direct contact. Nero gathered his élite force behind a hill; on the ridge he lined up a highly visible auxiliary unit and ordered them to shout and make noise.

Hasdrubal took his Ligurian and Iberian veterans and marched them to the portion of the ravine that could be crossed. He struck Livius Salinator's legions. His seasoned warriors carried the opening stage of the battle, fighting with extreme ferocity. 'There the greater part of the Roman infantry and cavalry were engaged to hold off the onslaught by the Spanish troops, the veterans well acquainted with the Roman mode of fighting, the Ligurians a hardy race of warriors. To the same front came the elephants, which had thrown the front lines into confusion by their initial charge and had forced the Roman standards back. As the conflict and shouting increased, the elephants were no longer under control and roamed about between the two battle lines, as though uncertain to whom they belonged, not unlike ships drifting without their steering-oars.'[3] When the elephants refused to obey their mahouts, they had to kill their beasts.

Heavily engaged, Hasdrubal failed to discover that another army was moving against his flank. Consul Nero, who was unable to cross the deep ravine, marched his legion behind the cover of low hills and circled around Hasdrubal's Hispaniards. Suddenly the Carthaginian army found itself caught between two Roman armies, and the men, who

---

[3] Titus Livius (XXVII, 48).

moments before had looked at certain victory, faced annihilation. The rush by Nero's men compressed the Hispaniards. The Roman archers poured continuous salvos into the cluster of men, piercing them right through, and burying arrows in horses. The Carthaginians halted, staggered and turned. Overawed by their sudden success against an army that had never been defeated before, the legionaries sprang forward and began to hurl their light spears after an escaping enemy. More and more Carthaginians crumpled like broken dolls, rolling down into the ravine, slithering and crawling away to die quietly under some bush or against a rock. Hemmed in from all sides, Hasdrubal could do nothing to stop the disaster. If an expression could be featureless, void of fear and dread, even hope, showing only resolve, or perhaps resignation, that was the expression on Hasdrubal's face as he watched the inevitable end. He was unharmed, sitting on his great charger, when suddenly the men around him saw the horse plunge forward. He uttered a savage yell and smashed the head of a centurion with his blade. Then he stabbed a rider with such force that his sword embedded itself in his victim. Lifting his foot, he kicked his adversary backward to free the blade. More Roman riders milled about him; he wheeled around and lifted his sword to ward off the coming thrust. He managed only to divert it before a blade whipped across his chest just as Hasdrubal lunged out, and both he and his aggressor went down in a tangle, yards from the precipice of the ravine. 'When fortune deprived him of all hopes for the future, Hasdrubal considered how, in case of total defeat, he might face his fate and suffer nothing unworthy of his career . . . and when the battle was lost, Hasdrubal rushed upon a Roman cohort, where he fell fighting valiantly, as was worthy of the son of Hamilcar and the brother of Hannibal.'[4] Along the shore of the

---

[4] Polybius (XI, 2).

Metaurus river, and in the ravine beyond, hundreds of vultures were floating on the afternoon thermals, waiting to swoop down and feast on a ghoulish meal.

Metaurus lit the funeral pyre to Hannibal's Italian dream. The relief forces he had counted on to bring his Italian campaign to a successful conclusion had ceased to exist. Hannibal was on his own, knowing that eventually he would lose against the forces building up against him. The man whose plan it had been to bring Rome to its knees by encircling Italy now found himself encircled. To add to his pains, in Publius Cornelius Scipio the Romans had found a general matching his own skills.

The Metaurus victory was significant in that it reversed the roles. From now on the Romans turned to attack. In the autumn of 204 BC, Publius Scipio debarked with thirty thousand well-trained troops at Utica, a harbour on the doorstep of Carthage. Hannibal's general, Hanno, who had carried himself so valiantly at Cannae, rushed there with a small force and was killed. Before Scipio could take advantage of this victory, another Carthaginian army threatened his line of communication, and he decided to go into winter quarters. The following spring he once again met the Carthaginian Hasdrubal Gisco. The general he had already confronted at Ilipa went down to defeat in the Battle of Bagbrades (203 BC). Thirteen years before Hannibal had endangered Rome; now Scipio was suddenly *ad portas* of Carthage. The Romans began to lay waste to the lands around the fortified city. Beset by panic, Carthage's Senate recalled Hannibal. It came as no surprise to Scipio, who kept himself well informed of his adversary's every move.

On 23 June 203 BC, Hannibal ordered all his horses and elephants killed. With his remaining fifteen thousand men, he sailed for home. His 'legendary march', one that had begun by overcoming the snow-covered Alps and brought Rome to its knees, had finally come to its close. In the end it had resolved nothing and gained nothing.

*   *   *

Rome wasn't sure it could win a protracted war on African soil, and therefore offered peace talks. It sent emissaries to Carthage; instead of a dialogue, Rome's ambassadors went straight into a dungeon. Scipio did not wait for his Senate's approval when he marched on the city at the head of a powerful Roman army. 'Hannibal save us!' Between Carthage and disaster stood only Hannibal's genius. But that was no longer enough. His victorious army was a thing of the past; he could no longer count on superiority in riders, his decisive weapon at Cannae. Hannibal, who had landed his army in Hadrumeta (Sousse) and knew that the decisive action would have to be played out in Numidia, marched on its capital Zama (Zowareen) in a desperate attempt to prevent what could no longer be put off. On 19 April 202 BC, the two armies met at the gates of Zama, in the valley east of Siliana. Though they were numerically roughly comparable, with 35,000 each, it was the first time that Hannibal commanded a force made up mainly of untrained call-ups, many of them slaves liberated for the purpose of doing battle. Everything depended on his elephants. Although he had one hundred, more than ever before, these were all untested young beasts without proper training. If these fearsome animals could create havoc in the Roman lines, and counting on his 15,000 Ligurian and Gaul veterans, he would stop Scipio from marching on his home-town.

Hannibal had won difficult encounters before, but against mediocre leaders. This time Rome's best general faced him. Both leaders knew that the outcome of the battle would rest entirely on the cavalry, only now the Romans could count on the assistance of Hannibal's former ally, the peerless Numidian rider General Massinissa. He was good, and so were his Numidian riders. Therefore Hannibal devised a plan that had some hope of success. Depending always in his tactical manoeuvres on his light and heavy cavalry, he

was too weak in mounts to use them as his *force de frappe*.
He ordered the cavalry commanders of his own Numidians
and Carthaginians to put up only faint resistance and then
turn and pretend to flee. This would pull the Roman
cavalry of Laelius and Massinissa from the battle theatre.
'We will attack before Scipio is in position. Launch all
the elephants and veterans at once, we haven't got the
cavalry to turn the Romans' wing.' He fell back on the
ancient Macedonian concept of shock by massed formation
– the phalanx of sixteen men deep, with no gaps in the line
and no faltering in the face of a head-on cavalry charge.
It had been proved that massed pikes could be more
terrifying to horse and rider than sabre-wielding cavalry
was to the pike-armed foot-soldier. All depended now on
the behaviour of his elephants; if they created enough
havoc in the Roman maniples, then with his Ligurians,
Gauls and Africans he would smash the Roman centre and
carry the day.

Scipio had superiority in mounted formations, and his
battle plan called for a mirror image of Hannibal's Cannae
envelopment. 'We must destroy his wings before we can
attack his centre! But first, we must stop his elephants.'
Scipio put his *triarii* in the centre, but behind his *velites*.
He then devised a clever way of rendering the predictable
charge by elephants less effective. He arranged his three
foot lines in columns instead of the usual overlapping
chequerboard formation; this was to allow for open lanes
into which the charging elephants could be funnelled. The
second task was more difficult to achieve. An elephant
was a two-edged weapon; it attacked in a straight line,
but if it could be sufficiently hurt and made to stampede,
then its reactions could not be predicted. Much depended
on the vulnerability of an elephant's thick skin and the
delicate manipulation of the mammoth by its mahout. To
this end the *velites* were equipped with long poles and
grapple hooks to pull the mahouts from their mounts,

plus pike-mounted blades to slash the elephants' vulnerable parts, such as the trunk and the tender skin below their rumps. Laelius's Latin cavalry and Massinissa's Numidians were placed on the wings to stop them from being put to flight by the elephants.

'Before nightfall they would know whether Rome or Carthage should give laws to the nations, not only for Africa or Italy, but the whole world would be the reward of this victory ... The ground was piled up in bloody heaps ... and when they had surmounted the obstacles, the two lines charged each other with the greatest fire and fury ... the battle was for a long time undecided, the men in their obstinate valour falling dead without giving way a step.'[5]

The sun rose in a glaring red ball, promising a hot African day. Rays reflected from steel cuirasses, bronze helmets and the wickedly sharp points of pikes. Through the morning haze both sides observed each other closely. A Carthaginian rider dashed up to Scipio: 'Our commander asks for a conversation, Consul.'

'So be it.' He pointed towards a spot halfway between the battle lines. 'On that hill.'

Unaccompanied, the two great generals met for the first time face to face. A young Scipio and an ageing Hannibal, the brilliant young pupil and the old master.

'The gods wanted it that I, who have carried war into the lands of Rome, and held victory so often in my grasp, have come to you to ask for peace. Of all the Roman generals that I have met victoriously, it is to your honour that you have made Hannibal take this step. We must not lose our will for quiet reflection. A certain peace is preferable to an uncertain victory.'

Scipio was observing the Carthaginian without showing

[5] ibid. (XV, 14).

emotion. But his bright blue eyes challenged him, showing will, bravery and persistence.

The Carthaginian continued: 'I, Hannibal, asked you for this peace.'

Scipio finally replied with the voice of a master; not one that negotiated but one that only dictated. 'Our fathers didn't begin this war, they didn't invade your homeland. You are an honourable man, but your Senate is treacherous. They talk peace and prepare for war. I know well the power of fate, Carthaginian, just as I know that everything in battle is left to chance. So be it. Let the gods decide.'[6] Scipio had obeyed the age-old rule that one does not trade with the enemy in wartime.

Slowly, both turned their horses and rode back to their lines.

Hannibal had missed his opportunity for surprise when he found Scipio's army already arrayed in echelons, screened by a thin line of archers. The Carthaginian heavy infantry had taken up its battle positions, but no major clashes had been reported so far, only the usual flurries between small troops of opposing cavalry. Hannibal's heavy *scutarii*, recognisable by their white tunics edged in purple, were massed in the centre, their long oval shields rammed into the ground. Across their front, Hannibal had concentrated all his elephants. Accompanied by his generals, he rode along the line and halted on a small rise. With a stentorian voice that belied his small figure, he shouted: 'Men of Carthage, you have covered yourself with eternal glory in many battles in the enemy's homelands. Now you must do the same at the gates of your own beloved city. You and you alone are Carthage's protectors. The time is now to show the Romans our sharpened swords.' A great clamour rose as they hailed their charismatic leader.

[6] M. Jelusich, *Hannibal*, Vienna, 1934 (after Titus Livius).

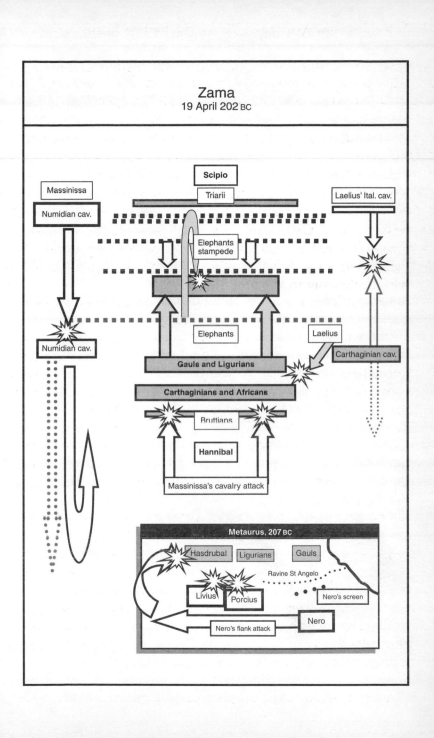

Scipio studied his enemy's line-up. He was about to address his troops, to inflame their patriotic enthusiasm and spur on their hatred of the enemy. But then something happened which upset his well-laid plans. Fired on by the speech of Hannibal, a small group of war-hardened Africans stormed ahead and entered into a skirmish with a group of Roman *hastati*, and before the flames could be put out this small incident had flared into a regular forest fire. The battle was on. The plans both leaders had laid were thrown out by a sudden spark that ignited a storm, a spark that would spread flames, blood and death all over the wide field. The sun was already unbearably hot when tens of thousands of steel statues came to life and advanced rapidly on each other. Nothing could now stop them. The field became an immense frieze as every legion and every infantry unit rushed ahead, their shields painted in bright colours to identify each individual unit. Only this was no fairytale make-believe; these were living, breathing men about to fall upon each other in deadly combat. Whoever fell was lost, dragged under and trampled by the following masses.

'Attack with the cavalry!' From the Roman flank phalanx came Massinissa's Numidian riders. They were immediately challenged by a similar attack from Hannibal's Numidian cavalry. But Massinissa's men seemed to win the race; his riders were just a little faster, or perhaps more lucky in their choice of terrain, and hit the Carthaginian Numidians side-on. A brief rider battle developed between the 'enemy brothers'. Massinissa not only had a numerical superiority but the fighting power of his troops had been honed to perfection by Hannibal himself in the many battles from Hispania to Cannae. Now they were using their experience against their former field commander. Within minutes they had scattered Hannibal's riders and put them to flight. Rather than wheeling inward, towards Hannibal's flanks, Massinissa led his horde in a wild chase after their enemy brothers down the field and, presently, took no more part in the battle with Scipio's foot-soldiery. Almost the same combat occurred on the other wing, where Laelius's Latin cavalry fought and chased after the Carthaginian cavalry, and then left Scipio without his precious riders.

On Hannibal's signal the master of elephants set his huge grey monsters crashing forward in an unstoppable juggernaut. They had been near indestructible before, but now the Romans had devised a new element: their phalanx split apart to allow for open lanes. With pikes and lances, the legionaries funnelled the elephants into these open channels; lithe *velites* ran alongside the trampling elephants, slashing at their trunks and underbellies with specially lengthened sickle-lances. They became so caught up in their deadly game that a number fell victim to their own daring. If an elephant turned in their direction, and the *velites* couldn't get out of the elephants' way quickly enough, they were squashed like beetles. Others jumped forth and took their place, and, as the mountains of flesh charged past them, stabbed javelins into their rumps. But nothing seemed able to stop the elephants; the sickle-thrusts only helped enrage the beasts. Their shrill trumpeting drowned out the screams of horror as they mowed down rows of Romans, leaving a welter of dead and dying in their wake. Following right behind the fearsome beasts came Hannibal's veterans, advancing with measured step, clashing their javelins against their shields and with trumpets blaring. At sixty feet from the enemy line they suddenly stopped, and through some gaps in the line dashed men with javelins. They threw a volley into the enemy line-up and then rapidly retreated before the heavies advanced, screaming their throats hoarse. With a tremendous din, the two shield walls crashed into each other. Then came a clash of steel and the thrum of arrows taking flight. The unified frieze dissolved into islets of different colours.

Nobody could escape the inferno of yells and pain and blood. The screams of the wounded and the shrill sound of pipes made for a terrifying music. Under Hannibal's inspired leadership, the determined Carthaginian phalanx attacked with cohesiveness and shock power. They were more ferocious and bloodthirsty than the Romans and pitted themselves against the legions' first-rank *hastati* in a struggle that was both fierce and bloody. The front ranks of the Romans gave under the pressure of the wild elephant charge, hammered into the ground by the fierce Gallic warriors in a massive tangle of flesh, bronze and steel. Scipio's battle formations began to break up; their feet heaved and strained for purchase upon the dry earth. His centre broke from within; his *velites* were mauled and slaughtered; the shield wall of ten was down to five, then three, then a hole. Ever more Ligurians and Gauls poured through the breaches to battle hand to hand with his *triarii*. A cry of dread rose from the terror-stricken pockets of *velites*.

That was when Carthage's fate was decided. It was a minor incident but the decisive one, and nobody could give a clear description of how it came about. This much was certain: a stout-hearted *velite* managed to ram his long pike into the soft behind of a particularly big and aggressive elephant; the pain-stricken animal reared up on its hindlegs and threw off its mahout before it whirled around and headed straight back the way it had come. The elephant must have been the leader of a pack, since in no time its turnabout was copied by a half-dozen maddened beasts; with their trunks upraised and ears wide spread, they plunged back into the line of the advancing Carthaginians and scattered Hannibal's veteran lines, leaving in their wake a mass of trampled bodies. The blaring trumpets of the stampeding elephants gave a signal to the entire herd, which raced out of control into the thick of the battle. In this whirling cauldron of trampling feet and death, fighters threw down their arms to get away from the madly trumpeting, turning elephants. A huge cloud of dust whirled up and fitfully covered this scene of madness; screams of agony were drowned out by the blaring of the mad beasts. There were no survivors who would ever recount the story of these terrible moments; those who managed to escape had been driven mad by the horror of it all.

Taking advantage of this chaos in his enemy's phalanx, Scipio immediately ordered his last reserves of *principes* and *hastati* to strike at the Carthaginian centre. The *hastati* became hopelessly entangled in close-up combat and could make no progress against Hannibal's solid veterans. For a heart-stopping moment everything hung in the balance. Despite the pressure from Scipio's third-line *triarii*, Hannibal might still have achieved victory had it been only an infantry action. But this was not Cannae; and it was no longer Hannibal's brother Mago and his daredevil rider charge of Carthaginians and Numidians who helped decide the outcome. On the same day as Hannibal's cavalry mounts had to be destroyed in Sicily, Mago had been thrown off his horse and killed. No, this was Zama – and the ferocious Numidian Massinissa had switched allegiance. But where was Massinissa? After the initial clash, Hannibal's riders had bolted with Massinissa's Numidians chasing after them until both groups were well out of sight of the battlefield. Scipio looked in distress after his quickly disappearing cavalry. There was no time to lose. It was vital to get Massinissa to attack the Carthaginians' rear. A concentrated rider charge would finish Hannibal more quickly than any amount of heroism by Roman *triarii*. While Scipio's infantry failed to penetrate Hannibal's veteran line, and the Carthaginians were once more gaining the upper hand, he sent two messengers galloping after Massinissa with the order to turn around.

Hannibal marvelled at the spirit of self-sacrifice that

propelled his men forward in suicidal patriotism. They advanced because they trusted him. He sensed that they were going to make it – their pace was quickening. Now again it was Scipio who was hard pressed. Hannibal's veterans had broken through his line and were beginning to encircle his back. The Romans were being swarmed over by maddened Carthaginians, poking in hot rage at the armoured shield wall, when the sound of drumming hooves came with an eerie unreality. When Hannibal looked back it was not forlornly but wildly, in helpless rage. That vile Massinissa, groomed by him for greatness, was stabbing him in the back . . .

Massinissa launched his Numidians at the ragged spear hedge, hastily put up by the surprised Carthaginian veterans. His riders thrust aside the lances and battered down the spearmen. In the cauldron the slaughter continued. The escape lanes were piled high with corpses. The Ligurians stood behind the piles of dead, facing the onslaught; soon they were pressed so close together that they could no longer use their weapons. The Numidians were pressing into them, exacting a terrible toll. Hannibal's veterans were cut down where they stood. The same riders that had destroyed Rome's legions at Cannae, and had then turned into Rome's allies, administered the killing stroke at Zama.

Hannibal rode slowly back to Carthage. Zama was the end of a long dream.

Scipio sat on his horse, his mouth set grimly. He thought he would enjoy watching those who had destroyed Rome's pride at Cannae die. But he could feel no joy. He had to stop the slaughter and give the Carthaginians the chance of an honourable surrender. To his aristocratic way of thinking it was beyond dignity to kill an enemy who could no longer defend himself. The wounded had to be looked after, limbs amputated, wounds cauterised. Those who had been slashed or stabbed beyond hope of recovery had to be put out of their suffering. Riderless horses had to be rounded up, and the dead tallied. Thousands of bodies were strewn over the sands of Zama, crumpled up, legs twisted grotesquely, blind eyes staring in death. Ravens flapped from one body to the next. 'On the Roman side there fell fifteen hundred, on the Carthaginian over twenty thousand.'[7]

The victors reacted in various ways. Some were angry enough to kill any wounded they found. Others simply stared at the carnage in sickening disbelief. Like Hannibal, Scipio climbed on his horse and rode off. He was Roman, not a barbarian revelling in a feast of blood. His last thought concerned the dead. 'Build a funeral pyre and burn those who fell.'

'What about the Carthaginians?'

'They fought just as heroically. In death, there is no difference.'

For Scipio it had been a close call. Hannibal lost, but not by much. One incident made the difference. In the end, the old master had produced his crowning masterpiece by giving his young rival a lesson in tactics. Trying to pull the Numidian riders from the field with a fake retreat was pure genius. It almost worked. Without Massinissa's last-minute intervention, the battle would have gone Hannibal's way. In the long run, the near run battle did save his city and induced the Romans to seek peace. Just as Hannibal couldn't take Rome by storm, Scipio refrained from attacking fortified Carthage, and a fragile peace was concluded.

Despite objections by the hostile Hanno clan, the people of Carthage chose Hannibal as their new governor. In the years that followed, this honest Carthaginian tried in vain to overcome the rot and injustice that plagued the city. He

[7] Polybius (XV, 14).

remained upright even when his enemies vilified him. His end came as the Oracle had predicted, when the mob turned on good men and true and then dragged their prophets to the altar of sacrifice. What Roman arms had never achieved, his jealous detractors did. His own betrayed Hannibal. Perfidious Carthage! Its Senate collaborated with Rome to hand him over, thinking that this would save their necks. To escape the indignity, Hannibal fled aboard a ship. The Romans chased him across the entire Middle East into Anatolia, where he had obtained the protection of King Prusias of Bythnia.[8] It didn't come for free; Bythnia was engaged in a war against its neighbour Pergamon. At stake was control over the vital straits from the Black Sea into the Mediterranean. Hannibal played a significant role in the Bythnians' naval victory when he filled earthen jars with vipers, which were thrown on to the ships of their enemies.

As for his nemesis, Scipio Africanus shone in preparation for a battle when Rome launched an army against Antiochus III, King of Seleucid Syria. In early 192 BC, Scipio crossed the Hellespont and invaded Syria. Before the time came to do battle, Scipio fell ill and had to relinquish his command to Gnaeus Domitius (Magnesia, 190 BC). The winning strategy was entirely Scipio's; the victory laurels went to Domitius. This war would have been forgotten had it not been for a truly historic event. Hannibal Barka and Publius Cornelius Scipio Africanus Major were to meet one final time. Contemporary historians recorded their encounter and placed it in Ephesus in 192 BC.

Scipio Africanus: 'Who do you consider the greatest military genius?'

Hannibal: 'Alexander of Macedonia.'

'And second place?'

---

[8] The Kingdom of Bythnia was located between the Black Sea and the Marmara Sea.

'Pyrrhus of Epirote.'

'So, who would you put in third place?'

Without giving it a thought, Hannibal replied: 'Myself! Already as a youngster I've conquered Iberia. After Heracles I was the first to cross the Alps. Then I moved into Italy and not one of you had the courage to confront me while I burned down 400 of your cities and even threatened Rome itself – and all that without the slightest assistance from Carthage.'[9]

Scipio thought it over. 'But which position would you give yourself had I not defeated you at Zama?'

'Well, in that case I would have put myself above Alexander.'

Scipio, now known as Africanus Major, returned to Rome. Weakened by age and illness, the grizzled warrior was of no more use. Enemies in the Senate accused him of embezzlement. The charges were false, but the shame of his people's betrayal pushed him into voluntary retirement. All vestiges of his personality were eradicated. That included proof of his victory at Zama.

'Scipio has been ousted. Does this bring you joy?' King Prusias of Bythnia asked Hannibal about the man who had beaten him in battle.

'Why would it bring me joy? He was the only Roman for whom I had respect.'

'How strange you are, Hannibal. It seems one must defeat you to gain your respect.'

In 183 BC, Rome finally caught up with Hannibal. In a shady political deal, Roman consul Flamininus promised King Prusias Rome's military assistance in Bythnia's on-going war against Pergamon. The price was nothing less than the head of Hannibal.

'He is my guest, and a guest's life is sacred,' replied King Prusias.

---

[9] A. Müller, *Gespräche zur Weltgeschichte*, Stuttgart, 1965.

'And the assistance you've asked for?'

'That it has come to this! I, mightiest of kings, have to ask a favour from a commoner.'

Flaminius looked angry. 'I am not a commoner! I am a consul of Rome.'

The sly Prusias retracted quickly. 'So be it, then. I shall prevent Hannibal from crossing my country's borders.'

'King, you grant something which Rome has already acquired by the might of its arms. No, the Senate expects you to give them proof that you have more than just your benefit on your mind. They demand Hannibal.'

'And what price is Rome willing to pay for it? My people love Hannibal. Should I betray Hannibal, they might betray me.'

'The day Hannibal is delivered to me, Rome will pay its debt.'

Perfidious Rome – in the Battle of Magnesia, Pergamonian cavalry had been instrumental in helping them defeat King Antochius of Syria, and now they traded their friendship for the head of one man. And so it was. Once realpolitik won over honour, Hannibal's fate was sealed.

The following morning the Carthaginian woke up to discover that his residence at Libyssa (Brousse) was surrounded by soldiers, that all exits were blocked and that his host was ready to hand him over to a Roman consul. Hannibal, tortured by self-doubts and old beyond his sixty-four years, had reached the end of his long 'legendary march'. But in his final moments there was something magnificent about the man who had defied antiquity's superpower for so many years. The great Hannibal seemed to be rising out of his tomb as much as preparing to descend into it. He saw the ghosts waiting for him – his father drowned in the flood, his brothers going to their death in battle. To die by violence was the fate of the Barkas. His turn had come.

'You, gods of vengeance, I call upon you to witness the

murder of an invited guest and to punish the death of a defenceless man. Cursed be the King of Bythnia who betrayed his guest. And may destruction rain on Rome.'

The young Roman centurion who had been sent for him was awed by the presence of the greatest of all enemies his country ever faced: 'Great Hannibal, do not leave with a curse on your lips. Go in peace.'

'Peace, my son, I have never known. I cannot help it, as long as I shall breathe lives in me an oath I have given as a child. But all this seems a thing of the past. Grass is already growing over our battlefields. A new generation has taken over, soon all will be forgotten. Our names will become the dust the winds scatter.' He could not have been more wrong. In the millennia to come, the name of Hannibal was linked with greatness, the eternal symbol of courage and genius.

Never was anything bolder than his countenance, never anything more defiant than the look on his face the moment he raised the poison cup to his lips, and drank it. His voluntary death was his last act of contempt in adversity, the ultimate gesture of veracity before himself and history.

When they came to tell Scipio Africanus, he looked at the sky: 'I mourn for the man, not for the Carthaginian.' The people of Carthage and Rome paid homage to Hannibal's immense courage. His coffin was carried by a detachment of Roman soldiers and he was laid to rest with great honours in a marble tomb at Heraclea on the shore of the Pontus Euxenius (Black Sea).

Scipio's words were engraved on the great Carthaginian's tombstone. '*Ingratia patria!* You do not even have my bones.' His stele stood for well over a thousand years, before rampaging Turks destroyed it.

It is one of the great ironies that two great men, true giants among history's military leaders, shared an almost

equal fate. Scipio, honoured in parades, cheered by count-
less thousands as the saviour of Rome, decorated on the
steps of the Forum with the victor's laurels and given
the honorific title of 'Africanus Major' by Rome's august
Senate, had become an outcast, living his final years in
seclusion on his Naples estates.

The Roman survived his Carthaginian rival by only three
months. Like Hannibal, Publius Cornelius Scipio Africanus
Major died alone. 'I want to be remembered for who I was
and what I fought for – nothing more and nothing less.'
History granted his last wish.

As for Carthage, its perfidy could not save it. The
city died thirty-seven years after Hannibal. Its end was as
swift as it was brutal. The hate prevailed. Cato, leader of
the Senate's majority, fired his people on with: '*Ceterum
censeo Carthaginem esse delendam* . . . I hold the strong
belief that Carthage must be destroyed.'

Had Hannibal's wise counsel prevailed over that of a
corrupt and weak Senate, Carthage might have been spared
the final spasm of terror; but gone were the days when a
charismatic Hannibal could inspire men to come to their
country's salvation. The fear and weakness of its rich traders and rulers were ruthlessly laid bare. Rome demanded
that the population of Carthage move inland and the city be
abandoned, an ultimatum launched by the Carthage-hating
senator Magnus Porcius Cato. The adopted grandson of
Scipio Africanus, Publius Scipio Aemilianus crossed the sea
to lay siege to Carthage. For weeks the city had been cut off
from all outside help by a ring of Roman legions. Starvation
and contagious diseases decimated it; nine-tenths of its
population had succumbed and the rest were confronted
with the prospect of death by Roman sword. In 147 BC,
on the evening before Scipio Aemilianus prepared his final
assault, he gathered his army and pronounced the *devotio*,
calling upon the infernal gods to punish Rome's enemies.

'Disperse them for ever, seed terror and fright on this

town of Carthage and its army which I am calling by its true name. Those who bear arms and launch their shafts against our legions and our army, make them disappear, and take away the light from this army, these enemies, their men of the cities, their fields and all the inhabitants of these regions.'[10] After almost seventy years to the day, the avengers of Cannae were ready, their eyes filled with hatred.

It was noon, and the town lay dead without shadow when the Roman army climbed over the walls and went murdering down the streets. In the last stage of the siege, Scipio Aemilianus tried to show some of the noblesse of his namesake, Scipio Africanus, but his Senate had given strict instructions to devastate the city. The Romans turned the white pearl of the Mediterranean into a ghost town, lifeless and desolate, with only heaps of rubble to mark where the houses of patricians had once stood. And beneath the pathetic mounds of stones and timber lay its owners, those who had betrayed Hannibal. For seventeen days the town burned. After which Rome's legionaries spread salt on the ground to render the earth infertile. No destruction of a major city before or after, including the destruction caused by the atomic bombs, came anywhere near what happened to Carthage. It vanished as if it had never existed.

It was left to Julius Caesar's geopolitical overview to recognise its location for its strategic and commercial importance. In 46 BC he laid the foundation for a New Carthage. Roman colonnades and amphitheatres replaced Baal's temple, and the language spoken was Latin. Following Caesar's assassination, Octavian completed his uncle's work, and, as Emperor Augustus, he forced his 'Pax Romana' on the world of antiquity, now possible thanks to the disappearance of Rome's greatest Mediterranean rival.

*   *   *

10 *devotio* from *devotare*, to cast an evil spell. Recorded by the Roman Proconsul of Africa Macrobius, *Saturnales* (III, 9).

The decision over who should rule the ancient world is the story of two battles.

First came Cannae, planned by one man, executed by one man and won by one man. It was perhaps the best example on record of a victory that did not depend on chance and stupidity. Hannibal's best troops had attacked his enemy's worst, whilst Varro's battle-hardened Roman legions in the centre were pinned down by Carthage's auxiliaries. Cannae was the classical set piece of annihilation. And yet the Battle of Cannae decided nothing. Zama decided everything, and thereby became the hinge of history. It was Hannibal's Waterloo, the result of the shock effect produced by the outcry '*Hannibal ad portas!*' It woke a complacent Rome and led it to its final greatness. When all seemed lost, the Roman phoenix rose from the ashes, created a mighty war machine and then used it to conquer the world.

Until the end, politics, and its relationship to Carthaginian power, was an integral part of Hannibal's strategy, but the analysis of his campaigns by his contemporaries, mostly Romans and Greeks, focused entirely on the purely military aspect. The impact of his campaigns on Rome had been so deep that the defeat in his final year did nothing to reduce his stature. Roman military leaders studied his campaigns and regarded them as the summit of warfare; they tried to elucidate the secrets of the Carthaginian's strategic thoughts and operational moves, not to understand what he had done but to prepare for future wars.

Hannibal's greatness lay in his extraordinary faculty for surmounting impossible odds. By getting inside the mind of his opponent, he proceeded from deduction to planning to action. He was prepared to take enormous risks, but he could also limit his ambition. His operational opportunism made use of no standardised, predetermined methods, only the fullest possible exploitation of openings by any means available to him. His consummate tactical and strategic skills under formidable odds, facing the most dynamic and militarily efficient of nations, reserve him a place as one of the three greatest generals of all time.

At the Battle of Zama, Scipio Africanus used his imagination to work out the strategy of his opponent before he engaged his forces in the decisive combat. Even that might not have worked but for an elephant that turned the wrong way. Luck is always on the side of the victor. 'To the Carthaginians it was a struggle for their own lives – to the Romans a battle for universal dominion and supremacy.'[11]

Before Metaurus, Rome was an Italian military nation; after Zama, it became antiquity's superpower.

[11] ibid. (XV, 9).

Part Four

The Caesars

102–44 BC

(Marius to Caesar)

'Oderint, dum metuant.'
('Let them hate so long as they fear.')
Cicero (106–43 BC), *Philippic*

9

The Guardian of Rome

Aquae Sextiae
2 July 102 BC

'On the field of battle it is a disgrace to the chief to be surpassed in valour by his companions, and a disgrace to the companions not to come up to the valour of their chief. The chiefs fight for victory, the companions for their chief.'

Tacitus, *Germania*

Consul Caius Marius was the guardian angel of Rome. On the basis of an objective look at history, Marius did more for the survival of Rome than others would ever manage. He saved it from certain destruction, nothing less. Fortunately for posterity, two Roman scribes recorded his exploits – Tacitus and Plutarch.

The men who led Rome's armies were subservient to the Senate. They were guided by the Senate and they executed the orders of the Senate, after which they were expected to retire to their estates, given to them by the Senate, to grow grapes, but never to enter politics. This changed suddenly under an aristocrat by birth and a populist by choice, Gaius Gracchus, who formed a plebeian party (135–121 BC) and then led the *populares* in taking over the Senate. Following his death on order of the patricians in the Senate, the *populares* elected an obscure general six consecutive times as their representative and consul. His name was Gaius Marius.

In 113 BC, according to the Roman calendar DCXL (or 640 years after the foundation of Rome in 753 BC), out of the dense forests along the northern bank of the Danube in Noricum (Austria) appeared suddenly vast hordes of blond, blue-eyed giants, so tall that the Roman garrison of Carnuntum on the Danube took only one look at them, threw away their arms and ran. These were the *Caempir* (in German *Kämpfer* or warrior, what the Romans called *Cimbri*) and the *Teuton*. Torrential floods had devastated their native lands (Schleswig-Holstein and Denmark's Jutland peninsula) and forced them to wander off in search of new pastures. They gathered their wives, their cows, their cooking pots and their swords and set off on a long march. From Austria, where they had been blocked by a Roman legion under the consul Papirius Carbo and soundly thrashed him, their huge masses moved into Helvetia (Switzerland), where they were joined by another warrior tribe, the *Ambrons*. All three were first reported in Gaul (France) in 110 BC, moving down the Rhône valley. The Roman consul Silanus met the tribal leaders, took a look at the huge mass, and haughtily denied their request for land to settle on. He greatly underestimated the potential threat to Italy by this human wave on the move. Silanus tried to bar their route, but his makeshift force, made up mainly of reservists and untrained call-ups, suffered the same disastrous fate as had befallen the men of Consul Carbo before him. Most of the 200,000 Romans died under the battle-axes of the blond giants. What Silanus could not achieve with 200,000, Consul Mallius Maximus next tried with 80,000 trained Roman legionaries. In 105 BC, he met the tribes at

Arausio (Orange) on the Rhône. It turned into one of
the worst disasters to befall Roman arms. Confronted
by the howling mass of Nordic giants, the legionaries
broke ranks and fled in terror. In their attempt to escape
across the wide Rhône, all were killed. After the battle, the
victors rounded up 40,000 Roman non-combatants and
butchered them.

Suddenly the spectre of an invasion of the Italian homelands loomed. Nothing stood between the blond barbarians
and the Italian peninsula, nothing but a few demoralised
cohorts cowering behind the walls of Massalia (Marseilles).
Rome's citizens shivered with fright, its Senate panicked
and called on their specialist, Consul Gaius Marius. He
was a man of solid peasant stock, a freeborn Roman citizen
but never part of the ruling patrician caste. With his rustic
smartness and a cool head in difficult situations, he had
climbed the military ladder. As Praetor he had subdued the
rebellious tribes of Spain. At the time of the Arausio disaster
he was in North Africa, busy dealing out bloody noses
to the ferocious Numidians. With its customary perfidy,
Rome had attacked the warriors, which had led Scipio
Africanus to victory over Hannibal. With his experience,
Marius became Rome's guardian, its last hope of salvation.
His first task was to stop the barbarians from invading
Provincia Romana (Provence).

Together with his staff, which included the young quaestor Lucius Cornelius Sulla, a man destined to play a
decisive role in the consul's life, he sailed for Massalia.
What awaited him on his arrival was a shameful episode,
which exposed the weakness of Rome's defences and the
cowardice of its troops. The handful of legionaries was disorganised, badly armed and their morale at zero. Marius's
initial task was to make them overcome their fright of the
Teutonic giants, and to instil confidence in their ranks.
There was nothing he could do about the barbarians until
his demoralised troops were reorganised. Luck was with

him. It was late in the season, and the Cimbri, Ambrons and Teuton decided to halt their drive south and pitch winter camp along the Rhône near Avignon, before attempting the dangerous river crossing in the coming spring. An intertribal quarrel made the Cimbri split off from the Teuton and Ambrons. They left to go looting in Spain, but were stopped in the Pyrenean passes by Celtic Iberians. The Cimbri's departure reduced the tribes' overall effective, but their numerical superiority was still ten to one.

Winter bought Marius precious months, which he used with rigorous training and indoctrination sessions. Thereby Marius became the initiator of psychological warfare. 'The Teuton are no super-race,' he kept drumming into his men in daily sessions. 'We will beat the barbarians.' He didn't say openly that they could never confront the huge Teutonic force in battle, unless the most favourable circumstances prevailed. The tribes had in excess of 200,000 tough, well-armed warriors, in contrast to his 20,000 legionaries.

Marius was a highly superstitious man who believed in the stars, in sacrifices and oracles, and he offered battle only after having received the divine blessing of a superior being. For this he always kept a personal oracle by his side, a woman known as Martha the Enchantress. In a purple robe, holding a spear garlanded with ribbons over her head, Martha offered animal sacrifices to the gods and divined the future from the ashes of their bones. She advised Marius to be patient, and Marius trusted her. In this he was well advised.

He passed the winter of 103/102 BC in camp at Ernaginum (St Gabriel in the Camargue). With the first warm rays of the spring sun, hordes of Teuton and Ambrons moved against his fortified camp. They didn't try to take it by storm, only taunted the Romans with insults to lure them outside their defences. Marius would have none of it; he was there to save Rome, not to engage in a silly skirmish that he couldn't possibly win. He even refused to be provoked into a one-on-one combat with a Teuton chief. Not to be accused of cowardice, Marius justified himself to his men: 'It is not a question of gaining personal triumphs and trophies, but of averting the storm of war and saving Rome.' When the Teuton chief kept insisting, Marius sent a gladiator to take his place. There is no record of the fight's outcome.

After some weeks of the two sides throwing spears and insults at each other, the undisciplined rabble became tired of lying in wait before Ernaginum's spiked defences. They gave up in order to continue their march south (102 BC). For six full days from his position up on high (Les Baux), Marius watched an endless stream of carts move past in the valley, before he set off in pursuit. The huge mass of warriors, women, carts and livestock threaded its way painfully through the many marshes and lagoons of the Camargue, before it crossed the Rhône unmolested and then marched along the River Durance. Marius and his twenty thousand legionaries, from safe positions on the ridge of the Luberon mountain range, closely monitored their slow progress. Since the Roman consul refused to enter into a fight, the next few months turned into a stand-off. The Teuton mocked Roman sentries lining the cliffs above them: 'Do you have any message for your wives? We shall soon be with them, sleeping in your beds.' The legionaries, condemned to inactivity on the high ground, began to suffer from lack of water. They displayed an increasing impatience, if not rebelliousness, to a point where they actually spoiled for a fight. That again suited Marius.

'Why don't you lead us down before our blood is parched?' his thirsty legionaries wanted to know.

'All in good time,' their consul answered. His strategy was quite simple: make the enemies feel complacent and, at the same time, increase the combative spirit of his own legions. Yet before he could even consider an attack he had to split the two tribes into a 'manageable size'. One of his young sub-lieutenants, Serorius, had been stationed on the Danube and spoke fluent Teuton; one night he wandered into the barbarian camp and pretended to have escaped from the Roman prison in Massalia. He whetted their appetite by telling them about a city of immense treasures, practically bereft of outer defences and theirs for the taking. This did the trick. Next day, near Aquae Sextiae Salluviorum (Aix-en-Provence), the Teuton decided to split from the Ambrons and head for the gold of Massalia. This separated the tribes by a day's march.

'My legions can take on the barbarians one at a time. But we must get them on to a decent killing-ground. Until now they've been too smart to get caught that way.' Even the smart make mistakes. A 'decent killing-ground' was found when the Ambrons reached the valley of the Arc, a lovely place with gentle slopes and warm springs. Roman families from Aix were using it as their favourite spa. The Ambrons camped in this paradisiacal valley near the wells, while the legionaries were up in the hills and still thirsty.

'Gaius Marius, we must have water or we shall die of thirst.'

'So you will, but you must earn your water with your blood,' replied their leader, and thereby guided them into action without them knowing it. The incident that followed was insignificant in itself but it helped change history. A Roman maniple, so thirsty that they were willing to break ranks, decided to tempt fate and take what was needed; with pails and buckets, and armed with their swords, they ran down the hill to fetch water. They met a bunch of tribal women doing their washing, protected by a handful of warriors. Since there were many more Romans than blond giants, the legionaries quickly took care of the barbarians. Their screams brought a few more Ambrons on to the scene, some of them straight from their luxuriating bath in the hot springs, unarmed and having to do battle with their bare fists. The well-trained, heavily armed Romans easily overcame them. More legionaries hurried downhill to help their comrades, and soon a regular combat developed as barbarians in increasing numbers rushed into the fray. The Ambrons kept arriving in mobs, the Romans in maniples. The barbarians didn't stand a chance against the disciplined legions. A well-orchestrated incident had removed the decision from Marius. Like an armoured flood, his legions rolled down the slopes and, with fierce determination, waded into the blond giants to split them up into smaller groups, to be hacked to pieces by a solidly anchored Roman phalanx. With their tribe's battle cry of '*Ambra!*', even the Ambron women picked up arms. To no avail – the idyllic Arc creek was choked with the bodies of dead and dying barbarians. 'A crying was heard from the defeated Ambrons all through the night, not the sighs and groans of men but like the howling and bellowing of wild beasts.'[1] And so the Ambron nation died.

Marius had no time to savour victory. His spies informed him that the frightful Teuton were near by. Their expected attack didn't materialise, but this still left Marius with the problem of handling the much bigger tribe of Teuton. Retreat into the hills? For that it was too late; a decision was forced on him forty-eight hours later. His scouts kept him abreast of the Teuton's every move. The tribe had entered a parallel valley. Just before darkness, Marius set off with a few companions. They slid from their horses and climbed the hill that separated his legions from the barbarians. The woods were deathly silent – no birds, no ground creatures and certainly no people; they had fled before the wave of Teuton. Ahead lay what looked like a pass. The slope leading up was steep but not impassable. Then they were on top, with a clear view of the valley

[1] Plutarch.

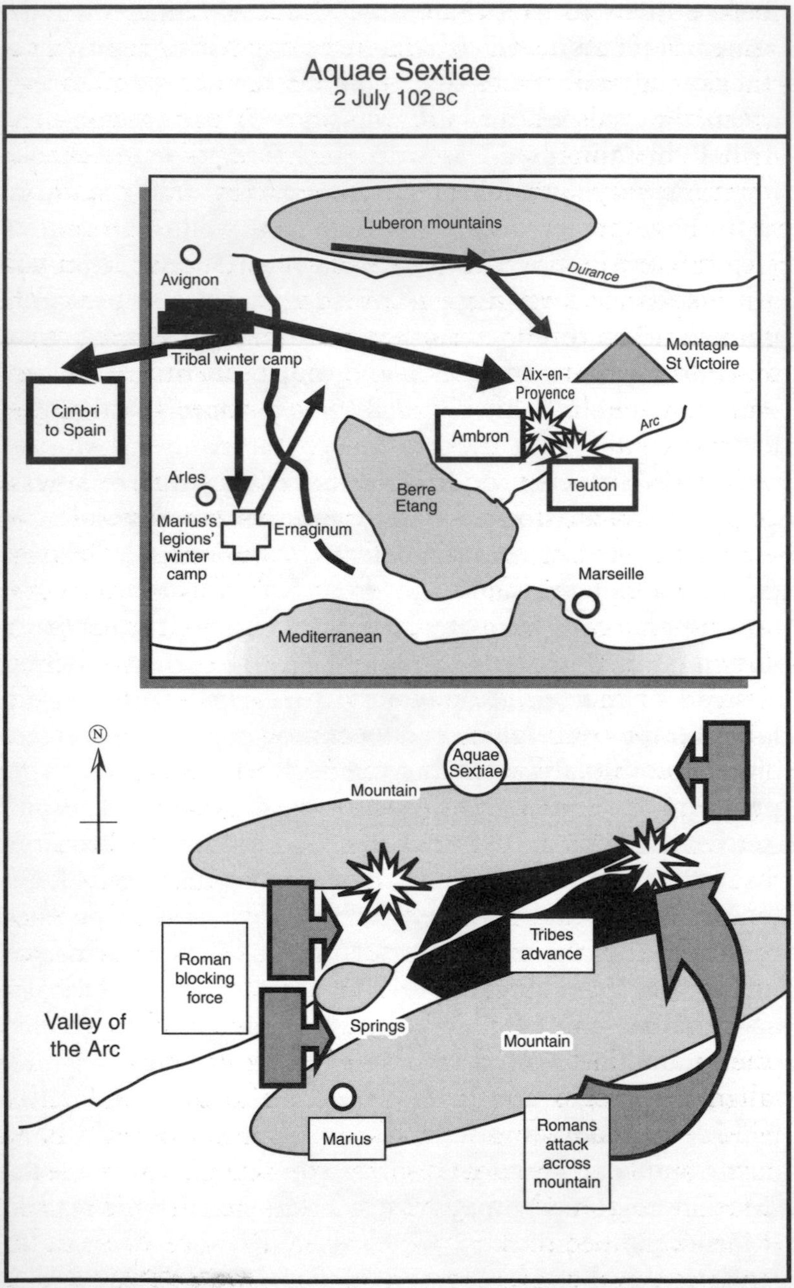

Aquae Sextiae
2 July 102 BC
Luberon mountains
Avignon
Durance
Tribal winter camp
Cimbri to Spain
Montagne St Victoire
Aix-en-Provence
Arc
Ambron
Teuton
Arles
Berre Etang
Marius's legions' winter camp
Ernaginum
Marseille
Mediterranean
N
Aquae Sextiae
Mountain
Tribes advance
Roman blocking force
Valley of the Arc
Springs
Mountain
Marius
Romans attack across mountain

before them and its thousands of campfires. Quite foolishly, the Teutonic force had settled down in an area where
they could easily be trapped – if there was an army to trap
them! For this Marius's legions weren't big enough. The
tribal chieftains had a right to behave confidently. In the
morning they would head from the valley and spread out
into the unprotected lands beyond. A feeling of imminent
death was in the air. Marius knew that he was defending
the last barrier between this immense horde and Rome. He
looked down on the massed forces and scoffed. He would
have to reorganise his men and plan something different
and new. He had a few ideas; he only hoped that the god
of war would grant him his chance.

Marius threw away the textbook. His plan was founded
on desperation. In war this is known as 'the best solution
in a series of bad options'. He would use each cohort as
an individual fighting force instead of integrating it into
a solid phalanx. Each cohort was to put up a frontage of
fifty men, with an interval of six feet between each fighter,
instead of the *testudo* of interlinked shields. This would
allow for more room to wield swords, and it lengthened
his line considerably. It also doubled the effect of available
manpower. And he added a surprise. If Hannibal could
move his elephants across the Alps, his men could surely
overcome a pine-covered mountain. During the night, he
ordered three thousand of his élite, with Tribune Claudius
Marcellus in the lead, to cross over the mountain pass
and be prepared to barricade the valley to the rear of
the Teuton while with his main force he marched around
the mountain to block the front exit from the valley. He
aligned his legions in his novel tactical order, the flexible
chequerboard line-up that was to revolutionise the Roman
army and bear his name over the following centuries – the
Marian Legion. Once all this was done to his satisfaction,
Marius climbed to the top of a hill so that every one of his
cohorts could clearly see him. He knew what the presence

of a general meant to the morale of the troops – many a battle had been forfeited because a leader had lost sight of what was happening on the battlefield and therefore failed to react to a rapidly developing situation. Perhaps it was less courageous to stand on a hill than to fight in the midst of the slaughter, but he considered courage a futile attribute when exchanged for a commander's overview.

He had given precise instructions to his first blocking screen; their advanced ranks were to make noise, then break and run as if stricken by panic, sucking the enemy into the trap. That was what they did, and the Teuton took the bait. With fierce battle cries, the giants of the North dashed after the fleeing Romans, as their womenfolk screamed encouragement and rattled their war drums.

'Sound the battle horns,' ordered Marius. At the blare of tubas a wall of pointed steel stepped from its hiding place behind the cover of a gully, to face the oncoming barbarians. At this critical moment, more Roman horns sounded; this time they came from the rear of the valley. The legionaries surged down on the blond giants with a violence that left no doubt about their determination. The Teuton were so surprised that they halted amid shouts and stares of bewilderment. The moral effect of this shock attack from their rear was devastating; the barbarians wheeled around in confusion, which got them hopelessly entangled. The Romans had bottled up both exits from the valley. Marius, a figure in the scarlet cloak of an *imperator* (general), stood out like a beacon on a promontory. He ordered his trumpeters to sound the call for advance. His cohorts wheeled into squares and bore down on the chaotic Teuton. The first two ranks used their stabbing pikes, while the rear ranks threw *pili* (javelins) into the enemy beyond. Most javelins were used several times, pulled by the advancing legionaries from corpses. With the Teuton compressed from front and back, between cliffs on both sides, the battle turned into carnage, the ground piled high with the bodies of the fallen. Plutarch recorded hundreds of thousands killed and eighty thousand women and children dragged off into slavery. The fact is that not many of the Ambrons and Teuton survived. Weak and wretched captives were becoming no longer just a nuisance that had to be fed, but a living threat to the security and even the lives of their conquerors in the shiny trappings of Marius's legions. Several hundred thousand were marched up the steep slopes of the Montagne St Victoire,[2] that huge blue-and-white rock rising steeply from the Provençal plain, and then pushed at sword point over the cliffs. They left the heaps of dead and dying, the thousands of naked, interlocked bodies, to rot in the summer heat, giving off a smell so putrid that it forced the citizens of Aix-en-Provence to flee the nauseating stench. Campi Putridi (Fields of Putrefaction) they called the area then, and the village that stands on its location today is still called Pourrières (French for rotten).

One danger still remained – that of the Cimbri, who had turned back from the Pyrenees and were headed for a confrontation with the Romans. Once more, Marius rushed to Rome's rescue, this time with a rebuilt Roman force. The battle against the Teuton had proved the value of his new tactical formation, and the Battle of Vercellae (101 BC) was a repeat of his previous victories; the consul's cohorts and his Thracian cavalry annihilated the Cimbri: 140,000 were killed or executed on the battlefield, and 60,000 non-combatants were sent into salt mines and their women into brothels. At Vercellae, as at Aquae Sextiae, Marius left behind heaps of corrupting dead.

After Aquae Sextiae and Vercellae, Marius was hailed as the guardian of Rome and elected consul six consecutive times. However, his political acumen did not match his

---

[2] Mons Venturi, known since the sixteenth century as Montagne St Victoire in honour of Marius's victory.

military talent, and his misrule led to a frightful civil war (91–88 BC), the worst in Roman history as it was fought on the streets of Rome. The adversary of the plebeian Marius was his former quaestor, the conservative Sulla, who carried the opening battle. Marius fled to Africa, but was brought back by the democrat Lucius Cinna. Marius instituted a reign of terror which found its parallel two thousand years later in Robespierre's Terror during the French Revolution (1794). Rome's civil war was eventually settled by Sulla (82 BC), who defeated a democratic force, seized Rome and declared himself dictator. The guardian of Rome, Gaius Marius, ended his days as an outcast in Africa, hunted down by Gnaeus Pompeius (Pompey).

Marius bequeathed to Rome a superb military reform. The disaster of Arausio (105 BC) had clearly demonstrated the necessity for a change in Rome's military system, and Marius was its reformer. The plebeian Marius abandoned all aristocratic distinctions within the military class and forced the Senate to appoint commanders by virtue of talent and not birthright. The average legionary was courageous, well fed and well muscled; his award for brave conduct was a plot of land from his *imperator*, its size according to the bravery shown. The *equites* (patrician cavalry, routed at Cannae), a unit reserved formerly to the sons of nobility, disappeared completely; it was replaced by a corps of professional cavalry, made up of foreign mercenaries from Numidia, Thrace or Hispania. They were formed into *alae* (wings) and officered by Romans. Though they lacked the patriotic ardour of Rome's former legions, they made up for it with their skill and professionalism. This helped Imperator Marius to create with his Marian Legion a system of interchangeable units of great operational flexibility and manoeuvrability, a powerful military tool which he passed on to his nephew, the man who was soon to follow in his footsteps and finally make Rome into a world power: Gaius Julius Caesar.

*   *   *

The two victories at Aquae Sextiae were brought about
by necessity. Owing to his inferior manpower resources,
Marius was forced to adopt a tactical system that became
the key to a sweeping military reform. Not realising the
full impact of his innovation, he provided the key element
for the Great Roman Conquest.

Marius had brought the barbarians to a halt at the gate
of Italy. Now it was up to a younger man to conquer
the world.

10

The Fury of Caesar
Treveri
14 May 55 BC

'Tu regere imperio populos, Romane, memento!
Pacique imponere morem! Parcere subiectis et debellare
superbos.'
('O Romans, be it in your care to rule the nations with
imperial sway.
To impose the rule of peace, to spare the humbled and crush
the proud.')

Virgil (70–19 BC), *Aeneid*

Anyone with authority or inspiration can push men into
battle. For this shepherding of sheep to the slaughter,
a practised demagogue holds a definite advantage. The
fundamental difference between Caesar and his opponents
was that Caesar would not give battle unless sure of an
initial advantage, and perhaps not even then, whereas his
opponents were ready to take to the offensive whatever
their disadvantages. He understood how to obtain more
profit at less cost. In this manner, Caesar was a master of
his art; his adversaries were not.

He did not possess the military brilliance of an Alexander
or a Hannibal, but then he had something just as vital
for success: luck. In the long history of warfare there is
no general that has ever been luckier. Granted, with his

audacity and overriding energy he made his own luck. Furthermore, he grasped the nature of warfare in his age, and formed his army into a devastatingly efficient instrument to deploy his special skills. In whatever endeavour he was engaged, be it in Spain, in Gaul, during the civil war in Rome or in Egypt, by his charismatic leadership he assured himself of the unquestioned loyalty of his troops. His talents were unique; never subsequently has anybody been able to combine the qualities of great captain, statesman, diplomat, lawgiver and author. He funnelled all the means at his disposal – men, money and politics – towards one end, and one end only: the grand strategy of winning power. His military successes were founded on a basic principle: act quickly before the crisis increases and the danger multiplies, and once you cross the threshold of force, strike with everything you've got and do not stop until the enemy is completely annihilated. Only once did his luck fail him. On that day he fell victim to the assassin's dagger. But he left history his name, which symbolises the highest authority of any state: a caesar.

Gaius Julius Caesar (born around 102 BC) was a democrat, and, like his uncle, Marius, showed military promise. At twenty the Senate crowned him with the *corona civica* for his amazing victory over the pirates of the Aegean and the part he played in Rome's triumph over King Mithridates (74 BC). In 68 BC he was named quaestor[1] of Hispania Ulterior. He suppressed local uprisings and ended his tenure by conquering the entire Lusitania region to become proconsul of Spain (61 BC). Given the shining example of courage he set, soldiers began to hail him as their *imperator*, an adulation that greatly disturbed the Senate – especially since Caesar was part of the minority popular faction. He was called back to Rome, where his

---

[1] In rank below proconsul.

acid wit quickly earned him the reputation that he was not to be tangled with in open debate. In the power struggle of Senate intrigues he was continuously challenged by Gnaeus Pompeius (called Pompey), recently given a triumphant reception after having stormed Jerusalem and conquered Judaea (63 BC). Caesar knew only too well that he couldn't fight the mighty Pompey on equal terms. 'If you cannot fight them, join them,' goes the saying, and he did, in a triumvirate (60 BC): Pompey, the victorious general from the war against Mithridates (66 BC), Caesar the upstart, and Licinius Crassus, the banker and Rome's wealthiest citizen. Though in no way a general, Crassus 'bought' himself an army, and with it he brutally put down the Spartacus revolt (71 BC), a feat he concluded by having every supporter of the rebel gladiator crucified along the Via Appia. This act went only to prove that Crassus was cruel, but not a danger to the political ascendancy of Caesar, who suggested to his triumvirate partners that they would best serve Rome, and fill their pockets, by looking after 'provinces of extreme wealth' – which happened to be far removed from Rome's seat of power – while he offered to sort things out at home, where riots were erupting and a civil war threatening. With his co-partners out of the way, stuck in some outlying province, Caesar got the Senate to appoint him proconsul of Illyricum (Croatia and Serbia), Cisalpine Gaul (the region north of the Apennine mountains and the Po valley) and Transalpine Gaul (the entire south of France with Provence, Dauphiné and Languedoc), whose former governor had fallen off his horse and died most conveniently, and from where, according to Caesar, 'barbarians were threatening Italy'. His claim carried substance, since only forty-four years before his uncle Marius had brought an invasion of Cimbri, Teuton and Ambron to a halt. There was more to Caesar's planning; his new position as proconsul of both Gauls gave him automatic control over a number of veteran legions.

His military genius was not based in new ideas, but he applied the schemes of other great generals – Alexander, Hannibal, Scipio and his own uncle Marius to perfection. Caesar studied the military reforms that Marius had undertaken, and he was intrigued by the implications of legionaries with space between the members of each cohort, unlike the former formations of the massive, tight phalanx, trained only to face forward and stay there, holding a section of the line with their spears. Caesar's new army was designed for rapid movement and increased strike mobility.

'*Gallia est omnis divisia in partes tres* – Gaul is divided into three parts,' he wrote in the introduction to his monumental commentary on the Gallic War, *De bello gallico*. As general, he saw things differently to the common soldier; as author a posteriori he surveyed the hurried marches, sieges and battles of the general. Caesar the author wrote about Caesar the general in the third person, but in fact he was the same man.

His initial plans were to expand Rome's possessions across the Rhine and march along the Danube, that mythical river which separated Rome's Alpine border from the northern barbarians. But a sudden migration by 385,000 Helvetians moving south along the Rhône and endangering Rome's jewel of Provincia Romana aborted his Danubian plans. With only 34,000 battle-hardened troops, he rushed to meet them. It was the first time he resorted to a strategy of blocking an overpowering enemy with a series of fortresses.

Caesar's scouts had done a thorough job of charting rivers and mountain passes, but here, in the deep forests of the Jura, his legions were stumbling along on tracks that were nothing like the roads the Romans had built to move their legions around their provinces. These were no more than cow trails, where branches whipped at the tunics of the legionaries and fatigue slowed the long column on its forced march. They were tired, but so was the enemy. The Helvetians had marched across ravines and mountains, which wasn't simple with their large train and all the camp followers. And when they set up camp it had no defensive plan to it; no ditches, no sharpened stakes, no neat rows of tents. Crude earthen shelters and hide tents sprouted haphazardly; goats, sheep, horses and pigs wandered about in great profusion. Caesar's men caught the Helvetians during their crossing of the River Arar (Saone). Thirty thousand, still waiting to be ferried on to the left bank, were annihilated, while the rest of the tribe had to watch the slaughter helplessly from the opposite shore.

In July 58 BC, Caesar's legions took care of the remaining Helvetians near Grenoble. With his 30,000 legionnaires, strengthened by 20,000 Gaul auxiliaries of dubious loyalty, Caesar attacked 70,000 Helvetians outside their camp. In a battle that lasted throughout the day, the Romans drove the Helvetians back into their camp, seething with hundreds of thousands of screaming women and children. Caesar used the bedlam for his final attack. It was the first time he showed his real character. The battle had been fierce, and at times it had even looked as if he could lose it. A sacrifice was called for, something to make the gods happy. If the bodies of his vanquished would do it, so be it. There were sacrificial prisoners aplenty. A dreadful scene unfolded in the camp as men, women and children were indiscriminately slaughtered by Caesar's order; 130,000 Helvetian warriors died. The Romans didn't count the women. A special envoy of Rome's Senate was shocked by what he found – a countryside strewn with the mangled corpses of an entire tribe. He demanded justification of the proconsul. Caesar was so convincing in arguing that his men had acted only in self-defence that the envoy declared himself satisfied.

Having eliminated the Helvetian threat, Caesar marched his army on Bibracte (Mount Beuvray) to deal with Chief Dumnoreix of the Eduens, the largest confederation of Gallic tribes in central France. 'For years this man had collected taxes, and had become extremely rich. He kept a personal bodyguard and household cavalry, and with their help, exercised his influence over the neighbouring tribes. He was married to a Helvete princess, and he nourished a personal hate against Caesar and all that was Roman. Furthermore, Caesar's arrival diminished his own power when he openly honoured his brother Diviciacos.'[2] Caesar used his great diplomatic skill to convince Dumnoreix of the grave danger to his rule posed by an invasion by Teutonic tribes under Ariovistus, a threat which, according to Caesar, only his Roman legions could prevent. For this venture he talked the Eduen chieftain into providing him with 4,000 of his Gallic cavalry. With his newly recruited auxiliaries, Caesar hastened to face Ariovistus. On 10 September 58 BC he met up with his 75,000 barbarians near Vesontio (Besançon). He thrashed the Teuton and chased them back across the Rhine. With that success ended the first year of the Gallic War (58 BC). Caesar passed the winter months in Besançon.

In 57 BC, Caesar rushed north and, with his 20,000 legionaries and 20,000 auxiliaries, invaded Belgica. In April, he crossed swords with King Galba's 100,000 tribesmen on the River Axona (Aisne). He thrashed the wild and undisciplined Belgiae, and was annexing their territory when in July he ran into an ambush by the Nervi. The attack came while his legions were strung out along the narrow wooded valley of the River Sabis (Sambre).[3] Seventy-five thousand Nervi tribesmen plunged down from the wooded hills and caught the Romans on

---

2 Caesar, *De bello gallico* (I, 18).
3 The Germans used the same approach in the blitzkrieg of 1940.

the riverbank. Despite the initial shock, Caesar managed to form up his legions and then took the initiative. At day's end, 60,000 dead Nervi floated down the Sambre. Caesar's losses were also considerable and, until he could replenish his legions, he had to postpone his plans for further conquest until the coming year. After his three decisive victories over the northern barbarians, eastern and central Gaul now acknowledged the supremacy of Rome.

While in winter quarters in the Loire valley, he planned a general campaign for 56 BC. He dispatched Publius Crassus with one legion to Aquitania (Aquitaine), Titurius Sabinus into Normandy, while his most talented subordinate, Legate Titus Labienus, faced German barbarians along the Rhine frontier. Caesar, at the head of a number of legions, marched against the Veneti situated in Armorica (Brittany).[4] Five of his officers in Roman regalia preceded him to negotiate a peaceful takeover. The Veneti slapped the Roman envoys in chains and dragged them in a cage all over the country to show their power. They had never before done business with Caesar. Informed of the arrest of his ambassadors, Caesar threatened the Veneti leaders with pillage and murder. The Veneti counted on their fleet to hold off the landlocked Romans. Caesar surprised them by ordering the construction of sixty vessels, and manned them with a legion under Decimus Brutus.[5] While the rest of Caesar's army stood on the shore, a naval battle took place in the Bay of Quiberon between Decimus Brutus and the Veneti. The hastily built Roman ships were no match for the fast, heavier ships of their enemy. The Veneti were gaining the upper hand when Brutus came up with the genial idea of ordering sickles tied to long poles with which the legionaries could slash their enemy's rigging. Soon the Veneti fleet was drifting helplessly in

[4] This episode has become the subject of a popular French cartoon strip, *Astérix*.

[5] Who was to gain notoriety by virtue of Caesar's final exclamation: '*Et tu, Brute?*'

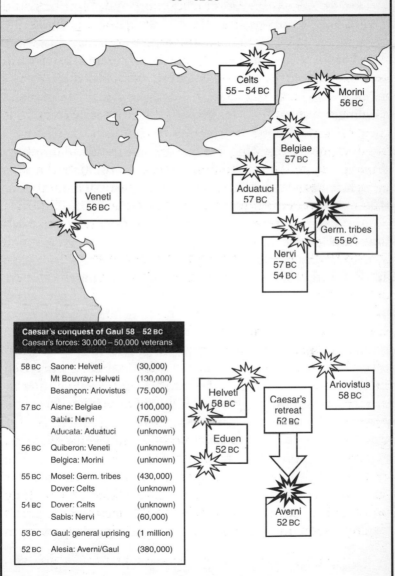

Caesar's Major Encounters in His Conquest of Gaul
58 – 52 BC

Celts
55 – 54 BC

Morini
56 BC

Belgiae
57 BC

Aduatuci
57 BC

Veneti
56 BC

Germ. tribes
55 BC

Nervi
57 BC
54 BC

Caesar's conquest of Gaul 58 – 52 BC
Caesar's forces: 30,000 – 50,000 veterans

58 BC	Saone: Helveti	(30,000)
	Mt Bouvray: Helveti	(130,000)
	Besançon: Ariovistus	(75,000)
57 BC	Aisne: Belgiae	(100,000)
	Sabis: Nervi	(75,000)
	Aducata: Aduatuci	(unknown)
56 BC	Quiberon: Veneti	(unknown)
	Belgica: Morini	(unknown)
55 BC	Mosel: Germ. tribes	(430,000)
	Dover: Celts	(unknown)
54 BC	Dover: Celts	(unknown)
	Sabis: Nervi	(60,000)
53 BC	Gaul: general uprising	(1 million)
52 BC	Alesia: Averni/Gaul	(380,000)

Helveti
58 BC

Ariovistus
58 BC

Caesar's
retreat
52 BC

Eduen
52 BC

Averni
52 BC

the bay. The legionaries boarded the Veneti vessels and killed their sailors. Caesar exacted terrible revenge for the mistreatment of his ambassadors.

During the winter months, Caesar pored over maps of Gaul to work out the manpower he would require for his coming spring campaign. With the snows gone, his legions faced little opposition in attempting to overcome the Morini and Menapi of Belgica (Flanders). With the last redoubt reduced, and the treaty with the Eduen King Dumnoreix holding, most of Gaul was now under Caesar's control. In 55 BC he turned his full attention to subduing the Germanic tribes of the Asipetes and Tencteri, which swarmed into Gaul from across the Rhine. With his hard core of 30,000, Caesar marched against the 430,000 Germans, of which at least 100,000 were armed warriors. Despite the impossible odds, Caesar was by now so convinced that nothing on earth could stand up against his legions that he decided to set an example in order to discourage all further trans-Rhenian adventures by barbarian tribes. Like a python, endless columns of Germans had wound through the valleys between the wooded hills of the Ardennes before they camped along the Mosel river at Treveri (Trier).

Caesar began by playing his diplomatic master card. Throughout the drawn-out talks, he had been purposely stalling the barbarians. He argued that the Rhine constituted a natural geographic demarcation line; the tribal chieftains didn't see it like that. But they couldn't agree on anything, they kept openly bickering, and Caesar exploited his enemy's moral disintegration for his planned offensive purpose. His political and military understanding told him from the beginning that nothing could be gained by negotiation; matters could only be resolved through battle. His long-range appraisal was that Rome could survive an invasion of Gaul for no longer than a year before the tribes from across the Rhine would move south and come knocking on Rome's door. While the talks with the tribal leaders were in progress, and the two forces camped within sight of each other, Caesar was being kept informed of the enemy's plans by a renegade Tencteri tribesman. He told him of the friction between the tribal heads. That suited Caesar well, until the day his spy told him that the barbarians were planning a surprise attack.

The moment had come when Caesar had to decide between attack and retreat. He would fight, but he would decide when. The mass of Germanic tribes was camped on a plain near a dense forest – good for an ambush by cavalry. Caesar had his Gallic auxiliary cavalry officered by Romans. 'They will take away your country.' He made certain they understood that Gaul was *their* country. 'We must stand together to save it,' he told the Gaul riders in a tone as seductive as that of the Pied Piper.

Caesar's preparations for a shock attack were a compound of many deceptive ruses. He diverted the enemy's attention from his steadily increasing troop strength by ordering seemingly useless cavalry parades and routine troop inspections in full sight of the Germans, while surreptitiously moving that same night an entire legion deep into the woods on the flanks of the Germanic camp. Great fires were lit to suggest the continued presence of this legion in camp. Meanwhile cavalry was filtering into the forest to the other flank, where they were concentrated in dense forest.

'We will surprise them,' said Caesar to his officers, then turned to his cavalry commander. 'Ride through the wood and cut them off before their whole army comes through. Jupiter will smile on you.' The tribune Lucius Mancinus spurred his horse into the forest where the cavalry stood. The men mounted as he rode up. The Germans never fought by night; Caesar planned to attack them while they rested around their campfires.

The proconsul was right. On military matters he was rarely wrong. His men were the sinews of his right arm, and they were in battle position, while the barbarians were indeed at rest in their camps, without sentries, without guards. Caesar's trumpets sounded. Everything was drowned out by a scream, bursting forth from many thousands of mouths, which vibrated in the air. It came from Caesar's legions. The barbarians were completely unprepared, and the surprise was total. 'The Romans are coming!' The Germanic chieftains, who had been drinking together, staggered to their feet, jumped on their horses and dashed to rouse the camp. 'Courage, brothers,' one yelled, 'those are the same Romans we've already beaten before. Remember your hatred of anything that is Roman. We shall be masters of this land. Fight, my brothers, fight!' They were already too late to save the situation. When some of the tribes rallied, the Roman ranks were only a javelin's throw away, letting go of their *pili*. A hail of javelins shattered the Germans. Swords flashed along the line of legions. In no time the ground around the camp was strewn with corpses. The Germans hesitated, retreated, and then ran, hotly pursued by Caesar's cavalry, hacking into unprotected backs. The legionaries stumbled after them over dead and wounded, slid in puddles of blood, hurt themselves on the weapons of the dead sticking from the ground. The barbarians were knocked to their knees, flailing their arms. The wave of Romans pushed on, jumping over the fallen. Some tumbled. The follow-up wave flowed over everyone, knocking the fallen ones to their faces and trampling over them. They swept almost unchecked over the stupefied defenders. In the mass of ditches around the camps, the horses of Caesar's cavalry became worthless. The Romans dismounted to attack the barbarians on foot from the flanks. They got in among the Germans, although many were cut down by swipes from vicious battle-axes as more of the Germanic warriors rushed from their campfires to join in the fray.

Caesar rode up to the confused front line and suddenly

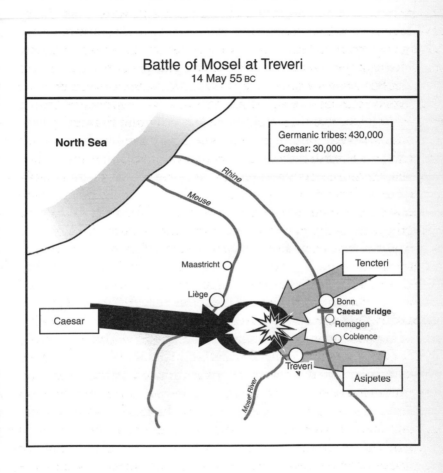

Battle of Mosel at Treveri
14 May 55 BC

North Sea

Rhine

Meuse

Germanic tribes: 430,000
Caesar: 30,000

Maastricht ○

Liège ○

Caesar

Tencteri

Bonn
Caesar Bridge
○ Remagen
○ Coblence

Treveri

Mosel River

Asipetes

found himself amid the barbarians. Hands reached out for him, scratched his skin, and tore off his purple robe. A barbarian with a huge axe thrust out at him. The blade went into Caesar's rearing horse and he was thrown off; before the German warrior could deliver his killer stroke, a legionary dashed to his proconsul's rescue. The German fell, pierced by a lance. Caesar had no time to feel fear; that would come later. Around him the slaughter continued. His legions on the flanks wheeled towards the camp, like a huge door swinging on its hinges. The hapless mob of Germans was swept before the legions and pushed back into their camp, creating terrible panic among their wives and children. Many were hemmed in with their backs to the Mosel, and in the panic a great number were drowned. The rest broke in wild flight. The thick forest country gave Caesar's soldiers the chance to bar the tribesmen's line of retreat. The legionaries stood behind heaps of dead, preventing anyone from escaping. The pressure on the legionaries eased, and now their initial fear was replaced by dull anger.

The tall, commanding figure of Gaius Julius Caesar appeared among his legionaries. His very presence induced pride. It was a splendid Roman victory. *Hail Caesar!* He bent over the body of Lucius Mancinus, his cavalry's tribune. For a brief moment, grief and fury distorted his face before it turned to stone, his eyes locked straight ahead. 'Rome will not be served well wasting the rest of my troops on a new attack. An example has to be made. Never again will Germanic barbarians be allowed to threaten Rome's vital interests. Never again shall they cross the Rhine.' With that single phrase, he sentenced four hundred thousand to die. He had every Asipete and Tencteri man, woman and child rounded up and massacred. A few he allowed to escape across the Rhine, so that they might spread the message of Caesar's terrible fury and therewith stop future adventurism on the part of other Germanic tribes.

Once news of this deliberate blood-bath reached the Senate, Caesar's enemies used it to weaken his political position at home, hypocritically expressing shock. The Senate demanded of Caesar that he defend the massacre. He didn't do much explaining; he simply stated that the amount of rebellious activity all over Gaul and Alemannia left him with no alternative but an expedient example to quell the growing menace and assure the safety of the citizens of Rome. His supporters made sure that his reply was broadcast throughout the city; instead of Caesar being condemned for the atrocities, his name was hailed throughout Rome. Caesar, the saviour.

As a direct consequence of his victory over the Germanic tribes, Caesar achieved his greatest engineering feat, one that wasn't widely talked about. In early June 55 BC he marched with his legions to the Rhine. His intention was to cross the river and penetrate deep into Germany to punish the other tribes. The problem of logistics was awesome. In order to assure steady supplies for his legions, he ordered a bridge thrown across the Rhine, a feat never attempted before. An immensely wide river and a strong current increased by spring rains confronted his engineers. Their task was to build a structure that would stand up to summer floods and assure Caesar's legions a safe return after their summer campaign.[6] Their first task was to divert the strong current in order to plant the bridging pylons. They solved this problem by planting a row of triple pylons as current protectors. Once this was done, a further row of pylons was laid across them, followed by a second row of double pylons angled to push against the strong current. Once both rows were in place, cross-beams were laid and covered with logs. The bridge was now ready, and Caesar

---

[6] By historical coincidence, Caesar's bridge was located near the famous bridge of Remagen, by which the US army finally crossed the Rhine in WWII.

crossed with his legions into Germany. His campaign was nothing like as successful as his bridge-building achievement. The tribes had had time to leave, and Caesar chased them into the backwoods of Alemannia without making contact. In midsummer he returned to Gaul. Once the last soldier had crossed the Rhine, the bridge was destroyed. There wouldn't be another bridge across the Rhine for a thousand years.

By August 55 BC Caesar was ready to invade a territory as yet untouched by the Roman eagle – the British Isles. While still inside Germany, he ordered the construction of a fleet to be assembled at Portus Itius (Boulogne). During a week of late summer calm he managed to cross the Channel to Dubra (Dover). On the shore he faced heavy opposition from a hastily formed alliance of Celtic tribes. Using ship-mounted catapults and ballistas, he managed to land some of his troops. After a two-week stand-off on the beaches, Caesar called it quits and sailed back to Gaul in order to prepare a more elaborate cross-Channel invasion for the coming year. In July 54 BC, Caesar's five legions with 2,000 cavalry – 22,000 men in all – made an unopposed landing on the Dover shore. It was shortly after everyone had safely been put ashore that a storm sank the invasion fleet. Caesar found himself cut off from his supplies and, at the same time, confronted by a sizeable force of Celtic warriors under their chief Cassivellaunus. While the Briton hesitated, Caesar swept past him inland and crossed the Thames somewhere north of London. Their rapid advance stopped Cassivellaunus from delivering a concerted strike and negotiations were initiated, which ended with the nominal submission of the Britons to Caesar and Rome.

During these negotiations, Caesar was under pressure since open rebellion had flared up in northern Gaul. With Caesar still in Britain, the Nervi had attacked the legion of Sabinius, and when the Roman asked for a truce their chief, Ambiorix, granted them safe conduct; but once the Romans had marched from their camp they were waylaid and butchered. To lose Sabinius was a severe setback. Fortunately for Rome, in Caesar it had a man used to impossible odds and capable of making lightning decisions. In order to solve the crisis, Caesar demanded from the Senate the right of one-man command; from that moment on, his operational staff never amounted to more than an organisation for assembling the information he required, and for transmitting his personal orders.

With only 7,000 men, Caesar hurried to an encounter with Ambiorix's 60,000 warriors. They met at the River Sabis (Sambre), where Caesar cleverly faked the goodwill for negotiations and feigned indecision, which enticed Ambiorix into an attack on unfavourable ground where his numerical superiority made little difference. Caesar's legionaries counter-attacked and drove the Nervi off the field. After his victory over the Nervi he turned against the Belgiae, and forced them into submission.

In 53 BC an unforeseen event shook Rome's solid bastions when the wealthy partner of the triumvirate, Crassus, led a foolish expedition against the Parthians under General Surenas – no Hannibal himself, but compared to the banker Crassus a great strategist. Crassus crossed the Euphrates and was caught by Surenas in the open desert near Carrhae (Haran). Instead of attacking and forcing a decisive result, Crassus foolishly formed his legions into the standard square. Surenas refused to give battle, but rode with his cavalry in circles around the squares, firing arrows into the dense legion masses. While the Romans were left to fry in the broiling sun, Surenas's riders tortured the thirsty legionaries by holding up goatskins and letting the water trickle into the desert sand. A frantic Crassus couldn't come to grips with the elusive foe while his army was undermined by heat and thirst. In an act of desperation, he dispatched his son Publius Crassus with a legion to fetch water. The Parthian cavalry feinted retreat, lured the six-thousand-man column into an ambush, and while they were between tall sand-dunes came down on them and wiped them out to the last man. As night fell, Crassus made a break, abandoning his four thousand wounded to the mercy of the Parthians. His retreat was stopped at sunrise. While sitting in Surenas's tent for negotiations, Crassus was run through by the Parthian's sword. Carrhae was a clear cavalry victory over the 'invincible Roman legions', a first indication that foot-soldiers could no longer stand up to the mounted archers from the East. The wild Parthian riders were the harbingers of the Huns and the Mongols. The political result of Carrhae was that Parthia took control of Armenia and Mesopotamia.

In the aftermath of Crassus's defeat, Rome's streets erupted in violence. Vociferous packs roamed wild, and anyone in their path was beaten up and robbed to the accompaniment of ribald laughter. Pompey was appointed dictator, and with his cohorts waded into the rowdy crowd. He bashed in some heads, had others crucified and established order in no time, much to the gratitude of the citizenry.

The defeat of Crassus came as no surprise to Caesar. In the beginning they had been three, a hero (Pompey), a banker (Crassus) and a diplomat (Caesar). Now they were only two, and one had to go. Caesar knew that in order to subvert Pompey's popular support he required a highly visible action, and one profitable for Rome. The most tempting target was Gaul, of which he was proconsul. His plan had always been to expand Rome's domain from Provincia Romana (Provence) north to encompass all of Gaul, which called for the elimination of the many independent tribes. Now this ambition took on a wider political dimension. Caesar never undertook an action without a fully worked-out plan. As the conqueror of Gaul he would be in a position to challenge Pompey for the laurels. There was only one more hurdle standing between Caesar and the popular acclaim that would surely lead him to ultimate power – an obscure Gaul leader by the unpronounceable name of Vercingetorix. Caesar's scouts had told him that the Averni were savage fighters and that Vercingetorix was a god to them. He could easily believe that. And so Caesar headed off for his greatest battle.

Caesar's success at the River Mosel in the face of incredible odds was due to his ability to exploit two factors in the art of war: mobility and surprise. More than a general, he was a leader, exemplifying Napoleon's dictum of two millennia later: 'The moral is to the physical as three to one.' His personal courage on the battlefield was sadly tarnished by an ignominious aftermath. The end result of his shameful deed was that the Germanic tribes were prevented for centuries from crossing the Rhine.

11

52 ... *L'Année Terrible*

Alesia
15 September 52 BC

*'Alors la Gaule, alors la France, alors la gloire ...
... alors le vieux titan celtique aux cheveux longs.'*
('Onward, Gaul, onward, France, onward to glory ...
... onward the ancient Celtic titan with his long hair.')
Victor Hugo, *L'année terrible*, 1871

The Bellum Gallicum, or the Rising of Gaul, began with the massacre of the Italian merchants at Cenabum (Orleans) in the winter of 53 BC. One after the other, Rome's Gallic allies defected; after the Eduens came the Segusiaves, Parisii, Cubes, Bellovaques, Senons, Ambarres. By far the most ferocious were the Averni under their leader Vercingetorix. Only the Averni had both the power and the organisation to take Gaul's destiny in hand, as most of the other tribes were either too weak or too divided among themselves to constitute a serious threat to Rome. Gaul fulfilled a vital dual military function for Rome; it held the Rhine border against the Germanic tribes and was a stepping-stone into Britannia.

What unfolded in this year of 52 BC – the year the French call '*l'année terrible*' – was a scenario virtually unknown until then. Rome's powerful triumvirate had fallen apart. Crassus had been killed, Pompey was preoccupied with his grab for ultimate power, and Caesar was bogged down in Gaul, trying to douse rebellious fires, which had sprung up in the four corners of the country. In one of his rare errors of strategic diagnosis, Caesar thought that the north-east could become the focal point of the uprising; but it was from the centre – the region where his alliances seemed strongest – that the menace came. Since the beginning of his invasion, Caesar had based his strategy around the alliance with the Eduen nation and its five main tribes. For his army's mobile striking force, he counted on his Gaul auxiliaries, especially the four thousand Eduen horsemen of King Dumnoreix. In July 54 BC, while waiting for favourable winds for his crossing to Britain, an incident occurred which was to have enormous consequences.

With good reason, Caesar was worried that some of his Gaul allies might forgo their allegiance and rise against Roman rule during his absence on his venture to Britannia. He resolved to leave behind him only the Gallic leaders he could fully trust, and to take along those who posed a threat. Of these, the most powerful was Dumnoreix, the Eduen. When Caesar 'invited him' to accompany him on the sea journey, Dumnoreix found all sorts of excuses: 'he was afraid to undertake a sea voyage', or 'he was retained by his religious duty to his people.'[1] When Dumnoreix found himself faced with Caesar's categorical refusal to leave him behind, he started an intrigue with his fellow Gaul chieftains to remain on the Continent. 'It is not without reason that the entire nobility of Gaul is to be taken from here. Caesar's aim is to massacre us all, away from the eyes of our brothers. He will bring us to Britain to make us perish.' Caesar was too preoccupied with his

---

[1] Caesar, *De bello gallico* (V, 6–7), as all subsequent quotes.

invasion preparations to take much notice of Dumnoreix. The day the wind turned favourable and he gave the order to embark, Dumnoreix abandoned camp and headed back home. Caesar was livid and decided to make an example of the Eduen 'because he expected nothing good from a man who had dared to disobey him, and that in front of the Gaul chieftains'. He suspended his fleet's departure and dispatched a detachment of Roman cavalry to bring back the King – alive! Within four days, the Romans caught up with the absconding Eduen, who was travelling at a leisurely pace in the certain belief that Caesar was already on the high seas. The Roman cohort surprised the sleeping Eduens in their camp. Dumnoreix heard the commotion and stepped outside his tent to face the threat, sword in hand. In the heat of the moment, and despite the express injunction by Caesar to bring his hostage back alive, a centurion flung his spear at Dumnoreix's breast. 'Traitor, your time has come!' As the Eduen spun around from the force of the thrust, more legionaries plunged their *pili* into his body. This murder happened in full view of the Eduen warriors accompanying their king. According to custom, the dead King's head was hacked off and taken back as proof of capture. Caesar was shocked, not by the brutality of the act, but by its utter stupidity. To kill a king in front of his countrymen could only lead to trouble. The story spread, and all of Gaul was in shock. As Caesar had predicted, following the murder of their king the treaty with the Eduen was abandoned. Then all other treaties with Gallic tribes were broken and Caesar found himself with only his Roman legions and no auxiliaries to do the fighting for Rome. This left him without cavalry, he could no longer count on provisions from his allies, and his men suffered from hunger.

In a meeting deep in the forest of the Carnutes, the tribal chieftains swore a sacred oath, putting aside their petty jealousies and resolving to fight one common enemy.

All it would take was for one energetic leader to step forward and unite the tribes. Such a man was the Averni prince Vercingetorix. He was born in Gergovia around 80 BC, the scion of a princely family. His uncle was King Gobannitio of the Averni, and his father the fierce Celtill, who had tried to usurp his brother's crown and was executed for it in public. Vercingetorix was in his late twenties, tall and well muscled, with flowing long hair and a golden beard that gave him the look of commanding fierceness of an ancient prophet in rage. He had served his military apprenticeship under Caesar as a *contubernales* (companion of the tent, in fact a hostage of noble parentage). Caesar had noticed the young man's leadership qualities and hoped to make him the leader of Rome's auxiliary armies. But Vercingetorix was trained by and for Rome – like the Teutonic Arminius some years thereafter – only to turn on Rome and take on its legions. The Averni hoisted him on a shield and pronounced him their king. His first step was to send embassies to the tribes of Gaul – the country counted three hundred of them, most based around an *oppidum* or stronghold – and he called on them to join his drive to free the country of the Roman invaders. His movement gathered momentum. Major tribes, like the Pictons, Parisii, Cadurques, Turons and Senons, joined Vercingetorix.

Caesar was caught unawares, but then reacted with his usual swiftness. He surprised the budding Gaul Confederation by crossing the snow-capped peaks of the Vivarais mountains in early February and invading the territory of the Averni. From there he marched his legions to Agedincum (near Sens). This was where the final phase of Caesar's War of Gaul began. It was set off when the Eduens refused to provide his starving legions with supplies. In early March he left Agedincum and marched on Cenabum (Orleans). In the middle of the night his army appeared before the city gates; a stream of panicky people jammed on to the narrow bridge spanning the Loire as legionaries hacked their way into town. Caesar allowed his men to loot Orleans before he put it to the torch. From Orleans he hastened to his next target, the heavily fortified town of Avaricum (Bourges), jewel of Gaul and capital of the Biturgies.

For Caesar, Avaricum was of double importance: as somewhere to show the tribes what he would do to any ally who dared to change allegiance, and as a source of precious supplies for his legions. The Roman proconsul was learning a lesson in how perilous it could be to undertake a campaign with an army dependent on horses before the grain harvest was in. It almost brought his train of siege engines to a standstill. To deny Caesar's army their forage, Vercingetorix had ordered a scorched-earth policy. On his order, his Gaul put thirty cities to the torch – but not Bourges. They refused to sacrifice 'the pearl of Gaul'. And so Bourges was left standing, a fatal flaw in the Gaul's strategy. For the first time, Caesar's siege genius came to the fore. It took his legionaries a mere two days to build a prodigious structure; working like ants, they put up two elevated terraces, each 100 metres in length and 30 metres in height. With their catapults they then decimated the enemy; the fall of the town was only a question of time. The defenders had left themselves with an option for escape, a secret tunnel. When they tried to make good their escape, the town's women raised such clamour that it gave away the tunnel's location and Caesar's men plugged the exit. The legionaries climbed unopposed over the town ramparts and stormed into the city, committing on their way horrible slaughter; of the 40,000 defenders, only 800 managed to get away alive. This Roman triumph wasn't due to the valour of the legions but to Caesar's inventive siege technique. What then followed added little to the glory of Caesar: he gave specific orders to massacre the entire population of Bourges, with special attention being paid to the religious druids. This brazen blood-bath backfired on Caesar. Resolving the crisis politically was now out of the question.

After two days' rest, and with his army fed and resupplied, Caesar marched on the *oppidum* of the Eduens at Decetia (Decize). He forced Cotos, the only ally he could still count on, to step down in favour of Convictolitavis. Caesar hoped that the latter would prove himself grateful and help protect the legion's rear. Instead Convictolitavis threw in his lot with Vercingetorix and Caesar found himself caught between two fronts, the mighty Eduen nation to his north and Vercingetorix in Gergovia.

Caesar was already calculating the cost of his next venture: the siege of Gergovia, the *oppidum* of the Averni (near Clermont in central France). He was aware that he must move quickly and strike decisively before the Eduens were on his back. On the way, Caesar tried to gather Rome's support for his scheme; he required the aid of powerful allies – not only the Senate's approval of his military plans, but their sanction of his larger aims as well. It wouldn't be the first time that a shrewd leader, having delivered a decisive conquest, then used it in his quest for ultimate power. With Vercingetorix down, he would go after Pompey.

Vercingetorix was getting ready to put his master plan into operation. By luring Caesar into a siege at Gergovia, he would tie the Roman down and then crush him between his own Averni and the mighty Eduen force.

Caesar's siege was a disaster from the beginning. He had fallen into a trap. With a huge mass of hairy Gaul, who greased their long braids with fat, wore leather vests over their bare chests and carried their long swords on belts slung over one shoulder, coming down on him, he abandoned the siege and pulled out. This was costly; he lost a thousand dead, including forty-six valuable centurions. But Caesar slipped the snare and managed to rejoin his second-in-command, Titus Labienus, who with his six legions had just achieved victory over the Parisii at the gates of Lutece (Paris). Caesar was still without the vital cavalry. His Gaul cavaliers had deserted him and everything pointed in favour of the 300,000 Gaul, including at least 30,000 to 40,000 horsemen. Caesar decided to abandon Gaul and make for his fortresses in Provincia Romana (Provence). More than anything he needed to protect his retreat from cavalry attacks. With his Gaul cavalry gone, he dispatched an embassy with bags of silver across the Rhine to engage five thousand of the utterly ruthless Germanic riders, a daring gamble since barbarian mercenaries were known to ride for whoever paid the most. Once they were across the Rhine, Gallic gold could easily turn them against his Romans. But he judged correct, and soon these barbarians were to prove their value.

While Caesar hastened south, more warriors swelled the Gallic forces, like brooks feeding into a large stream. However, the main force was still too far north to come to the immediate assistance of Vercingetorix, and it was left to him to block Caesar's route to Provincia Romana. He did this on the Armançon river (near Montbard). In this hilly Burgundy countryside, the Gaul cavalry split into three columns – two suddenly appeared on the Roman flanks while the Gallic foot troops barred Caesar's advance. His Germanic mercenaries entered the fray. In a brief but furious battle the Germans took a height from where they rode down on the Gaul. The attack by the Germans came so suddenly that Vercingetorix was not given time to deploy; his blocking unit on the Armançon river was overrun and 'the German barbarians did unto them terrible carnage'.

Caesar called a meeting of his legion tribunes. 'We march through a hostile land when a wolf calls out: "I, Vercingetorix, will eat you!" Well, a wolf, even wounded, is still a wolf. Gaul are in our front and Gaul are in our backs. Let us chase this lonesome wolf as long he lacks support. If he retires into a fortified position, then we will surround him and starve him out.'

'And when the great host comes to his help?'

'Then we will build a second line of defences and fight against them as well.'

'Hail, Caesar, and may the gods be beneficial.' That was all they said, since they knew that only Caesar's will counted. While the Romans were already laying plans for a siege, Vercingetorix reached a fateful decision. This time he would set a trap superior to the one at Gergovia, from which Caesar had slipped. He would block the legions' way and await the arrival of the Gallic host from the north to crush Caesar like corn between the stones of a mill. 'After the rout of his cavalry, Vercingetorix at the Armançon ordered an immediate retreat and took the road to the *oppidum* of the Mandubians at Alesia.'[2]

Since then, historians have pondered why Vercingetorix shut himself up inside the *oppidum* at Alesia. It made no sense in strategic terms. He had more than enough effective to block the only road leading to the south through the mountains of Burgundy, an ideal ambush position. He had 80,000 and Caesar had only 35,000. The simple explanation is that he was badly shaken by his near-escape at the Armançon river, where he had witnessed the efficiency of Rome's disciplined legions, and that he planned to tie Caesar down in a siege position and hold out, since by now all of Gaul was bearing down on Caesar to smite the Roman eagle. That, and only that, could have been his strategic motive. He ignored the principal danger. Should something go wrong, it would leave him trapped on a rock. But how could anything go wrong? His scouts informed him that the main Gallic force of several hundred thousand was but a few days' march to the north.

---

2 ibid.

'Caesar cannot march south past us or we will harry his rear. We sit squarely in his path. He must attack us, and this is a strong place. But he will be coming with fire and steel and the gods only know what other dark powers.' Whatever his reason, the leader of the Gaul was preparing the stage for a battle of epic proportions.

The *oppidum* at Alesia[3] was located on a rocky promontory, the Mont Auxois (418m), surrounded by four hills roughly equal in height: Mont Rea (386m), Montagne de Bussy (426m), Mont Pennevelle (405m) and Montagne de Flavigny (421m). Before it stretches for some three miles a pasture, the Plaine des Laumes, crossed by the Brenne river. Today it is dotted with fields and farms and a motorway to Dijon; then it was a prairie with patchy cornfields to feed the population of the *oppidum*.

In the summer of 52 BC the weather suddenly took a change for the worse. It began to rain, the rivers swelled and the ground became waterlogged. This was to become one of the crucial factors in the forthcoming confrontation. While Vercingetorix waited for the huge Gaul army to close the trap on the Roman legions, which were camped before Mont Auxois on the open, indefensible plain, muddy roads greatly slowed the advance of the relief force and gave Caesar time to prepare for the encounter. The *oppidum* at Alesia was virtually unassailable. And yet Caesar recognised its weakness: if his legions couldn't get up the hill, by encircling the entire Mont Auxois with a breastwork he would in fact prevent Vercingetorix from coming down. This again would deprive the besieged of their source of water, two small streams, the Ose and the Oserain,

---

[3] Until the middle of the nineteenth century, the exact location of Alesia was a mystery. Napoleon III ordered excavations which located what Caesar described as a *murus gallicus*, or Gallic wall, near the village of Alise Sainte-Reine. Final proof was provided in the mid-1950s by use of aerial photography, which clearly showed the outline of Caesar's walls. Today's visitor will recognise the place from far away by the giant bronze statue of Vercingetorix, the masterpiece of the French artist Aimée Millet, which looks out over the Bourgogne countryside.

which passed through the valley. By diverting their water supply he would bring the fortress down. The master of siegecraft ordered the most gigantic siege battlements the world had ever seen: 2,000,000 cubic metres of earth were moved to construct two circular *vallations* (walls or ramparts), a *contravallation* to cut Alesia off from the outside, and a *circumvallation* to stop the relief army from reaching their besieged brothers on Mont Auxois. The rain-soaked ground made it easy to dig up the enormous volume of earth it took to build such monstrous ramparts. A basic structure made from cut trees was filled in with wet earth; once dry, it took on the consistency of concrete. The legionaries, stripped to the waist, worked on the fortifications. Their axes and shovels rose and fell in rhythm. With every legionary cutting, digging, dragging and building, both ramparts were finished in record time. Caesar knew that he was safe from a surprise sortie by Vercingetorix; his plan was to wait for the rest of the Gaul to arrive. The *contravallation*, stretching along the base of the mountain for ten miles, was put up in less than one week. This eliminated any hope of the inhabitants leaving the *oppidum* and, unless soon relieved, the garrison was condemned to slow death by thirst and starvation.

For the two battlements, Caesar designed a complicated, highly effective system of defences. The ramparts were reinforced with twenty-three *castelli*, wooden towers manned with archers. Directly below the ramparts, deeply embedded in the steep mud walls, were five rows of thorn branches (like barbed wire); on a sixty-foot-wide glacis, the space between rampart and moat, thousands of *cippis*, fire-hardened spikes, were driven into the ground. The saplings of an entire forest had gone into these traps. The area was peppered with *lilias*, five-foot-deep holes hidden under branches to break the legs of horses. Two twenty-foot-deep trenches fronted the glacis, filled with water diverted from the two rivers. These moats served

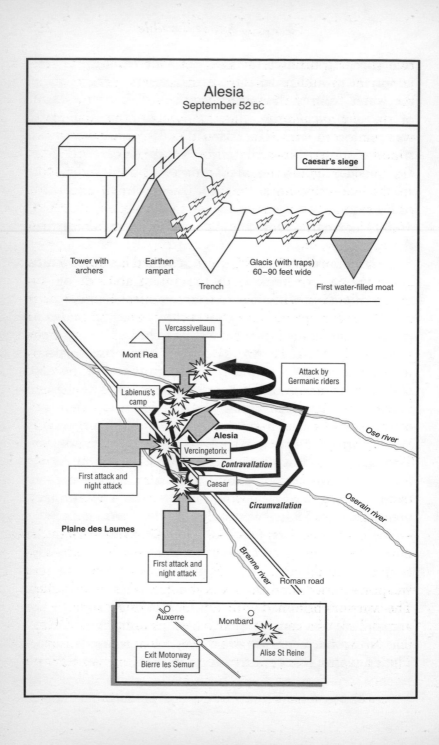

Alesia
September 52 BC

Caesar's siege

Tower with archers

Earthen rampart

Trench

Glacis (with traps) 60–90 feet wide

First water-filled moat

Vercassivellaun

Mont Rea

Labienus's camp

Attack by Germanic riders

Ose river

Alesia

Vercingetorix

Contravallation

First attack and night attack

Caesar

Circumvallation

Oserain river

Plaine des Laumes

First attack and night attack

Brenne river

Roman road

Auxerre

Montbard

Exit Motorway Bierre les Semur

Alise St Reine

two specific purposes: to slow up foot troops and subject them to archery fire from the towers, and to divert
the water from the besieged *oppidum*. The entire length
of the *circumvallation*, the rampart fronting the plain,
was reinforced with Caesar's artillery, *scorpions* (massive
tripod-mounted bows that fired bundles of metal bolts)
and *onagers* (giant slingshot catapults hurling masses of
stones like grapeshot).[4] Finally, Caesar's men and those
of his second-in-command Labienus, altogether 30,000 to
35,000 legionaries plus supply units, were camped between
the two *vallations*.

In the meantime, Vercingetorix installed his 80,000 men
along the eastern flank of the mountain and not on top
in the *oppidum*. This was a severe tactical blunder as it
gave Caesar a strong indication as to where the principal
attack would come from, and he relocated his own troops
accordingly. He knew that he didn't have months or even
weeks but at the best days to finish the defences. He
had pressed and cajoled his thousands of bare-chested
human ants to dig trenches and put up yard after yard
of wall. He was right – four days made all the difference.
Four short days and history would have been rewritten.
The delay caused by heavy rainfall and dithering Gallic
leadership sufficiently slowed the Gaul army to prevent it
from catching Caesar's legions unprepared on a wide open
plain. Caesar's luck held.

The Gallic relief army, all of 248,000, arrived from the
north-west. They didn't move like an army but more like
a mighty herd; the horses neighed, swords clinked and
weapons rattled, and the air was filled with ribald jokes.
The warriors brimmed with confidence; this was more the
atmosphere of a carnival than a serious military undertaking. No wonder – they hadn't seen a Roman in a month.
Their advance units rode to the top of Mont Rea; before

---

[4] Both these siege engines can be seen on Trajan's Column in Rome.

them, a few miles across a flat prairie, rose the sheer cliffs of Alesia. They stared at the smoke from their brothers' campfires, rising into the sky from the Alesia promontory. They saw something else, below the cliffs: a double enclosure of ramparts and towers! And between these two walls, more fires – an entire circle of them. This prevented the Gaul leaders from communicating with Vercingetorix up on the *oppidum*.[5] That evening, the leaders of the Gaul held a meeting. Present were the three principal chieftains, the Atrebate Commios, the Averni Vercassivellaun and the Eduen Eporedorix, as well as the leaders of the lesser tribes. The meeting was stormy as everyone wanted to advocate his own strategy. 'Our task is to free Vercingetorix.' Most had agreed on that when a voice cut across the babble of dissenting opinions. 'No! We are not here to free our brothers. We are here to annihilate Caesar and his army, and we must not stop before the last Roman is dead!' This was more surprising in that the voice was that of Vercingetorix's cousin, the Arverni Vercassivellaun. For him it had become a question of honour to protect the glory of his clan. To free Vercingetorix was secondary to his personal hatred of anything remotely Roman, a blind hatred that was to lead to a lack of strategy. 'Yes, kill every Roman!' Attack, certainly, but where? That problem was given no thought. Armies have gone down to defeat because they didn't have the most elementary notion of the terrain in which they operated. This was the Gaul's land, but the drummed-together Gallic army was not from Burgundy; because of its vast numerical superiority it had done nothing to scout the area and find out about Caesar's defences.

Caesar sneered in contempt at this oversight, which could only help him, but still, the distribution of forces

[5] The Romans had a unified long-distance signalling system using mirrors or smoke; the Gaul, being an assembly of various tribes, had nothing of its kind.

was hardly reassuring. Not only was he faced with a huge mass of foot troops, some of his enemy forces represented the most fearsome cavalry since Hannibal's Numidians. Caesar's veterans were superior in discipline, tactics and battle experience, but he couldn't afford to fight a drawn-out battle, one that he couldn't win. His aim was to show the enemy that tackling his *vallation* fortifications would prove too costly and persuade them to wander back to their tribal lands, after which he would depart for Provincia Romana.

Next morning, the plain was curiously still. For weeks it had rung with the sound of hammers forging iron heads for lances and arrows. Now the hammers were silent, and there were no shouts or curses from centurions or engineers. The time for building was over; the seriousness of combat was near. As he towered above his legions on his horse, the proconsul's voice carried conviction: 'Soldiers of Rome, you of the proud tradition, there have been many emergencies before, and it was always the valour of our legions that carried victory. Let it be so this time. The enemy is in front of us and the enemy is behind us. We have no choice but to fight in order to survive. Hold the battlements and fight if must be to the death. Every one of you must remember: *civis Romanum sum* – I am a Roman.'

It was good to have trust in him and it was good to believe.

The Gaul launched their first assault without preparation, without plan or overall leadership. They just came. Thousands upon thousands poured down from the hills (today Mussy-la-Fosse) into the Plaine des Laumes. Soon the entire plain was filled with milling riders. From the top of Mont Auxois they presented a splendid spectacle, and Vercingetorix's men had much to cheer. The riders forded the Brenne river, closely followed by men on foot running hell-bent for the Romans. Caesar had aligned two legions, the 10th of Legate Caninus Rebilus and the 11th of Legate Antistius Reginus,[6] in front of the ramparts to stem the flood. For hours the Roman wall of shields and spears stood fast and prevented the Gaul from crossing the moat. The walking wounded crawled through the gate so fast and in such numbers so that they couldn't be cared for in time. In the summer heat, gangrene set in quickly. Many died of loss of blood; their corpses were stacked against the palisade of the *circumvallation*. And when there was no more space in which to stack them, the corpses were dumped over the walls, adding to the visual horror. The combat seesawed until nightfall, when pressure became so fierce that the legions were forced to retreat behind their protective walls, leaving hundreds of their wounded and dead outside the ramparts. That first day both sides suffered great losses; but while the Gaul could afford it, the Romans could not. They had no reserves.

The first day's battle had taught the Gaul about the many traps buried in the defences of the *circumvallation*. They spent an entire day preparing the material necessary to overcome the obstacles: earth to fill in the moats and the leg-breaking foxholes, ladders and grappling hooks with which to scale the ramparts. During the following night, thousands of Gaul crept towards the first moat of the *circumvallation*. In their coats they carried earth as fill and passages were made across the ditch. The defenders failed to detect the sheer extent of this hectic activity. For one thing, the Romans were too exhausted after two days of fighting to be adequately watchful, and no alarm was sounded until the assault force had reached within a few yards of their final objective. Suddenly, masses rose from the ground in a frightful clamour, rushing to the assault.

---

[6] Napoleon was to use the example of their stand to incite his Vieille Garde.

They poured a furious hail of arrows on to the top of the ramparts.

The noise rising from the plain was Vercingetorix's first indication of the renewed attack on the *circumvallation*. He roused his own troops and led them down to launch an assault on the *contravallation*. Romans hurried to man their assigned posts. Using the stacks of prepositioned munitions, they riposted with rock showers from their siege catapults, but they could do very little to reinforce the weak angles in the wall's defences. Their saving grace was that the Gaul attacked everywhere at the same time, rather than concentrating their efforts on one specific point of the rampart. Soon so many had jammed into the narrow glacis between the two moats and the rampart that, despite the dark, the Romans found easy targets and the Gaul suffered terrible losses. That saved Caesar's legions that night. That, and the incredible valour and leadership of two legates, Gaius Trebonius and Marcus Antonius (later triumvir and lover of Cleopatra). By their example they inspired their men on the defences. As long as the Gaul stayed outside the 'mined territory', the glacis between water-filled trench and rampart, they held the advantage, but as soon as they crossed the first moat their freedom of movement was vastly restricted by space and traps. Their main losses came from the tremendous forward rush during which they were impaled on the spikes embedded in the ramparts. Caesar ordered Legate Titus Labienus to launch a diversionary attack with two full legions outside the *circumvallation* and ease the pressure. Labienus's two legions were immediately attacked by waves of howling Gaul on the open field and physically shoved back towards their camps. The battle on the ground increased to fever pitch. Most of the Gaul had by now crossed the moat and found themselves jammed in between the water on one side and the rampart and a marching legion on the other. They couldn't climb over the walls and they couldn't get back

across the water-filled ditch. Compressed, they offered
a perfect target for Roman missiles; rocks rained down
on them and arrows hissed through the air, thumping as
they struck, piercing the men and sending their horses
mad. Many steeds began to buck, rearing up on their
hindlegs to be pierced by another shaft through the soft
underbelly. The Gaul began to waver and the disciplined
legions pushed forward in a well-drilled phalanx and cut
through waves of attackers. The sortie by two legions
decided the night attack. The Gaul left thousands of dead
behind, impaled on traps or floating in the water of the
moat. Once the fight around the *circumvallation* had come
to a halt, Vercingetorix was left with no choice but to pull
back into his mountain *oppidum*. For the second time, a
major attack had failed. Never two without three, Caesar
knew, and he prepared for a last stand.

It finally dawned on the Gaul that to 'kill the Romans'
took more than bravery. They elected a leader; their choice
fell on Vercassivellaun. The local tribe of Mandubians had
told him of a way around the Roman camps, and his scouts
had discovered a weak spot in the Roman wall. Labienus's
camp was on a strip of level ground without traps and
gave access to a gate in the *circumvallation*. Shortly after
midnight on 15 September 52 BC, Vercassivellaun took
sixty thousand of his best fighters and most of the Gallic
cavalry on a detour around Mont Rea so as not to arouse
the suspicion of Roman sentries. Before first light his force
was in position atop the mountain. Below them they saw
the ring of fires the Romans had lit as a precaution against
another surprise night attack. Vercassivellaun allowed his
men a rest until noon. When the sun was at its zenith, he
gave the signal for a general advance.

For the Romans manning the ramparts, it must have
been a frightening sight, the massive waves rolling down
from the surrounding hills, then banging their swords
against their oval shields and chanting Celtic war hymns

at the tops of their voices. The Gallic cavalry broke out of the forest of Mont Rea and came down the long slope; their horses splashed across the Ose river. There were so many that their mounts were pressed against one another. They headed directly for the camp of Legate Titus Labienus, held by the 30th Legion, with close support from the 31st and 36th. Before reaching the moat, the Gaul riders twisted their upper bodies, pulled the string on their bows, leaned way back in their saddles and let loose a cloud of arrows into the Romans manning the rampart and the lined-up cohorts just behind it. The riders were followed by masses of Gallic foot-soldiers. This time Vercingetorix had been forewarned of the coming attack by a signal flashed from a polished shield, and now he swooped down from Mont Auxois with all of his remaining warriors to attack Caesar from the inside.

The moat presented no obstacle as it had been filled during the two previous attacks; every time the Romans had tried to empty it, their work teams had been decimated by feathered shafts. From his observation tower, Caesar watched the opening of a battle he knew would prove decisive. The stakes were tremendous – his legions' demise or the conquest of Gaul. Caesar's emphasis was on massive fire from the ramparts and towers. The steady crash from trebuchets sent thousands of rocks and iron balls spinning through the air. The Romans suffered heavily; arrows struck the battlements and men spilled on the ground. What he had feared now came to pass – his men were caught between their own walls. Once again, Caesar was lucky. The attack by Vercassivellaun and Vercingetorix had never been co-ordinated, and rather than launch a concerted effort in the same sector their forces attacked separate portions of both outer and inner walls. The supreme moment was at hand; the Gaul would lose should they fail to break down the Roman breastworks, and the Romans knew they were lost if the Gaul poured across the ramparts. In the sector under attack by Vercassivellaun a serious chance of a breakthrough developed. For once his warriors attacked in unison; the archers peppered the walls and the foot-soldiers crept steadily towards the rampart under the protection of a 'turtle' of shields raised above their heads to ward off Roman missiles. While Vercassivellaun sent more and more fresh troops into the fray, the Romans had to hold with what they had; anyone who could still stand, wounded or not, was pressed into service. Between the walls there was much confusion; conflicting orders had soldiers running in all directions, plugging holes or carrying armloads of arrows.

Caesar raised his head to peer over the wall. He saw a great number of Gaul making their way towards the Labienus gate. 'Hold the gate!' he yelled, hurrying over to add support with his personal presence. He had only one more reserve, his precious Germanic cavalry, which he had kept out of sight of the Gallic army. Those 5,000 Germans were his iron ration, and he would use them at the timely hinge of battle. It took great discipline to do this, but Caesar was a man with an iron will. Other than the 5,000 riders, his total manpower availability to plug a breach was down to six cohorts or 3,000 men – to stop an onslaught by perhaps a hundred thousand!

Meanwhile, Vercingetorix had vigorously attacked the Oserain side of the *contravallation*, where Caesar had put young Decimus Brutus in charge of the defences. One of the most vulnerable portions lay between two towers, held by a thin line of battle-weary legionaries from the 30th Legion. To them the combat seemed like a surrealistic play, seen through the haze of exhaustion and the smoke from Greek fire. The archers on the towers picked off the Gaul as accurately as they could, and as fast as they could notch arrows in their bows. Nothing seemed to stop their fury; on they came, again and again, in droves, in hordes. And still they had failed to reach the top of the ramparts.

Caesar's siege engineers had done their job well; their fortifications were well prepared and deeply stacked. This offensive went on hour after hour. Gains could be counted in yards. Vercingetorix rotated his troops every half-hour but the Romans didn't have the luxury of replacements, they just carried on. The Gaul began to feel the pressure; the new units that went in were green and began losing the ground that veterans had gained, so the old fighters had to go back in and continue the struggle. After hours of confusion and five futile attempts, Vercingetorix moved his men farther down the wall to attack another portion of the *contravallation*. As the mass of Gaul moved along on the outside, in full view of the defenders, the Romans gathered their troops out of sight of the Gaul and moved alongside them, thereby leaving great portions of the wall almost without defenders. And again, Caesar's luck held: this time the Gaul no longer possessed the necessary reserves to attack everywhere at once, or perhaps they didn't think of it in the heat of combat. Where the ramparts were now virtually undefended they could have scaled the walls without opposition.

At the Labienus gate, things were desperate. The Gaul were swarming around and had come within a few feet of the top of the ramparts. Caesar had dispatched his very last six cohorts under Gaius Fabius Maximus when a rider dashed up to the proconsul to announce that for Legate Labienus it was a matter of minutes before his forces would crumble before the onslaught. Caesar quickly switched the six cohorts from Brutus to Labienus, who now commanded thirty-nine cohorts, half of Caesar's effective; in a final effort, he gathered them inside the gate, which was about to give under the continuous onslaught. Suddenly the doors swung open and out poured his fifteen thousand legionaries in a daring sortie. Instantly his Romans faced hordes of bawling, red-faced devils; then they were upon each other, screeching like banshees and flailing their arms. They snarled like human dogs, biting, snapping and gouging. Punch drunk, they tore at each other's hair and eyes. Some of those dying were held standing by the pressure from both lines. But there were too many Gaul for the Romans.

Labienus was re-forming his decimated legions. Those the Gaul thought had been defeated were standing in perfect formation; this so surprised them that for a few moments all fighting stopped. Labienus came walking out from behind the line, his shield on his left arm, with only two men as his guard. He gave the signal and the thinned line came on with levelled lances. There was nothing hasty in their advance. His legion kept its lines trim and steady in their metal grey and leather brown. After another signal they pulled to a halt, the cohorts ranged, stolid and unmoving. That was when the Gaul gave out their fierce war cry and dashed at them.

While this battle raged, another emergency was materialising on Caesar's flanks. He could see masses of Gallic cavalry trotting off to his right to pass around Labienus's legions, manoeuvring into position to launch a charge.

The real crisis of the battle was at hand. For now Vercingetorix could have launched a concentrated counter-charge. If only he had been able to reorganise his men quickly for an attempted breakout, he would certainly have succeeded. He left it too late, and the moment was gone.

Labienus's sortie bought Caesar some precious time while he pulled every available man from the safe portions of both ramparts. This created four additional cohorts, two thousand men in all. Caesar himself took the lead. Astride his charger, he made a conspicuous figure, dressed in the flowing *paludamentum*, the purple mantle of a Roman general. The sight of their leader fired up the legions; a great shout rose from the battlements and the Romans threw themselves with renewed vigour at the Gaul. Sword in hand, the lead centurion let loose a shout. It was the greatest sound he would ever make. At the head of his century, he bounded over dead and dying and wounded. The Gaul were surprised by the new onrush; some froze and then quickly turned. A giant of a Gallic warrior, full bearded and tall, barred the way of the Roman; they came at each other in a blur of clanging blades; the centurion stumbled over a body, fell, and was pierced by the giant's sword. Two legionaries jumped the tall warrior. Then he too was down and the Gaul began to fall back ... then they were running, fleeing as the barbarians always did before a concentrated Roman assault.

This was the critical moment Caesar had been waiting for. If he could make the Gaul break and run, there would be chaos. It was time for his Germanic riders. Caesar was finally committing his precious mercenary cavalry. He issued an order of last resort: the cavalry were to ride around the *circumvallation* and smash into the enemy, now heavily engaged in the battle with Labienus's legions, from the rear. It was a desperate gamble but it had to work or all was lost, for Rome and for Caesar.

At a blare from horns, his mercenary cavalry formed into two massive blocks. Another horn signal and the Germanic cavalry raced from their position, faster and faster, until their horses were covered in foam. Every rider had his long sword across his saddle and both hands on the pommel. Sword clashed with sword, body with body. The battle-fresh Germans rode over the Gaul. That first wave of riders was followed by a second wave, coming around the Alesia hill from the opposite direction and catching the Gaul army from the rear. The German riders drove like a howling storm into the mass of their opponents; the Gaul fought like wild beasts. Body armour split under mighty two-handed sword strokes, bolts rained down on man and horse. A tribune sat on the ground, holding his stomach where he had been struck by a lance. Blood poured from his mouth before he fell forward.

'At last the German riders coming from behind the mountain pushed the enemy before them wherever they found him. They pushed him all the way to the river where the Gaul chieftains had taken a stand with their infantry, and there did frightful massacre.'[7]

Caesar rode up a hillock from where he could survey the entire field, just in time to watch the cavalry charging around the Gaul and into their rear. The Gallic army was collapsing before his eyes. Everywhere the Gaul scattered and fled, throwing away their weapons for a faster getaway. His Germanic mercenaries, now almost without opposition, rode down the fleeing masses, their long swords rising and falling. Many Gaul warriors were killed, none were taken prisoner. Mountains of slaughtered piled high in front of the rampart, and those who weren't already dead soon suffocated under the mass of bodies falling on top of them. Then fighting went on all along the *circumvallation*, individual hand-to-hand combat. The tribal warriors had fought well throughout the afternoon, but they were getting increasingly tired, having used all their strength in the futile attempt to storm the rampart earlier in the day. The mountain of corpses hampered their retreat. Many more were caught and slaughtered.

All day long Vercingetorix had been in the front line of the battle. His clothing was torn in many places from sword cuts and sticky with patches of dried blood – that of his enemy. He would have no time to clean up until after his plans were settled for the morrow. The green field below Mont Auxois was dirtied with heaped bodies, and far across the plain the relief force was falling back in a speckled flood, making for the safety of the distant hills. His own men were pulling back, flooding past

---

[7] Caesar, op. cit.

him, not looking at him. He was an island in the stream of retreat. Many of his men had gone to their deaths against Caesar's wall in the bright sun of a brilliant afternoon. An emotionless voice in him, untouched by the rage that burned him up, told him that the cursed rampart could not be taken. It was over – along with the horror of loss, the weariness and a helpless rage. His men had died for nothing and he had sent them to their deaths. Down in the valley, out of the smoke of the many fires, rode a figure in a crimson mantle. His face was hard and pale, his eyes bright and hot as he stared across the emptiness of death to where stood the lone figure of Vercingetorix. The Gaul turned away. Enough of this. He walked up the hill, into the evening breeze. He was suddenly aware of the tears blurring his eyes. His troop leaders gathered around him, standing immobile, absorbing the knowledge that began to pass among them without words that it was over. The sun began to sink, red like blood, and with it came a slow darkness which flowed over the field and up to the cursed rampart, moving along the dead and the dying like the shadowy wings of a giant bird. The Gaul's vast host was routed and the slaughter was great. Their bones were left to turn to dust on a field in Burgundy.

Vercingetorix flexed his sword hand; the long blade dangled down to his ankle with the carved pommel on the strap around his shoulder within easy reach. What good was a sword against the pain of hunger? His men were worn out and they were hungry, and if he were to try again tomorrow he would lose half of them; they were exhausted beyond endurance, with a thick tongue from thirst and a mouth too dry to chew food. But they had to go out; he would allow them all the rest they needed *after* they had broken through that cursed rampart. He would have to drive them out again, before they were ready, because, if not, they would all die of thirst and hunger. There was a rage in his brain like that of a fighter who has been down once and is up again, looking for an opening. It was a silent rage. With night came the sound of wailing women, mourning their husbands and sons. Vercingetorix looked at his suffering people. 'We can only die. What else can we do? I see no choice.'

It was not to be. Vercingetorix held out another fortnight before he arranged for a meeting with Caesar, to arrange for free passage from the *oppidum* for the greatly suffering women and children. The Roman proconsul remained merciless. Putting pressure on the non-combatants had become a powerful weapon to force the Gaul leader to his knees. 'Have pity on the women and children,' Vercingetorix pleaded.

Caesar only looked at the warrior. 'Pity is a word I know not.'

When Vercingetorix went back up the hill, he knew that all was lost.

It is true that Vercingetorix shut himself up, together with 80,000 men, inside the fortress of Alesia, which in itself wasn't very big. When he sent off his cavalry, why did he not send off three-quarters of his infantry? Twenty thousand men would have been sufficient to reinforce the garrison of Alesia, located on a rocky spur and which included already a large population of non-combatants. He didn't have provisions for more than thirty days. Alesia was a strongpoint that had nothing to fear but hunger. If instead of 80,000, he'd have had only 20,000, he would have had food for 120 days, while the rest of his 60,000 warriors could have roamed the countryside and harried Caesar's besieging forces. Instead, it took 50 days to assemble a new Gallic army, by which time Vercingetorix' locked-up army had run out of food.

In a desperate move to save his army from a painful death, Vercingetorix had all non-combatants forcibly removed from the *oppidum*. They wandered aimlessly between cliff, rampart and wall to find a morsel of food and a drink of water while awaiting death.

'In those days of the siege and before Lord Vercingetorix rode off into death and the oblivion of legends, we spent our time looking at our dwindling food, looking out for smoke on the horizon and listening to the sound of a horn by night that never came and the rumour by day, that from somewhere out there relief was coming to alter the course of the siege. But light was fading fast and the deep night was approaching with giant steps.' Such was the account of one of the survivors.

Personal triumph was all that counted for Caesar; nothing else mattered. The combat on the plain had turned into siege by thirst. All Caesar had to do was to sit on the bottom of the hill – and wait. It was an extraordinarily hot autumn and Alesia's cisterns soon ran dry. When too many of his men fell over dead of thirst and hunger, the Gaul chieftain finally gave in.

It was a great calamity that thousands of young Gaul had died in vain. Vercingetorix had tried to improve the lives of his people. But he had gambled, and now the whole country was in mourning. At Gergovia he had spared the Roman enemy he knew would now kill him.

On the twentieth day the Roman guards at the gate shouted and pointed at a figure that sat on a horse before them as if chiselled in stone. A helm was strapped to his chin; his chain-mail was dull and dented and scarred from battle. And Vercingetorix, the Gaul King himself and the symbol of Rome's glorious victory, came through the gate on his warhorse in his most splendid armour, rode in a circle around Caesar, who was sitting on a platform, jumped from his horse and threw his sword at Caesar's feet: 'Take this, most valorous of warriors, victor over a valorous warrior.'

Caesar's mouth grew hard. 'Come to bend your knee?'
And the Gaul warrior remained on his knees until Caesar
handed him over to the guards in his ultimate moment of
triumph.[8]

The dream of a Gaul delivered of the Roman yoke had
been within reach; that dream ended one day in September 52 BC. Julius Caesar, the master of siegecraft, had
seen to it. The *bellum gallicum* was nearly over.[9] With
the *année terrible* began for the people of Gaul 'the long
night of the *ténèbres* [darkness]'. Rome's domination of
Gaul was to last five hundred years.[10]

Caesar was deified. He returned home to celebrate a triumph, as decreed by the Senate, for he had pacified the great
country north of the Alps. Many chariots, heaped with the
spoils of war, passed in triumphal procession before the
Temple of Saturn. On one of them was Vercingetorix, with
a chain around his neck, followed by a train of equally
chained captives. The crowd cheered Caesar and made
him their hero of the day. But soon intrigues began and
his political influence waned. He still lacked the power
to face both a hostile Senate and his rival, Pompey. He
returned to Gaul to join up with his faithful legions. Over
the next two years (51–50 BC) Caesar turned Gaul into a
Romanised province, and as such it remained an integral
part of the Roman Empire for the next five hundred years.

---

[8] Plutarch.

[9] The best and probably most accurate account of all these events can be found
in Caesar's own *De bello gallico*, Book VII, written by him shortly after the
events in his winter quarters in Bibractum in 52–51 BC. All the participants,
including the imprisoned Vercingetorix, were near him. Of course, it is the version
of Caesar, the victor. All other accounts, Titus Livius, Asinius Pollionus, Florus,
Plutarch and Dio Cassius, were written 150 years later and certainly borrowed
from Caesar's writings.

[10] When Gaul was finally 'liberated' by the Francs, they saw in the Frankish King
a reborn Vercingetorix.

Caesar's greatest achievement, as he wrote himself, was the conquest of Gaul. In ten years he had conquered eighty major cities and subjugated three hundred tribes. One million Gaul went into slavery to serve their Roman masters.

When one looks at the events of the *année terrible*, the overall impression is that of an incredible reversal in the fortunes of war. A priori, Caesar's legions were condemned, certainly after their setback at Gergovia and the defection of Gaul's largest nation, the Eduens. With a country in open rebellion, its principal roads cut and his army deprived of supplies by Vercingetorix's scorched-earth policy, Caesar fled headlong towards the safety of the Roman fortresses in Provence; he found his route barred, he stood, fought, and then reversed the situation.[11] Was Vercingetorix a bad strategist? Three times he used the 'abscess of fixation strategy', which consisted of luring his enemy into a fixed siege position around a friendly central fortress (Bourges, Gergovia, Alesia), then assembling a maximum of friendly forces around the enemy to annihilate him by a concerted action from the outside. At Bourges, the Gaul didn't as yet have the necessary forces and Caesar took the fortress; at Gergovia, Vercingetorix counted on the Eduens to catch the Romans between two pincers, but Caesar recognised the danger and slipped from the closing trap; at Alesia, Vercingetorix finally had all the pieces in place for achieving victory. The relief army was to be his principal element in the extermination of the legions, crushing them inside their own ramparts. But faced by a situation of 'victory or death', the legendary Roman legions proved to be

[11] A similar situation occurred at Agincourt in 1415. Henry V, with a decimated force, tried to reach his fortress at Calais, was stopped by the French and then achieved an astounding victory. And the French at Dien Bien Phu in 1954, trying to lure the Viet Minh into a siege trap and then annihilate them from the outside, were themselves annihilated.

better disciplined and better motivated, and they resisted. Intervention by a relief force, whatever its size, could no longer bring about a Gallic victory. Caesar recognised the rich potential of his success. It was not Gaul he was after, but Rome.

Vercingetorix, above all else, was a man of flesh and blood. He cut across intertribal feuds and transcended the inconsistencies of men less far sighted and less able than himself. He may have been an opportunist, but one so Gallic in manner as to suggest in him the presence of a much deeper strain of altruism and honour. He was the picture of a brave and resolute warrior with vehement passions. In the end, a master of superior diplomatic skills and quick decisions outwitted him. With Caesar's victory at Alesia, Gaul lost its Celtic identity. Its language became Latin based (which it still is) and its popular customs Latinised.

For six painful years, Caesar made Vercingetorix suffer all that a mortal could suffer. The Arvernii was locked away from sunlight and clean air in the dungeon of the Tullianum. The pain that his body suffered at the hands of the jailers may well have been surpassed by that which his spirit endured. In late 46 BC, at the height of his glory, Caesar ordered the prisoner strangled. For the noble Gaul death was perhaps deliverance, that of the chained eagle whose soul was set free.[12] As for the mighty Caesar, he survived his prize captive by only sixteen months. On the Ides of March, the Gaul's curse was finally fulfilled.

What would have happened had Vercingetorix achieved victory in those humid autumn days of 52 BC? It is unlikely that the eventual course of history would have changed.

12 At excavations at Alesia, ordered by Napoleon III, a small bronze was discovered. It shows a Gaul warrior lying on the ground, his arm covering his face. Roman in origin, it is known as 'The Dying Gaul'.

The economic, political and strategic interests of Rome would have determined that. Gaul had a direct border with Rome. With great obstinacy, Rome's legions would have returned, and Gaul would have found itself inescapably integrated into the Roman Empire.

The glory of Caesar has been sung in fable and text. Vercingetorix was soon forgotten, and yet it was he who had once incarnated an authentic form of patriotism. His quest was that of a samurai, his watchword '*honneur et patrie*'. It was to be seventeen centuries before his name appeared again as a brief mention in Jacques de Cassan's book about ancient Gaul kings.[13] In 1873, Paris acquired a rue Vercingétorix, and in the dark days leading up to the Second World War Charles de Gaulle used the Gaul warrior to warn the French of Hitler's growing menace: 'When Vercingetorix threw his arms at the feet of Caesar, perhaps he intended that his desperate homage serve his race as an immortal lesson.' Following France's defeat in 1940, writers recalled the gesture of the Arvernii chief in clandestine pamphlets, holding him up as the example of '*le premier résistant* [the first resistance fighter] in the history of France'.

It is as men that both must be judged. Both were brave and resolute, both driven by power and hunger for distinction; both showed vehement passions and were capable of heinous crimes. One thing is certain – Vercingetorix and Caesar were worthy of one another, in glory as in defeat. Caesar was freely to admit in his *Commentaries* that his decisive victory over Vercingetorix hung by a thin thread.

The failure of the Gaul attack exemplifies the eternal problem of a stronger force with too many heads pitted against a weaker force directed by a single man. The

---

[13] J. de Cassan, *Traité des anciens rois des Gaulois et des Français depuis le déluge*, Paris, 1621.

controversies over the opportunities thrown away at Alesia have never been resolved and are obscured in a haze of romance.

The crucial factor at Alesia was the astuteness of Caesar in awaiting the propitious moment to release upon the enemy the fury of his Germanic cavalry.

Sixty years thereafter, the grandsons of the same Germanic auxiliaries who had borne Rome to dominance over Gaul wrote *finis* to Rome's rule beyond the Rhine. In a decisive encounter in the Teutoburger Wald (AD 9)[14] they smashed Rome's legions and changed for ever the destiny of central Europe.

---

[14] As described by the author in his *The Weather Factor* (Hodder & Stoughton, 1999), the Battle of the Teutoburger Wald took place between the legions of Varus and Arminius, the German.

12

The Die is Cast

The Rubicon
11 January 49 BC

'*Iacta alea est* – the die is cast.'[1]
Caius Julius Caesar, 11 January 49 BC,
while crossing the Rubicon

'*Silent enim leges inter arma* . . . laws are dumb in a time of war.'[2] Accordingly Caesar did what no Roman general had ever dared before. He flaunted Rome's laws, took his army and crossed the Rubicon. With one step, he had cast the die.

Like Greece, the cradle of democracy, Rome was governed by a few ruling families, the *patres*, or patrician families with seats in the Senate, an assembly of elders, from the Latin *senex* for old. The *proletarii* (landless) and *plebs* (urban class), who were directed to follow their masters, were left empty handed. It took 250 years before the *plebs* managed to achieve representation of their demands. When eventually revolts against the ruling patricians broke out, they proved to be vicious and bloody, since there

---

1 Actually quoted by Suetonius in his *Divus Julius*.
2 Said by his contemporary Cicero (106–43 BC) before the Senate.

was no guiding example by which to settle the problem through discussion. A few Romans were millionaires while millions were impoverished. It took a disgruntled pair of patrician brothers to shake the impoverished from their lethargy. The tribunes Tiberius Sempronius Gracchus and his younger brother Gaius formed neighbourhood committees into the *populares* party, and when they tried to give land to the landless, the patricians murdered them, together with hundreds of their followers. The plebeians took to the streets. A terrible civil war broke out between the populist consul Gaius Marius, the lion of Aquae Sextiae, and his equally bloodthirsty counterpart, the patrician Lucius Cornelius Sylla, who was the first to openly overthrow a senatorial command and march with his legions on Rome (88 BC). Sylla entered the city and exacted a terrible vengeance on the followers of Marius: 'The cadavers without heads rotted in the streets, left there to make all those against his rule tremble.' A trembling Senate voted Sylla in as dictator. This didn't put a halt to the fratricidal strife that was tearing the country apart. By the time both of these pitiless men died in their beds, they had managed to decimate the population of Rome.[3] History would record them as the gravediggers of the Roman Republic.

Two generals, who knew much about the business of war but nothing about creating a peace, fought it out. The Republic was tottering. Consul Marcus Tullius Cicero, a brilliant orator whose greatest achievement was regularly to switch allegiance and march behind the winning flag, held the view that politics must always override the decisions of the military: '*Cedant arma togae, concedat laurea laudi* ... Let the weapons give way to the togas [civic robes] and the laurel to the paeans.' Indeed, war is

[3] Plutarch, *Vies: Marius*, Paris, 1971.

too serious a business to be left to generals. Cicero, claiming to have discovered a plot against the august Senate, was granted exceptional powers, which he then used to eliminate the supporters of his enemy, the patrician Lucius Sergius Catilina (63 BC). In just four famous speeches – 'O tempora, O moris . . . what times, what habits' – Cicero harangued Catilina to his death (62 BC). Five years later, once the apparent danger had passed, Cicero himself was condemned. (In 43 BC, after changing sides once more, Cicero was murdered on the orders of Marcus Antonius.)

Time was ripe for the emergence of 'the strong man'. The man about to appear was not only a general, he was an astute politician. With civil war hardly at an end, and Rome still uneasy, a new challenge arrived in the person of Consul Marius's nephew, the only one Sylla had failed to eliminate during his rampage. His name was Gaius Julius Caesar. This brilliant young member of the plebeian *populares* was ambitious and power hungry. His timing was perfect. While several men fought for control as dogs fight over a bone, three emerged victorious when they formed a coalition, or triumvirate (60 BC). A general, Pompey, a banker, Crassus, and Caesar. The driving force was Caesar, who had inveigled the Senate into having himself pronounced consul by the simple expedient of having the Senate's president arrested and thrown into chains. Caesar was still too feeble to strike out on his own. Therefore he helped Crassus to recover his personal fortune lost during the civil war and diverted the monies destined for retired legionaries to Pompey. And he reserved the plum for himself: he was nominated to take sole command over the two Gauls, north and south of the Alps. This was where Rome's veteran legions were located; it was the short cut to Rome. He achieved this with a series of brilliant victories over the Germanic and Gallic tribes. By 52 BC, Caesar had become a power, worshipped by the people and bequeathed the laurel wreath by the Senate.

In 52 BC, while Caesar struggled against the Averni in Gaul, and against any law governing the Roman state, his great rival Pompey had himself elected sole and unique consul by the Senate. One of his first steps was to order Caesar to disband his auxiliaries, relinquish command over his victorious legions and return to Rome – or face being branded a traitor and being hunted down as such. To forestall the hostile ambitions of a power-mad military commander, Roman law forbade a general from entering Italy accompanied by his legions without the prior consent of the Senate. Caesar refused to be summoned before a toothless Senate to answer charges of disobedience. In the wake of his great victories, he was not one to be ordered around by a jealous rival. Caesar's camp was overflowing with officers who showed blind obedience to their overlord, and by calling his soldiers 'my companions' he persuaded them to fight for him even without pay. They knew that he would amply reward them. With only one legion – but certainly the best fighting force Rome had ever seen – he marched from Ravenna and reached the border between Cisalpine Gaul and Rome, marked by a small river flowing into the Adriatic Sea, the Rubicon.

Meanwhile, while warring with the tribes in Asia Minor, Crassus got himself conveniently killed in an ambush by Parthians (53 BC). This, plus fear over the growing popularity of Caesar, had provoked Pompey into making his move. A showdown between the two power-hungry partners was now inevitable. While Pompey never considered using his legions to overthrow the constitution, Caesar had no such qualms. But he did hesitate before invading Italy, not because of concerns about the legality of such a move but because of doubts about his chances of grabbing power.

On 11 January 49 BC, Julius Caesar crossed the Rubicon. Cicero, who met up with him to join what he considered to be the coming force, flattered him: 'When I see his carefully combed hair and his honest stare, I cannot imagine that Caesar carries in him such a perverse notion as the destruction of the Roman constitution.' But, as Caesar had clearly avowed: '*Iacta alea est* . . . The die is cast.' And it was. With this step he started the Great Civil War.

Their first encounter went to Pompey. At Dyrrachium, Caesar attacked Pompey's fortified camp and his nose was bloodied. A few months went by before they met again. On 9 August 48 BC, at Pharsalus by the shore of the Enipeus river, Caesar once more faced Pompey in battle. Caesar commanded twelve undermanned legions, 30,000 men at the most, and very little cavalry, while Pompey could field Rome's army of over 60,000 men and 7,000 riders. But Caesar would never face an enemy with all his cards on the table. '*Dolus an virtus, quis in hoste requirat?* . . . Trick or force, what would not be permitted to the enemy?'[4] Pompey had discarded surprise; he completely ignored this key element espoused by all the great captains of history. He remained faithful to the theory of frontal attack. A fundamental defect in his plan was the width of his fighting front; he fed his legions into a bottleneck which would become utterly congested. For Caesar, the means by which surprise could be achieved lay behind a hill, strategically located between the town of Pharsalus and the Enipeus river; it was ideally suited for hiding a force for a surprise attack from behind its cover into the open flanks of his opponent. In the meantime, Caesar had split off six cohorts and scraped together two thousand men from his already depleted legions and put these into reserve behind the hillside. He then spaced his two battle lines to cover Pompey's entire front line. This left big gaps in the centre. Caesar, one of the most enterprising of history's generals, didn't wait to get trampled by the weight of the opposing force but ordered his trumpeter to sound the signal for attack. His legions advanced, throwing

4 Virgil (70–19 BC), *Aeneid* (II).

their *pili*, and then dashed at the wall of Pompey's lances. These were Caesar's veterans from the Gallic Wars, facing a hastily recruited force. In no time they had battered aside the spears to come within sword range. Pompey countered their breakthrough by throwing into his centre more seasoned reserves, and the tide of battle tilted in his favour. For Caesar, who was closely observing the battle from a hill, sitting on his horse visible to all next to his *primipilus* (flag carrier), the situation became critical. But the legion at his centre held, although the rest of his line was in flux. Some of his veterans tried to withdraw in order to regroup and protect their right flank, because it was there that the sheer weight and numbers of the adversary were mauling Caesar's thousand riders.

While Pompey watched the defeat of Caesar's cavalry on the wing, hesitant to take the initiative, Caesar sallied forth at the head of the six cohorts, the very élite of the legions. Their shield wall and spears caught Pompey's cavalry by surprise and created havoc. His soldiers hacked away at the legs of the horses and brought the entire cavalry formation into disarray; they fled towards the back of Pompey's formation, chased by Caesar's cohorts. If Pompey had only taken the initiative now, and put in all his remaining reserves, another four legions, Caesar's fate would have been sealed because a gaping hole had appeared between his advancing six cohorts, his cavalry and his centre. But Pompey, the general who had always reacted with speed and courage, became so preoccupied by the plight of his precious cavalry that he failed to react. It was the prelude to disaster, because Caesar now ordered his third-line reserve to advance through the holes in his two forward battle lines. He concentrated on Pompey's flank and took the enemy in enfilade, then rolled him up. The attack from a new, fresh force, combined with the surprise created by the six cohorts, was triumphantly successful and decided the battle. Pompey's rearward ranks crumbled, their troops reeling under the surprise attack. What had been a forward-moving battle line minutes before broke in panic and became a disorderly mob running for their lives. Caesar's legion allowed them no respite but pursued the fleeing rabble. It was typical of Caesar's style of warfare that he had forbidden, on pain of death, any plunder of Pompey's camp before the enemy's army was completely annihilated; letting them get away to reassemble farther to the rear would have rendered the victory pointless. Pompey's army was routed; it suffered 15,000 killed while Caesar lost a mere 230.

Caesar imperator! The Roman provinces declared one and all for Caesar. Pompey fled to Egypt, where he asked King Ptolemy XII and his co-regent and sister Cleopatra for asylum. With the final elimination of the only man who still stood between him and ultimate, unshared power uppermost in his mind, Caesar embarked with four thousand men and chased Pompey to Alexandria. On arrival in Egypt he was met by the guardian of King Ptolemy, Theodotus, with the phrase: 'Dead men don't bite!' He presented him with the head of Pompey. It was in Alexandria that Caesar fell under the spell of the beautiful Cleopatra. Her arrival in Caesar's life was as spectacular as it was unique: her servant Apollodorus entered Caesar's bedchamber, carrying a precious carpet across his shoulder. 'A gift, great Caesar!' He then unrolled the carpet and, lo and behold, out rolled the beautiful Egyptian queen, probably still a virgin at the time, since her husband and brother, King Ptolemy, was only ten years of age. That night, Cleopatra became the Roman's mistress and subsequently bore him a son. She followed Caesar to Rome, where he installed her in one of his palaces where he spent his nights – although for strictly political reasons his official residence remained that of his wife Calpurnia.

As for the notion that Julius Caesar was simply inspired

by a desire for personal glory or by a Spartan sense of heroic duty, it was certainly true that Rome admired and extolled heroism and did not always consider discretion to be the better part of valour. Caesar was able to observe the advice given by antiquity's greatest generals, Alexander and Hannibal, that the surest test of a great leader in battle is to know when to retreat. Many times he fretted and stormed when the 'mutinous Gaul', or other indolent auxiliaries under his command, resisted his attempts to impose upon them legionary Roman discipline. He never truly came to understand his foreign subjects and always judged them by Roman standards.

Caesar, the brilliant exponent of mass and mobility, perfected his uncle Marius's military techniques, which essentially were timeless and not affected by technological development. He understood the effectiveness of striking at the core of his opponent's power. Once the enemy's main army was defeated, and his economic centres occupied, all else would follow. He recognised that the surest means of achieving his goals was to raise a sizeable force and concentrate it on the essential objectives. This military power, in combination with political reality, reflected Caesar's psychological need for conquest and absolute domination. The full-blown nationalism of Caesar's times provided the new mass armies of Rome with a reliable motivating force, which Alexander or Hannibal had known only in rudimentary form. It was in Caesar's temperament to achieve personal glory through public recognition. 'Rome has never produced such a man as Caesar, and should he continue to observe the same drive and principles in his future policy, he must surely conquer the world.'

Caesar's victories were no less Greek than those of Alexander, his strategic principles no less classical than those of Hannibal. But his army, his weapons and siege engines had changed beyond recognition. He did not lack physical courage, nor was he ever obsessed with his personal safety.

Time and time again he proved it when he led his men from the front. Caesar was far from perfect – he dealt most brutally with the people he conquered, particularly in Gaul. Those were deeds that blackened the heart and weighted it with lead. But never Caesar's.

'*Veni, vidi, vici* . . . I came, I saw, I conquered.'[5] Caesar conqueror, Caesar dictator, Caesar *imperator*. Caesar had developed the personality traits that were bound up with the title. There was an aura of greatness, of heroism about him, not just as the result of his astounding victories. There was something mystical, unexplained and immeasurable about it. Even without his military achievements he could have won himself a place in the pantheon of the great.

He possessed neither the nobility of Alexander nor the military acumen of Hannibal. But he was certainly a wilier statesman, seeking to bargain for what would allow him to rule Rome, and rule it alone. To this end he lavished gifts on Senate and people, demonstrating that he had the discernment and largesse of spirit to rule wisely and well. His enemies weren't so sure of his goodwill. 'A man in Caesar's presence must step carefully if he cares to keep his head on his shoulders.' In 46 BC, now aged fifty-four, Caesar was presented by the people of Rome with the mantle of a *praefectura morum*, the dictator of moral manners, which permitted him even to stamp coins bearing his effigy. A veritable cult surrounded his personality; like the gods he gave his name to a month, and like the gods he was venerated at religious ceremonies. 'And this man is now become a god . . .'[6] He was named *imperator* for life, the highest judge in peacetime and supreme warlord in time of war. He assured himself of massive support by granting entire provinces the right to call themselves Roman citizens. He created a mighty army, increased

[5] Dispatch by Caesar to Rome after his victory over the Bosphorans at the Battle of Zela (2 August 47 BC).
[6] Shakespeare, *Julius Caesar*.

the salary of his legions and replaced every important functionary with one of his own officers. Caesar was a winner, and the crowd carried him on their shoulders to seize power in the Forum. There were still tribunes and senators, quaestors and consuls, but in title only. Gaius Julius Caesar was dictator of Rome, and with it the world of antiquity.

His charisma was overpowering; his soldiers adored him and no woman could ever resist him. The crowds loved him, and he enjoyed every minute of adulation; wherever he went, they chanted: 'Caesar . . . Caesar . . . Caesar . . .' Most of all, Caesar was a man of overbearing ambition with an ungoverned lust for raw power. The conquest of Gaul became the vehicle designed to carry him to domination. His unique goal was to be the master of Rome, and he conspired to destroy all his political opponents. Pompey was murdered in Egypt; Pompey's son was beaten in Spain; Cato went to Africa, where he was beaten and then killed himself. One survived, because he knew how to adapt to Caesar's ambition: Cicero. Once Caesar achieved the status of *imperator*, no power on earth could stop him, and no man could tell what his next move would be. And yet there were those who felt that the usurper had to be stopped. More than one man made that decision.

Julius Caesar was a talented and prolific writer who wrote his own history; others, who adored him, wrote of him with expressions of the most abject flattery. Those who abhorred his abominable deeds and dared to tell the truth about an usurper who wandered over corpses to achieve ultimate power found their words silenced. Caesar was the Great Manipulator. With extraordinary dexterity he changed the minds of the cheering crowd to prepare them for 'slavery under an Imperial despot' which they were to endure for centuries.

Already, in 62 BC, Cicero had tried to warn the people of Rome: 'Wherever you are, remember that you are equally within the power of the conqueror.' When challenged by friends as to what made him suddenly change his mind about Caesar, Cicero quipped: '*Cuiusvis hominis est errare! Nullus, nisi insipientis, in errore perservare* . . . Every man can err; only the unwise remain in error.' The meteoric rise of Caesar proved him right. The hour was near when the God of Victory, with Caesar as his high priest, would reveal himself to the Senate and people of Rome.

Caesar's 'deity complex' led him truly to believe that he was the chosen of God – a politician not averse to committing crime, but also a man of passion and dreams who was about to fall victim to his ultimate goal: his uncontrollable hunger for power.

13

An Honourable Man

Rome, the Theatre of Pompey
The Ides of March, 44 BC

*'Marcus Brutus, having the goodness of disposition,
had not his equal in honesty and pureness of purpose.'*
Plutarch

It is a quirk of history that antiquity's greatest republic
should have been founded and brought down by two
members of the same family clan, the Junii. Both men
carried the name of Brutus: Lucius Junius Brutus and
Marcus Junius Brutus. Between these two events five centuries passed.

In 535 BC the tyrant Tarquinius Superbus usurped the
throne of Rome. His first act was to kill off all those who
supported his predecessor, including the elder of the two
Junii brothers. Having been forced to observe the public
execution of his brother, the younger of the Junii plotted
revenge. He needed to wait for the appropriate moment,
in the meantime playing dumb. It saved his life but earned
the young Junius the sobriquet of Brutus – Latin for dumb
brute. From that moment on he was known only as Lucius
Junius Brutus, the dumb.

When King Tarquinius sent his sons to consult the

Oracle at Delphi, they took along as plaything their stupid cousin, Lucius Junius Brutus. The Oracle gave them a strange prophecy: 'He who kisses first his mother will earn supreme authority over Rome.' The royal brothers, most anxious to be the first to kiss their mother, were eager to get back to Rome. While awaiting their ship, one of them stuck out his leg and cousin Brutus fell to the ground. Thereby Lucius Junius Brutus was the first to kiss his mother – Mother Earth.

For years Lucius Junius waited patiently for the opportunity to take revenge and deliver the kingdom from the usurper. In 510 BC Brutus was given his chance. Although murder in high circles was likely to be overlooked, especially when committed by a member of the royal family, adultery and rape were not.

A prince of royal blood, Sextus Tarquinius, lusted after the wife of his cousin, the young senator Lucius Tarquinius Collatinus. Her name was Lucrecia Collatinus, and she was of exquisite beauty and honoured by all as a woman of impeccable virtue. One night, Prince Sextus broke into her husband's home and stole into the room where fair Lucrecia was reclining. 'Lucrecia,' he murmured, putting his hand on her naked breast, 'not a sound. I am Sextus Tarquinius and I am armed. Do not make a sound or I shall most certainly kill you.' Lucrecia stared at him with frightened eyes; she could hope for no succour as her husband had been dispatched on the King's business. Sextus confessed his desire for her and demanded that she give herself to him, in vain; not even on pain of death would she commit such a shameful deed. So he took her against her will.[1]

The following morning, the ravaged Lucrecia called on her returned husband, confessing the story of her

---

[1] Titus Livius, *Ab Urbe Condita* (I). This work was written six hundred years after the events.

shame, and demanded revenge of him. Whereupon she pushed a dagger into her heart and died at her husband's feet. Collatinus collapsed in sorrow over the body of his wife and called for the only friend he could trust, Lucius Junius. Whilst her husband mourned his beloved wife's death, Brutus pulled the dagger from Lucrecia's breast and rushed to the Forum, where the story had already preceded him and a great crowd had gathered. Waving the dagger, he exhorted the crowd: 'By the blood of Lucrecia, more chaste than any and shamed by a tyrant's offspring, I swear by this dagger and the fire and everything else which gives strength to my arm, that I shall track down Tarquinius Superbus, his evil wife, his cursed brood, and that I shall never let him, his descendants, nor anyone else ever again reign over Rome.'[2] The martyrdom of Lucrecia led to the foundation of antiquity's greatest republic.

There is perhaps a truer version of this certainly honourable tale. By the sixth century BC, the teachings of the Father of the Republic, the Athenian Solon (590 BC), had begun to infiltrate Roman society. When the tyranny of Tarquinius Superbus became unbearable, the families turned to Brutus, who possessed all the requisite qualities to lead the revolt – honesty, patriotism and political acumen. Certainly, he was after revenge, but at the same time he was also out to save Rome. His endeavour called for the full support of patrician families and the *populi*. The people of Rome followed him, as did the army (which Lucius Junius Brutus had persuaded with patrician gold to switch allegiance), and they chased out the King and his brood. Once that was achieved, and Rome had been liberated from its monarch, Lucius Junius Brutus did something highly unexpected. Not wanting to become another usurper, but rather someone who kept his promises and his integrity, he refused the crown, which was his by right. He could foresee

<hr/>

2 ibid.

the threat of a civil war should he disallow the *populi* what they wanted in exchange for their continuous support while at the same time pacifying his own aristocratic class.

His greatest challenge came from within his own family. His two sons plotted to re-establish a monarchy. The plot was discovered, and the plotters arrested. It was left to Brutus to dispense judgment. Not for a moment did the great patriot hesitate to choose the Republic over his family. To set an example for generations to come, and ensure that never again would there be a revolt against the SPQR, the senators and people of Rome, the founding father of Rome's Republic had his sons publicly executed for treason. 'And Brutus, first of his name, was an honourable man . . .'

With political wisdom, Lucius Junius Brutus went on to build Rome on the Greek republican model. Two magistrates, elected annually, were to act as *consuli*. By these means he divided their power and eliminated the dangers of the tyranny of one. The system worked and became the forerunner to the modern twin seats of power. The Romans' faith in their constitution was unshakeable, and indeed for the next five hundred years it worked to perfection.

Rome went on to conquer Italy, it survived foreign wars, barbaric invasions, natural disasters and internal upheavals. It survived Hannibal and the Helvetes. But suddenly Rome was faced with a challenge that could bring down the Republic and its ideas.

It was at this juncture that another Brutus arrived on the scene. Marcus Junius Brutus, the eventual leader of the anti-Caesarian conspiracy, spent his youth reading the Greek philosophers who had passed on their thoughts regarding a true and indivisible Republic. Yet, despite his pure republicanism, this second Brutus was to contribute as much to the restitution of the monarchy as his great ancestor had been responsible for its destruction. Having witnessed the death of Caesar – a friend, perhaps even a foster father figure – he was to live long enough to note that the death of Caesar only delayed the inevitable.

Marcus Junius Brutus, the first honest governor of Cisalpine Gaul, was shocked by the political corruption he discovered on his return to Rome when he was recalled to take over the highest function in the city, that of praetor. Thirty-six years of age, as cultured and civilised as the man he admired most, Julius Caesar, and imbued with the same spirit, he was suddenly faced with the prospect of having to condone illegality on the part of all those who bent the law for their own purposes under the mantle of legality. That Brutus retained an authentic love for Caesar is undeniable; however, he looked on with dismay as his idol changed. Caesar had certainly the most seductive personality of all despots. He would order an entire tribe killed without showing remorse, and, at the same time, forgive his personal enemy. His faculty for decision-making and his tenacity in adversity earned him the reputation of a military genius; on a political level he was without compare. As *censor*, Caesar manipulated the Senate at will. Worse still, in recognition, the Senate had bestowed upon him the title *pater patriae*, Father of the Nation, though he preferred the title *imperator*. Legally speaking, that made all the people of Rome subjects of Caesar. As *pontifex maximus*, he could manipulate religious teachings to aid his political objectives, and as *praefectura morum* he used his title to pass any law he pleased. With his acerbic wit, Cicero reported on the manner in which Caesar misused his political office: 'At one o'clock, Caesar announced the election of a consul to serve until 1 January – which was the next morning. So I can inform you that in Canninus' consulship, nobody had lunch. Still, nothing untoward occurred while he was consul: such was his vigilance that throughout his consulship, he did not sleep a wink!'

While, as *imperator*, Caesar was worshipped and admired by the ordinary people, he engendered in the ruling classes a feeling of resentment and betrayal. Saviour to one, he became the 'enemy from within' to others. They felt an increasing need to stop the demon who was destroying all the democratic values they held dear. They whispered that he had polluted the ideas of liberty, fairness and justice, and they were ready to do anything to stop him. Marcus Junius Brutus tried to warn Caesar that his ruthless ascent to supreme dictatorship was repugnant to Roman republicanism, but the dictator dismissed his warning with contempt. Marcus Brutus himself was not a danger to Caesar, but some of his friends would soon make him so.

Signs that pointed to his megalomania were increasing. During the Roman games of 45 BC, his effigy was carried into the arena before those of the gods. This was blasphemy, and it upset the patricians. A conspiracy was taking shape, but it was still without a charismatic leader. Brutus was hesitant, until the day he was invited by Caesar's mistress, Queen Cleopatra, together with twenty thousand Romans, to a sumptuous dinner. The occasion was arranged to sound out the people's reaction to re-establishing Rome as a monarchy. After dinner, Brutus overheard many of the invited guests addressing Caesar respectfully as *Rex*. Despite his love and admiration for the great Caesar, Brutus finally took the decision to join the conspirator Longinus Cassius. With this step, Marcus Junius Brutus became the obvious leader of the conspiracy, 'which took less arms than audacity and the reputation of an honest man such as Brutus to assure by his presence justice from the beginning to the end'.[3] As praetor of Rome, controlling the entire authoritarian apparatus of the capital, Brutus had the chance to strike the fatal blow. But 'Brutus was an honourable man' who spent weeks

[3] Plutarch, *Brutus*.

in anguish, torn between conscience and inclination. He finally became the last man in the history of Rome to choose fidelity to the constitution over loyalty to a benefactor. He found himself in the role of a misfit, driven by his own weariness of the affairs of the Republic into a circle of conspirators for whom he had nothing but contempt.

In February 44 BC, the Senate, whose membership Caesar inflated from the ranks of his cronies to nine hundred, named him *dictatus perpetuus*. Being dictator for life meant that Rome had now effectively reverted to absolute control by a single man. He became the focal point of passionate hate on the part of the Roman ruling class. Later that same February, Caesar declared that he would leave for a campaign in Spain. He set a date of 18 March. This panicked the conspirators into a rash decision. He couldn't be allowed to gain more popular support through yet another victory. In fact, had Caesar and the conspirators ever been able to discuss their problem in a sober atmosphere, free of the bitter animosity that civil strife engenders, they would have found much common ground. Both had the interests of Rome at heart and, in their different ways, wished to see Rome returned to stability, under one dictator or two consuls. Caesar's whole existence was a continuous conflict between innate idealism which led him to seek to carve out a super-realm for Rome and the iron discipline of a dictatorial conqueror.

One of the main causes of the drama that occurred on the Ides of March in 44 BC was the 'affair of the crowns'. It happened during the feast of Lupercal, when Caesar's master of cavalry presented the *censor* and *imperator* with a crown in front of the huge audience. This coronation scene was repeated by Marc Antony before an august crowd in the Forum. When Caesar coyly refused the crown, the crowd cheered. So Caesar asked them to take the laurel crowns into the Capitol. In the first days of March 44 BC, a senatorial supporter of the dictator (probably

Marc Antony himself) placed the same diadems on two of Caesar's statues at the entrance and then called for Caesar's installation – as King of Rome. This so upset the patricians in the Senate that two tribunes, Marullus and Flavius, snatched the crowns and removed those who had saluted Caesar as their king by force of arms. Their gesture had shown that the Senate and people of Rome loved Caesar but didn't care much for kings. Caesar was furious, and had the two tribunes removed. For the conspirators, the time had come to put their plans into action. They didn't dare confront him openly in the Senate, but Caesar had to be stopped. He who thrived on luck was to be lucky no more. *'Conversa subite fortuna est . . .* The luck has changed.'[4]

'If heaven has eyes, he won't live long enough.' Thus spoke Casca, one of the conspiracy leaders. Brutus frowned, but his eyes held a pensive, meditative look. He could see the pitfall. Bloodshed would only serve to create a martyr figure. They picked the date of 15 March, because Cassius had been informed that the *imperator*'s supporters in the Senate were to pronounce him King the next morning.

The night before the Ides of March, Caesar took part in a gluttonous feast at the house of his friend Lepidus. Next morning, as he arrived at the Theatre of Pompey, he was still under the influence of too much wine and not a man who could confront a menace or end a mutiny with sharp words. Brutus, surrounded by his conspirators, was waiting for the *imperator* on the steps of the theatre. Their principles were noble; everything else was less glorious. The scene, which took place before the statue of Pompey, defied the uprightness of the honourable Brutus. As if in a stage play about murder in the arena, twenty-three togaed patricians jumped on Caesar and his ambition fell victim to their daggers' thrust.

---

[4] Cornelius Nepos (99–24 BC).

. . . Tillius Cimber, laying hold of Caesar's robe with both his hands, pulled it down from his neck, which was the signal for the assault. Casca gave him the first cut in the neck, which was not mortal nor dangerous, as coming from one who at the beginning of such a bold action was very much disturbed; Caesar immediately turned about, and laid his hand upon the dagger and kept hold of it. And both of them at the same time cried out, he that received the blow, in Latin: 'Vile Casca, what does this mean?' and he that gave it, in Greek to his brother: 'Brother, help!'

Upon the first onset, those who were not privy to the design were astonished, and their horror and amazement at what they saw were so great that they durst not flee, nor assist Caesar, nor so much as speak a word. But those who came prepared for the business enclosed him on every side, with their naked daggers in their hands. Which way soever he turned he met with blows, and saw their swords levelled at his face and eyes, and was encompassed, like a wild beast in the toils, on every side. For it had been agreed they should each of them make a thrust at him, and flesh themselves with his blood; for which reason Brutus also gave him a stab in the groin. Some say he fought and resisted the rest, shifting his body to avoid the blows, and calling out for help, but when he saw Brutus' sword drawn, he covered his face with his robe and submitted, letting himself fall, whether it were by chance, or that he was pushed in that direction by his murderers, at the foot of the pedestal on which Pompey's statue stood, and which was thus wetted with his blood. So that Pompey himself seemed to have presided, as it were, over the revenge done upon his adversary, who lay here at his feet, and breathed out his soul through a multitude of wounds, for they say he received three-and-twenty.

When Caesar was dispatched, Brutus stood forth to give reason for what they had done.[5]

Among the horde of assassins was Caesar's kinsman and naval leader, Decimus Brutus – not to be confused with the conspiracy's leader, Marcus Junius Brutus, but the 'younger Brutus', son of Caesar's former mistress Servilia, who had defeated the Veneti at sea. It was to him that Caesar spoke in a dying voice: *'Et tu Brute?'* 'When the murder was newly done, there were sudden outcries of people that ran up and down the city, which indeed increased the fear and tumult,' reported Plutarch. When the site was clear and all the hostile senators had fled out of the hall, Brutus thought he might easily press home his advantage. But then people began to arrive amid much shouting. The news had raced through the city and a huge crowd gathered before the theatre to pay the slain Caesar their last respects. Brutus realised that he couldn't possibly become the Senate's new leader without exciting sedition and perhaps a civil war in the city. One of the conspirators, the Republican Lucius, was quick to justify the murder as a necessary sacrifice: 'People of Rome, observe the countenance and admire the high spirit of one who set you free from the dictator. Do not betray your liberty, or the defender of it.' Yet popular opinion remained that this had been a brutal assassination of a great man, especially once they became roused by the fiery eulogy of Marc Antony, standing over the corpse of the slain . . . 'and Brutus is an honourable man . . .'[6]

Brutus's greatest fear was justified. In death, Caesar became

---

[5] Plutarch's account of the murder, in the Dryden translation of his *The Lives of the Noble Grecians and Romans*, published by *Encyclopaedia Britannica*, Chicago, 1952. Plutarch lived from AD 46 to 102, and his version can be considered the closest to a description of the actual event.

[6] Shakespeare took this from Plutarch.

a martyr, and what the conspirators had been so desperate to stop was now inexorably under way. The fickle populace of Rome grieved for their *imperator* as all good subjects would grieve for their king. The murder of Caesar pushed Rome into another civil war. In the years to follow, many more Roman soldiers died at each other's hands than ever did during Caesar's war against the Gaul.

The struggle between pro-monarchists and pro-republicans did not end there. Marc Antony, the seasoned general, aligned himself with Caesar's nephew Octavianus, the astute politician, against the republicans Cassius and Brutus. At the head of an all-Roman force, Marc Antony caught up with the republican legions in swampy terrain near Philippi.

On the eve of the battle, Brutus turned to his friend Cassius: 'If Providence shall not dispose what we now undertake according to our wishes, I resolve to put no further hopes or warlike preparations to the proof, but will die contented with my fortune. For I already have given up my life to my country for the Ides of March – and have lived since then a second life for her sake, with liberty and honour!'

On the morning of 3 October 42 BC the first battle began. Brutus was successful along the whole line, but not Cassius, who commanded the right wing. Brutus attacked and had soon pushed back the combined forces of Octavianus and Antony. But by attacking before Cassius was ready to strike he had put a dent into their battle formation and was separated from Cassius by a trench line, put up by Marc Antony's soldiers. This created a fatal gap. Meanwhile, fully unaware of the danger, Brutus advanced and, in a surprise march around Octavianus's wing, entered his enemy's camp. Brutus thought the battle decided in his favour, but he had never received the message from Cassius asking him to rush to his succour. While all was going well for Brutus, who faced an indecisive Octavianus, Cassius was pushed into a swamp by the able leadership of Marc Antony and his legions. It was the decisive moment of the battle. How history would have changed had Brutus dispatched even one legion. Cassius, left without a relief force, thought that Brutus was also losing his part of the combat. With his legions being pushed farther into the deadly swamps, and severely mauled, Cassius, seeing that all was lost, entered his tent, pulled his mantle over his head and bared his neck. He then asked his friend Pindarus to deliver the deadly blow.

Before they were given a chance to ransack Cassius's camp, Marc Antony rallied his soldiers to turn his full force against Brutus. In this he expected strong support from Octavianus in order that they might catch their opponent in a vice. Brutus was unaware of the grave danger of being crushed between two forces. Still the battle could have gone his way, had he turned immediately against Marc Antony and his legions; because now an incident occurred which once again altered the outcome. The night before the battle, Octavianus had been told of a dream by his friend Artorius, who had seen Octavianus carried from camp on a litter, pierced by many arrows and agonising in death. This so frightened Octavianus that, when Brutus entered his camp and his two thousand Greek mercenaries were killed, Octavianus panicked and fled. Brutus, on entering his tent, found it empty, although some of his soldiers presented their bloodied swords to him and told him that they had killed Octavianus. By running away, Octavianus had robbed Marc Antony of certain victory, and it left the battle unresolved, making another inevitable.

For the next twenty days, the armies of Marc Antony and Brutus camped in sight of one another. On 23 October 42 BC, in a surprise move worthy of Hannibal, Marc Antony left Octavianus holding the front while he led part of his army through the swamp and caught Brutus's legions from the rear. Once again, the outcome of the battle proved indecisive, since Octavianus had failed to follow up Marc Antony's success with the legions under his command. The politician, soon to become Emperor, was simply not up to decisive military action. Yet this battle shattered all hopes for the restoration of the Republic; the 'honourable Brutus' was despondent over the failure of the people of Rome to rise and lend him their support. They had been blinded by Octavianus's empty promises to keep the Republic alive, a pledge the ambitious Octavianus would not keep. The Republic was dead. Brutus was at an end; there was nothing he could do to stop the process. God, his god and that of the Republic, had decided to condemn the only man who could have opposed with his republican spirit the absolute power of a king – or, in this case, an emperor.

Marcus Junius Brutus was as much responsible for reinstalling the monarchy as his illustrious forebear Lucius Junius Brutus had been for bringing it down. That thought made him so despondent that he threw himself on his blade. 'I do not weep for my own misfortune but for that of the *patria*,' were his parting words.[7] His body was found by Marc Antony, who covered it with his richest mantle of purple, and when a thief tried to steal the mantle he had him instantly put to death. The noble Brutus was burned with great honour and his ashes were sent to his mother Servilia.

Brutus wanted to die, and he wanted to pay for the sins of a tottering Republic he had believed in and then tried to sustain. With his death the Republic died, to be replaced by an *imperium romanum*.

The circle was closed. A monarchy ceded to tyranny, tyranny gave way to a republic of the aristocracy; thereafter the aristocrats yielded to one more democratic republic,

---

[7] It could also have been that Brutus asked Strato, his friend, to run him through, because Strato was brought before Marc Antony by one of Brutus's tribunes who said: 'This, O Caesar, is the man that did the last friendly act to my beloved Brutus.'

until another monarchy threw out the old values and brought back the tyranny of the absolute monarch.

The differences between our century and the ancient world are profound, but not enough to render an analogy superficial. The five-hundred-year experience of the Roman Republic is much too valuable to be overlooked. Much had come to pass in these five centuries: the great conquests – Italy, Carthage, Greece, Gaul; Cato and Scipio, Regulus and Cincinnatus; and the fight for the establishment of one of the best-formulated constitutions in republican history.

With the world's most famous assassination, the master of performance and façade, self-confident visionary, arch deceiver and manipulator of noble or desperate causes fell victim to his own ambition. Gaius Julius Caesar was one of those inexplicable phenomena which emerge at rare intervals in mankind's history. He mesmerised the Roman nation as a people have rarely been before or since.

The Ides of March sounded the death knell to the Roman Republic, which had served throughout five centuries as the basis of a just Roman society, in which, ever since the fall of the monarchy, the state motto had been *Senatus Populusque Romanus* – the Senate and the People of Rome.

One assassination was enough to alter profoundly the next five centuries of history.

Part Five

The Emperors

27 BC–AD 81

(Augustus to Titus)

*'From battle and murder and
from sudden death . . .'*
The Litany from the Book of Prayers

14

A Season for Murder

Domus Aureus, Rome
9 June AD 68

'Quid leges sine moribus vanae proficiunt?'
('What help are empty laws without morals?')
Horace (65 BC–AD 8)

Of the first ten Roman emperors, all but two came to a violent end.

Augustus	29 BC–AD 14	killed Caesar's son Caesarion
Tiberius	AD 14–37	strangled
Caligula	AD 37–41	murdered
Claudius	AD 41–54	poisoned
Nero	AD 54–68	committed suicide
Galba	AD 68–69	beheaded
Otho	AD 69	committed suicide
Vitellius	AD 69	murdered
Vespasian	AD 69–79	died in bed
Titus	AD 79–81	murdered
Domitian	AD 81–96	murdered

Poor SPQR. The Republic of the 'Senate and the People of Rome' was dismantled. What followed was a succession of brutal, murderous rulers. There were many ways in which imperial power could reproduce itself: by election, violence, usurpation and natural inheritance. The best way to seize the purple was to kill your brother, and then your entire family. Murder in imperial families never stopped.

Their corruption and military oppression were to replace the liberal notion of the dignity of human nature. The end result was moral decadence and an inclination to indulge in all available appetites, preferably sexual. The emperors luxuriated in the wealth they robbed from their people, disguising murder with the formality of dispensing justice, violating the basic rights of their *populus* while shielding behind words of patriotism.

The Emperor was god. Caesar's nephew, who was to become the first emperor called Augustus, showed the way. 'You dare call me a mystic?' asked Octavian (Octavianus) of an augur at a place of sacrifice which had challenged him: 'Don't you believe in a god?'

'I have nothing against this or that god in particular. Of course, god is a hypothesis, but I must admit a god is vital to the harmony – universal harmony that is.' After a moment of silence he added: 'Perhaps we should invent a god . . .'

And with one phrase he set the course of imperial Rome for the next four centuries. A god, an *augustus*, 'one that is raised to the sky'.

Religious mania is the outcome of a devouring vanity, the illusion of power without limit, and a first disposition towards paranoia. When their will had been fully done among mortals, the Roman emperors declared themselves to be God. Their reign was mostly one of fear and panic, ending in perfidy and murder. '*Quid leges sine moribus vanae proficiunt?* What help are empty laws without morals?'[1]

Caesar's nephew did not venture forth to avenge the 'foul deed' done to Caesar; that had already been achieved by Marc Antony at Philippi. The outcome of the struggle was that the victorious Antony shared power with Octavian. The deal was sealed when Antony married Octavian's sister Octavia. All counted without the beautiful Cleopatra. Caesar's humour had attracted her in a way more passionate men could not. With Antony it was different; an immortal, if foolish, fast-burning love between bouts of remorse. For the love of an Egyptian queen Antony cast off his wife Octavia, and this much to the publicly professed anger of his jilted wife's brother, who managed to turn the former, much-celebrated mistress of his uncle Caesar into a harlot and outcast. In fact, for Octavian the affair was a heaven-sent pretext to wrestle power from Marc Antony and achieve dictatorial power, like his murdered uncle. Volatile and uncompromising, he openly encouraged violence against supporters of his opponent. Marc Antony had relapsed into total despair. The one he had promised his friend Caesar that he would always protect, the one he had so ably assisted to reach the summit of power, that Octavian, a cynic from a world that had outgrown the pure spirit of a republic, was out to crucify him. Their armadas of four hundred vessels each clashed on the open sea near Actium (2 September 31 BC). Octavian had bought with gold the loyalty of a number of Antony's captains, who, soon after the start of the battle, surrendered their ships to Octavian's general Agrippa. Cleopatra and Antony fled to Egypt, hotly pursued by Octavian. When Antony took to the field to check Octavian's advance on Alexandria, he was (falsely) informed that his beloved Cleopatra had killed

---

[1] Horace, *Odes*, Book III, Ode XXIV.

herself; in utter despondency over his loss he committed suicide. Octavian took Cleopatra prisoner and informed her that she was to be paraded in chains through the streets of Rome. This proud woman, who had conquered Caesar and became the great love of Marc Antony, refused to be subjected to such infamy. She pressed the poisonous asp to her bosom.

In 29 BC, Octavian returned in triumph to Rome and took on the title of *imperator*. Added to it was another title: *princeps rei publicae*, the First Citizen of the Republic. Two years later, in 27 BC, the Senate took the predictable step of raising him to the status of an earthly divinity. With this, the Republic was abolished. Octavian changed his name to Caesar Augustus, or 'the one raised to the heavens'. His achievement lay not in territorial conquest, as did that of his forebears, but in stopping the civil war and ensuring the security of the state. The guarantor of this was a strong defence force. He reformed the army – and created a monster; political decisions by any emperor depended from now on entirely on the goodwill of the legions. It was the army, and not the state or the Emperor, which decided and maintained the 'Pax Romana'.

With his death in AD 14, the War of the Diadochi[2] broke out over his succession. The period that followed Emperor Augustus did nothing to improve the glory of the empire. 'It is almost superfluous to enumerate the unworthy successors of Augustus. The dark, unrelenting Tiberius, the furious Caligula, the feeble Claudius, the profligate and cruel Nero, the beastly Vitellius, and the timid inhuman Domitian are condemned to everlasting infamy. Rome groaned beneath their unremitting tyranny, which exterminated ancient families of the republic and

---

[2] Fought by those who tried to claim for themselves the empire of Alexander the Great.

was fatal to almost every virtue and every talent that arose in that unhappy period.'[3]

The emperors were content to keep their dominions safe from incursions by the Parthians and Jews in Asia Minor, and the barbarian tribes north of the Danube and beyond the Rhine. Those hardy Teutonic warriors had shown the price a Roman emperor had to pay for his territorial ambitions when his legions tried to subdue them. In AD 9, the united Germanic tribes under Arminius, a Cheruscian prince and honorary Roman officer and citizen, annihilated the three legions of Varus in the Teutoburger Forest.[4] In a furious onslaught that was decided by a fluke of weather, a sudden thunderstorm, Arminius ambushed Varus and his legions in a dark forest, slaughtered the legionaries and nailed his captives to trees. This Roman disaster, one of history's decisive battles, put an end to all Roman territorial expansion plans beyond the river borders of the Rhine and the Danube, and the two major rivers became Rome's *termini imperii*, the border which nature had imposed on it. After that terrible defeat, Emperor Augustus had no more taste for war. In Asia Minor, in order to recover the lost legion eagles of Crassus, he preferred to pay a ransom to the Parthians rather than confront the wild horsemen in open battle. When Augustus died, his testament was read from the steps of the Forum. In it he established the boundaries of the Augustinian Empire, based on natural bulwarks such as rivers and deserts: the Rhine and Danube to the north, the Atlantic to the west, the Euphrates to the east and the wide strip of North African desert to the south. And so remained this *imperium romanum* for the next four hundred years.

The imperial interests of Rome were defined by the necessity of protecting the empire's blood and soil. That

---

3 G.M. Low, *Gibbon's Decline and Fall of the Roman Empire*, London, 1960.
4 See the author's *The Weather Factor*.

was why all the legions were strategically placed around its vast borders and kept in camps; more often than not a legion was stationed without its general, since an *augustus* did not need a general who commanded greater respect from his legion than did the Emperor. A military leader's initiative was never encouraged, and that again led to a decline in the legions' efficiency and discipline. The legions, eternal defenders of Rome, were watered down. No longer did their ranks carry that feeling of comradeship of arms and the fervent patriotism that had helped Rome survive terrible storms and led it to greatness. A war allowed the Emperor to take advantage of the desires of men otherwise outlawed for many sorts of crime; they joined up just to regain their freedom within the law, the 'law of the emperor'. A pardon was granted to anyone willing to fight. This swelled the ranks with those who would otherwise be found guilty of foul deeds, and who became legionaries for no better reason than to escape punishment. The poor flocked into camps to ensure a daily meal for their starving bellies in garrison canteens. Others joined the army to seek their fortune. The young patricians, born into the officer class, who depended neither on wealth nor booty, were out for personal glory – or strictly for the fun of it. In war they could kill and rape, and all in total legality. Garrison boredom was interspersed with hectic bouts of warfare and plunder. Camp life was the long wait in between. A legionary's time was passed mostly in lazing about. Precious little drilling was done, and his tackle was allowed to deteriorate; the rest of the day was passed in whoring, sleeping, boasting, eating and drinking. There was also the language barrier between the many ethnic components within a legion; quarrels broke out and private accounts were settled with the arms they were supposed to use on their empire's enemy.

This displacement left the heart of the empire vulnerable. Only a few legions were on hand to suppress internal trouble. The Emperor's and the city's protection were put entirely in the hands of ten thousand selected men of the Imperial Praetorian Guard. This proved to be a dangerous move. While the army kept the citizens and slaves from creating trouble, the praetorians kept the army under control, and the *augusti* spent their time worrying how to keep control of the praetorians. Because not only were the praetorians the bodyguards of the Emperor; they soon began to decide who should actually *be* Emperor. Thereby the emperors themselves created the situation that frequently led to their downfall or assassination.

As for the ordinary masses, the emperors were stripping their subjects' lives bare of the social mechanism that had worked so well under the Republic. They transformed the country into some autonomous, pitiless machine, which established a state of affairs that suited them better. And whenever the great *populi* became restless, the emperors gave them bread and games and a few bothersome Christians to be devoured by lions. This new religion posed a challenge to the power of the Emperor. Sooner or later there would be insubordination, or even worse, and the Emperor outlawed all instruction in Christianity. Which made matters only worse; Christianity went underground and continued to spread and flourish. Rome became a viper's nest of intrigue and murder. And so it came about that the emperors were more concerned with ensuring their own survival by killing off any opposition than running the empire.

All menial work was done by armies of slaves, hundreds of thousands from all corners of the empire. Slaves did not dare revolt, and if they so much as ventured to complain about their inhuman treatment, the praetorians displayed their utmost brutality. While Romans were strangled behind prison walls, slaves were publicly crucified along one of the main roads leading from Rome, and then left hanging there for the crows to pick at. The best way to achieve his freedom was for a slave to render valuable service and hope for the generosity of his master. Unfortunately Roman avarice stopped this from being a realistic prospect. A slave was a slave, a man without a country, and an inexpensive worker.

The Senate was a powerless tool of the despot; their meetings were brief and did nothing more than ratify the Emperor's decision and vote a new accolade for their *augustus*. The ordinary Roman had no part in government, and, in contrast to their ancestors, wanted none. They were happy to go to the Coliseum to watch gladiators do each other to death. '*Ave imperator, morituri te salutant* . . .'

Intrigues were everywhere, and death came quick, by poison or dagger. Almost none of the Roman emperors or pretenders to the throne ended their days in peaceful sleep. Emperor Tiberius's relations with Germanicus, pretender to the imperial crown, became strained. Germanicus was exiled as troop commander to the East, where, following a meal served to him by one of Tiberius's slaves, he fell down dead. His successor as Emperor left his name as a symbol of utter brutality. Grandson of Tiberius, he had the Emperor strangled in his sleep to usurp the crown (16 March 34). Gaius Caesar, better known as Caligula, son of Germanicus and a vicious sadist, was persuaded that his life was guided by cosmic forces; he listened to no other voices than those from heaven, which echoed his own thoughts. Whatever ascendancy he may have gained over his nihilistic courtiers by killing them off indiscriminately, he never controlled the uncontrollable praetorians, by whose favour alone he held his crown. His firm belief in his messianic mission drove him mad. He continued his killing spree, disposing of suspected rivals and, to the same degree, his closest supporters. He finally lost control and was murdered by officers of his own Praetorian Guard. Claudius, a relatively decent man as Roman emperors went, followed him. He was married to Messalina, whose spectacular beauty was as legendary as her sexual debauchery. Her husband was more interested in historic writings than in spending his time performing his masculine duties. In search of fiery oblivion, Messalina staggered towards self-destruction, reverting to the wild and promiscuous way of life for which she had been notorious before she married Claudius. Her parties became the talk of Rome, always ending in an uproarious state of disorder. And every morning she cast aside her lovers, bringing on headaches, nausea and more craving. She bribed her way into schools of gladiators, where she gave herself to dozens of young, eager male bodies. She searched for solace in dungeons, rutting with all those condemned to die the following morning. When she began quite shamelessly to take the Emperor's praetorians to her bed, Claudius finally had her killed by one of her former lovers while she was in the arms of yet another man.

Claudius acted extremely naïvely when he next took as his wife the sister of the mad emperor Caligula. Agrippina was a much more lethal woman than his previous spouse – she was ambitious, and within no time she had grabbed the reins of power. This upset the Romans, so she changed her plans. Agrippina's past was no example of righteous womanhood. She had had ample opportunity to 'taste the forbidden fruit' with a string of lovers, from generals to ordinary soldiers in camps, and it had left her with a son; how she remembered her screams of agony while giving birth to the child. It was the curse of Jupiter, the people whispered – the sister of that demoniacal Caligula had begot a pit of vipers. Now she had forced her timid emperor husband to adopt her bastard son, who was bestowed with the noble name of Nero Claudius Caesar Drusus Germanicus. This step put the monster in line for the throne. But for him to succeed it would be necessary to eliminate all those on the ladder ahead of him.

Throughout his life, Nero was haunted by the blood-bath that had brought him to power. Once Nero had been adopted and legalised by Claudius, the Emperor had to die before Claudius's own son by his wife Messalina, Britannicus, reached the age at which he could rule. A plot unfolded. Its driving force was Nero's mother Agrippina, a woman who had taken lessons from her brother Caligula. On 13 October 54, Empress Agrippina arranged for a private feast of a special kind.

'The most noble lady wishes your audience,' announced Claudius's captain of the guard.

The queen entered. 'You have been avoiding me, my dear husband.'

'The affairs of the empire keep me occupied,' he replied.

'Not tonight, my love.' She clapped her hands and one of her servants entered with two goblets of wine. Agrippina had been careful to take the antidote before entering the Emperor's chamber. She knew that she was safe from the poison. 'You do not trust me?' She laughed and emptied her cup. The wine made her dizzy; she knew that she had to be patient and wait for him to drink. He did, and fell to the floor, moaning and gasping, his face contorted, before he closed his eyes for ever. On the way out of his chamber, Agrippina looked at the slumped guards and the spilled goblets of poisoned wine. With Claudius out of the way, there was only Messalina's brat Britannicus to deal with. Four months after his father, he fell over dead after partaking of a spiced dish, and Nero became undisputed heir to a huge empire at the age of seventeen. He continued his mother's tradition of eliminating all bothersome members of his own family. In the following years he murdered two wives plus his harpy mother, because Agrippina had committed the unpardonable error of grabbing for herself the reins of imperial control.

The Emperor became the slave of men who hated and

despised him. The barbarous excesses committed by his praetorians may have disgusted him, but he was glad of any valid excuse to justify his own irresolution. He spent each morning at his usual duties, including approving the next batch of executions. Lulled by positive reports from his courtiers, who told their emperor what he wanted to hear, Nero continued his lascivious lifestyle. Orgies and murders followed one after the other. He must have been blind to overlook the growing thunder.

He was obsessed with distrust and its attendant neurosis. His corruption of power was reinforced by a fear of treachery. To stop himself from breaking down under the strain of such a life, Nero relied heavily on drugs. His augurs managed to cover up their emperor's exhaustion by means of stimulants, an approach that completely ruined Nero. A powerful constitution could have preserved him from early physical and mental collapse, but soon changes in his physical condition became apparent and his sustained outbursts of anger took on the form of aggravated madness. He suffered increasingly from stomach cramps. His augurs, the very ones who supplied him with their soothing poisonous concoctions, winked at each other over the obsolete religious ceremonies which they solemnly celebrated in the presence of the Emperor, and then fed him more drugs to calm him down. Nero spied conspiracy everywhere – many of his courtiers, eminent senators, even members of his family had to pay for his paranoia with their lives. They were charged with treason and executed. Should a treason charge fail, they were simply murdered. Nero's imperial household teemed with foppish courtesans. He entertained them with readings of his poetry, they were made to listen to his music, and they procured his lovers, more often than not their own sons and daughters. His court was crowded with parasites; his perfumed flatterers helped decide policy. 'The bad jokes of Fortune – village Pierrots yesterday, arbiters of life and death today, tomorrow keepers of the public latrines.'[5]

Impressed by the great achievements of Caesar, Nero launched his army on an expedition against Parthia. Command over the legions was handed to a good general, Gnaeus Domitius Corbulo, who took over an army weakened by years of inaction and formed it into an efficient fighting instrument. Under Corbulo's able guidance, the army soon took on form and purpose, and began to challenge the dominance of Nero's court sycophants. This so frightened the mad Emperor that he had Corbulo replaced by a complete military idiot who was not about to become a challenge – Caesennius Paetus. He came, he saw, and he was crushed at Rhandeia (AD 62) by the combined Parthian–Armenian forces of King Tiridiates. The fact that Parthian riders continually surrounded them, dashing around them like flies while keeping their distance, Paetus interpreted as a sign of fear, and he considered his force strong enough to dispense with a vanguard. He even neglected to send forth scouts. His legions, which had fallen back into their lazy routine following the dismissal of General Corbulo, simply refused to continue their march before they were given a lunch break, and this despite a report from an outrider who had seen three great masses of men and horses, gleaming with lances and armour. Paetus halted, and his men were lolling about around the cooking stoves when a shower of arrows struck the camp. A moment before there wasn't a man to be seen, and now suddenly a thousand archers were standing behind shrubs and low hillocks, having seemingly risen from the ground. They lit a ring of fire which immediately caught in the dry grass, flames shooting high into the air. A brisk wind rose and whipped up the flames, until the valley looked like the pit of hell, a tangle of smoke and crackling flame. It trapped

5 Juvenal.

the remaining Romans inside the cauldron. And through the flames came flight after flight of missiles. Safety lay ahead, through the screen of archers and slingers, but those who tried to reach it died in the flames or were shot at point-blank range by the Armenian archers. Because of the chaos, and the incessant attack from the missiles, it was every man for himself. The legions were buried under a shower of arrows. Shafts the length of a tall man's arm, with a tip hardened by fire, sped from bows drawn by men who had used them since childhood to hunt animals. Now they were hunting the greatest animal of all, their fellow man. The legionaries screamed in pain and their centurions in rage. The slaughter was great. Arrows pierced horses and saddles; some men fell, others stumbled over the fallen horses. The camp was in chaos – everywhere lay bodies and spears, swords and dead horses. One cohort of cavalry managed to saddle up and ride through the flames. They were immediately engaged by a vast horde of Parthian riders, which cut them from their saddles. Poor foolish Paetus was one of the last to die. He was captured and put to death. The Parthians and Armenians had no time to take prisoners. After the slaughter at Rhandeia, Emperor Nero reinstated Corbulo, who rebuilt the legions and with them invaded Armenia to establish Roman order.

From Emperor Augustus on, all rulers became the object of a religious cult, elevated to the rank of divinity. But an *augustus*'s power was brittle, built entirely on the loyalties of his Praetorian Guard, of the army, and of a broad spectrum of the *populus romanus*. If an emperor did not live up to their expectations, and since as a god figure he couldn't be voted out of his job, there was but one practical way to get rid of him – liquidate him. Such a fate had befallen all before Nero, especially his mother's brother, the evil Caligula, and now the good patricians had a valid reason to get rid of Nero. He was more interested in presiding over races at the hippodrome than being present on a field of battle. He frequented the lowest of drinking dens and bordellos, always dressed as a slave, to pick up occasional street lovers. His orgies became the talk of Rome. Virgins of noble birth were coupled with animals; the Emperor, dressed in women's clothes, made a spectacle of himself by being publicly violated by stroppy legionaries. But his speciality was sodomising young boys, strangling them with a silk cord during his ultimate frenzy. At one point he organised a wedding where he was the bride and his favourite lover the bridegroom. This was bound to lead to public outrage, especially after he forced prominent citizens, even senators, to join him, offering their wives and daughters to a series of specially selected muscular men wearing grotesque masks.

A dark chain of events led to the fall of Nero. In AD 64 a grave catastrophe befell Rome – a blaze broke out in a warehouse. It was never established how the fire started, whether by accident or deliberately. It raged quickly out of control and engulfed a large portion of the town, especially the poorer section, which was built from wood. Much of Rome was destroyed. Only the great patrician estates of stone and marble were untouched by the blaze – a symbol of the extreme tension that existed within Roman society, the great divide between rich and poor. A rumour spread throughout the poorer section of the city that Nero had started the fire to derive artistic inspiration for a composition dedicated to one of his lovers. Whether this was true or not, people began to believe in such tales because they wanted to believe. Gangs of toughs began roaming the streets, beating up the supporters of the Emperor (more to rob them than to inflict permanent harm), while the Praetorian Guard stood idly by and watched, hoping to carve their own power centres out of the general chaos. Patricians fled in fear to their country estates, while Nero ignored the people and their discontent. But he committed a fatal error when he ordered for himself a new palace, the *domus aureus*,[6] to be built on the still-smouldering ashes, and on property owned by some of the wealthiest Roman families. To cover the outrageous costs of this spectacular palace, he simply confiscated private property and increased public taxes. This brought him into a final conflict with the patricians. They had tolerated in silence his orgies and the murders of members of his family. But once his conduct touched their personal fortunes, it became everybody's business. Since they didn't dare openly oppose the divine person of the Emperor, slur campaigns were started. They achieved the desired result, and soon the broad masses had had enough of his excesses.

General Corbulo was not only a brilliant soldier, he was trained in the greatest military tradition of the ancient world, and was therefore faithful to his superior commander, the Emperor. In AD 67, when increasing signs pointed to a threat to his august person, Corbulo still supported the arbitrary moods of a despot corrupted by the exorbitance of power. To safeguard Nero's person, he suggested placing his loyal legions around Rome in order to forestall any adventurous designs on the part of the patricians, the populace or the fickle praetorians. But even as he was doing his duty, he knew what his reward would be. 'Caesar will have my head no matter what I do,' he said to his tribune. And so it was. Nero's paranoia had reached such a pitch of frenzy that he could see only treachery; he took Corbulo's well-meaning offer as an attempt on the crown. 'A traitor,' Nero fumed, and he publicly shamed Corbulo to such an extent that he forced him to commit suicide (AD 67). With Corbulo's death, Nero had dug his own grave.

Even in the last weeks, when his power to compel or

6 Recently it has been opened to the public and is well worth a visit. It is located across from the Coliseum.

reward was gone, Nero thought he could still reign by decree. He signed his own death warrant when he tried to dismiss the Senate. The emasculated Senate dared show a spark of courage when it bribed Rome's Praetorian Guard with bags of silver lashed to the backs of donkeys and dispatched into their camp and declared Nero 'Rome's public enemy' (AD 68). Rioting erupted; many were killed in a rampage when the patience of the population cracked under the strains of imperial oppression. Rich men were jostled by the rioting crowd who, with the cry: 'Slaves, back to your toil!' that had always before been directed at them, thrashed their masters. Many people died. Then a deep voice shouted: 'And you, the dead, return into your hell!' The Senate was dissolved owing to the clamour of the masses. The fickle Praetorian Guard heeded the *vox populi*, especially as they felt that they had been deprived of their fair share of the wealth doled out by their emperor; they switched sides and came after Nero. In final desperation, the Emperor called on his legions, but they would not respond to his plea. How Nero must have regretted ordering only months before the execution of the one man who would certainly have led his steadfast legions to his assistance – the victor of Armenia, Gnaeus Corbulo.

From outside his splendid palace, the *domus aureus*, the mob could be heard shouting for his death. 'I am not to be disturbed,' the Emperor told his servants as he entered his chamber that 9 June 68. Nero, the monster, lay down on his bed, his face darkened by distress, tossing and turning. He stared at the ceiling and saw visions of betrayals, foul murders and of the deaths he had ordered. Voices of those long dead whispered in his ear. He buried his face in trembling hands, biting his knuckles and sobbing miserably. His litanies, the gifts bestowed on his personal guards, the endless human sacrifices – all seemed vain and meaningless now. And yet, even with his executioners' footsteps pounding up the stairs, Nero still found time to arrange a spectacle for his apocalyptic ending. He dressed in flowing robes as if in the last act of a Greek tragedy, and then ordered his personal slave to run him through with a gold dagger. While the praetorians, with swords drawn, rushed towards his chambers, he was heard to cry out: 'What great artist dies with me.' Still the intruders dared not touch him, awed by the nearness of the imperial presence, writhing and moaning in the agony of his wound. Only when he was still did they grab his lifeless hand and rip away his rings, as well as the golden necklace and bracelets from his neck and arms. Outside the crowd roared: 'The scoundrel is dead. Rome is saved.' These were the same people who had cheered him and had enjoyed his spectacles in the arena, the fickle crowd of Rome. He created the lasting image of the mad Roman Emperor, luxuriating in perversion. There were other *augusti*, good rulers, who created wealth and prosperity for their citizens. But none ever achieved the same notoriety as Nero.

With Nero died the Augustan line. It was not surprising that after the steep decline in morals and the years of perversion, perpetuated by the likes of Messalina and Agrippina, Caligula and Nero, dispirited and embittered men turned against each other, bitter struggles broke out, and Romans turned upon each other in their wounded rage. With his death, civil war broke out between the leading generals and legates, who fought for the crown as dogs fight over a bone. AD 69 was the year of greatest confusion, when no less than four of these provincial legates claimed the right to become Emperor.

Galba, Otho, Vitellius and Vespasian. From the very beginning, each had a different concept of how best to achieve power. Servicius Sulpicius Galba was the quickest off the starting blocks. He had himself elevated to imperial rank by his Spanish legions and was accepted as such by Rome's Praetorian Guard. But he handled them so badly that they shifted their allegiance to Marcus Salvus Otho, who had taken a substantial loan from a banker to pay them off. Otho had Galba murdered by praetorian officers while the Emperor was carried into the Forum to make sacrifices to Jupiter. Fabius Fabulus, a simple legionary, cut off Galba's head and presented it to his general, Marcus Otho. After which Otho's men went on the rampage and killed all of Galba's men. The deed done, Otho took the purple. In the meantime, another legate holding the German border, Aulus Vitellius, claimed the right, and marched with his legions on Rome. The new Emperor Otho, on the throne for only thirty days, met him in the First Battle of Bedriacum (Cremona, April AD 69). Otho's army was defeated and he was captured and allowed to die by his own hand. Before he fell on his sword, he said: 'I can die with more honour than I can reign. By dying, I shall establish peace and unanimity and save Italy from another unhappy day.' By his victory Aulus Vitellius became the de facto Emperor. But – history is full of buts – in the Danube garrisons of Pannonia (Hungary) was another legate who did not care for Aulus Vitellius. His name was Antonius Primus, but since he was a man behind the scenes he called on his friend, legion general Vespasian, to become Emperor. As Vespasian was still busily engaged in a war against the Jews in the Middle East, Antonius Primus marched his legions against the usurper Vitellius. In the Second Battle of Bedriacum (October AD 69) Antonius defeated Vitellius, who managed to escape but was killed shortly afterwards by an angry street mob. With the slate cleaned, General Titus Flavius Vespasianus (Vespasian), who had distinguished himself during the conquest of Britannia and Judaea, was declared Emperor by Rome's Senate. His first act was to disband four disloyal legions. He dispatched Gnaeus Agricola to Britain to extend Roman rule to Scotland and Wales (AD 77–84).

When Vespasian ran out of cash to pay his legions, he

instituted a tax put on public urinals. Titus reproached him: 'How can you, Father?'

The Emperor held out a coin and replied: '*Non olet!* It has no smell . . .'

Following Emperor Vespasian's sudden death (AD 79), his son Titus Flavius Sabinus Vespasianus (Titus), who had taken his father's place at the head of the legions in the Middle East, became the obvious next in line for the coveted crown. He returned to Rome and his followers organised a triumphant victory parade, something more grandiose than had ever been seen. In fact he had good reason to celebrate, this conqueror of holy Jerusalem.

The first century of the *imperium romanum* saw the emergence of ten emperors, of which all but two died a violent death. It seems incredible that these power-mad rulers believed that the stars would protect their own god-image, or that a stroke of brutality such as the blatant murder of their families could save them. It is clear that they never understood the certainty of their ruin. By killing off his only hope of salvation, a loyal general, Nero sealed his own fate.

15

They Shall Fall by the Sword
Jerusalem
8 September AD 70

'. . . the days will come, in which there shall not be left one stone upon another, that shall not be thrown down . . . And when ye shall see Jerusalem compassed with armies, then know that the desolation thereof is nigh . . . for there shall be great distress in the land, and wrath upon this people. And they shall fall by the edge of the sword and shall be led away captive . . .'

Luke (21, 6–24)

The fate of Israel was already sealed in 63 BC when Pompey marched into Judaea and, following a three-month siege, entered Jerusalem. Judaea thereby became a Roman province and the independence of the Kingdom of Israel was at an end. In the wake of Pompey's replacement of Jewish judges with Roman procurators, and his attempts to impose his pagan gods on the image of the One Lord, the 'zealots' started out as a party of Jews who combined zealous observance of the Jewish Law with militant opposition to Roman rule. For this they were not loath to use the dagger. The zealot party first appeared in an organised form when they resisted the census of Galilee ordered (AD 6) by the Roman governor of Syria, Cyrenius. They preached open rebellion, willing to lay down their lives for independence from Roman domination.

With Herod the Great (62–4 BC), the Romans put in charge a man they thought they could trust. Herod did try to calm the fervour of religious fanatics by restoring the Second Temple of 520 BC to its former splendour, but other than that his only heritage was one of extreme cruelty which inspired the people with hatred for his regime. 'He was no king but the most cruel tyrant who ever ascended to the throne. He murdered a vast number of people and the lot he left alive was so miserable that the dead might count themselves fortunate.'[1] He ruled for thirty-six years, and his reign became famous for the fact that not a single day passed without his condemning someone to death, including his wife Mariamne (after whom he named one tower in his palace), and his sons Alexander, Aristobulus and Antipater. The King, 'who ruled like a wild beast', left only one relative alive, a nineteen-year-old girl, the beautiful Salome, who, according to the Bible, danced before his son, Herod Antipas, in exchange for the head of John the Baptist. His most infamous act may well have been the murder of the Innocents of Bethlehem (Matthew, 2, 16).

The people's hatred for the tyrannical house of Herod[2] was exceeded by an even stronger loathing of the occupation forces of Israel, represented by an immensely corrupt Roman procurator, Pontius Pilate, who held the sole authority to pronounce a death sentence. When Jesus, the Christos (which comes from Greek and means 'the anointed one', after a translation of the Hebrew word for 'messiah'), preaching his evangelism (in Greek: 'giving good news'), was dragged before the tribunal of Pontius Pilate, the latter announced: 'I find no fault in this man'

---

[1] Flavius Josephus.

[2] Herod the Great was followed by his son, Herod Antipas, King of Galilee (4 BC–AD 30), and Herod Agrippa II, King of Judaea (AD 28–91).

(Luke, 23, 4). In fact the Roman wasn't overly concerned with religious squabbles among Jews. But the crowd of Pharisees, fired up by their high priest, Caiaphas, who had much to fear for his own exalted position in the challenge of a religious revolutionary, wanted none of it. Jesus had said: 'I am the way, the truth, and the life: no man cometh unto the Father, but by me' (John 14, 6). This was cited as an example of blasphemy, and Caiaphas and the Jews called Jesus of Galilee a false messiah, ready to usurp Caesar's crown, and therefore demanded his death. 'The Jews cried out, saying, If thou let this man go, thou art not Caesar's friend: whosoever maketh himself a king speaketh against Caesar' (John 19, 12). Pontius Pilate knew that treason against his Roman *augustus* was punishable by death, and unless he acted his own life was in danger. 'When Pilate therefore heard that saying, he brought Jesus forth, and sat down in the judgment seat, in a place that is called the Pavement, but in the Hebrew, Gabbatha [Golgatha] . . . Then delivered he him therefore unto them to be crucified' (John 19, 13–16). 'And it was the third hour, and they crucified him' (Mark 15, 25).[3]

(Although the date of Jesus's crucifixion is uncertain, it is undeniable that, in Roman times, crucifixion was meted out as punishment for offenders who had committed crimes against the Roman state. The mass execution of slaves during the Spartacus revolt is an example.

In the summer of 1968, while construction work was under way on a hill known as Givat Hamivtar, a bulldozer inadvertently opened up an ancient burial site, containing several human remains. One of the skeletons, believed to have been that of a certain Johanan ben Hagalgol, displayed a smashed skull. But one may imagine the initial shock of the machine operator when he found the

---

[3] The date of Jesus's crucifixion must have been between AD 29 and 33, as Pontius Pilate held office from AD 26 to 36, and Caiaphas from AD 18 to 37, during the reign of Emperor Tiberius (AD 14–37).

victim's feet cut off from the body, with a nail driven through them and still fastened to fragments of wooden board. When informed of the find, the Israeli authorities, realising the implications and the arguments this could set off, sent two eminent independent experts, archaeologist Vassilios Tzaferis and pathologist Nicu Haas, to examine the remains. They discovered similar signs of penetration by nails, not through the palms but through the man's forearms, near the wrists. They concluded that the body weight would have caused the tissue to tear had the nails been driven through the palms. They found another gruesome and apparently inexplicable injury: the victim's shinbones had been smashed. The scientists concluded that this was probably not an additional torture but a *coup de grâce*, intended to bring on shock to end the crucified's life more quickly.[4] The possible 'quick death' factor sparked a series of heated discussions and counter-charges by the Church about the manner in which Christ died on the cross.)

During the reign of Emperor Claudius (AD 41–54) more religious trouble erupted. It was an unfortunate fact for many future generations of Jews that zealots sought to export their revolution to every corner of the Roman Empire. If the revolution had stopped at rhetoric, perhaps the Emperor could have looked the other way. But once it reached Rome itself, something had to be done. Dissidents who were attracting attention couldn't be tolerated, and Emperor Claudius 'drove the Jews out of Rome'. Survivors from that initial pogrom fled to Israel, and the trouble quickly spread throughout Galilee, where zealot fanatics demanded the removal of everything Roman from their homeland. The spark was ignited in May AD 66.

The initial cause was minor, the result was not. One of

---

4 J. Landay, *Silent Cities, Sacred Stones*, New York, 1971.

the many inept Roman procurators, Florus, no better than the corrupt Pontius Pilate, demanded payment of seventeen talents from the treasury of the Temple. His demand was rejected. Florus dispatched a dozen Roman soldiers to forcibly collect the tax. They committed the unspeakable offence of breaking into the Jews' most sacred Temple, and thereby stirred an outcry, followed by a rebellion that flared quickly throughout Judaea. Led by zealots, the terror spread to the cities. Violent rioting erupted in Caesaria and Jerusalem, where many supporters of Rome were murdered. With an adroitness and skill their Roman overlords had always stated they did not possess, the Jews mounted a guerrilla offensive of remarkable subtlety. In a series of hit-and-run attacks, they burned Roman villas and ambushed Roman patrols. Encouraged by their initial successes, more Jews flocked to the standards of the zealots. In October AD 66, a great disaster befell the Roman garrison at Bezetha, when their camp was overrun and most of its six thousand occupants killed. Before an all-out anti-Roman rebellion was allowed to spread throughout Asia Minor, a major Roman expedition was mounted from Syria to suppress the Jewish uprising. The man put in charge of quelling the rebellion was the Roman governor of Syria, proconsul Cestius Gallus, who rushed with one legion plus a number of auxiliaries to the rescue of the Roman procurator, besieged inside Jerusalem. By the time his troops arrived before Jerusalem, the town had fallen to an uneasy alliance of Jewish moderates and fanatic zealots. The 'Jewish War' was under way (AD 66–73).

Joseph ben Matthias, a Hebrew philosopher and historian, well known under his Roman pen name of Flavius Josephus (through the patronage of Emperor Vespasian, he later became a Roman citizen), was appointed commander-in-chief of the Jewish resistance forces in Galilee. He established his defences around Jotapata.

Wealthy Romans throughout the Middle East, fearing

the spread of the revolt throughout the entire region, implored their emperor to dispatch a competent commander. Emperor Nero showed little concern about affairs in his far-flung provinces of Asia Minor, yet he spared enough time from his orgies to appoint a competent general Vespasian 'to look after order in Asia Minor'. Vespasian acted with speed and energy. The region where only a few years before a certain Jesus had preached peace among all men became the opening scene of a vast act of butchery (October AD 67). Any Jew arrested for unusual behaviour, which included looking furtively at a Roman legionary, was condemned without a chance to defend himself. By December of that year, the defences of Jotapata, which had held out for forty-seven days, were overrun by Vespasian's sixty thousand legionaries and Flavius Josephus taken captive. He was one of the few Jews to escape crucifixion, and was therefore able to leave history an account of events in his monumental work *The War of the Jews*. His life may have been spared owing to a curious circumstance. Legion general Titus, the son of Vespasian and second-in-command, had ordered a number of captives thrown from the Mountain of Moab into the Dead Sea. Inexplicably, as often as they were thrown from the cliffs into the water they came drifting back to shore. This so amazed the Roman commander, who believed it the work of a Jewish devil, that he suspended the execution of the rest of his war captives.[5]

The news arriving from Rome was worrisome. With Nero's death and a brutal civil war looming, Vespasian's soldiers hoisted him on their shoulders with a lusty '*Vivat Caesar*'. Vespasian departed for Alexandria to organise the conquest of Italy, and left his son Titus, an extremely able

[5] The phenomenon may be explained by the high salt content of the Dead Sea, which makes the human body float. A more logical explanation is that Titus wanted to preserve the Jewish leader to parade him in Rome.

young man, to handle the problem of Judaea, its Jews –
and Jerusalem.

Titus was a tall, stocky man, with the demeanour of a
tough, determined individual, the toughness of one who
had, by his father's side, lived his life in war situations.
His outward manner was deceptively soft, but when he
gave orders he did so with the austere bearing of the
professional soldier. Rome was full of romantic stories
of his successful exploits. He had established a reputation
for efficient ruthlessness which even gave his father some
qualms. His present task was the restoration of Roman
authority in its provinces of Israel and Judaea.

In the spring of AD 70, leading a force of 80,000 men
with 340 catapults (in other words a sledgehammer to
squash a fly), Titus appeared before the walls of Jerusalem.
It was during the holy time of the year; thousands of
faithful had congregated to celebrate Passover and the city
was jammed beyond its capacity by pilgrims from all over
the Middle East. Titus's men encircled the city and cut
it off from the surrounding countryside. His call for the
city's surrender was answered by insults to the person of
his august father. The ballistas and catapults went into
action, slinging huge stones against the fortifications. Battering rams hammered at the foundations, whilst inside the
beleaguered city rival factions of zealots fought moderates
for control. Only when the walls began to show gaping
holes did they cease their internal strife. The leaders of the
rival parties, the moderate Simon bar Giora and the zealot
John of Gishala, agreed on a temporary suspension of their
internal problems – 'until the enemy was taken care of' –
and established a mutual command over the defence of
the walls. With the population swollen by the pilgrims
from many of Israel's warrior tribes, the two leaders could
count on more than enough defenders to man the walls and
towers. The rest they left in the hands of Yahweh, who,
so their priests kept assuring them, would not abandon

His children and His utmost Holy, the Tabernacle in the Temple.

At the beginning of May AD 70, four legions surrounded the town on all sides and began their assault. A human wave of men from the Vth, Xth, XIIth and XVth legions moved towards the walls. They clawed their way over the rock-strewn hillside and began to issue frenzied cries as they approached the high walls. Some paused to take shelter from the hail of stones raining down on them as their centurions screamed at them to keep moving. The closer they got to the wall, the more they suffered from rocks and other kinds of missiles. One kind of defence proved especially efficient; as the Jews needed their diminishing water supply for drinking purposes, and it couldn't be wasted by boiling it to pour on to the attackers, they came up with an ingenious solution: sand, of which they had plenty. They heated it in bronze kettles and deluges of the fine, burning substance scalded the attackers, stuck to their skin and fried a great number like chickens on a spit.

The first Roman attempts to overcome the walls were not crowned with success. Only once 120-foot siege towers were built from solid timber, covered with wet donkey hides to overcome the effect of flaming arrows and pushed within javelin range to keep the heads of the defenders down were the legions able to bring their iron rams into position. But their troubles continued; the defenders cut the ropes of the rams' pendulums with sickles tied to long poles. The siege seemed to be heading for a stand-off, especially as the Jews managed to supply the town with foodstuffs smuggled in through the gaps between the various Romans camps. The Romans began to wonder: what kind of soldiers were these who could fight so savagely in spite of impossible odds?

Titus, in an attempt to save as much of the city as possible – not out of humanitarian considerations but

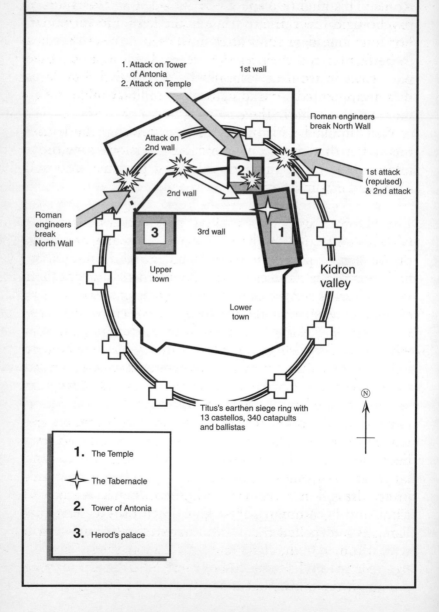

Jerusalem
8 September AD 70

1. Attack on Tower of Antonia
2. Attack on Temple

1st wall

Roman engineers break North Wall

Attack on 2nd wall

2nd wall

1st attack (repulsed) & 2nd attack

Roman engineers break North Wall

3rd wall

3

1

Kidron valley

Upper town

Lower town

Titus's earthen siege ring with 13 castellos, 340 catapults and ballistas

N

1. The Temple
The Tabernacle
2. Tower of Antonia
3. Herod's palace

for plunder, and furthermore to keep its walls intact for use as a Roman fortress – ordered an impressive military parade of a size that had never before been seen outside Rome. This mighty display was intended as a weapon of psychological warfare, to frighten the Jews into surrender. For four long days, unit after unit, their armour polished to perfection and their legions' eagles held high, marched past Titus in front of Jerusalem's North Wall. But Titus was disappointed – parading Rome's military might failed miserably to achieve the desired effect.

Well supplied with provisions, the Jews on the battlements felt that they could hold out for months, without taking into account the thousands of pilgrims who had swelled the population.

Just before a great storm there often comes a time of perfect clarity. It was the holy day of Sabbath, and most of the Jewish population, those not guarding the walls, had been to the temples to hear the word of the Lord. The zealots harangued the crowd with slogans of defiance. And although Jewish moderates tried to make their people listen to reason, suggesting that these reach an accommodation with Rome, which was still feasible, their conciliatory voices were shouted down by the extremists, who roused the masses to follow them into tragedy and disaster – as extremists have in all situations and ages.

Fired up, the populace committed an unpardonable sin, which was to cost them dearly. Thousands of excited Jews lined the walls and rooftops to shout debasing remarks and laugh at the Romans' polished armour, 'like a woman's pretty dress, but a woman without courage'. To incense Titus and his Romans, they spat down on the marching Romans and pelted them with manure and refuse. For a while the men of the Xth Frentesian Legion, tough veterans from Sicily to whom the honour had fallen to parade that day, took the abuse, but then came their tribune carrying the legion's eagle. As the flag-bearing group passed near a portion of the ramparts, lined with hardcore zealots, the insignia was pelted with foul refuse. It achieved what the zealots had intended, but the end result was not what they could possibly have wished for. The Romans had stoically accepted all the insults during their march past, but this was an insult neither the legionaries nor their caesar, Titus,[6] were ever likely to forget. Titus found himself with his mouth gaping open and clamped it shut. *By Jupiter!* was his only clear thought; the rest was a muddle of rage and the realisation that there were thousands of witnesses to this infamy. The insult raised the wrath of Titus and that of his legions to a height that bordered on ferocity, inspiring a desire to kill every Jew present. Every legionary felt personally outraged, and this gave an entirely new flavour to what before had been a routine siege. This event, unfortunate as it may have been, led to one of the dramatic turning points of history.

Titus immediately called off the parade and instead prepared for an assault. He needed to breach the walls surrounding the northern sector. The legions' engineers went into action; during weeks of hard work they honey-combed the foundations of the walls with a number of tunnels which they shored up with timber. Once they set fire to the timber struts this created a space under the walls' foundations, and the weight of masonry led to the collapse of a portion of the North Wall. Soldiers manned the battering rams and dealt death from siege towers as their 350 catapults lobbed avalanches of heavy stones onto the helpless city. The legionaries grabbed their spears and prepared for the assault. To little avail – for a long time the Romans were unable to scale the walls. The Jews displayed great obstinacy, and discharged showers of arrows from the top of the battlements on to the Romans.

---

[6] Caesar here is his rank, second only to *augustus* (emperor).

The legionaries fell, slain or sorely stricken, without ever seeing the men who slew them. The steep slope leading up to the walls became strewn with their corpses. With pressure mounting, the Jews launched a surprise sortie. It caught the Romans unawares and the raiders burned a number of siege towers and catapults, but they could do little about the tunnels under the walls. Rapid intervention by Roman cohorts encircled the raiding parties before they could return behind the safety of the walls. Those caught were crucified without judgment.

Still the Jews defended well and covered the breach. But there came a moment, as happens so frequently in siege situations, when the defenders were worn out and succumbed to sleep. A segment of the North Wall was unguarded and a group of legionaries forced their way across the partly demolished wall into the northern part of the city. More cohorts of the Xth Legion, assisted by the XIIth, rushed after them, pounding pell-mell through the breach and spreading out into the rabbit-warren of narrow lanes beyond. Their killing spree created panic and jammed more refugees than it could possibly hold into the upper city section, protected by a wall that led from Herod's palace to the Temple. This made the situation hopeless for the defenders still remaining in the northern sector. But the gates in front of them, leading through the second wall, had been shut, and all those caught outside the second wall were rounded up by the Romans and killed. A wail arose from the battlements where the Jewish skirmishers looked down on their comrades' brutal end. Now the Jerusalem of the zealots was greatly reduced to the section inside the middle or Temple wall, and the southern ramparts. Huge siege engines were brought close to the walls and fired tons of stone blocks into the city, killing a great number.

The loss of the northern section was almost immediately felt, since it robbed the defenders of almost all their precious food stores. Famine approached with rapid strides. Unwholesome food and the impure air of the many rotting corpses engendered pestilence, and carried the defenders off more rapidly than the stone balls from Roman catapults. Titus next ordered the building of a *circumvallation*, a wall manned day and night, which had proved so successful for the great Julius Caesar at Alesia. The Romans tore down a great number of houses and built from the rubble an earthen wall that completely surrounded the town and cut it off from all potential aid. Jerusalem was now condemned to a slow death by starvation. The news of the imminent arrival of a relief force from some of the mountain tribes inspired the Jews to a great last effort, every men fighting as if upon himself alone depended the fortunes of Jerusalem. But when this force failed to show up, and turned out to be nothing but a rumour born of desperation, the people's hopes collapsed and their enthusiasm for more combat dissipated.

With the situation hopeless, and no help coming from the outside or from the zealots' god, Titus tried one last time to reason with them. During the battle for Jotapata, his legions had captured Flavius Josephus, the Jewish leader of Galilee. Not only had Titus been superstitious about the Jews' bodies floating back to shore, thus sparing the lives of the remaining ones, but Flavius Josephus had also been kept alive so that he could be used as a pawn to negotiate the Jews' surrender. He was first given a tour of the *castellos*, which showed the hopelessness of further resistance. This was backed up, for his benefit, by a sustained bombardment from the quick-firing *scorpionis*, before Titus dispatched him as his envoy to the city's walls. 'Oh, you hard hearted men, throw away your weapons and have pity on your country that stands on the edge of the abyss!'[7] he pleaded with them, and pointed out the

7 W. Keller, *The Bible as History*, London, 1965.

bleakness of their situation, but they wouldn't listen to his wise counsel.

Adjacent to the Temple complex was the Tower of Antonia, a strongpoint held by the hardcore zealots of John of Gishala. In height it overlooked the sacred Temple enclave, and it became the key to the Temple complex. Under protective timbered roofs, the Romans rolled their heavy rams right up to the middle wall. Day and night the pounding continued, and eventually the wall began to show cracks. On the crammed city fell an incessant rain of shot from the Roman siege engines, while famine and epidemics decimated thousands, pilgrims and warriors.

The incessant pounding by the siege catapults and the vibration caused by the impact of its missiles helped to dull the senses of the damned. Jerusalem the Holy was being pounded back into the Stone Age. But the military action was nothing compared to the suffering of the population – thousands died each and every day of starvation. People killed other people to eat their flesh. The midsummer heat had nearly dried out the rest of their water supply and people drank their own urine, which led to painful cramps, and death. The worst was the hunger.

The terrible famine that increased in frightfulness daily annihilated whole families of the people. The terraces were full of women and children who had collapsed from hunger, the alleys were piled high with the bodies of the aged. Children and young people, swollen with lack of food, wandered around like ghosts until they fell. They were so far spent that they could no longer bury anyone, and if they did they fell dead upon the very corpses they were burying. The misery was unspeakable. For as soon as even the shadow of anything eatable appeared anywhere, a fight began over it, and the best of friends fought and tore from each other the most miserable trifles.

No one would believe that the dying had no provisions stored away. Robbers threw themselves on those who were drawing their last breath and ransacked their clothing. Their hunger was so unbearable that they were forced to chew anything and everything. They laid their hands on things that even the meanest of animals would not touch, far less eat.

And Flavius Josephus cried out in horror in the final line of his account: 'But why should I describe the shame and indignity that famine brought upon men, making them eat such unnatural things?'[8]

Josephus, basing his description of the tragic events on his own eye-witness experiences, and writing only five years after the event (AD 75–79), reported that a group of zealots who had manned the middle wall were so weak from hunger that they could no longer lift the heavy stones to hurl on to their aggressors. They were looking for food when they suddenly smelled roast meat. They stormed into the house of the wealthy Beth-Ezob family and found the old couple lying dead on the floor. But their daughter Maria was very much alive, curled up in a corner, still with fright. When they threatened the young woman, she handed them the roast meat. It was the corpse of a half-eaten child – her own.

Inside the city, the very earth seemed poisoned and putrescent with the stench of death, disease and defecation. The narrow lanes stank with the odours of crowded humanity while the air resounded with painful wails. Bearers of ill tiding in the form of flocks of vultures circled over the town to feed on the thousands of putrefied corpses. To prevent the outbreak of epidemics, the dead were unceremoniously dumped over the walls, adding to the overall horror with their foul stench. Ghostly skeletons tried to make their escape from the city by having

8 Flavius Josephus, *War of the Jews*.

themselves lowered at night over the walls. Whoever was caught was nailed to the cross. The Romans cut down the beautiful olive and fig orchards to use the trunks for the crosses. They did need a lot; five hundred a day died in this horrible manner, until a forest of crosses ringed the city. 'The war has turned all this country's beauty into wilderness,' lamented Flavius Josephus in his account of the siege. And for those not dying of hunger or nailed to crosses when caught awaited an equally horrid end. A rumour spread that Jewish refugees were swallowing their jewels to prevent their discovery during searches. In one night alone, greedy legionaries cut open the bellies of two thousand Jews in their search for treasure. When Titus heard about this outrage he had every single member of a rapacious unit put to death; after that the slaughter of Jews continued, but in silence. Now there would be more stacks of naked corpses piling up before the walls, vile in contorted death, or left hanging from crosses like ragged pennants of despair. All the more reason for the Jews to hold out; death itself was ironically the life-force of the zealots.

In late July, Titus prepared for the final assault. His force came sweeping up the hill and topped the rise before the wreckage of the walls. The legions broke through the middle wall and stormed the Tower of Antonia. Romans were pounding each other on the back in triumph. The news spread from man to man: the second wall had been breached. The legionaries were ordered to fan out and make sure that the serpentine lanes were not sheltering zealot fighters. All they found were weeping, praying, bloodstained women, clutching wailing children to their bosoms. Only the short third city wall and the strong walls around the Temple Mount remained in Jewish hands. By now the defenders' situation was utterly hopeless, but they wouldn't give in. The forest of crosses planted around the ramparts, intended to arouse eternal fright in the last defenders, clearly demonstrated how psychological warfare could have the opposite effect to that intended. The defenders were not given a choice and knew that only death awaited them, either on the barricades or by execution. And so the butchery continued with no pardon given or expected. The last defenders were holed up behind the Temple's walls, close to their most Holy of Holies. With its labyrinth of tunnels, galleries and courtyards, it proved a formidable barricade. Perhaps it was to appease his own gods that Titus gave strict orders to preserve the sacred shrine and prevent all damage to the sanctity of the Tabernacle. Or perhaps he was aware that his rams would prove powerless against the huge slabs of rock with which Herod had built the Temple. One last time, Flavius Josephus tried to make the zealots give up. In vain.

On 7 September AD 70, the legions, led by the Xth, launched their final attack to Titus's order of the day: 'Take the Fortress. Spare the Sanctuary.' The terrible catapults did not broach the Temple's inner sanctum itself, but a hail of metal bolts from the ballistas, fired down from the taller Tower of Antonia, pierced hundreds of defenders inside the courtyards. They were left lying on the polished pavement of the wide Temple courtyard, their blood spread over the pavement normally reserved for fervent prayer by thousands of pilgrims. The Temple was no longer a place of refuge and faith, but one of death and despair.[9]

Given its inviolate walls, Titus ordered that the massive wooden Temple gate be set afire. Under the protection of a 'turtle', a roof made of shields and held over the heads of the engineers, bales of straw and oil were placed against the oak-and-bronze door and lit. It took a full day before

[9] The sequence of events that finally led to the Temple's destruction is buried in the mists of time. Flavius Josephus, in his *War of the Jews*, was the only contemporary eye-witness to record the dramatic events, but seeing he was a Jew his account cannot be considered that of a neutral observer.

the door was sufficiently ravaged by fire for the Romans to break through. When the gap was sufficiently wide, the centurions of the Xth didn't have to give an order; their cohorts poured through as water floods through a hole in a dike. The legion's tribune thought that the defenders were less prepared for the assault than they really were. He was faced by a wall of zealots who fought for every inch of hallowed ground, every wall, every opening, as if possessed by the Devil himself. The centurion who had been first to climb through the still-burning gate was instantly killed, but those following on his heels jumped over his prostrate body and through the still-flaming door. Resisters came at them, but futilely. The Romans cut them down and swarmed over the first courtyard, taking it. The first cohort was followed by a second, then a third, careening across the polished stones of the great courtyard made slippery by the blood of the many slain. The front ranks were running at full tilt at a wall of defenders, jamming their stabbing lances into chests and bellies, while knocking out the last barricade erected before a steep staircase that led to a walkway high on the wall. A centurion who had taken over from his fallen comrade climbed with a cohort to the top, where they submitted to their rage, embittered by the deaths of so many of their comrades, hurling any defender they caught over the wall, to crash to his death in the Kidron valley hundreds of feet below. Only one more wall around the sacred Temple itself separated the Romans from the most Holy of Holies, the Tabernacle. Around that last wall the carnage was most frightful. Each man was alone in a world of ear-splitting mayhem. The earth seemed to move under them. Jews and Romans fought and fell, one on top of the other, until most of them lay dead or dying, jammed across the entrance. In the confusion of this final assault the unimaginable happened:

'One of the soldiers, without waiting for orders and without any sense of the horror of his deed, seized a blazing torch and, hoisted on the shoulders of one of his comrades, flung it through the Golden Window that opened into the rooms which lay beside the Holy of Holies ... however great their dread of what Caesar[10] had forbidden them to do, their hatred of the Jews and their eagerness to fight them was equally great. Thus the Holy Place was burnt down without Caesar's approbation.'[11]

Indeed, Titus had given strict orders to spare the Sanctuary. Centurion Liberalius came running towards Titus, gesticulating, yelling: 'The Temple is on fire!' Titus quickly gathered a great number of soldiers and hurried through the burning gate, across the courtyard littered with corpses, to douse the flames, which hadn't as yet reached the rooms containing the Tabernacle. Too late. Although the soldiers attacked the blazing timber with staves, nothing could any longer save the wood-panelled rooms; by now the fire had reached the inside and the big jars, filled with sacred oil, exploded 'like shooting stars'. Their bright flames set off an inferno no man dared come near. From the belly of the building, through the smashed opening that no longer protected the most Holy of Holies from spying eyes, spilled forth a blinding light, brighter than a thousand suns, followed by a deafening roar like the pained cries of a horde of furies.

The Romans froze on the spot when they saw one of the zealots clamber over the collapsing stairs, heading straight into the blaze. One last time, the man turned his face, his eyes filled with hate and his mouth open in a scream. He was calling out something that was drowned by the roar of the flames, and his accusing finger pointed straight at the Roman caesar; then he disappeared behind the curtain of roaring flames. Titus wanted to avert his gaze, but something forced his eyes to stare in the direction

---

10 Caesar as in Titus, who was caesar under Augustus Vespasian.
11 Flavius Josephus in his *War of the Jews.*

of the blinding curtain of fire that had just devoured a living being.

While the struggle for possession of the Temple walls continued, John of Gishala and a few dozen of his followers managed to make good their escape through a secret tunnel and were now putting up a final, if desperate, resistance in the three remaining towers of Herod's palace. Titus was forced to deploy for one last time his siege engines, which reduced Herod's splendid royal residence to rubble, before the defenders threw down their arms and months of fighting and suffering were brought to an end. The last of the emaciated zealots were rounded up, chained, and kept for the victory parade.

Nobody could afterwards tell with certitude how many among the 600,000 who were in the city at the beginning of the siege died during the fighting, how many starved to death and how many were slaughtered during the pillaging and rape of the city by Titus's legions.

With the ashes still smouldering, the legions planted their golden eagles in the courtyard of the most Holy of Holies, now cleared of the debris of war, and made sacrifices to their god of war, Mars. As punishment for the daring stand against Rome's might and the insult to its honour, Titus ordered that Jerusalem be razed.

'Destroy everything! Leave no stone unturned. Bring the buildings down. We'll wipe out every trace of the Jews. This city shall be levelled, never to rise again.' The Roman soldiers were crazed by the prospect of the wealth they expected to find in the houses. Hammers and chisels, used to create beauty, bit mercilessly into vases and ornaments, rendering them into shattered bits of stone and plaster. Axes fell upon delicately inlaid walls, making them crumble to dust, because behind every wall, so they believed, was a hidden treasure. Clouds of dust boiled upward into the blue sky. The soldiers wreaked havoc in the remains of temples, scraping the gold layers from walls. Those who begged the raving soldiery to halt the destruction of their shrines lay hacked and bleeding, next to the many bloating bodies, reeking with the stench of death and covered by flies. 'Shall we not bury them?' asked a soldier of the Xth. 'Let them lie,' replied his centurion, 'they are not fit to be buried. They all believed they could stand up to us. Let them be the food of jackals and vultures.'

The City of David, once magnificent in its beauty, was lying in ruins. Only the towers of Mariamne, Hippicus and Phasael, which fortified Herod's palace, were left standing to provide storage space for Rome's war matériel and comfortable quarters for the legions' officers. Their servants were the same Jews who, in the days before the siege, had enjoyed the hospitality of kings, such as Herod the Great, in these very rooms. They had to bear silent witness while their daughters were forced to provide sexual comfort and give birth to the bastard offspring of legionaries as the result of unremitting rape.

The captured leaders of the Jerusalem rebellion were dragged before Titus. John of Gishala's clothing was tattered, his beard, symbol of his romantic resistance, matted. His haggard face and sunken eyes reflected his exhaustion and hunger. A few days later, some legionaries located Simon bar Giora hiding out in a cave. Both John of Gishala and Simon bar Giora were messianic men whose followers had been fanatically devoted to them. Other than that, any similarities between the two ended. Though both were ostensibly equally nationalistic, and each professed to espouse the aim of liberating Israel and Judaea from the Romans, their ultimate goals were totally different. Both had failed. They had dared to gamble against the might of Rome, and they had lost. A pitiless caesar had taught them not to trifle with Rome.

Black clouds rose from the Temple Mount. Smoke poured from the rocky heart of the land. The clouds bore the message to all of Israel about the end of their Temple.[12] The Jews had accepted hardship and hunger, even death, but the destruction of their Temple was more than they could bear. For them it signalled the end, and a shocked hush fell across the land of Judaea, the silence of death. The hecatomb of human lives was terrible: 1,100,000 perished during the war years, of which 580,000 fell in combat. The rest starved. The surviving 300,000 were sold as slaves. From that day onward, the worldwide scattering of the Jews began.

Titus was awarded a monumental victory procession in Rome, where he paraded his prisoners in chains. But nothing could take the place of his prize booty, a golden, seven-branched candlestick. A replica, hewn in stone, can still be seen on his triumphant arch in Rome. Nothing is known of the fate of this candelabrum. It is likely that this reminder of a holocaust that destroyed a sacred Temple and sent its faithful to their deaths was robbed during the barbarians' sack of Rome and melted down for its gold value.

For three more years, resistance continued. The end came on a mountaintop overlooking the Dead Sea – Masada. Titus's legions laid siege to it. For many months Eleazar ben Ya'ir and a few hundred fighters held out, until the Romans built a ramp to reach the heights, and its nine hundred defenders and their families – rather than fall into the hands of the Romans – killed themselves. This was the final act in the War of the Jews, and it brought down the curtain on the Promised Land (AD 73).

Under pain of death, the Romans forbade Jews from ever walking again in the grounds of the razed city. On its ruins, using materials from its original buildings, Greek architects and Jewish slave labour, Emperor Hadrian ordered a new

---

[12] To restore the Temple has become the messianic aspiration of Judaism.

city to be built, Aelia Capitolia. Where the Temple had stood they put up a statue of Jupiter. And on Golgatha hill, where Jesus was crucified, a likeness of the goddess of love, Venus.

The Xth Legion which had breached the city walls, set fire to the Temple and brought Masada down remained as Judaea's occupation force for sixty years. They left their mementos carved in stone, while the Jews left nothing. Despite centuries of archaeological digs and much research, no real evidence of Israel's existence following the sack of Jerusalem in AD 70 has ever been uncovered. No Jewish cemetery, no Hebrew inscription, no tombstone. It was as if the Lord had determined to erase all trace of his children. Destiny, and Rome's heavy hand, had done the rest, leaving nothing. The ancient Jewish civilisation was crushed under the heavy boots of Roman legions. Yet while their temples were being reduced to cinders, a new religion was taking root; a Jewish rabbi from Galilee who preached forgiveness and love had started it. And although he came into the Land of Israel without a sword, his message was to outlast the Roman eagle by many thousands of years.

Titus succeeded his father Vespasian on the throne. He became the next victim of the Roman emperors' curse. While taking a bath, he was murdered by men loyal to his brother, Titus Flavius Domitian, who, after usurping the crown, was killed by his wife's lover.

As for the tribes of Israel, '. . . they shall fall by the edge of the sword, and shall be led away captive into all nations . . .' (Luke 21, 24). The Jews had to wait two thousand years before the prophecy of Ezekiel came true. 'And the desolate land shall be tilled, whereas it lay desolate in the sight of all that passed by. And they shall say, This land that was desolate is become like the garden of Eden' (Ezekiel 36, 34–5). Yet even today, peace is still a long way off.

*   *   *

The decision to destroy Jerusalem was taken during a legion's parade under the walls of the besieged city. If Titus had ever shown signs that he wished to preserve Jerusalem, the insult to his legion's eagle by fanatical Jews was an indignity too far, an outrage and a slur that a Roman Caesar could never tolerate. It was in the fury of a moment that he decided to punish the Jews by destroying Jerusalem. And he did.

Part Six

The Barbarians

AD 375–410

(Fritigern to Alaric)

16

Chaos in thc Empire

Adrianopolis
9 August AD 378

'*Nox ruit et fuscis tellurem amplectitur alis.*'
('Night came down and wrapped the earth in its dusky wings.')
Virgil, 70–19 BC

Chaos ruled throughout the Roman Empire. For nigh on two hundred years now, the many claimants for the rank of *augustus* had murdered each other. One emperor followed the next; sometimes there were even two or three contenders at the same time. The legions in the North elected Maximinius, the Senate picked Balbinus and Pupienus, and the troops in Africa chose eighty-year-old Gordianus as their emperor. Gordianus committed suicide on hearing that his son had been killed by Maximinius; Maximinius was killed by his troops; the two senatorial emperors were killed by their Praetorian Guard; and the grandson of Gordianus ascended to the throne, to be murdered by his bodyguard. That butchery was followed by the 'Age of the Thirty Tyrants' – actually only nineteen – who all suffered death by violent means.

Another power began to make itself felt, the Christian Church, which had gained vastly in importance. Much of this had to do with the disorder in the imperial court and its loose morals. Worship of Jesus soon began to supersede the worship of ancient deities – and some created emperor-gods. A kind of religious mania was rife, the outcome of an all-consuming vanity on the part of a series of *augusti*, the illusion of power without limit, and an inclination to paranoia. When their will had been fully done among mortals, the Roman emperors declared themselves to be God. The strict order that had brought Rome to greatness and then become the governing tenet of Roman society began to break up. Empresses were unrestrained in their behaviour and rutted shamelessly with a series of lovers. The wives of citizens followed their example and demonstrated equal sexual licence. With the code of morality broken, and everyone immersed in scenes of debauchery, other vices followed. Excessive indulgence in the passions of the soul swept through the nation like a plague.

Long ago, Roman citizens had stopped serving as common soldiers in order to amass great fortunes in the lands conquered by their valiant legions. As slaves were ineligible for service, the levies came from still-unconquered lands north of the Danube, in Illyria and Hispania. A special case was the terrible Goths. They had wandered from the Baltic regions and settled in the Danube delta states and the Ukraine. Their guile and skill served them well as expert hunters and warriors, with an uncanny intuitive ability to lay traps and set up ambushes. Goth warriors were the ideal human resource to satisfy Rome's voracious appetite for staffing its auxiliary legions. They were excellent horsemen and fighters, and from their midst came a great number of mercenary legionaries who flocked to the banner of legalised plunder. In all the Roman battles of that period, the Goths claimed a superior share of honours, but also of danger. But this provided them with great experience in conducting the business of war.

In essence, the political basis of Emperor Augustus's reign was a defensive military policy. To protect the empire's borders, he created twenty-five legions, or 150,000 men under arms. To support this Roman legion force, he called into being an equal number of auxiliary troops, which was eventually increased to some 400,000; they were engaged to serve twenty-five years and paid considerably less than an imperial trooper. Yet pay was not the main problem; Rome's training of its potential enemy in the art of war was. Subsequent emperors made few changes to the military set-up, apart from importing an even greater number of auxiliaries, called the *federati*, until barbarians became the main component of a Roman legion. The brightest military minds were used to instruct barbarians how to fight. They proved themselves bright and eager students who, on their return from service, took their know-how back to their tribes. In this way, Rome contributed largely to the final overthrow of the *imperium romanum*. It must be a tribute to Rome's political skill that this situation took four centuries to develop.

Most of the *augusti* were possessed of an empty idea of self-worth. All were spoiled by wealth and power, posturing as emperors, but once confronted with reality their façade collapsed and they saw no way to stop the headlong descent into disaster. Then they fell on their knees to beg, 'Help me!' And those being addressed would look at them ironically, and then do nothing, whether for the Emperor or his empire. Hence the irony that it was the barbarians who held the power of transformation. They became the principal actors, pursuing their conception of their own tribal interests, such as the expansion of lands for their herds, or, more often than not, easy spoils.

'The discipline of the legions, which alone, after the extinction of every other virtue, had propped up the great-ness of the state, was corrupted by ambition, or relaxed by the weakness of the emperors. The strength of the frontiers, which had always consisted in arms rather than fortifications, was insensibly undermined; and the fairest provinces were left exposed to the rapaciousness or ambition of the barbarians, who soon discovered the decline of the Roman Empire.'[1]

Thus an external force determined the pace of internal upheaval: the advance into Roman territory of tribes of wandering barbarians. By the beginning of the fourth century, Roman order was in systematic crisis. The emperors were no longer the sole drivers of the imperial system. The Goths and Vandals, who supplied most of the legions' manpower, developed their own agendas and tailored them to their needs. The consequences were profound. Together with the disorder created by an ever-increasing military despotism and the weakening of Roman emperors, who became little more than puppets tolerated by the barbarian mercenaries, emerged a new threat to the empire: the wandering of nations, original inhabitants of the great plains stretching eastward from the Elbe, the Danube and the Don, or from the high North along the dark and rock-ribbed waters of the Baltic. They were the people of a vast and mysterious wasteland of lakes, forests and marshes, who spoke their own strange language and worshipped their heathen gods. The biggest tribe of all was the Goth.

It wasn't the Goths' military efficiency which was the overriding cause of the looming disaster. Legions were certainly better armed than the barbarians. Great technical strides had been made in the process of smelting weapon-grade iron, and every hundred men could count on support from a catapult or ballista. But the patriotic fervour that had led Rome to world domination was now lacking. The empire's defence was no longer safeguarded by Romans but by *limitanei* (frontiersmen) and *comitatenses* (militia

---

[1] E. Gibbon, *The Decline and Fall of the Roman Empire*, New York, 1953.

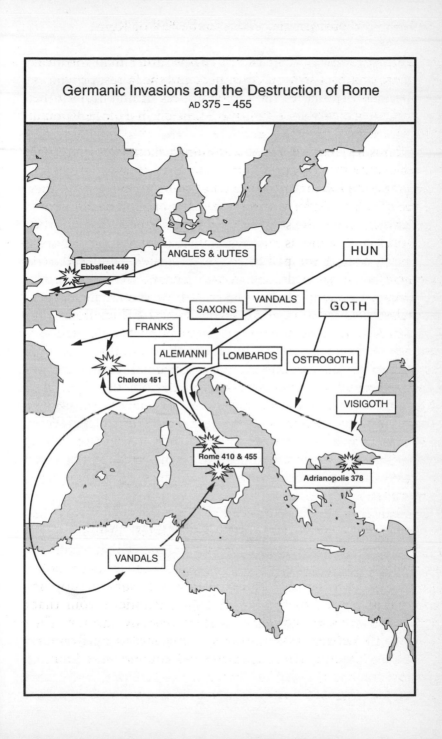

Germanic Invasions and the Destruction of Rome
AD 375 – 455

ANGLES & JUTES

HUN

Ebbsfleet 449

VANDALS

GOTH

SAXONS

FRANKS

ALEMANNI   LOMBARDS   OSTROGOTH

Chalons 451

VISIGOTH

Rome 410 & 455

Adrianopolis 378

VANDALS

of the interior). With this increasing recruitment of tribal warriors, especially in the officer corps, barbarians soon became the highest power in the empire. They showed no particular allegiance to the Roman eagle. Whose eagle was it anyway? Scipio and Caesar's Roman legionaries had been suckled with the patriotic milk from Mother Rome, and then had gladly offered their lives in order to protect *their* country and *their* families, or to conquer a land for the glory of Rome. The same could not be said of Illyrians, Thracians or Goths; they could hardly be called upon to 'protect Rome', a city which most couldn't even have located on a map. For centuries now, all of Rome's fighting had been conducted by its auxiliaries – Raetians, Gaul, Alani, Goths or Vandals, who were sometimes unwilling to engage in action against their own tribal brothers.

For one last time the Roman Empire was returned to its former glory, under Emperor Constantine. His rule was being challenged by the consul Maxentius, who had declared himself Emperor. Constantine decided that Maxentius was too dangerous an enemy to be allowed to live, especially since he had taken possession of Rome, and he took to the field. Before their confrontation on the banks of the Tiber at the Milvian bridge (AD 312) Emperor Constantine saw a cross in the sky and a voice said to him: '*In hoc signo vinces!*' ('With this sign thou shalt win'). He vowed that should the Christian god lead him to victory, he would convert to Christianity.

The forces were aligned at either end of the wooden bridge. Constantine led his troops in a strong attack across the bridge. Men fell on both sides, for given the narrowness of the span the fighting was body to body and sword to sword. The slaughter was great. Men pushed ahead with no thought in mind but to get across. At the height of the combat, Maxentius was thrown off the bridge and pulled down by his body armour. Constantine marched into Rome as the victor and kept his promise; he was aware that with one shrewd move he had united a great portion of Rome behind the Lord's, as well his own, banner. In AD 325 he called for the first Council of Christian Churches. This watershed event took place at Nicaea (Iznik in Turkey). Christianity became Rome's state religion and the people were baptised. With Constantine's death (AD 337) the empire's candle began to flicker, waiting for the storm that would snuff it out.

While the *augusti* were busy butchering each other, the barbarians from the north began to take advantage of the situation. Rome's borders were constantly raided by Quadi, Heruli and Saxons (the latter came mostly by sea to Britannia). However the main peril for the *imperium romanum*'s survival came from three big Teutonic tribes: Franks, Alemanni and the biggest tribe of them all, the Goth. Still it required something to ignite the spark.

That something arrived on horseback from the inner steppes of Mongolia. In AD 372, a horde of riders on small, agile ponies appeared in White Russia, homeland of the Alani and Ostrogoth. They were from the Hsiung-nu tribe, a word the Goths couldn't pronounce, and so they simply called them the Hun. Nothing stood up to them; their avalanche overwhelmed the Alans at the Battle of the Tanais River (AD 372), from where they continued their rampage, threatening the Ostrogoth. While trying to stop the Huns from crossing the Dnieper river, the Ostrogoth chieftain Ermanaric was killed. A million Ostrogoth, led by their princes Alatheus and Saphrax, streamed towards the border of their Goth brothers, the Visigoth. The Visigoth chief, Athanaric, appealed to the new Roman Emperor Valens for intervention to prevent the multitude of Ostrogoth from swamping Visigoth lands. Valens hesitated, by which time the Visigoths were bunched up against the Danube. The Roman Emperor then agreed to let the Visigoths cross into his empire, as long as they surrendered their weapons and all youths of military age. As talks were in progress, promising to drag on, two young Visigoth princes, Alavius and Fritigern, roused their people not to give in to the exaggerated Roman demands. A million Visigoths followed their call; 200,000 were well-armed and trained warriors who pushed aside the Romans, forcing their way into Thrace.

While the Romans were busy in Thrace, a mass of Ostrogoth reached the Danube in the middle of winter (AD 376); here blocks of ice had created an ice jam. On the opposite shore was the Roman garrison of Carnuntum, held by one legion. The leader of the Ostrogoth, Prince Saphrax, waited until all were ready, then raised his sword. A flaming arrow soared high and a hundred thousand lances rose into the air. He gave out his tribal war cry and was answered by a joyous clamour, metal hitting on metal and wood banging on wood. The noise floated on the cold winter air towards the Roman legionaries guarding the opposite shore. Never before had there been such a mass of people – of nations, tribes and warriors – ready to invade the Western Roman Empire. The immense body began to move; with their wives and children of all ages, domestic animals, horses and thousands of wagons, they came down to the river's shore and then across the ice.

It was evident that soon these two huge Goth masses – basically of the same blood yet two enemy brothers for generations – had to collide, most likely in a profusion of blood. That was what the Roman Emperor counted on. But they didn't collide, at least not with their swords. The Ostrogoth Alatheus and Saphrax met with the Visigoth Alavius and Fritigern and formed an alliance that welded the two tribes into one nation; only united could they present a common front against the Roman legions. Emperor Valens found himself caught in a trap with two huge warrior armies descending on

Constantinople. He tried to outsmart them, with disastrous results.

The war between the Goths and Romans began during a parley between Emperor Valens and the Visigoth leaders. Under the guise of wishing to engage in peace talks, Valens had lured the princes to his camp. While they were sitting down at a welcome dinner, the Emperor's man stormed into the banquet hall. They killed the Visigoth Alavius but bungled the murder of Fritigern. The Visigoth guards put up a fight in which they died to the last man, but in the mêlée Fritigern managed to escape through an unguarded door, jump on his horse and dash off into the night. He rallied the tribes. Before he linked his Visigoth forces with those of the Ostrogoth, he fought an encounter with a Roman force at Marianopolis (Shumla in Bulgaria, AD 377). He won easily, because the Goth way of fighting relied on mobility and a powerful cavalry. After the battle, Visigoth and Ostrogoth joined up and then went on a rampage throughout East Roman Thrace.

'If we annoy them enough, the Romans will bring out their army against us,' warned Alatheus, the Ostrogoth. 'The empire is a giant beast best left unawakened. Do you want to fight them?'

'Yes,' replied Fritigern, 'and we shall beat them in battle.'

'Indeed, we have beaten them on the river and in the mountain passes,' stated Saphrax, the second leader of the Ostrogoth, 'but no one has ever beaten the legions in the plains. I cannot even recall the last time anyone tried.'

'We could put a lot of men against the empire, and our people would sing about it for a thousand years,' countered Fritigern, whose main purpose was to exact revenge rather than going after loot.

'Not all the tribes would answer your call.'

'Enough would if we promised them the riches of Constantinople!'

There was a shocked silence. Go for Constantinople! Fritigern must be mad! But Fritigern knew what he was talking about. Legions on foot could never face cavalry. And though the empire had the foot-soldiery, the Goths had the riders.

'A properly trained rider force can beat the legions!' Slowly he brought the others around to his point of view. And thus it was decided.

A weak, indecisive Emperor Valens was finally pushed into reacting; he called up an army with which he moved on Thrace to stop the Goths from laying waste to the entire province. While marching via Constantinople to Adrianopolis, with his forces concentrated in the eastern part of the *imperium romanum*, an event took place along the Rhine–Danube boundary which was quite unique for its time. Whether engineered by the warring Goths or brought about by spontaneous contagion, it resulted in every single Germanic tribe going on the warpath, and all along the Rhine–Danube frontier Rome's outlying garrisons were hard pressed. Valens called on assistance from his co-emperor, his nephew Gratian, who rushed to the Rhine, where the Alemanni had crossed into Gaul. Gratian defeated the barbarians at Argentaria (Colmar); 40,000 Alemanni, including their king, Prianus, paid for the invasion with their lives. While Gratian was victorious, things were not going at all well for Emperor Valens in far-off Thrace, especially after a combined force of some 300,000 Goth were joined by a contingent of highly trained Goth auxiliaries, supposed to fight for Rome, but who had killed their Roman officers before abandoning the Emperor's army. They brought with them their weapons, but even more important they delivered the Emperor's war plan.

With this, the war changed tone. Tribune Sebastianus, holding the empire's last line of defence in Thrace, was informed by his forward scouts that there might be a large body of barbarians coming on fast behind a cavalry screen.

His scouts had tried to penetrate this, but were repulsed with great losses. Such a rapid advance was most unusual; normally these barbarians came on like a flood, looted whatever they could, then rested to enjoy their spoils. Sebastianus dispatched more cavalry patrols to keep track of the enemy's movements and, at the same time, sent a messenger to warn the Emperor.

Sebastianus's scouts had been right. For once, the Goths had not stopped in order to loot the countryside. They were making straight for Adrianopolis. 'By nightfall they will have reached our forward bastions.' Tribune Sebastianus sighed. A dozen years ago he would have had three legions to do the job, but ten years of internal bickering and strife had robbed him of half that number. Also, nowadays emperors did not care to keep armies larger than absolutely necessary, for fear they would rebel, elect their own emperor and turn against their rightful *augustus*. Sebastianus had to make every effort to stop the Goths before they reached Adrianopolis. The Emperor would never forgive the tribune who allowed a Roman city to be sacked by barbarians. He had to delay the enemy and hope for the timely arrival of a relief force. Emperor Valens was coming up from Constantinople, but if he didn't arrive in time Sebastianus's men would be crushed under the hooves of Goth steeds.

In the first days of August AD 378, the Goth's march suddenly came to a halt, a mere ten miles outside the city of Adrianopolis. In a series of rolling hills and wide vales they set up camp.

The Roman determination to extract the utmost advantage from their superb road system was a key to their strategy. By making full use of the cobblestoned military roads, they could rush armies over hundreds of kilometres to meet more ponderous enemy forces, formidable if only by their overwhelming number. Rome's generals had always been able to raise a large enough force to inflict an immediate and massive defeat on their enemy. The greatest exponents of this strategy had been Marius and Caesar. But that was five hundred years ago, and Emperor Valens was no Caesar.

The future of the empire was changed by a bout of insane jealousy. Valens was envious of the successes that his nephew Gratian had scored over the Alemanni, and also those of his subordinate, Tribune Sebastianus, who, with a relatively minor force, had managed to delay the Goths in a series of daring sorties. With fifty thousand troops, the Emperor reached Adrianopolis on the eve of 8 August AD 378. There he was informed that he was confronting only the Visigoths, and he saw a good opportunity to set matters straight. In fact the Ostrogoth had gone off on a raid. Valens didn't care to have anyone else share in a victory that would elevate him to the summit of Rome's glory pyramid. He took a rash decision not to await the arrival of the second Roman army under his co-ruler Gratian, who was bearing down on Adrianopolis from the north. Gratian was only three days off, and with his additional fifty thousand trained and well-armed legionaries, their ballistas and catapults, Emperor Valens would not only enjoy a crushing majority, he would trap the Visigoth between two pincers. But at what price? He would have to share his triumph with that upstart nephew of his. Without allowing his men a rest, Valens marched his army straight for the Goth's encampment. 'I want to wipe them from the face of the earth, not merely defeat them. I want to kill so many that they will tremble at the very thought of Augustus Valens.'

A single incident decided the issue. Five days before Valens showed up with his legions, Fabius Tullius, an envoy of Tribune Sebastianus, met up with the Visigoth leader Fritigern. His task was twofold – to try and stall the advance of the Goth tribes by offering them concessions, and, more vital still, to report on the size and placement of their forces. While being led to the tent of the Goth leader, Fabius Tullius had a quick look around the wagon camp. What he spied didn't impress him; it looked more like a gypsy caravan than a well-organised army.

'Prince of Goth,' said the envoy, 'you would do better to protect your lands against the Hun plague rolling in from the East than to confront the forces of the Emperor.'

Fritigern, in the company of tough-looking warriors, looked sternly at the Roman. 'It seems to me that your tribune is rolling in the dust begging for peace. Let it be your *augustus* who rolls in the same dust. Turn around and ride back to your superior. Tell him it is us who have to exact revenge for the vile murder of our prince by your *augustus*.' The warriors nodded their heads and stomped their feet. Fritigern added with a grin, 'And furthermore, there is no treasure to be found with the Huns.'

As Fabius Tullius had met only the Visigoth Fritigern, and saw only Visigoth warriors in the camp, it left him with the erroneous impression that the tribes had split up and that the Visigoth were all that the Roman army would have to face. On his return, he relayed his observation to Sebastianus, who passed it on to his emperor. It was a typical case of a battle being precipitated by one of the belligerents acting on faulty intelligence. Because what the Romans didn't know was that Fritigern had been chosen by both tribes as their overall commander, albeit sharing military decisions with the Ostrogoth princes Alatheus and Saphrax. The day of Fabius Tullius's visit, many of the Visigoth warriors were away hunting for fresh meat, and the Ostrogoth had gone off on a looting spree.

Fritigern counted on Valens staying at Adrianopolis to await the arrival of Gratian's army, and was surprised when informed that the Emperor had bypassed Adrianopolis and was heading straight for him. Fritigern lost no time; he sent couriers to catch up with Alatheus and Saphrax and call in the Ostrogoth. To stand a chance against the Emperor's legions, which he believed were already boosted by Gratian's men, he needed the Ostrogoth by his side in the battle that he knew must now be fought. It was too late to break up the encampment and move off; the many women, children and livestock would make a rapid strategic retreat almost impossible. Fritigern could only hope that his message would reach the Ostrogoth leaders in time.

On all the hilltops surrounding the encampment, fires were burning brightly into the young morning. When the initial rumour about the Romans' approach spread through the camp, an immense crowd gathered in front of Fritigern's tent. He had to reassure them.

'When Rome was still invincible, the only difference between their leaders and the ordinary soldier was a strip on the tunic. But today, the same patricians wear flowing dresses of silk and purple, they ride no longer the horses but put these before a painted wagon and then have themselves carried on silk cushions to their great estates all along the coast. And their emperors, every one of them wants to see his image in the tallest and most impressive statues, placed in the midst of town squares, and they are only satisfied when the people decorate their stone image with gold.'

He played on the fact that the Goth, being a wandering people, had no use for permanent symbols. The crowd shook their heads; not even the greatest of kings would ever think of having a statue put up in his honour! 'But you know what is the worst?'

'Tell us, Fritigern,' yelled the people.

'The worst is that they do not honour their wives but take pretty boys for their pleasure . . .' The masses howled with disgust; for them nothing was more base than sexual perversion.

'There is gold and there are women for the taking. And

they took it all. The power of the *imperium romanum* is due to luck. That, and acting at the opportune moment. Will and strength alone are not sufficient to conquer. The same holds for us. And our opportune moment is now!'

The Goth raised their weapons. 'Beware of us, Romans, beware of us, because we are the Goth, we are the terror, we are the Devil . . .'

Fritigern rose in his saddle. In his face shone pride, but also anger. It was as if he had just discovered that there could never be peace between the Romans and his Goth. It was true; they lived under the same stars, but in two separate worlds.

Augustus Valens had been joined outside Adrianopolis by Sebastianus, and with this combined force he advanced straight for the Goth's encampment. He had 60,000 men to the Visigoth's 200,000. But his men were better trained, much better armed, and disciplined. Their marching route was leading them along a valley bordered by rolling hills; he had chosen the valley since this represented the best battleground for his formation, predominantly made up of foot troops. The night before the confrontation, many of his cavalrymen, tough Goth horsemen in Rome's pay, had abandoned his camp and joined their blood brothers. The situation was insane: riders clad in Roman uniforms and wielding Roman swords would come against him. Once the battle was won, he would have all of them put to death. But first he had to achieve victory.

9 August AD 378. The sun climbed quickly over the horizon. Many would not see the sun set. The battle opened as a free-for-all. The Romans walked into it without plan or preparation, and the Goth responded likewise. Like two giant turtles crawling towards each other, heavily armed Roman auxiliaries suddenly met up with a number of Visigoth warriors. The fighting began with the two

Adrianopolis
9 August AD 378

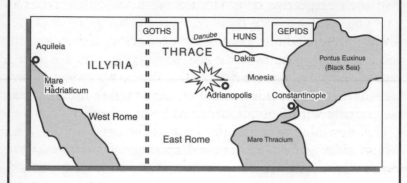

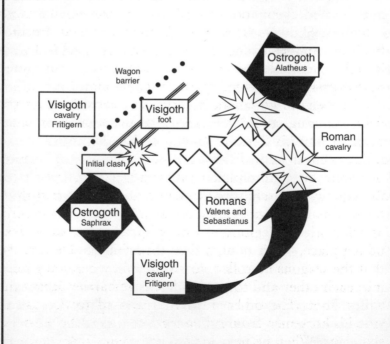

sides screaming insults at each other; the ground forces crashed into each other; nobody wanted to give. Matters got completely out of control as ever more warriors jumped into the fray, until a regular battle was under way – all without the slightest interference on the part of their respective commanders, who sat on their horses as confused as were their fighters on the ground. There wasn't the slightest possibility of victory, either for one side or the other; nobody was willing to lower his sword to get into battle formation. The muddle was so great that even their commanders could no longer tell friend from foe, especially with Roman uniforms being worn by deserters. This thrashing around lasted for about half an hour until both sides were so exhausted that they began slowly to disengage. The Romans, better disciplined and trained, were the first to react; they formed into battle formations and backed their foot-soldiery with siege engines and catapults. Showers of steel projectiles from the dreadful ballistas came whistling through the air, striking full blast into the mass of leaderless Visigoth. Dozens of men rolled on the ground, shredded by the steel missiles.

The Visigoth commander, Fritigern, dashed across the field, shouting commands, trying to get some semblance of order into his lines. A Roman charge, he knew, would follow almost immediately. All he could do was to look on while his undisciplined rabble rushed forth to meet the equally undisciplined Roman auxiliaries in a furious hand-to-hand struggle. It did not help Valens, who couldn't attack with his legions in line while this sideshow was taking place, but it bought time for Fritigern. He ordered that the wagons be rolled down the hill, where they piled into each other and formed a defensive barrier across the valley floor. The other thing he managed to do was to stop his horsemen from riding forth to join in the senseless slaughter. When he next looked across the valley floor he saw how the centurions had managed to get their men under control. With their phalanxes readied and their battle flags unfurled, for the Goth the critical moment was near. Fritigern was still without news from the Ostrogoth. Unless he could get his warriors disentangled from this useless encounter and formed into a solid line in front of the wagons, a disaster was in the making.

Valens knew that his men were vastly superior to the bunch of wild warriors facing him. Even if they were slowly being formed into a line, this pack of hounds could just about bite his hand, but they would never come out victorious. They had spat on the contracts signed with his *imperium romanum* because they thought that they were stronger than Roman legions. Such thoughts were dangerous, as they gave strength. Valens didn't only want to win a battle; he wanted to annihilate the tribes. Still, he made sure not to commit a fatal mistake, as his brother Valentinian had done when he went to his death. Along the Danube border, Valentinian had underestimated the Goth's will and courage. It was an old nation with inbred customs and beliefs, and one of these beliefs was in their own invincibility.

Valens raised his hand to stop his guards. He wanted to ride out alone and look into the eyes of this presumptuous Visigoth before he made him bend down and put his foot on his neck. He had hardly advanced a few paces when the tubas of the Goth began to sound. He turned in the saddle to face his men, who gave him a gusty cheer.

'Our men grow restless, Augustus,' his tribune Sebastianus tried to warn him.

'Damn them. Leave time for fear to grow among the barbarians,' Valens said. He had hoped that the barbarians would either charge his lines or break at the sight of the massed legions and run. They weren't doing either. The Emperor raised his hands. Step by syncopated step, thousands of legionaries advanced behind their wall of shields. It was a fearful sight, one that had struck terror into the hearts of their enemies over many centuries. And suddenly they hesitated, then halted; there seemed to be unrest among the troops as they stared at some point in the distance, at the blinking of much armour in sunlight, too far off to recognise the colour of the battle flags. This was certainly co-emperor Gratian's vanguard, which had moved faster than expected. Many Roman units let out a cheer. Their reserves were coming up from the enemy's rear; they would trap the cursed Goth in a vice and their battle would be a simple walkover.

Fritigern had also noticed something unusual. He looked past his men, at the line of legionaries that was again slowly advancing through the wide pan between the two rolling hills. For Fritigern it was high time to instil impetus in his warriors. He dashed along the line of tightly packed wagons. 'Be brave, Goth warriors. We fight for everything or we must die.' With a wild outcry, the Goth lifted their shields and swords and then stormed from the wagon wall straight at the Roman phalanx. Ahead was Fritigern on his massive charger, hurtling across the wet ground, throwing up mud from its hooves. He made straight for a Roman centurion with purple feathers on his helmet, marching slightly ahead of his line. The Goth leader gathered the reins in his left hand and drew his long barbarian sword. With one stroke he severed the centurion's head, a feat watched in awe by both Goth and Romans.

The Romans had pushed their shields into the ground and formed into a solid wall. Then they waited for the impact. For minutes their world stood still ... Valens called for his available Roman cavalry; a few hundred came riding around the right wing, faster and faster. The roar became deafening ... the Goth came on and then stumbled in their hundreds. The deadly fire from Roman bows managed to paralyse the warriors. In no time they had turned, trying to escape the hail from Valens's frightful catapults. Valens sent dispatch riders to the legions to order them into a general advance.

They were within three hundred yards of the Goth encampment when a rider came dashing over the hill, his body swaying wildly in the saddle. Blood was pouring from a vicious wound across his chest. In great pain he slid off his horse and came reeling up to the group around his emperor. 'Augustus, the barbarians are coming . . .' he managed to whisper before he fell over. What barbarians? The man was dead and dead men give no news. Valens's face was haggard and haunted. The barbarians? It couldn't be.

When his lead elements were a mere hundred paces from the line of wagons, and the legions' war horns were sounding the final attack, there was suddenly a flash of movement on the hillsides above the battlefield. Barbarians! The Ostrogoth horsemen had arrived from the East! Indeed, as when out hunting wild animals, they had concealed their approach by swinging around in a wide circle. They had followed the sound of battle and, once they could hear the metallic clang of swords, they had split up into two groups, one under Alatheus, the other commanded by Saphrax. The surprise was total. Their masses appeared like a wave over the crest of the two hills – close, much too close for the advancing Roman legions and their commanders to be able to react in time. Valens ordered his legions to make a turnabout and face the flanks of the Ostrogoth cavalry, but it was too late for such a manoeuvre to be effective. The Goth riders came down the hills on both sides of the valley. There were so many riding so close together that their knees touched.

Before they made contact, they spread out in open order with Alatheus in the centre. Twenty paces behind them came another line of Goth horsemen. They were thus spread over a wide area, but still able to circle around the Romans. At the same time the Visigoth foot-soldiers had reached the Roman line; sword clashed on sword, body on body, making it virtually impossible for the legions to turn about and face the horsemen. The Roman trumpets sounded a frantic retreat, but for far too many there was no retreat possible. A dense cloud of dust covered what was best described as mass slaughter.

Two entire legions, commanded by Roman officers but made up of Illyrian and Thracian auxiliaries, laid down their swords and gave up. They were quickly rounded up and driven back behind the wagon barrier by a number of warriors. There they had to face a mass of hysterical Visigoth women, screaming and swearing and armed with anything from pitchforks to kitchen knives. It took some hefty pushing by the Visigoth guards to keep their womenfolk from murdering the prisoners. For them the war was over and their future uncertain. If the Romans won, they would be executed for cowardice, and if the Goths emerged victorious they'd be their slaves.

The surrender by Valens's auxiliaries left a gaping hole in the Roman right flank. Fritigern, rallying his Visigoth cavalry, circled behind the battle scene and crashed into the rear of the Romans. They came sweeping down on the legions as a sandstorm sweeps over the desert. Those of the Romans who faced the Visigoth cavalcade were simply driven into the ground. Axes came down on heads, body armour split under the welter of sword strokes, and lances impaled hundreds. Abandoned by their auxiliaries, blocked in front by a barrier of carts and thousands of Visigoth foot troops, hammered in the flanks by two wings of Ostrogoth cavalry, and attacked from the rear by the Visigoth riders, the Romans fought on, but what had seemed like certain victory was quickly turning into a race with death. The furious attacks on their legions had split the Roman battle formation into separate cohorts, until only small groups fought on. In these brutal moments of hand-to-hand brawls the sword cuts didn't distinguish between friend and foe. It was small consolation that they had no way of knowing who had been slaughtered and by whose sword. The legionaries began to weaken, their strength sapped, as around the cohorts heaped the bodies of their fallen. It wasn't so much the silence of the dead as having to listen to the painful cries of the wounded, condemned to certain death, which drained the Romans' will to fight on. Their only thought was to save their lives by running away. They found every exit lane barred by the madly circling Goth rider hordes, slashing deep into the backs of the escapees. Not a single one was spared.

The noise abated; the field was dotted with heaps of corpses where brave men had made their final stand. When the sun stood at its zenith, the war horns of the Goths sounded the end of the victorious battle. They left the enemy dead and near-dead for the jackals and buzzards. In the evening a wind began to blow and covered the field, littered with bodies, with a film of fine dust.

Later, as human scavengers stripped the fallen of valuables, a Goth patrol found Augustus Valens wounded but still alive. Dragged before the victorious Fritigern, he offered the Goth a huge ransom for his safety. The Goth prince refused; he wanted to avenge the shameful deed the Roman had committed, nothing less. How a Roman emperor was put to death history does not recount, only that he and his faithful tribune Sebastianus, together with all the Roman captives, were killed.

With victory won and Adrianopolis within their grasp, the Goth were about to head for the town when a scout rode into camp, announcing that Gratian's army had finally arrived and that the city was defended by a strong force of legionaries. The Goth, basically a fast-moving rider army which had never learned to cope with the stout walls of fortresses, turned away from Adrianopolis and laid waste to all of Thrace. Their wanton destruction of the fabulous ancient Greek treasures, the temples, monuments and scriptures, immortalised them in history as 'the barbaric Goth'.[2]

In one of the numerous running battles between the pillaging Visigoth and the Roman holding forces of Tribune Promotus, Prince Fritigern was killed (AD 383).

By annihilating the 'last Roman army' of Emperor Valens, the Battle of Adrianopolis became a watershed in history. It stripped the *imperium romanum* of its defences and was to lead gradually to its collapse. And it started a revolution in military history: the eclipse of infantry by horse-mounted formations. Rome's legions were crushed under the hooves of barbaric riders. 'On several occasions in her history Rome had suffered as overwhelming a disaster, yet never so decisive a one. For the battle of Adrianopolis was an epoch-making conflict. The Empire was rocked to its foundations.'[3] More than Hannibal's threat after Cannae, the Battle of Adrianopolis proved a decisive turning point in history. Following Valens's defeat, the Roman Empire as it had stood for half a millennium was faced with dissolution.

The drama of Adrianopolis began when a spy made a mistake and an emperor based his strategic move on faulty intelligence. It was aggravated by the negation of common tactical sense, when this victory-mad emperor pushed his army against a divided enemy, without scouting out the whereabouts of the enemy's other main force. And a fluke, with the sudden and unexpected appearance of overwhelming rider masses, decided it.

The battle made the Goths a major power, dispelling the Roman belief in the inferiority of the barbarian race. At

---

[2] The term Gothic for a type of medieval cathedral was intended to express a barbaric style, and came from the raid by Goths throughout Thrace.

[3] Prof. M. Bang, *Cambridge Medieval History* (vol. 1).

Adrianopolis, the last Roman army had been destroyed, and with this the end of the *imperium romanum* was unavoidable.

17

When Rome Falls, the World will Fall

Rome
24 August AD 410

'Adest Alaricus, trepidam Roman obsidet, turbat, irrumpit.'
('Alaric appeared before trembling Rome, laid siege, spread
  confusion and broke into the city.')
Orosius, *Seven Books of History against the Pagans*, AD 414[1]

The Roman prefect in charge of the Julian Alps region
was annoyed. His border had been quiet for years and,
just as he was counting on retiring to his rich estates
near Herculaneum and letting someone else worry about
the cursed province, he was shaken from his reveries
by a rider who dared to announce an invasion by barbarians. The scout had seen only a handful of outriders,
but he thought there might be a bigger force coming up
behind them.

'We have to go into the hills to teach them a lesson,'
said Prefect Julius Gaius Licinius, who knew that he was
no great general. 'It's been a long time since we had an
expedition. This time we will destroy these barbarians, not
defeat them, but kill so many that they will never come
back!' He felt that with his garrisoned legion of Illyrian

---

1 Orosius, *Historiae adversum Paganos*, transl. Rome, 1882.

auxiliaries he could quickly take care of the incursion. It would give those sloppy legionaries, currently lazing about, something to do. But Julius Gaius Licinius didn't realise, nor did he try to find out, what was coming at him. Several weeks later he was dead, and so was what remained of his legion. They had confronted not some insignificant little tribe of barbarians, but the victors of Adrianopolis, the Goth!

With the regency of Western Roman Emperor Honorius, an excessively sly and unsavoury character, began the end of the Roman Empire. The effeminate climate at his court quickly infected the legions. Legionaries complained not only about low salaries, but also about the weight of their protective armour and helmets. Discipline broke down;[2] training was abandoned and military exercises frowned upon. The terrible Roman sword had lost its sharpness; ever since the disaster at Adrianopolis, Rome's emasculated army abased itself before its enemies. When faced by a courageous foe, they preferred the ignominy of flight to the resolution that had led their ancestors to greatness. Once again they were to face such an enemy, a fierce warrior nation willing to use raw force and naked violence to sack Eternal Rome. They were led by one of the great warriors of his time, Alaric the Goth.

Alaric, prince of the Visigoth, had joined Emperor Theodosius's army as a rider commander. While serving in the Roman army, young Alaric used his time well to learn all he could about military strategy, which, all along, he planned to use against his military instructors. In AD 390, he led a Goth raiding party across the Danube, the first time this future nemesis was to test Rome's defences. Emperor Theodosius, challenged for the crown by Valentinian II

2 Vegetius, a contemporary military historian.

and having to fight a civil war, managed once more to stop Alaric's advance by offering peace talks. In the meantime, a Roman general, Magnus Clemens Maximus, had usurped the crown of Gratian and faced Theodosius in battle. With the help of a brilliant young Vandal general, Stilicho, Theodosius defeated Maximus. With this victory, the empire was for one last time united under one ruler, Theodosius, who resided in Constantinople. Stilicho became his de facto 'keeper of the peace'. With the death of Theodosius, the empire was split between his two inept sons, Arcadius in the East and Honorius in the West.

Honorius had become the new Western Empire *augustus*, but he was Emperor in name only; all the power rested with Stilicho, a military commander of great skill and daring. Emperor Honorius hated Stilicho for his success, his nobility and his popularity, but he was the only one capable of saving the empire. His policy of tolerance kept the barbarians at bay, and they continued to supply Rome's legions with soldiers. He became so well liked by the auxiliary legions that they considered him their father, and fought for Stilicho like some private army.

While civil unrest kept the two Roman empires occupied, a new danger began to loom ominously in the East: the Huns of King Uldin were running out of grazing land for their immense pony herds and beginning to push westward. As a result the newly elected King Alaric of the Visigoth broke the treaty he had previously agreed with Stilicho and launched a new raid into Thrace (AD 395). He roamed the countryside at will, his Goth plundering and murdering. In an attempt to save what could be saved, Stilicho marched with his legions against him, but was ordered out of Thrace by Eastern Emperor Arcadius, who was more concerned with the presence of a Vandal general and his private army than the devastation caused to his lands by Goth raiders. In one respect he was right – Stilicho was the man of the hour, and only his excellence kept the tottering *imperium romanum* from total collapse. But the pressures on the outlying provinces increased and with them the danger to the heart of the empire.

In AD 401, Alaric accepted payment of a large ransom by the envoys of Emperor Arcadius to vacate his part of the empire. Alaric set his sights on the rich upper Italian towns. This meant a confrontation with the Western legions of Count Stilicho. Before his legions could be positioned, Alaric surprised the thin Roman line on *limes* duty[3] and crossed the Danube, and his army came flooding across the Julian Alps. Panic broke out when it became known that Alaric's final destination was Rome. Emperor Honorius fled the Eternal City for Ravenna, a fortress surrounded by high walls and miles of impenetrable swamps. He barricaded himself inside his palace, surrounded by frightened advisers.

'They're coming! They have raided the empire before, but never like this,' said a quivering *augustus*. 'Of what religion are they?'

'Some barbarians call themselves Christians, but the Christians of the Eastern Empire say they are not.'

'The barbarian auxiliaries in my armies certainly are . . . they will stop the pagans from doing harm to their Christian emperor . . .' They did not.

Alaric had the determination of a wolfhound, and from those who served under him he exacted a loyalty that verged on fanaticism. To fight for the great king was the ultimate challenge for any young Goth. For his gigantic raiding party Alaric had selected the best among his warriors. Having pushed aside the legion of Prefect Licinius and crossed the mountain range that separated the Danube valley from the Adriatic sea, Alaric captured the major

---

[3] *Limes* was the defensive wall put up by the Romans along the Danube and Drau.

Adriatic city of Aquileia,[4] which he put to the torch. An unusually early winter brought his march on Rome to a halt. He set up winter quarters in the Po valley. He left it up to the Romans to guess whether, come spring, he would move on Ravenna, Milan or Rome.

The winter's delay allowed Stilicho to travel personally through the Brenner Pass and call for *confederati* among the Raetia tribe on the Upper Danube. Roman gold bought Stilicho an army and, by early spring, he was leading his levies across the St Gotthard Pass and heading for Milan, now under siege by Alaric.

'Don't forget, King Alaric, Rome can count on his friendship with the Alemanni and Raeti.' It was true – Stilicho's name inspired confidence and trust among many of the barbarian tribes. 'They might come to the assistance of Stilicho and stop us conquering West Rome.'

'We haven't come to conquer a country. Our wars are never directed at taking the land but at carrying away the loot.' If asked to advance with great speed, he knew that his men would obey him and follow him instead of stopping at frequent intervals for loot. They were deep inside the enemy's domain, and if they stopped off to loot and divided their forces, they'd all be killed.

From the Upper Danube, Stilicho had put out the call for Rome's garrison legions in Gaul and along the Rhine to join him in Milan. When the Goth king heard about Stilicho's plans, he marched against him, leading to three inconclusive encounters. The first was in March AD 402 near Asta. Stilicho carried it. Three weeks later, on 6 April, Stilicho suddenly attacked Alaric's camp near Pollentia, while the Goths were immersed in their Easter celebration. The initial encounter went to Stilicho, until Alaric got his Goth cavalry together and then inflicted great losses on the

---

[4] Located between Trieste and Venice, it still has its most splendid cathedral with a fabulous mosaic floor. Any visitor to Venice is well advised to make the detour.

Romans and their *federati*, the Alani. While this battle was going on outside the camp, Stilicho and a detachment of Roman cavalry cut their way into the camp and devastated it, taking a number of hostages, including Alaric's favourite wife. Once again, nothing was decided, and Honorius paid a ransom to get Alaric out of Italy. Within the year the Goth were back. In June 403, Stilicho faced Alaric near Verona, where he finally managed to stop Alaric's advance into central Italy. Following this battle, which bled both sides dry, the two leaders began to horse-trade. Alaric renounced his 'allegiance' to Eastern Emperor Arcadius in return for being appointed Western Emperor Honorius's governor-general for Illyrium. In this way Western Rome grabbed Illyrium from Constantinople, since Alaric had been its governor all along, albeit appointed by Arcadius.

The Western Emperor signed the parchment sealing the deal. To avoid any occasion for further offence to the Goth and their king, Emperor Honorius complied with all their whims and demands. If this showed his weakness, he had only himself to blame. Popularly he was regarded as a mere voluptuary, another perfumed Nero fiddling while Rome burned, while, owing to the insincerity he showed in his various acts of bribery and cajolery, the Goth mistrusted him completely. The corruption of power and the complacency of the Emperor began to consume the empire.

While Stilicho was warring with Alaric, a simple Roman soldier on garrison duty in Britain, Constantinus, had himself pronounced Emperor of Britannia and Gaul and established himself by sharing control with marauding barbarians. Constantinus's revolt ended Rome's rule over Britain and, without the protection of Rome's legions, left the island vulnerable to many invasions by Picts, Scots and Saxon sea rovers.

Alaric and Stilicho were opponents in the field, but they also admired each other as warriors do. The Vandal and the Goth, both barbarians, spoke with the toughness of leaders of men. Their decisions for settling conflict were taken without referring to an emperor cowering behind the walls of Ravenna. This inspired tantrums in the insanely jealous Honorius, who believed that he was being left out of affairs of state. Having been locked up for months behind his palace walls, without any notion of what was happening on the outside, only increased his paranoia.

Honorius conspired with three patrician Roman generals, Turpilio, Varanes and Vigilatius – an unsavoury character who left his name to an instrument of terror: the *vigilanti* – to do away with Stilicho, then remove all barbarian legion commanders and replace them with men loyal only to Honorius. The murder was carefully planned so that his closest lieutenants would be caught in the same trap. The trio didn't give a thought to the fact that all competent field officers had risen from the auxiliary barbarians and that such a purge could weaken Rome's legions beyond recovery.

The assassination of Stilicho (AD 408) finally brought about Rome's demise. Honorius gave a feast in Stilicho's honour. While he was sitting at his emperor's table, armed guards burst into the hall and buried their swords in Stilicho and his companions. Cavalry units, the *vigilanti*, then roamed throughout the legions' garrisons in Upper Italy to slaughter most of Stilicho's lieutenants. Auxiliary units of Raeti, Alani, Illyrian and Gaul were caught in a desperate situation; their families, settled in Italian cities, were taken hostage by the *vigilanti* to stop the legionaries from reacting. In this hour of need, they turned for help to their erstwhile foe, the Goth Alaric. Alaric was an opportunist and recognised the opening that would allow him to fulfil his dream – the capture of Rome.

In AD 409, Alaric, at the head of a mighty host, crossed the Alps and entered the principal town of Aquileia, where he was cheered on arrival by the auxiliary legions. He continued his march down the length of the Italian boot without meeting opposition. Betrayed by his conspirators, Emperor Honorius fled once again behind the walls of Ravenna and left Rome to fend for itself.

The great hall was almost empty. Honorius, cowering before a fire trying to warm himself, faced a tribune. 'Tell me, how are the barbarians armed?'

'With lances and swords, Augustus.'

'Then they are only horsemen and cannot scale the walls.'

'We believe so, Augustus.' The thought of his continued and assured safety cheered the Emperor. The last time the barbarians had bypassed the tall walls of Ravenna, and they would do so again. At least, so he hoped. Honorius stripped the surrounding countryside of its food supplies and called upon his few loyal soldiers to assemble around him in Ravenna – thereby continuing to leave Rome to fend for itself.

By the autumn of AD 409, Alaric was camped around Rome, a city of 1,200,000 inhabitants, protected by formidable walls and accessible through twelve gates. It was a fact that the only weakness the barbarians showed was that they were ill equipped to take fortified places by storm. They had no siege engines and no techniques for scaling walls. But there were other means to overcome ramparts; one didn't have to climb over them to take a city. Alaric didn't have the troops to storm the walls, but he had the means to blockade the gates. All the city's supplies arrived by ships on the Tiber river from the port of Ostia. By cutting off the supply line, Alaric condemned Rome to death by starvation. It didn't take long before the people began to go hungry.

The persons of both sexes, who had been educated in the enjoyment of ease and luxury, discovered how little is requisite to supply the demands of nature; and lavished their unavailing treasures of gold and silver to obtain the coarse and scanty sustenance which they would formerly have rejected with disdain. The food the most repugnant to sense or imagination, the aliments the most unwholesome and pernicious to the constitution, were eagerly devoured, and fiercely disputed, by the rage of hunger. A dark suspicion was entertained that some desperate wretches fed on the bodies of their fellow creatures that they had secretly murdered; and even mothers are said to have tasted the flesh of their slaughtered infants![5]

A delegation of citizens came begging. Alaric refused to consider allowing sections of the population to leave the epidemic-ravaged city. 'The thicker the hay, the easier it is moved,' he replied. 'I shall reconsider only if you deliver to me all the gold and silver in your city. Every precious possession and all of my brothers you hold as your slaves.'

The patricians were shocked. 'Your demand is great, great king. What do you intend to leave us?'

'Your lives!'

A few Romans had managed to escape from the city. They brought to Ravenna tales of the misery they had endured and the utter hopelessness of continuing the resistance. The Emperor commiserated with them, but otherwise did nothing, leaving the people of Rome to fend for themselves. When the news reached the beleaguered city that they could no longer count on help from their emperor, it increased their frustration. All horses and other animals had been slain, and dogs and cats were being sold at enormous prices. Even vermin were becoming scarce. With famine came disease. While epidemics ravaged Rome and

5 E. Gibbon, *The Decline and Fall of the Roman Empire* (XXXI), New York, 1953.

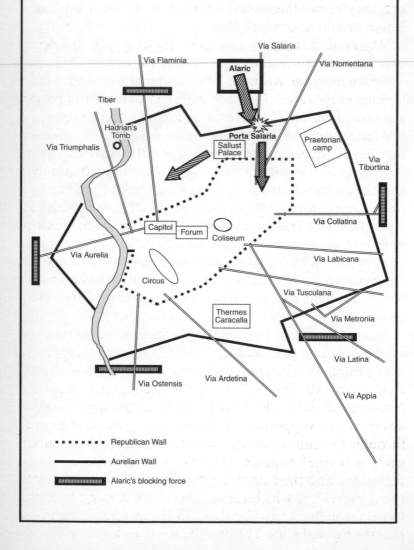

Imperial Rome Surrounded by the Aurelian Wall
24 August AD 410

Via Salaria

Alaric

Via Flaminia

Via Nomentana

Tiber

Hadrian's
Tomb

Via Triumphalis

Porta Salaria

Sallust
Palace

Praetorian
camp

Via
Tiburtina

Via Collatina

Capitol Forum

Coliseum

Via Aurelia

Via Labicana

Circus

Via Tusculana

Via Metronia

Thermes
Caracalla

Via Latina

Via Ostensis

Via Ardetina

Via Appia

········· Republican Wall

——— Aurelian Wall

▨▨▨▨ Alaric's blocking force

its will to fight was reduced by famine and fever, Alaric left part of his army to continue the siege. With the rest he took up winter quarters in Tuscany. In the spring, Alaric didn't go for Rome; he marched on Ravenna.

'Ravenna is strong, my liege.'

'I know, and I am missing some of my best warriors, they're holding down Rome, but we shall now take Ravenna and afterwards Rome.'

'My king, it is never reasonable looking to two sides at once,' one of his advisers dared to point out.

'Spare me your wisdom. Yes, we might lose one side by looking at the other. But once we take Ravenna and punish a traitor, Rome will fall without a fight.'

Alaric's adviser had been right; he couldn't take on two great cities at the same time. He tried to storm Ravenna and failed. In large part this was to do with the mosquito-infested swamps, which sapped the strength of his men, who were falling victim to fever (malaria). After weeks of frustration, he led his army back south to reinforce the siege of Rome. This time he no longer needed a sharp sword to overcome the city's ramparts; help came from the inside. In a daring sortie, some Romans managed to get through the defences by floating down the Tiber river. They gave Alaric some welcome news.

'King Alaric, our brothers will overpower the garrison at the Salarian gate and open the doors to your army,' they promised. The coup was planned for the night of 24 August AD 410. The Goth sympathisers gathered in several houses near the walls. In the middle of the night, several dozen armed supporters of the Goth king made their way through the rabbit-warren of lanes towards the Salarian gate. In a brief struggle, they overpowered the surprised defenders, and then slashed through the rope that held up the drawbridge, which came down with a bang that was heard throughout Christendom. Goth rider hordes stormed into the Eternal City. The first the Romans knew of the fall of their town was blaring Goth war horns and the noise of hooves on pavements.

'*Adest Alaricus, trepidam Roman obsidet, turbat, irrumpit* – Alaric appeared before trembling Rome, laid siege, spread confusion and broke into the city.' A barbarian king had achieved what no one before him had managed. Never before had a foreign invading army entered sacred Rome; not even Hannibal had accomplished that. Alaric's insolence carried him to the very throne that had been occupied by Rome's emperors for four centuries.

Alaric and his men came not to conquer, but to loot. His triumphant entry was followed by the 'sack of Rome' – six days of looting, burning and rape. Frustrated for months before shut gates, the Goths now released their pent-up ferocity. Rome was subjected to the horrors that follow when victory, brutality and licentiousness are linked. Every evil passion was allowed to parade with impunity; revenge, lust and avarice ruled the day. 'Rome no longer exists . . .' In the most gigantic plunder in the history of mankind, Rome, the centre of the universe and keeper of all its stolen treasures, was put to the sack. Nothing and no one was spared. Temples and churches were robbed clean of icons and silver chalices; splendid mansions were emptied of treasures. Anything that could be carried was stacked high on to wagons, and what couldn't be removed was smashed, or piled up and burned. Goth warriors drove around in splendid carriages, dressed up in foppish clothes. Wine cellars were emptied; fights broke out among the drunken looters.

In the poorer sections of the city, where little of value was found, the plundering Goth were so infuriated that they torched the houses. Strong winds fanned the fires and sparks flew across rooftops, and many other parts of the town burst into flame. As entire sections were devoured by the fire, the people stood by in apathy. The splendid

Palace of Sallust fell victim to the conflagration. A thick, oily cloud hid the horror; the acrid stench of smoke and death was everywhere. As always, the worst was reserved for the hapless population. Noble matrons were stripped naked and driven along the streets to suffer the agony of brutal rape by hordes of drunken men. Young girls were savaged in front of their families. The city's leading patricians were rounded up like cattle, nailed to the cross or made to collect the many mutilated corpses rotting in the hot summer sun; they became infected by handling the dead and were shortly to die in horrible agony. Women were dragged into warriors' tents or pushed into cages to be sold on slave markets. As for 'the worthless', those who under normal circumstances were left alone, even they were sold or slaughtered. And those whose lives were by a miracle spared, they would never again behave normally; their minds had been deranged by the horror they had had to live through.

There was one notable exception. Alaric wasn't exactly an atheist, because atheism was not a survival trait in a world with several thousand gods, he just didn't much care for any of the gods. But there was one prophet they called Christus, and too many were following his teachings for him to be overlooked. The Goth king thought it wise not to confront the one and only Christian God and his representative on earth. Therefore he had given strict orders, on pain of death, to protect the sanctity of the basilicas of St Peter and St Paul. Many lost and terrified souls, hoping that being near their God would save them, had fled into the crypt and were cowering in fear around the altar when a group of drunken Goths stormed in. A giant of a warrior stood on the steps and swung his long blade. He did it perfectly calmly, as if he were chopping wood. When Alaric was informed of the incident, he sent a patrol and had all those participating in the desecration of the holy place executed on the steps of the church. He then ordered that their corpses be left lying among their victims as an example to others.

St Augustine, Bishop of Hippo (Bona in Algeria), living in voluntary seclusion in a small cell to contemplate the ways of the world and religion, was sufficiently horrified by the sack of Rome to write in his *Retractions*: 'Rome, meanwhile, by the invasion of the Goths under their king Alaric, was overthrown with a crash of a mighty slaughter. Inflamed with zeal for the House of the Lord, I am determined to write a treatise on the City of God.'

Their stay in Rome did Alaric's men no good. For six days they gave themselves up to the most unbounded extravagance. Bickering, fights over spoils and the influence of the depraved and luxurious way of the Romans threatened to destroy their fighting spirit, and it left King Alaric with no option but to forcibly remove them from the eternal City. The Goths were not loath to apply torture to force confessions of hidden treasures, and it became so bad that they even murdered one another over the possession of valuables. After six days of cruelty, lust and rapine, Alaric ordered his hordes to quit the city.

There has never been an exact account of how many fell victim during the sack of the city. It is commonly acknowledged that most of its honourable citizens ended up as slaves. But as the barbarians preferred gold to slaves, some could repurchase their freedom for a relatively modest sum. Those who couldn't be sold to Syrian slave traders, or who proved otherwise useless or too old, were simply done to death before the great host set out on their march into Campania. For its beautiful capital, Capua, a similar fate was reserved. The city was plundered, but its citizens were spared. By now the Goths had learned to enjoy the warmth of southern sunshine and the pleasures of good wines. Their years of hardship along the Elbe and Danube were forgotten. The Huns were but a memory of a distant past.

The conqueror was not allowed the time to enjoy the fruits of his plunder. Probably during the earlier siege of Ravenna, a malaria-carrying mosquito had stung him. As he was ready to cross over into Sicily, he came down with a high fever. He hung on for days, tossing on his camp bed, bathed in sweat and shivering with cold. In his final hours, he called for Athaulf, to whom he bequeathed his kingdom. Four months after the sack of Rome, Alaric died of the fever. Many claimed afterwards that it had been the Lord's way of punishing the heathen.

His funeral was as spectacular as his life and displayed the ferocious character of the barbarians. Thousands of slaves were forced to build a dam in order to divert the waters of the River Busento, which passes under the walls of Consentia. The construction was a gigantic undertaking during which many drowned. The royal sepulchre, stuffed with the golden spoils of Rome, was lowered on to the empty riverbed and then the waters were restored to their normal channel. To safeguard the tranquillity of their conqueror king in death, and to conceal the site from treasure hunters, the Goths sealed his sepulchre with inhuman barbarity; they slit the throats of every one of the thousands of slaves who had worked on it. Nobody has ever discovered the secret and Alaric's treasure of the Busento still lies somewhere to be found.

With the death of Alaric ended a chapter in history. His successor, Athaulf, married the sister of Emperor Honorius, Galla Placidia, and then left with his men on a conquest of Gaul and Spain (AD 415). After many years of wandering, the Visigoth finally settled in the region of Aquitaine (France), where they established the first barbarian empire. Athaulf was murdered, and Wallia, who replaced him, became the first King of Toulouse (AD 419). There the Visigoth remained, peacefully settled, tilling their fields, until a new danger forced them from their complacency to face their most terrible enemy yet on a field of slaughter. In AD 451, King Theodoric the Visigoth met up with Attila the Hun.[6]

In 452, Attila the Hun invaded Italy. Divine intervention in the person of God's representative on earth, Pope Leo I – and his bag of gold – saved Rome. Then, in AD 455, Rome suffered yet another sack from a Germanic tribe, the Vandals under their king, Gaiseric.

It went like this: a jealous Emperor Valentinian murdered the 'last of the Romans' in the person of Aetius, who had been victorious over the Huns. Aetius's protégé, Petronius Maximus, murdered Valentinian and usurped the crown by forcing the Emperor's widow, Eudoxia, to marry him. Eudoxia appealed to Gaiseric the Vandal King, Gaiseric killed Emperor Petronius Maximus, and his men sacked Rome. For a grand finale, Gaiseric abducted Eudoxia.

Alaric's heritage was terrible. Rome had survived onslaught by Etruscans, Carthaginians, Cimbri, Helvetes, Gaul and Belgiae. But none of them was like the Goth, who turned out to be the foe that finally delivered its death stroke. Eternal Rome as it had existed for centuries, the splendour of great emperors' courts, of amphitheatres and magnificent public baths cut from marble, of residences housing the treasures of the globe and white temples with their slender columns pilfered from the shrines of Greece, that Rome was no more.

'The temple is overthrown, the gold has been pillaged, the wheel of fortune has accomplished her revolution, and the sacred ground is again disfigured with thorns and brambles. The hill of the Capitol was formerly the head of the Roman Empire, the citadel on earth, the terror of kings; illustrated by the footsteps of so many triumphs, enriched

---

[6] See the author's *The Hinges of Battle*, Hodder & Stoughton, London, 2002.

with the spoils and tributes of so many nations . . . the public and private edifices that were founded for eternity lie prostrate, naked and broken, like the limbs of a mighty giant; and the ruin is the more visible from the stupendous relics that have survived the injuries of time and fortune.' These words were written a thousand years later, in 1430, by Poggio in his *De varietate fortunae*.

Rome, the only power that for centuries had transcended national boundaries, which had ensured law and the survival of Western civilisation, was dead. And with it died hope for the immediate future in a world gone mad.

The fall of Rome happened not by dint of bravery but through stealth and betrayal. A few dozen men overpowered the guards and dropped the drawbridge, and Rome's auxiliary legions refused to fight for the empire's survival.

It wasn't only the Goth, Vandals, Huns and Langobards who were pounding on the door. The demise of antiquity's superpower was inevitable once the moral collapse of Rome, its society and their *augusti* set in.

The day the 'glory that was Rome' died, the Dark Ages began.

Epilogue

Vae Victis!
'Woe to the Vanquished!'
Livy (59 BC–AD 17), *History*

'There will be no end to the troubles of states, or indeed, dear Glaucon, of humanity itself, till philosophers become kings in this world, or till those we now call kings and rulers really and truly become philosophers.'

Plato, *The Republic* (fourth century BC)

From Armageddon to the fall of Rome. A walk through the fringes of hell.

We have a propensity to exalt the past – the Golden Age. We are missing many pieces in history's greatest puzzle. Not much has withstood the ravages of time and barbarism. Magnificent edifices, exposed to the convulsions of nature, have survived storm, rain and earthquake, but not the wanton destruction by man. The ruins of antiquity lie scattered over uncultivated fields. The Babylonians left only a temple's wall; the Greeks destroyed Persepolis; the Romans dumped salt on Carthage, then managed to set fire to the many volumes of Western philosophy in Alexandria; and the Catholic Church stripped the Coliseum of its marble. 'Behold the relics of Rome, the image of her pristine greatness. Neither time nor the barbarians can boast the merit of this stupendous destruction: it was perpetrated by her own citizens, by the most illustrious of her sons. They have done with the battering-ram what the Punic hero could not accomplish with his sword.'[1]

The ancients also left us their idea of civilisation, the good and the bad. They were patrons of beauty and paragons of virtue; but they were also the barbarous products of a brutal age. They erected temples, unsurpassed in their splendour, and then practised a licentiousness that violated with impunity any law. This led to a breakdown of morals, and the fall of great empires. Nothing was eternal.

Time has played some interesting tricks on our interpretation of antiquity. We look upon the Egyptians, Greeks and Romans as the heroic representatives of some incredibly noble time, the central plot in a Sophoclean drama, a biblical message where goodness wins out over evil. However, in all these ancient tales of goodness and splendour, one element has gone missing: the violence, ferocity, ignorance and cruelty that shook the world of antiquity. Wars were conducted with utter brutality and the vanquished were slaughtered to the last man, woman and child. Pity was unknown; the blood of the innocent desecrated holy lands and sacred grounds.

The key to greatness was (as it still is) conquest. Many of the great battles of antiquity were fought for territorial gains. Others were stimulated by passion and revenge. More often the motive was transient possession of portable wealth, which was followed by wanton indulgence of lust and cruelty, battering to the ground the magnificent edifices of the caesars or burning the inspiring principles of Greek philosophers. The prime example is the destruction of the world's greatest monument to free thought, the Library of Alexandria. Everyone participated in its destruction: Caesar, barricaded inside its walls, trying

---

[1] Francesco Petrarca (Petrarch), 1304–74.

to protect himself behind a screen of flames from irreplace-
able manuscripts; the Christian bishops, who considered
liberal ideas philosophic idolatry; and the disciples of
Mohammed, inspired by the ignorance of the fanatic.
Before the Great Library was put to the torch, Caliph
Omar ordered: 'If these writing of the Greeks disagree
with the Book of Allah, they are pernicious and must be
destroyed.'

Invasion of foreign soil was followed by brief, intense
encounters and short bouts of feverish combat. Its repercussions extended far beyond the particular time and
region. The military chaos that always followed a political
upheaval in the 'cradle of civilisation' tempted others to
invade, conquer, or simply settle scores with bigger, more
populous neighbours, as Alexander did when he invaded
Persia. The Pharaoh Thutmosis needed to protect his trade
routes and therefore conquered Palestine. They did not
always end in victory; there were failures aplenty. Darius
and Xerxes swamped the Aegean with their mighty hosts,
only to discover that reports of Greece's military weakness
were greatly exaggerated; Hannibal failed to obtain control
over the Mediterranean because he was betrayed by his
own country. It was left to Caesar's major land campaigns
to seize and retain all of Europe and thereby consolidate
Rome's hold over antiquity. And then Valens lost it all
when he acted on faulty intelligence. The 'barbaric hordes
from the East or the North' were no more brutal or unjust
than the Spartans or Romans – but perhaps a bit 'more
foreign'.

It is strange to find Caesar's nihilistic carnage among
the conquered tribes granted the same patriotic status as
Rome's fight for survival against Hannibal. The overriding
message was: all wars are ennobling, especially if you die in
one. Such a lack of proportion stemmed mainly from the
deep-rooted desire to elevate battle death above ordinary
death, so that the soldier who died from the thrust of

sword or lance must be accorded eternal honour. Some men actually believed that it was more heroic to die in an epic battle like Thermopylae than in bed, because dying in bed seemed to them all prose and no poetry. At best, such a romantic vision of war may be childish nonsense, but it played into the hands of those who were trying to get others to fight for them and were eager to dispatch young men to an early grave.

No period of history has used up more people more quickly and more thoroughly than antiquity, with its pitiless slaughter of all by all. Its campaigns leave us with a spate of military lessons and political implications – failures of strategy, the role of armaments, and the fighting ability of the armed forces. By delving into the past we may learn for the future.

Then (as now) four principal themes run through historic battle situations:

Manipulation of men.

Strategic innovation.

Conquest of mind.

The flexibility to adopt new options when those planned fail to achieve results.

The basic themes and principles of warfare have never changed. Then as now, creative leadership, wisdom and courage were the three pillars of victory. Paralytic hesitation led invariably to disaster, as did foolish bravado. A great general had to know that risk was inherent in war, and that there was a clear difference between a calculated risk and a reckless gamble. Some believed in the cause of righteousness; they resisted foreign invaders with an intensely nationalistic spirit and demonstrated it through their willingness to give their lives for the *patria*. The common error of both was their belief that they were defending a just cause and killing for a just cause. Some reduced everything to a simple formula: kill as many of your enemy as you possibly can and break his morale.

They gauged their progress by the piles of twisted corpses they left behind. And when they had made a desert they called it peace.

In the ancient game played for the laurels of world history we find many actors, the good and the villains. They were pharaohs and philosophers, dictators, kings and barbarians. All were visionary, heroic, barbarous, creative and destructive. All were ambitious and all were empire-builders. Their empires rose and their empires fell. A king was the symbol, but a symbol only lasts a lifetime. The sacrifices they made and the victories they won made them great, just as great as the limits to which they exercised their military power and imposed their brutal will.

It was always war which established economic, political and cultural hegemony. And these wars were conducted with a brutality we cannot even imagine, ending invariably with the annihilation of the enemy nation. Rome's legions had shown that the wandering tribes in search of territory could expect nothing but death. In time the *imperium romanum* became the playground of corrupt emperors and their clique of court officials. It was a time when emperors lost their heads, or they themselves killed off their legion commanders. The means by which an emperor could hang on to his power was to engage tough Northerners, that emerging cast of barbarian generals who could be kept under control because of their intense rivalry with one another.

Nothing is eternal, and the end of antiquity arrived with lightning speed. A furious struggle broke out over the corpse that was once glory; the tottering vestiges of a Roman empire were crushed by the millstone of a gigantic *Völkerwanderung* – the wandering of nations in search of pasture. The outcome was predictable: no winners, only losers – the curtain-raiser to a bleak and dark future, the Middle Ages.

This much is plain. Whether it was the decline of Egypt, the making of Israel, the successive ravages of Assyria and Babylon, the rise of Persia, the glory that was Greece, the conquest of Carthage, the subjugation of Gaul or, in the end, the fall of Rome, the shape of our present-day societies was forged by the people of antiquity in a series of bloody cataclysms.

'*Vae victis!* Woe to the vanquished!' By this formula, which knew no pity, empires emerged which built their glory on the ashes of those they had torched. For us remain only their monumental towers by which we may judge their greatness, from the Great Pyramid of Cheops to the Coliseum of Titus.

> *As long as the Coliseum stands, Rome shall stand.*
> *When the Coliseum falls, Rome will fall.*
> *And when Rome falls, the world will fall.*[2]

All the great heroes and villains died, but they remain in our memory.

[2] The Venerable Bede, AD 673-735, also quoted by Lord Byron in his *Childe Harold's Pilgrimage*.

Bibliography

The Bible

The Old Testament dates from around the time of Moses and the great kings (1200–800 BC) and was first written in Hebrew. It comes in three parts: The Law (Torah), The Prophets (Nebiim) and The Writings (Ketubim). The threesome is known as Tanach, for the first letters of the three parts.

The New Testament was written after the death of Jesus, and follows the ancient testament with the addition of the Gospels – Matthew (AD 42–50), Mark (written during the Jewish revolt, AD 66–70), Luke (written after the destruction of Jerusalem, AD 80–85) and John (AD 100), the Epistles and Revelations. For quotations from the Bible, the Authorised King James Version was used.

Megiddo

The Old Testament.
The Cambridge Ancient History.
Gale, R. *Great Battles of Biblical History*, London 1968
Keller, W. *The Bible as History*, London 1956
Kempinski, A. *Megiddo – a city state and royal centre in North Israel*, Munich 1989
Loud, G. *Megiddo II*, University of Chicago, 1948
Nelson, H.H. *The Battle of Megiddo*, University of Chicago, 1913.
Noth, M. *System der Zwölf Stämme Israels*, Darmstadt 1930

Petrie, W.M.F *A History of Egypt*, London 1896
Rutgers University Press, *World History of the Jewish People*, 1971
Yadin, Y. *The Art of Warfare in Biblical Lands*, London 1963.

Marathon/Thermopylae/Salamis

The three major works quoted are the translations by Lewis Campbell, George Rawlinson and Richard Crawley, all nineteenth-century English scholars, from the contemporary Greek accounts of Aeschylus (525–456 BC), Herodotus (*History of the Persian Wars*, 486–420 BC) and Thucydides (*The History of the Peloponnesian War*, (465–395 BC). Nineteenth-century experts on Persia's wars were J. Arthur Munro and G.B. Grundy.

Campbell, L. (transl.), *The Persians (Aeschylus)*, London 1890
Crawley, R. (transl.), *The History of the Peloponnesian War by Thucydides*, London 1874
Durant, W. *The Life of Greece*, New York 1939
Fonara, C.W. *Herodotus*, Oxford 1971
Fuller, J.F.C. *Decisive Battles of the Western World*, London 1954
Grundy, G.B. *The Great Persian War*, London 1901
Munro, J.A.R. *The Campaign at Marathon*, London 1899
Rawlinson, G. (transl.), *History of Herodotus*, London 1880
Sealey, R. *History of the Greek City-States*, Berkeley, 1976
Selincourt, A. de (transl.), Herodotus, *The Histories*, London 1972

Alexander

Source material for Alexander is relatively easy to come by. His contemporaries lauded his exploits – Flavius

Arrianus (Arrian's) *Anabasis Alexandri*, Quintus Curtius's *Historiae Alexandri*, Plutarch's *Alexander*, as well as Aristotle's *Athenaion Politeia* and Xenophon's *Hellenica* and *Anabasis*. Arrian's description is probably the closest to the truth. His records are correct in topographic details and his accounts of the King's orders are precise, backed up by the writings of Ptolemy, who served under Alexander as commander of the Companion cavalry. Polybius borrowed much material from Callisthenes, Alexander's court historian. Unfortunately, many of the original accounts were lost in the great fire at the Library of Alexandria.

The famous encounter between Alexander and the family of Darius after the Battle of Issus was depicted by Veronese in 1565 and hangs in London's National Gallery.

Babbit, F.C. (transl.), *Plutarch*, London 1926

Fuller, J.F.C. *The Decisive Battles of the Western World*, London 1954

——— *The Generalship of Alexander the Great*, New Brunswick 1958

Hammond, N.G.L. *Three Historians of Alexander the Great*, Cambridge 1983
Alexander the Great, Bristol Press, 1989

Jacoby, F. *Die Fragmente der griechischen Historiker*, Berlin 1923

Miller, W. *Xenophon Anabasis*, Cambridge, Mass. 1914–25

Oldfather, C.H. (transl.), *Diodorus Siculus, Bibliotheca Historica*, Cambridge, Mass. 1933–67

Paton, W.R. *Polybius Histories*, Cambridge, Mass. 1922–7

Robson, E.I. (transl.), *Arrian's Anabasis Alexandri*, London 1929

Rolfe, J.C. (transl.), *Quintus Curtius Historiae Alexandri*, London 1946

Seibert, J. *Alexander der Grosse*, Darmstadt 1972

——— *Untersuchung zur Geschichte*, Darmstadt 1969

Tarn, W.W. *Alexander the Great*, London 1948
Wicken, U. *Alexander der Grosse*, Berlin 1932

Hannibal

The best sources are the Greek historian Polybius (205–125 BC), *General History of the World*, and the Roman Titus Livius (64 BC–AD 17), *History of the Origins of Rome*, Cornelius Nepos (99–24 BC), *De viris illustribus*, Dio Cassius (AD 155–255), *Historia Romana*, and Roman Proconsul of Africa Macrobius, *Saturnales*.

Boularés, H. *Hannibal*, Geneva 2000
Cottrell, L. *Hannibal, Enemy of Rome*, New York 1961
Dodge, T.A. *Hannibal*, Boston 1891
Foster, B.O. (transl.), *Livy*, London 1929
Groag, E. *Hannibal als Politiker*, Vienna 1929
Hoffmann, W. *Hannibal*, Göttingen 1960
Jelusich, M. *Hannibal*, Vienna 1934
Lazenby, J F. *Hannibal's War: History of the Second Punic War*, Warminster 1978
Liddell Hart, B.H.A. *Greater than Napoleon: Scipio Africanus*, Boston 1927
Mahjoubi, Prof. Ammar, *Dictionnaire des Antiquités*, Tunis
Mommsen, T. *Die Geschichte Roms*, Berlin 1895.
Moore, F.G. (transl.), *Livy*, London 1949
Müller, A. *Gespräche zur Weltgeschichte*, Stuttgart 1965
Polybius, *Histories*, Paris 1977
Shuckburgh, E.S. (transl.), *The Histories of Polybius*, London 1899
Titus Livius, *Ab Urbe Condita – History of Rome*, transl. London 1830
Toynbee, A.J. *Hannibal's Legacy*, London 1965

Marius/Vercingetorix/Caesar

Background material can be found in Plutarch (AD 46–120), *Marius* and *Caesar*, in the Dryden translation, published by *Encyclopaedia Britannica*, Chicago, 1952, Suetonius (AD 69–125), *The Twelve Caesars*, Cornelius Tacitus (AD 55–120) *Annales*, and, of course, Caesar's own *De bello gallico*.

Caesar, J. C. *Caesaris commentarii de bello gallico – Guerre des Gaules* (transl. Constans), Paris 1926, and (transl. Kraner, Dittenberger) Berlin 1964

Cambridge University Press, *Libertas as a political idea in Rome*, 1961

Carcopino, J. *Alesia et les ruses de César*, Paris 1958

Cassan, J. de, *Traité des anciens rois des Gaulois et des François depuis le déluge*, Paris 1621

Colomb, G. *L'énigme d'Alésia*, Paris 1922

Dodge, T.A. *Julius Caesar*, Boston 1892

Goudineau, V. *Caesar et la Gaule*, Paris 1990

Graves, R. *The Twelve Caesars* (transl. Robert Graves after Suetonius), London 1957

Gundolf, F. *Caesar, Geschichte seines Ruhms*, Berlin 1924

Harmand, J. *Une campagne césarienne: Alésia*, Paris 1967

Jullian, C. *Vercingétorix*, Paris 1901

Le Gall, J. *Alésia, Archéologie et histoire*, Paris 1990

Musées Nationaux de France, *Vercingétorix et Alésia*, Paris 1994

Napoleon III, *Histoire de Jules César*, Paris 1866

Reddé, M. *L'armée romaine en Gaule*, Paris 1996

Roman, D. and Y. *Histoire de la Gaule*, Paris 1997

Syme, R. *The Roman Revolution*, Oxford 1939

Thierry, A. *L'histoire des Gaulois*, Paris 1828

Fall of the Roman Empire

The principal source for this chapter is the work of Edward Gibbon, *The Decline and Fall of the Roman Empire*, which he finished in 1787. Since then, there have been numerous abbreviated versions and interpretations of his monumental work. Gibbon no doubt used references from Orosius's *Seven Books of History against the Pagans*, and the *Ecclesiastical History* of the Venerable Bede. Also used were Tacitus, *The Annals*, Dio Cassius, *Roman History*, and Suetonius (AD 69–140), *Caesar Augustus. Lives of the Twelve Caesars (c.* AD 121), which recounts the histories of Julius Caesar and of Rome's first eleven emperors, from Augustus to Domitian. A readable combination of fact and unverifiable rumour drawn from ancient sources, the *Lives* serves to illuminate the social climate of early imperial Rome.

Albertini, E. *L'Empire romain*, Paris 1938
Bang, Prof. M. *Cambridge Medieval History* (vol. 1)
Gibbon, E. *The Decline and Fall of the Roman Empire*, New York 1953
Flavius Josephus, *Wars of the Jews*
Keller, W. *The Bible as History*, London 1965
Koebner, R. *Empire*, New York 1961
Low, D.M. *Gibbon's The Decline and Fall of the Roman Empire*, London 1960
Momigliano, A. *Nero in the Augustan Empire*, Cambridge 1934

Titus

The principal record of the fall of Jerusalem was kept by the Jewish commander and historian Flavius Josephus in his *Antiquities: The War of the Jews*, written AD 73–75. Also consulted were the Gospels according to Mark, written during the Jewish revolt AD 66–70 but *before* the destruction of the Temple, and Luke, written about AD 80–85 *after* the fall of Jerusalem.

Flavius Josephus, *Antiquities: The War of the Jews*, transl.

H. St John Thackeray, R. Marcus, L.H. Feldman, New York 1929–65

Galling, K. *Textbuch zur Geschichte Israels.*

Henderson, B. W., *Five Roman Emperors*, Cambridge 1927.

Istrin, V. *La prise de Jerusalem de Josephe le juif*, Paris 1934–8

Kenyon, K.M. *Digging up Jerusalem*, London 1974

Landay, J. *Silent Cities, Sacred Stones*, New York 1971

Moscati, S. *Geschichte und Kultur der semitischen Völker*, 1953

Noth, M. *Geschichte Israels*, 1974

Thackeray, H. St John, *Josephus, the man and the historian*, New York 1929

Yadin, Y. *Masada, Der letzte Kampf*, 1967

Alaric

The Greek monk Orosius, a philosopher and educator, was probably an eye-witness to the sack of Rome by Alaric. His work, *Historiae adversum Paganos*, reflects many facets of Roman life of the period, and was written a year after the sack of Rome (*c.* AD 411–14).

Claude, D. *Geschichte der Westgoten*, Stuttgart 1970

Courcelle, P. *Histoire littéraire des grandes invasions germaniques*, Paris 1964

Diesner, H. *Das Vandalenreich*, Stuttgart 1966

Gamillscheg, *Romania germanica, Siedlungsgeschichte der Germanen*, Berlin 1934

Jordanes, *De originae actibusque Getarum*, transl. as *The Origins and Deeds of the Goths*, AD 551.

Latouche, R. *Les grandes invasions et la crise de l'Occident au Ve siècle*, Paris 1946

Lot, F. *Les invasions barbares*, Paris 1937

Mazzarino, S. *La Fine del mondo antico*, Milan 1959

Orosius, *Historiae adversum Paganos, c.* AD 414, transl. Rome, 1882

Index

References to maps are shown in italics.